The Great Leap Forward (GLF) of 1958 to 1960 must be considered one of the great tragedies of Communist China. It is estimated to have caused the deaths of between 14 million and 28 million Chinese. Intended to transform China into a leading economic power, the radical utopianism of the GLF instead brought on economic disaster.

In this book, David Bachman examines the origins of the economic policies of the GLF Whereas standard accounts interpret the Great Leap as chiefly Mao Zedong's brainchild and a radical rejection of a set of more moderate reform proposals advanced in the period 1956 to 1957, Bachman proposes a provocative reinterpretation of the origins of the GLF that stresses the role of the bureaucracy. Using a neoinstitutionalist approach to analyze the economic policy making leading to the GLF, he argues that the Great Leap must be seen as the product of an institutional process of policy making. This book's radical reinterpretation of one of the most important episodes in the history of the People's Republic of China provides a framework within which to analyze the role of institutions more generally in the political economy of that nation.

Bureaucracy, economy, and leadership in China

Bureaucracy, economy, and leadership in China

The institutional origins of the Great Leap Forward

DAVID BACHMAN
Princeton University

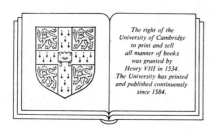

The right of the University of Cambridge to print and sell all manner of books was granted by Henry VIII in 1534. The University has printed and published continuously since 1584.

CAMBRIDGE UNIVERSITY PRESS

Cambridge
New York   Port Chester   Melbourne   Sydney

Published by the Press Syndicate of the University of Cambridge
The Pitt Building, Trumpington Street, Cambridge CB2 1RP
40 West 20th Street, New York, NY 10011, USA
10 Stamford Road, Oakleigh, Melbourne 3166, Australia

First published 1991

A portion of the present work, primarily in Chapter 4, appeared in
David Bachman, *Chen Yun and the Chinese Political System,* China
Research Monograph no. 29 (Berkeley: Institute of East Asian Studies,
University of California, 1985). © Copyright 1985 by The Regents of
the University of California. Reprinted by permission.

Printed in the United States of America

Library of Congress Cataloging-in-Publication Data
Bachman, David M.
Bureaucracy, economy, and leadership in China: the institutional
origins of the great leap forward / David Bachman.
     p.   cm.
Includes bibliographical references.
Includes index.
ISBN 0-521-40275-1
1. Bureaucracy – China – History – 20th century.   2. Industry and
state – China – History – 20th century.   3. China – Economic
policy – 1949–   I. Title.
JQ1508.B28   1991
338.95′009′045 – dc20   90-49810
                                                                  CIP

British Library Cataloging in Publication applied for

ISBN 0-521-40275-1 hardback

For Mom and Dad,
Ann and Victoria

Written under the auspices of the Center of International Studies, Princeton University

Contents

Preface

This book is about the way institutions affect policy making in China. In particular it looks at the role of coalitions of economic bureaucracies in shaping Chinese macroeconomic policy in 1956–1957, and at how these institutions contributed to the Great Leap Forward. In contrast to most accounts of the origins and development of the Great Leap, this work finds that many of the economic policies associated with the Leap were in fact first advocated by a coalition of planning and heavy industrial interests. Instead of Mao's formulating ideas on self-reliance, industry's aiding of agriculture, emphasis on medium- and small-scale industry, and decentralization, the two top planners of the People's Republic of China, Li Fuchun and Bo Yibo, were the first to suggest and champion these policies in the spring and summer of 1957. To be sure, Mao bears ultimate responsibility for the catastrophe caused by the Great Leap and its millions of deaths due to starvation and malnutrition, but he did not formulate some of the most salient actions of this frenetic period of Chinese history.

This finding, that the planners advocated what later were called Maoist economic policies, raises fundamental questions. First, why would the planners advocate a platform of economic measures that seem to undermine their own role in the political and economic system? Second, why would Mao and the Chinese Communist Party (CCP) adopt such a package? The answer to the first question is that in fact many of the proposals of Li Fuchun and Bo Yibo actually strengthened the position of the planning and heavy industry coalition. Li and Bo put forward these ideas for both economic and political purposes. Economically, they saw the policies as addressing the problems of lagging agricultural growth and the inability of China's limited resources to meet all the demands put on the economic system. Politically, they advocated the policies in response to an attempt by a coalition of financial, agricultural, commercial, and light industrial officials, led by Chen Yun, Li Xiannian, and Deng Zihui, to alter the macroeconomic management system in China. In what amounted to China's first efforts at economic reform, this coalition, which I refer to as the financial coalition, advocated use of the market, price incentives, more investment in light industry and agriculture, and the use of financial indicators (rather than the material balances characteristic of the Soviet model of economic development) to govern macroeconomic policy making. The coalition advocated stable, slow advance. It was quite successful in late 1956 and early 1957 in making inroads into the power and resources of the planning–heavy industry coalition, and in early economic plans for 1958 it appeared that heavy industry and other interests would not receive preferential treatment. Li and Bo, leaders of the planning and heavy industry coalition, saw this fundamental political challenge and responded to it with their own program for aiding agriculture and using increased resources for heavy industry to solve China's economic problems.

Why, then, did Mao and the Party adopt the planners' program? First, this book argues, Mao and other top generalist leaders were largely ignorant of economic affairs and were relatively dependent on the bureaucracy and economic specialists to draw up plans for them. Second, the reform program of the financial coalition had apparently failed. Agricultural growth slowed even further during the period when the financial coalition held sway. This may not have been a fair assessment, and it is doubtful that price incentives had been given enough time to work, but nonetheless when the time came to evaluate the performance of the economy under the reform measures, output figures worked against the financial coalition. Moreover, there was significant overlap in the views of Party critics, as expressed in the Hundred Flowers Campaign and by the financial coalition. When Mao and the CCP condemned the Hundred Flowers criticisms as a manifestation of class struggle, many of the measures associated with the financial coalition were defined as ideologically illegitimate. Finally, the Party adopted the planners' program because there seemed to be no alternative.

While this interpretation of the origins of the Great Leap Forward fundamentally revises conventional views about the nature of the Leap, this book has a larger purpose as well. It aims at formulating an institutional approach to understanding the Chinese political economy. As noted, it identifies several key coalitions of bureaucracies that played dominant roles in the making of economic policy in 1956–1957. These coalitions were present not only in this period but throughout the Mao era and into post-Mao times as well. Moreover, these coalitions have held essentially the same policy positions throughout the history of the People's Republic. This book attempts to explain the origins of these coalitions and why they have persistently advocated the same policies. To put it simply, these institutions and interests are results of the dynamics of China's relative economic poverty and the original missions of these organizations. Coalitions of interests and institutions formed because individual bureaucracies were seldom powerful enough to advance and defend their specific interests. With the help of the senior leaders charged with overall supervision in each major area of endeavor, there emerged a broad tendency, or program of policies, around which groups of bureaucracies could organize themselves. Because their tasks and the resource environment in which these organizations operate have not changed fundamentally since 1949, these coalitions and their interests have also persisted with little change.

When I began working on a dissertation on the Great Leap Forward, more than ten years ago, such an interpretation was hardly in my mind. I did start my research with certain hunches and assumptions. Perhaps the most important of these was the view that economic decision making and economic questions deserved more attention than they were getting in much of the literature on Chinese politics at the time. I also began with the view that there was much in the history of the People's Republic that remained unexplained. China scholars are often preoccupied with analyzing the most recent epochal event – whether the Cultural Revolution, when I started graduate school; economic reforms, when I finished my dissertation; or the Tiananmen massacre, shortly before I finished writing this book. Given the tendency for a thorough documentary record to emerge only years after the fact, I felt I should avoid contemporary subjects and focus on an earlier period – that of the Great Leap Forward.

My hunches and assumptions were reinforced by several developments. First, a casual reading of several of the ministerial journals of the 1950s suggested a number of complex developments that the existing literature on Chinese politics did not seem to take into account. Soon thereafter, I received a copy of a volume of materials by Chen Yun then circulating internally in China. The importance of this volume to my thinking about this period cannot be overestimated. Finally, I started my dissertation research and writing at a time when "the state" was a reemerging field of concern in political science. While little of this literature focused on state socialist systems, there were many insights to be drawn from analyses of advanced and underdeveloped capitalist states.

These were the concerns that drove the original doctoral dissertation on which this book is based. I hope that many of the findings of the original work have been strengthened by the additional documentation coming out of China since the early 1980s and by a more mature understanding on my part of the nature of politics in general and of politics in China in particular.

Acknowledgments

How extensively should one acknowledge and thank those responsible for one's intellectual genealogy? There are only so many ways to say thank you, and words in my case must fail to convey the debts and the gratitude incurred in the course of intellectual discovery. I could, even should, acknowledge my debt to my teachers going back to first grade, and to the author of every book or article that engaged or provoked me. Colleagues of all sorts have further refined my thoughts. It is truly impossible to thank you all by name, but my gratitude to you all is profound.

Some contributors to my work have been so formative that they must be singled out for special mention. At Swarthmore College, where I was an undergraduate, Kenneth Lieberthal and Lillian Li were the first to excite me about China, and without their example I would be doing something else today, certainly not teaching and writing about Chinese politics.

At Stanford University, where I went to graduate school, John Wilson Lewis and Alexander George served as both mentors and dissertation advisers who inspired and encouraged creative thinking about China. My fellow graduate students at Stanford were no little source of support and comfort. They included Bill Joseph, Carl Walter, Horace Nash, Maria Morgan, Don Koblitz, Tom Gottlieb, and Frank Hawke. Tom Fingar was an unofficial adviser who helped me along each step of the way at Stanford.

At Princeton, my feelings for my fellow members of the junior faculty are indeed hard to express. John Ikenberry, whose work on the state has helped me a great deal; Anne Norton, whose understanding of politics helped me to see things in a different light; Atul Kohli; Peter VanDoren; and Ken Oye deserve special mention.

I wish to thank Forrest Colburn, Atul Kohli, Henry Bienen, George Downs, and the junior faculty reading group at Princeton for reading parts of this manuscript and improving it more than they know. I owe a special debt to Lynn White for his ceaseless optimism, encouragement, and all-round good nature, and for reading the whole draft. David Lampton, Barry Naughton, Dorothy Solinger, and two anonymous referees read the entire work and, despite my stubbornness, forced me to face critical problems in the analysis.

Other friends and colleagues in the China field who helped me are too numerous to mention. Yet this book is part of an ongoing dialogue with all of them, and without their work and their words of criticism and support this book would be seriously diminished.

Four people deserve special thanks. They are Roderick MacFarquhar, Li Cheng, Harry Harding, and Ann Fenwick. Their influences on this project were the greatest, and my debts to them are the greatest.

One simply cannot write about Chinese politics in the 1950s without truly appreciating the work of Roderick MacFarquhar. His first essay on the period this volume covers was written in 1958, and he has made seminal contributions with major works in each of the succeeding decades. He and I disagree on a number of things; this was made clear when he agreed to serve as a commentator on a shorter version of this book presented at the 1985 Association for Asian Studies convention. I hope this work does a better job of persuading him of my views than that paper did. I do not know Professor MacFarquhar well, but his works and his kindness in serving as a commentator on my paper (and providing an early draft of MacFarquhar, Cheek, and Wu, 1989) were indispensable to my whole approach to politics in China in the 1950s.

Li Cheng served as a research assistant during one crucial summer of the writing process. Perhaps no one knows the Gest Oriental Library at Princeton better than he. He uncovered all the post-1979 writings available at Princeton and brought them to my attention. He read and commented on my original dissertation and on an early draft of this volume. His own work on leadership in China has enriched my understanding of Chinese politics.

Harry Harding was my principal dissertation adviser, and he has had the greatest impact on my understanding of Chinese politics. During one of our innumerable lunches at Stanford, he suggested that I think about a dissertation on the Great Leap, and during many of the others he hammered away at the shortcomings of my logic and understandings. His analytical clarity and eloquence were great influences on me. It is unfortunate that the student did not match the teacher.

Finally, my wife, Ann Fenwick, has lived through this work since its inception, first as a fellow graduate student at Stanford and now well into our married life. She has been the perfect blend of sympathetic critic, editorial craftsmaster, and at times skeptical onlooker to the bizarre process by which her husband goes about thinking and writing. I could not have done the dissertation or this book without her.

I should also thank the following institutions for support: The East Asia Collection at the Hoover Institution and Chen Fumei and Mark Tam provided all the material I needed for the doctoral dissertation. I was then awarded a postdoctoral fellowship at the Center for Chinese Studies of the University of California, Berkeley. Outgoing Chairman Lowell Dittmer and incoming Chairman Joyce Kallgren conspired to force me to finish my dissertation; as Joyce said then, I would thank her for her efforts, and I am doing so. C. P. Chen and Annie Chang at the Center library were also indispensable in helping me ferret out materials. At Princeton, the Center of International Studies and its director, Henry Bienen, provided money for research assistance and a home base that sheltered me from some teaching pressures. Martin Heijdra at the Gest Oriental Library was very responsive to my requests to obtain materials. Andrew Walder and Jean Oi helped me obtain material at the Fairbank Center library at Harvard and put me in touch with Nancy Hearst, who has been most generous. Finally, I wish to thank Emily Loose and Martin Dinitz at Cambridge University Press for encouraging me to submit this manuscript to the Press and for seeing it through its production so quickly and beautifully.

Chronology of major events and developments, July 1955 – July 1960, with special emphasis on 1956 and 1957

July 5–6, 1955   Li Fuchun, chairman of State Planning Commission, presents First Five-Year Plan (FFYP) to second Session of First National People's Congress (NPC). Plan follows Soviet model of development.

July 31   Mao Zedong speaks to provincial Party secretaries of Chinese Communist Party (CCP), urging more rapid agricultural cooperativization than envisioned in the FFYP. "Socialist upsurge" in Chinese countryside begins.

October 4–11   Sixth Plenum of Seventh Central Committee (CC) convened. Mao again encourages faster formation of cooperatives. Deng Zihui, head of Party's Rural Work Department, criticized as a "rightist."

November 16–24   CCP CC Conference on Transformation of Capitalist Industry and Commerce discusses effective nationalization of all remaining privately owned enterprises in China.

November 1955 – January 1956   Twelve-Year Agricultural Program, or Forty Points on Agriculture, formulated by Mao and provincial Party secretaries, calling for rapid increase in agricultural production.

December 1955 – June 1956   "Small leap forward" to achieve "more, faster, better, and more economic results" launched. Huge increases in targets announced; widespread mobilization undertaken. Collectives formed throughout countryside; "socialist transformation" of private enterprises completed.

January 14–20, 1956   CCP CC Conference on Intellectuals. Mao and Premier Zhou Enlai speak, advocating better working conditions for intellectuals and greater freedom of academic discussion, especially in science.

February 25   Nikita Khrushchev delivers secret speech denouncing Stalin and "cult of personality" to Twentieth Congress of Communist Party of Soviet Union.

April 5   After series of Politburo meetings, CCP publishes "On

	the Historical Experience of the Dictatorship of the Proletariat" – CCP's response to Khrushchev. Essay says "certain systems" must be established to prevent arbitrary rule.
April 25	Mao delivers speech "On the Ten Major Relationships" after being briefed by most main ministerial officials in China. Speech urges more balance in economy, moderation in polity. Mao also proposes slogan "Let a Hundred Flowers Bloom, Let a Hundred Schools of Thought Contend," reflecting his desire to enliven intellectual activity in China.
May 12	State Economic Commission, under direction of Bo Yibo, established and charged with yearly planning and supervision of plan implementation.
May 25	Lu Dingyi, head of CCP propaganda department, publicly discusses Mao's "double hundred" policy.
June 15–30	Third Session of First NPC: speeches by Chen Yun, chief economic official of PRC, on defects in socialist transformation; Li Xiannian, minister of finance, criticizing "rash advance"; and Li Fuchun, disagreeing with aspects of Mao's Ten Major Relationships.
June 20	*Renmin Ribao* (People's Daily) editorial criticizes both conservatism and rash advances, marking effective end of small leap forward. Economic officials try to cool down overheated economy.
Summer	Preliminary proposals for Second Five-Year Plan drawn up.
September 15–27	Eighth National Congress of CCP convened. Major addresses by China's number-two leader, Liu Shaoqi, Zhou Enlai, and rising leader Deng Xiaoping on political and economic policies for medium term. Speeches by Chen Yun on economic reform, Li Xiannian on price reform, Deng Zihui on agricultural consolidation, Bo Yibo on macroeconomic control, and Li Fuchun on planning. Congress concludes that main contradiction in Chinese society is between backward economy and advanced political system, that class struggle is not important, and that economic development should be focus of all work.
September 28	First Plenum of Eighth CC elects new CCP leadership. Mao, Liu, Zhou, Zhu De, Chen Yun, and Deng Xiao-

	ping elected to Politburo Standing Committee, with Deng serving as Party general secretary.
Second half of October	Nationalist uprisings in Poland and Hungary. CCP gives Soviet leadership advice.
November 10–15	Second Plenum of Eighth CC discusses Eastern Europe, growing economic problems; launches policy of economic retrenchment. Chen Yun, named minister of commerce around this time, revives and expands use of markets.
November 18, 1956 – February 6, 1957	Zhou Enlai abroad; Chen Yun acting premier in his stead.
December 29, 1956	CCP issues "More on the Historical Experience of the Dictatorship of the Proletariat." Discusses contradictions among leaders and led in socialist states.
January 7, 1957	People's Liberation Army literary officials criticize "double hundred" policy.
January 18–27	Conference of Provincial Party Secretaries: Chen Yun speaks on January 18 and introduces "three balances" – budget, credit, and materials – to readjust and control economy. Li Xiannian speech supports Chen. Mao speaks on blooming and contending; generally supports Chen's economic policies.
February 27	Mao speech "On the Correct Handling of Contradictions Among the People" encourages citizens to voice their discontent with government and CCP to improve their functioning.
March–April	Mao, Liu, and other major leaders tour country, expounding on contradictions among people and need for CCP rectification.
March 9	Chen Yun, addressing Third Session of Second Chinese People's Political Consultative Conference on increasing production and practicing economy, says "tense balance" will characterize economy for foreseeable future.
April 27	CCP issues directive on Party rectification, allowing ordinary citizens to participate (published April 30).
April 30 – June 8	Large-scale blooming and contending as intellectuals, non-CCP figures, and students raise increasingly severe criticisms of CCP.
May	Bo Yibo and Li Fuchun enunciate economic policy based

	on self-reliance, medium- and small-scale industry, and decentralization during provincial tour.
June 8 – end 1957	Anti-Rightist Campaign launched by CCP to crush its critics. More than 550,000 persons officially branded as rightists and subject to punishment.
June 26 – July 15	Fourth Session of First NPC: speeches by Zhou Enlai, Bo Yibo, and Li Xiannian. Zhou defends CCP; Li attempts to defend three balances; Bo reiterates ideas he and Li Fuchun articulated in May and calls for revival of Forty Points on Agriculture.
Early–mid July	Mao speaks in Qingdao to provincial leaders. He agrees with Bo on Forty Points and on industry aiding agriculture, calls for attacks on CCP's critics, and then goes into seclusion until late September.
August 18	Rural free markets closed.
September 23 – October 9	Third Plenum of Eighth CC: Deng Xiaoping reports on rectification and Anti-Rightist Campaign. Chen Yun grudgingly introduces decentralization measures but resists planners' and Mao's ideas on economic development. Mao, in closing speech, calls for "more, better, faster, and more economic results" in economic construction. This marks beginning of Great Leap Forward.
October 4	Soviet Union launches first sputnik.
November	Mao in Moscow declares that "east wind now prevails over the west wind," meaning that balance of power has now shifted to socialist states and that they can pursue their policies more aggressively.
December 2	Liu Shaoqi proclaims that China will catch up with Britain economically in fifteen years; is supported by Li Fuchun on December 7.
December 19	Bo Yibo suggests "positive balance" as key to economic planning and activism in economic work. This invites inflation of planning targets.
Mid January 1958	Nanning Conference: Mao and others formulate sixty articles on work methods, with theme of "uninterrupted revolution." Mao criticizes conservatives and experts identified with Zhou Enlai and Chen Yun. Escalation of economic targets begins.

March 9–26	At Chengdu Conference, Mao criticizes intellectuals and bourgeois experts and urges greater mass mobilization and increased enthusiasm. Further rise of economic targets.
May 5–23	At Second Session of Eighth Party Congress, Liu Shaoqi outlines Great Leap Forward program in public. Internally, CCP urges even higher targets than Liu states openly, with goal of catching up to United States economically in short order.
Summer	Large rural people's communes begin to emerge in countryside. Fantastic plans to develop the steel industry formulated.
August 17–30	Beidaihe Meeting: height of Great Leap utopianism. Communes authorized (and created nationally in six weeks). Steel production targeted to double 1957 figure. CCP claims "sprouts of communism" are developing throughout country.
November–December	First Zhengzhou Conference, Wuchang Conference, and Sixth Plenum of Eighth CC begin to retreat from Leap utopianism. Some targets are lowered but remain grossly unrealistic; ideological claims about communism are disavowed.
February 27 – March 5, 1959	At Second Zhengzhou Conference, Mao calls for thoroughgoing rectification of communes but remains very optimistic.
February–May	Chen Yun returns to high policy-making position, urging unified planning and reduced steel production. (In early summer, Mao will endorse Chen's ideas on economic balance.)
February–July	CCP gradually cuts back on Leap excesses, but bad policies, organization, and weather cause agricultural production to fall precipitously, marking onset of "three calamitous years" of famine.
July 2 – August 1, August 2–16	Lushan Conference and Eighth Plenum of Eighth CC. Defense Minister Peng Dehuai attacks Leap and indirectly Mao. Mao rebuts and forces CCP to choose between himself and Peng. Peng is ousted from leadership; Leap is reintensified, exacerbating looming agricultural and industrial disasters.

July 1959 – July
1960

Sino-Soviet relations deteriorate. All Soviet advisers in China are recalled in July 1960. Leap collapses in early 1960, but remedial action does not begin until second half of year. Famine intensifies; industrial production falls markedly. Economy is in depression.

1

Introduction

One of Mao Zedong's more memorable post-1949 sayings was "Where do correct ideas come from?" They do not fall from the sky, he stated, nor are they innate in the minds of men. Instead, he argued, correct ideas emerge from social practice, and social practice alone.[1] Using the terminology of present-day political science, Mao's words might be paraphrased: "Where do political preferences come from?"[2] This book takes the position that preferences and policies in China also emerge from social practice, and uses this insight to examine the interplay of economic, bureaucratic, and leadership factors that gave rise to the Great Leap Forward (GLF) of 1958–1960. Particular attention is paid to the period from September 1956 to October 1957, one of the great turning points in the history of the People's Republic of China (PRC).

Beginning in mid 1956, and greatly accelerating after the Eighth National Congress of the Chinese Communist Party (CCP) in September 1956, reformist ideas appeared on China's political agenda. In the economic realm, Chinese leaders called for the market to supplement the planned economy and challenged the heretofore dominant position of heavy industry as China's top economic priority. The leaders may also have tried to orient their country's foreign trade toward broader relations with noncommunist nations. In the political realm, even more fundamental changes were considered. For a brief time during the Hundred Flowers Campaign, the Party encouraged Chinese citizens, especially intellectuals, to come forward and voice their opinions about the state of the nation. The CCP even tolerated criticism of itself, at least temporarily. A new relationship among the Party, the government, and society appeared to be in the making, but these reformist policies were abruptly terminated in June 1957. By the following

---

1. Mao, 1971, p. 502. This does not mean that Mao actually behaved according to this precept. Solinger, 1981, begins with the same quotation.
2. See, for example, Wildavsky, 1987, and Laitin and Wildavsky, 1988.

September the Party had radically shifted course, having embarked on a new line of development almost directly antithetical to reform efforts. This new path was, of course, the Great Leap Forward.

This study argues that many of the fundamental economic policies of the "radical" Great Leap Forward, one of the most extreme, bizarre, and eventually catastrophic episodes in twentieth-century political history, are explained in important ways by the workings of China's bureaucracies. Moreover, the bureaucratic perspectives that helped to launch the Leap persisted in Chinese politics for an extended period, and they still resonate within the political system today. A coalition of economic planners and heavy industrial leaders formulated in 1957 an innovative series of policies that appeared both to meet China's economic problems and to defend this group's interests from attack by another coalition, composed of leaders in the fields of finance, commerce, agriculture, and light industry. This second coalition advocated many economic reform measures, including expanded use of the market as a key supplement to economic planning. Mao and other leaders, after weakly embracing the reformist program, took the planners' policies as their own after the collapse of the Hundred Flowers Campaign.

The Great Leap Forward may be defined in a number of ways. Perhaps the best overall definition is: the two-year attempt, from early 1958 to the end of 1959, to implement a communist utopia in China. The Great Leap Forward was energized by the belief that through one titanic effort everything could be accomplished at once. Not only was China to be economically transformed by mobilizing labor (and turning it into capital) in communes and by producing steel in backyard furnaces, but cultural life was to be remade as well. Mass poetry writing, the elimination of illiteracy, encouraging everyone to make scientific and technical discoveries, and the establishment of new social patterns by forcing peasants to live and eat in dormitories and mess halls were all part and parcel of the Leap. The Leap was a package of policies stitched together, and to a remarkable degree acted upon, in order to create a communist utopia. Every component aspect of the Leap grew more and more grandiose until the whole mélange disintegrated with the collapse of the economy. The Leap was built on denial of the laws of economics, and when at last it became clear that those laws could no longer be wished away, as all unpleasant truths were during 1958–1959, perhaps 30 million persons, or about 4 percent of China's population, had starved to death.[3]

3. The term "Great Leap Forward" has a number of other meanings. First, it stands for the historical period 1958–1960. It also signifies a particular strategy of economic development and resource allocation. This strategy includes high levels of investment, high production and in-

Paradoxically, this seemingly irrational tragedy grew out of a number of policy streams that were quite creative and responsive to narrow economic and bureaucratic concerns. The planners gave Mao Zedong a series of policies that emphasized the construction of medium-size and small industries instead of large factories; self-reliance instead of dependence on the Soviet Union for advanced technology; industry aiding agriculture instead of industrial neglect of the rural areas; and decentralization instead of the rigid centralization prescribed by the Stalinist model of development. These policies were sensible economically and politically, and did not require a real break from the patterns and practices of resource allocation that had characterized the Chinese economy in the mid 1950s. In fact, they defended the Soviet model by seeming to jettison it – for example, technology imports from the Soviet Union actually increased during the Leap, and heavy industrial investment, both absolutely and as a relative share of total budgetary outlays, grew substantially. In addition to being responsive to China's economic woes, these policies also defended the political interests and power of the planning coalition. Because the planners were able to convince Mao and other leaders not only that the economy did not have to be readjusted and slowed down because of fundamental agricultural problems but also that "to do more with less" was possible, Mao and other leaders took the planners at their word and did much more than the planners ever imagined. Heavy industrial interests were served by the Great Leap.

Historically, the Leap was one of the distinctive eras in Chinese politics.

vestment targets, decentralization, industry aiding agriculture, self-reliance, and emphasis on medium- and small-scale, as opposed to large-scale, factories.

Technically speaking, the GLF was only one of the "three red banners" that were the core elements of Chinese politics from 1958 to 1960. The other banners were the people's communes and the General Line for Socialist Construction, which was defined as "going all out, aiming high, and achieving more, faster, better, more economical results" in building socialism. (See Liu Shaoqi, "The Present Situation, the Party's General Line for Socialist Construction, and Its Future Tasks," in *Communist China, 1955–1959*, 1971, pp. 416–38.) In other words, in its narrowest sense, the term "Great Leap Forward" was used to mean a massive upsurge in economic development aimed at changing China's "poor and blank" countenance forever. This precise meaning of the term has been used by almost no one except Chinese writers of the late 1950s.

Roderick MacFarquhar suggests another definition. He sees the Leap as a state of mind, a definition he provided when discussing my paper "The Bureaucratic Origins of the Great Leap Forward" presented at the 37th Annual Meeting of the Association for Asian Studies in 1985. MacFarquhar did not fully develop this point, and the description above may not do full justice to his ideas on the subject. Presumably, this state of mind means the utopian goals set by the Party and the belief that an unprecedented level of mass mobilization would bring these goals to fruition. Other elements fit into this mind set: denigration of technical expertise, a charged ideological atmosphere, the idea that through struggle anything was possible, and the belief that physical laws did not necessarily apply to properly indoctrinated citizens. In his book on the GLF (1983), MacFarquhar seems to use "GLF" to refer to two things: the historical period 1958–1960 and a style of Party rule.

The Chinese leadership swore that China would catch up with and exceed Great Britain's production of major economic goods within fifteen years. The Chinese people were mobilized to do battle with nature, to transform China's "poor and blank" condition fundamentally.[4] Chinese leaders, symbolically demonstrating their commitment to converting mobilized labor into capital, engaged in the construction of the Ming Tombs Reservoir. Peasants were organized into rural people's communes composed of thousands of households. These were not just agricultural units but also industrial, governmental, educational, cultural, and military organizations. The whole country was exhorted to produce steel, and very small backyard steel mills were set up in the communes. Massive increases in production were announced, but demands for even greater upsurges were continually made. A millenarian spirit gripped the land.

That the Great Leap was one of the great disasters in the history of the People's Republic is now beyond question. Millions died of starvation or of diseases related to malnutrition. According to official Chinese sources, the famine of 1959–1961 caused 14.1 million excess deaths (or about 2 percent of the entire population), but most Western demographers estimate the toll at about twice this figure.[5] The old and the young were particularly susceptible to the effects of famine. While all provinces and areas suffered, Anhui, Gansu, Guizhou, Henan, Shandong, and Sichuan provinces appear to have been particularly hard hit.[6] Industrial and agricultural production all but collapsed. (See Table 1.) Agricultural production regained 1952 levels only in 1962, and considering population growth in the interim, real living standards were still below those of the early years of CCP rule. Other data could be marshaled to show that the already low standard of living deteriorated further.[7] Huge urban migration in 1958 so worried the CCP that it banned further movement and forcibly returned newly arrived city dwellers to the countryside. For the next twenty or so years, peasants were bound to the land in an almost feudal way. With urban inflation caused by the Leap and

4. Mao argued in 1956 and 1958 that the Chinese people, especially the peasants, were poor and blank. This, he argued, was not a bad, but actually a good, thing, for poverty would impel them to seek advance, and blankness, or lack of learning, would allow them to receive advanced knowledge easily. See Schram, 1974, p. 83, and Mao, 1971, p. 500.

5. See Kane, 1988, ch. 6.

6. Ibid., pp. 94–98.

7. Assessments of the effects of the GLF can be found in Wang Ping, " 'Da Yuejin' he Tiaozheng Shiqide Renmin Shenghuo" (People's Living Standards during the "Great Leap Forward" and Readjustment Period), in Liu Suinian, ed., 1982, pp. 162–78; Liu Suinian and Wu Qungan, 1984; Sun Yefang, "Consolidate Statistics Work, Reform the Statistical System," *Jingji Guanli* (Economic Management), 1981, no. 2, trans. in Foreign Broadcast Information Service, *Daily Report, China*, March 26, 1981, L 4 – L 9 (see L 5); Joseph, 1986; Bernstein, 1984; Whiting, 1975, pp. 20–28; and MacFarquhar, 1983, pp. 326–32.

Table 1. *Total product of society, 1957–1962 (in billion yuan and index figures, with 1952 = 100)*

	Total		Agriculture		Industry	
	Yuan	Index	Yuan	Index	Yuan	Index
1957	160.6	170.9	53.7	124.8	70.4	228.6
1958	213.8	226.7	56.6	127.8	108.3	353.9
1959	254.8	267.4	49.7	110.4	148.3	481.7
1960	267.9	280	45.7	96.4	163.7	535.7
1961	197.8	186.2	55.9	94	106.2	331.1
1962	180	167.6	58.4	100	92	276

Source: State Statistical Bureau, 1986, pp. 24–25. Total product of society (or global social product) is the sum total of gross output produced by agriculture, industry, construction, transportation, and commerce. See p. 735. The chart uses comparable prices (p. 737).

its aftermath, real worker incomes did not exceed 1957 levels until the early 1980s. The political repercussions of this catastrophe contributed significantly to the launching of the Cultural Revolution, a different kind of cataclysm the Party inflicted on the Chinese people (and on itself).[8]

The juxtaposition of a moderate reformist period in late 1956 to mid 1957, on the one hand, and the GLF, on the other, suggests that the radical Leap was based on total rejection of the more liberal period and that there were few or no continuities between the two phases of Party rule. Indeed, this view is central to standard interpretations of the Great Leap.[9] This approach locates the origins of the Leap in the collapse of the Hundred Flowers Campaign of public criticism of the Party and the subsequent attack by the Party on its critics during the Anti-Rightist Campaign. According to this view, the radical utopianism of the Leap was the outcome of the Party's suppression of its antagonists (seen as hostile to socialism), the deleterious effect of the Anti-Rightist Campaign on vertical communication within the Chinese bureaucracy (during and after this campaign, no one dared to contradict the views coming down from above for fear of being sentenced to labor reform), and the ultraleftist proclivities of certain Chinese leaders.[10] The suppression of criticism or questioning of any Party policy created amplifying feedback. Lower levels reported to superiors what they thought superiors wanted to hear, reinforcing the radical predispositions of the political center and lead-

8. MacFarquhar's third volume (in progress) will deal extensively with this issue. See also Teiwes, 1979a; Chang, 1975; Ahn, 1976; Harding, 1981; and White, 1989.
9. In addition to MacFarquhar, 1983, see idem, 1974; Vogel, 1971; and Prybyla, 1970.
10. In addition to the sources already cited, see Das, 1979; Schram, 1971; and Schoenhals, 1987.

ing Mao and other Chinese leaders to flights of fancy that ultimately proved calamitous for society and the Party. In short, this view holds that the Great Leap Forward emerged out of the political trends in Chinese society in 1957 and developed like a fever (to use a favorite post-Mao phrase describing the excesses of the Leap) from Mao's brain.

There is merit to this approach, but at the very least it is incomplete, and it blinds analysts to some of the more complex, perplexing, contradictory, and inadequately studied aspects of the Leap itself. The standard explanation focuses a great deal of attention on Mao Zedong and other radical leaders in the political system while downplaying the importance of institutional concerns in the polity and economy. It has difficulty explaining where the economic planks of the GLF program came from and why they were adopted. Although economic concerns were central to the Leap, these concerns do not figure prominently in the standard, largely political, interpretation of the GLF. The conventional view has trouble explaining why the Leap, a movement often seen as China's attempt to assert its independence from the Soviet model of development and perhaps from the Soviet Union itself, saw record levels of Sino-Soviet trade. Similarly, this interpretation cannot tell us why China's trade turnover during the Leap reached levels surpassed only in the early 1970s, despite emphasis on self-reliance from late 1957 on. The GLF, according to Liu Shaoqi in the most extensive exegesis by a major Party leader, was supposed to redress the problems of economic imbalance found in the Soviet model, with its emphasis on heavy industry, neglect of light industry, and exploitation of agriculture. The Leap, however, further compounded the disproportions in the Chinese economy.[11] The usual political interpretation of the origins and development of the Leap does not account for why such a radical reversal of Party policies in the summer and fall of 1957 met with relatively little intra-elite opposition. Finally, the conventional view has difficulty explaining why Mao Zedong, whose prestige and authority were severely jolted by the Hundred Flowers Campaign, could within months so easily reacquire the power to launch another major initiative.

These puzzles, contradictions, and complexities are the starting points for this work. How can they be explained? Or, paraphrasing Mao's question at the start of this chapter, "Where do policies come from?" The answer presented here is that the economic policies associated with the GLF were the result of a complex political process involving bureaucratic coalitions in China's political economy. Political leaders coopted the policies put forward by

---

11. Liu Shaoqi, "The Present Situation" (n. 3).

the winning coalition and added their own concerns to the position of the winners. But ultimately the interests of bureaucratic organizations were decisive in explaining the pattern of economic policy making in China during 1956 and 1957 and in structuring many of the economic choices made in 1958 and 1959. Mao's responsibility for the catastrophe caused by the Great Leap cannot be denied, but the competing activities of the Chinese bureaucracy and Mao's subordinates gradually discredited moderate alternatives to the Leap.[12] The Soviet model had been tried, but rural China could not support further "primitive socialist accumulation" or severe exploitation to finance industrialization. In 1956–1957, a modest reform program with market elements was attempted and also found wanting. Potential critics of the Leap had few alternatives to offer. In other words, paraphrasing Marx, Mao made his own Great Leap Forward, but he did not make it as he pleased; he did not make it under circumstances chosen by himself, but under conditions directly found, given, and transmitted by the bureaucracy.[13]

The analytical approach used here is in the "new institutionalism" school.[14] It adds significantly to our understanding of politics in China by suggesting how political organizations affect political life. Despite the enormous impact of Franz Schurmann's *Ideology and Organization in Communist China* (1968), structural approaches to Chinese politics concentrating on the role of political organizations have not been common. Only in recent years have works in this vein begun to appear.[15]

The full impact of political institutions – how they structure, channel, and constrain political action in China – has yet to be discussed systematically. The application of the "new institutionalism" framework in a Chinese context is perhaps the main goal of this book and is presented most fully in Chapter 3. Moreover, this framework is applied to a critical case study. Other than the Cultural Revolution (and perhaps the Tiananmen massacre), it is hard to think of cases in PRC history where institutional politics is less likely to be the dominant mode of policy making. If I can show how institutions help to explain the political economy of the Great Leap Forward, the sa-

---

12. This view was suggested by an anonymous reviewer who cited the work of the revisionist German historian Hans Mommsen, whose ideas on the development of the Holocaust are similar to my arguments about the origins of the Great Leap Forward. Most of Mommsen's work is in German (which I do not read), but the gist of his views can be found in Mommsen, 1986. I am grateful to the reviewer for bringing Mommsen's ideas to my attention.

13. Marx, 1972, paraphrasing p. 437.

14. March and Olsen, 1984; Ikenberry, 1988; Krasner, 1984; and Evans, Rueschmeyer, and Skocpol, 1985, are major statements of the "new institutionalism."

15. The most important work on the interplay of institutions and society in China is Walder, 1986. See also Kenneth Lieberthal and Oksenberg, 1986, republished with generally minor changes in Lieberthal and Oksenberg, 1988. As is discussed in Chapter 3, bureaucratic politics approaches are not synonymous with institutional approaches, although they do overlap.

lience of the approach for other periods will be strengthened, even without detailed case studies of those periods.

This work also has aims more historical and interpretive in nature. It revises and supplements existing works on the origins of the GLF. Among the major points developed in the course of this work are: (1) When Mao Zedong first considered an original path for Chinese socialism, his preference was for a more market-oriented, participatory model, not a radical leftist one. Only when he concluded that the "Bukharinist" position of combining economic planning with the market[16] had failed did he adopt extreme leftist ideas about Chinese socialism. (2) The major economic policy-making and administrative organizations in China were organized into two coalitions, one headed by Chen Yun and Li Xiannian and the other headed by Li Fuchun and Bo Yibo. Each group produced innovative thinking about, and provocative solutions for China's economic problems. Each group was prepared to part company with aspects of the Soviet model of development. (3) The planners, Li Fuchun and Bo Yibo, played a central role in defining many of the economic policies associated with the GLF. They did this for reasons having as much to do with the interests of the planning and heavy industry coalition as with objective economic conditions or promptings from the top leadership. (4) Economic officials largely controlled the economic agenda of the PRC. Mao and other generalists could modify the options put forward and, perhaps most important, decide on the pace of developments, but by late 1957 the key economic policy-making bureaucracies generally defined the range of policy choice available to the central leadership. (5) Finally, a fairly stable alliance between the planning and heavy industry coalition and the Party dominated Chinese politics from the 1950s until the late 1970s, if not longer. When this alliance was faced with external challenge, the result was increased suppression of domestic political critics and very large increases in investment. Indeed, as will be suggested in the conclusion, this pattern of alliance and threat accounts for the emergence of other leaps in the Chinese political economy.

A final set of aims reflects the perspectives of the reforms of the late 1970s and the 1980s, and their termination as symbolized by the Tiananmen massacre of June 1989.[17] The reforms of 1956–1957 and 1978–1989 and their

16. Named for the Bolshevik leader Nikolai Bukharin, 1888–1938, who took such a view in the mid 1920s. The definitive biography of Bukharin is Stephen F. Cohen, 1980.

17. Chinese leaders (and President Bush) deny that the Tiananmen massacre means the end of reform, but the ideological revival after June 4, 1989, makes fundamental economic changes highly unlikely and basic political changes from within the Party leadership impossible. Chinese leaders, having observed the changes in Eastern Europe and Nicaragua, know that democratizing the system will inevitably lead to their loss of power. Moreover, with the example of Ro-

failure color the ways in which we think about reform in China generally, and the specifics of each period of reform condition our understanding of other eras. This study of the reforms of 1956–1957 raises the following questions – which may defy answer – for analyzing later reform episodes: If the reforms of the 1950s had succeeded, what would China be like today? Was the failure of the 1957 reform inevitable? Were the mass suppressions in 1957 and 1989 caused by the same political processes? Why did the reforms of the 1950s and 1960s fail to take root? Have the reforms of 1979–1989 been sufficiently institutionalized to persevere even though reform efforts have been halted? How are reform and its termination today different from reform efforts and their failure in the past? Have the interests of key institutions changed significantly between the 1950s and the 1980s? Since many of these key institutions were responsible for the subversion of reform in the 1950s, are they still opposed to reform now, and if so, what is the significance of this opposition? Although a number of these questions are discussed in the concluding chapter, definitive answers to some, if not all, of them may not be possible. Nonetheless, it is hoped that this study of an earlier period of reform and its failure, highlighting inadequately studied aspects of the Chinese political economy and written in light of the existence of current reform efforts and their suppression, will increase understanding of contemporary developments, if only indirectly.

This study of the origins of the Great Leap Forward is organized analytically rather than chronologically. Part I, composed of Chapters 2 and 3, provides the necessary historical background and the conceptual framework needed to understand economic policy making in 1956–1957. Chapter 2 provides an overview of developments in China up to mid 1956 and previews developments in 1957, thus supplying the indispensable context needed to understand subsequent events. Chapter 3 develops the institutional perspective employed throughout the text. The reasons for adopting such an approach, the specific institutional interests of each major bureaucratic coalition, and patterns of bargaining and alliance behavior are all introduced here. Part II, consisting of five chapters, presents a case study of the rise and fall of reform and the rise of the Great Leap Forward. *Rashomon*-like, each of its first four chapters examines the perspective of each of the major coalitions and groups separately. Chapter 4 looks at the views of the finance–commerce–agriculture–light industry coalition. Chapter 5 focuses on how the planning and heavy industry coalition responded to efforts to reduce its

---

mania's Ceaucescu in mind, several individuals in the leadership must fear that any "reversal of verdicts" on the massacre will bring about not only their fall from power but also trials for murder.

primacy in the making of Chinese economic policy and in the allocation of resources, and on the counteroffensive it launched, which ultimately embodied many of the economic programs associated with the GLF. These included industry aiding agriculture, self-reliance, decentralization, and more emphasis on medium- and small-scale industry. Chapter 6 discusses the views of the Party with respect to its role as the entity responsible for social transformation. Chapter 7 studies the thoughts and actions of the top leadership to see why it first supported reform and then opted for a Great Leap Forward. Then Chapter 8 brings the perspectives of the various coalitions together in discussing the Third Plenum of the Eighth Central Committee (September 20 – October 9, 1957), where the reformist view was decisively defeated and the Great Leap Forward was initiated. This chapter also provides a brief overview of the Great Leap itself. Finally, Chapter 9 offers conclusions specific to the case at hand, suggests how the conceptual framework may be more broadly applicable to the study of Chinese politics, raises more general issues about the nature of political economy and reform in China, and offers some brief comparisons of Chinese political and economic developments in 1957 and 1989. A short appendix considers the nature of the constraints on Mao's ability to direct economic policy making, as well as providing evidence that those constraints indeed existed.

Part I

Historical background and conceptual approach

2

Overview: Chinese politics and economy, 1956–1957

The convocation of the Eighth National Congress of the Chinese Communist Party (CCP) in September 1956 marked a fundamental transition in the relationship between the Chinese state and Chinese society. By mid 1956 the outcome of the transition to socialism had been decided. All the institutional arrangements the Chinese leadership then associated with a socialist state (collectives in the rural sector, effective state ownership of the means of production, and an articulated bureaucratic structure) were then in place.[1] These institutions and the policies that had spawned them were not functioning very well, but the transition period had been completed.

Chinese leaders were justifiably proud of the rapid progress they had made. But once the clear and well-defined tasks of the transition period were accomplished – a decade or more ahead of schedule – the historical experience of the Soviet Union and the existing ideological and policy visions of the Chinese leadership became much less relevant. The fundamental goal of building a powerful socialist state remained, but that goal would not be achieved in the near future, and its attainment seemed to require the somewhat mechanical process of adding new industrial facilities. To be sure, the leadership was concerned about the problems caused by abrupt collectivization of the countryside and the transition to socialism in the urban areas, and many officials were preoccupied with trying to make the new institutions work more efficiently. But the convocation of the Eighth Party Congress on September 15, 1956, marked the beginning of a year-long debate in the leadership and the key organizations of Party and government over the nature and basic policies of an increasingly mature socialist state.

The debate was carried on in two largely separate arenas. In a heretofore unprecedented development, the Chinese political agenda split. On one track, key generalist leaders and involved specialists grappled with the issue of

1. In 1958, the leadership, especially Mao, felt that collectives were insufficient, and merged collectives to form communes.

state-society relations. The other area of contention was the strategy and tactics of economic development for both the short and long term. The participants in each forum were aware of the state of discussion in the other. But economic specialists were not active in the broader political discussions of state-society relations, and the generalists did not intervene in the economic debates.

A. *The pattern of politics before September 1956*

Chinese politics before 1954 is best described as a highly successful ad hoc decision-making system. The CCP and its leadership responded successfully to almost total economic, political, and social disruption caused by nearly a half-century of warfare on the Chinese mainland ended only by the CCP's victory in 1949. In relatively short order, land reform was carried out, inflation halted, the economy restored, and industrial construction begun. The Party organization grew rapidly, and by 1954 Party branches penetrated all levels of Chinese society. The governmental structure became more fully articulated, and the end of the Korean War in 1953 enabled the CCP to channel all of its energies into economic construction and social transformation.

In September 1954, the first constitution of the People's Republic of China (PRC) was promulgated, symbolizing the development of a more regularized political system. The Chinese party state resembled that of the Soviet Union in all important respects. But although structures were similar, the relationship among leaders in China was different from that in post-Stalin Russia. China was led by its revolutionary generation of political elites, most with limited formal education and little foreign travel. These leaders were men of tremendous confidence. They had defeated superior Kuomintang forces to win the Civil War, they believed they had defeated the Japanese in the war in China, and they had fought the United States to a standstill in Korea. Leadership relations were generally stable. Mao Zedong's position and prestige were unchallengeable, and only the issue of his health seemed to precipitate intraleadership struggles.[2] None of the other Chinese leaders sought to displace a healthy Mao, and their rankings and specialties were quite stable. Struggles for power within the leadership were rare in the 1949–1956 period.

2. On Mao's ill health, see Mao, 1977, p. 92 (this also reveals Mao's unrivaled power within the leadership – he had the right of approval of all Central Committee documents); and Schoenhals, 1986a (see p. 115, where Mao reveals he had had a stroke). The only major leadership struggle of the early and mid 1950s is thoroughly discussed in Teiwes, 1979a, ch. 5. On Mao's relations with his colleagues, see Teiwes, 1988, pp. 1–80.

While the CCP had extensive experience in the rural areas, it lacked knowledge of how to manage industrialization. In the early 1950s, the Party copied the Soviet model of development; China's First Five-Year Plan (FFYP) began officially in 1953, although it took two and a half years after the nominal starting point of the plan before its text was published. The plan was a mirror of five-year plans in the Soviet Union, concentrating overwhelmingly on the development of basic industries. The centerpiece of the Chinese plan was 156 whole plants imported from the Soviet Union. Most of these plants were in the heavy industrial sector, and they were the building blocks on which China's modern industry was to be constructed. The FFYP also called for the complete collectivization of Chinese agriculture by 1967 (the end of the Third Five-Year Plan) and for the complete nationalization of capitalist industry, handicrafts, and commerce by that time too. The basic industrialization of China was also slated for completion by 1967.[3]

Yet by the time the FFYP was published, signs of acceleration of the pace of advance set out in the plan were already present. Responding to criticism by a leading Chinese intellectual in late 1954, Mao Zedong launched an attack that ran counter to the relatively liberal policies toward culture and intellectuals that had been in existence since late 1953. The campaign against intellectuals who opposed Party rule (the so-called Hu Feng Clique) was expanded in early 1955 into the Campaign to Eradicate Hidden Counter-Revolutionaries. At the same time, rural rectification was launched.[4] These campaigns created incentives for cadres to overfulfill targets, thereby proving their political reliability.

Less than a month after Li Fuchun, chairman of the State Planning Commission, announced a goal of one million agricultural cooperatives by the end of the FFYP, Mao proclaimed that this figure was too low. Mao not only contradicted Li Fuchun's position; he overturned what had been in mid spring 1955 his own evaluation of the situation. He called for building 1.3 million co-ops by the end of the plan. This represented a 100 percent increase over 1955 levels. Because of the various campaigns Mao sanctioned in early 1955 and the inflammatory language he used to describe those who opposed his position – he singled out the Party's Rural Work Department and its leader Deng Zihui – Mao's speech launched a frenzy of activity in the rural areas, and his goals were greatly overfulfilled by mid 1956. Not only was coopera-

3. See *First Five Year Plan for Development of the National Economy of the People's Republic of China in 1953–1957*, 1956, and Li Fuchun, "Report on the First Five Year Plan for Development of the National Economy of the People's Republic of China in 1953–1957," in *Communist China, 1955–1959*, 1971, pp. 42–91.

4. See Mao, 1977, pp. 172–83. For a full treatment of the campaign, see Merle Goldman, 1971, ch. 7; on rural rectification, see Vogel, 1971, pp. 133–38, 142–46.

tivization just about completed by mid 1956, but co-ops were also turned into collectives.[5] Thus, the top item on the CCP's agricultural agenda was implemented more than a decade before the time specified by Li Fuchun.[6]

Mao and many other Chinese leaders were so encouraged by the successes of collectivization that they greatly sped up the timetable for the socialization (essentially the nationalization) of remaining privately owned industry, commerce, and handicrafts and for the rate of industrialization, creating the "small leap forward" of late 1955 and early 1956. "Socialist transformation" was thus also completed well in advance of its 1967 target date. Not surprisingly, the rapid institutional transformation associated with the "socialist high tide" created many problems.[7] The small leap saw a huge increase in investment funds (more than 60 percent over 1955), a tremendous rise in output targets, and other efforts to mobilize workers and staff to increase economic construction greatly.

In late 1955 and early 1956, Mao and a number of provincial first Party secretaries drew up the "Draft National Agricultural Program," or Forty Points on Agriculture. The goal of this twelve-year plan was one of more than doubling the agricultural output of China, using a variety of means. In fact, the document became a hodgepodge of measures, reflecting such social aims as the elimination of illiteracy as well as setting concrete production targets. The National Agricultural Program was flawed and, coupled with the pressure to fulfill targets years in advance of the schedule, led to serious problems in the rural areas.[8]

As Mao mobilized the Party to complete socialist transformation, Nikita Khrushchev denounced Stalin to the Twentieth Congress of the Communist Party of the Soviet Union. Khrushchev's criticisms of Stalin raised the larger

5. In co-ops of about twenty households, peasants were rewarded according to their contributions of property and capital as well as their contributions of labor. In a collective, averaging about two hundred families, the only criterion for remuneration was labor contributed.

6. Mao, 1977, pp. 184–283. On Mao's position in the spring of 1955 and on general agricultural policy before his July 31, 1955, speech on collectivization, see Deng Zihui, "Zai Quanguo Disanci Nongcun Gongzuo Huiyishangde Kaimuce" (Opening Address to the Third National Rural Work Conference), and Qiang Yuangan and Lin Bangguang, "Shilun Yijiuwuwu Nian Dangnei Guanyu Nongye Hezuohua Wentide Zhenglun" (Preliminary Discussion of the 1955 Inner Party Debate on Questions of Agricultural Collectivization), *Dangshi Yanjiu* (Research on Party History), 1981, no. 1, pp. 2–9, 10–17, respectively, and Bai Jianjun, "Yijiuwuwu Nian Xiatian Dangnei Guanyu Nongye Huozuohua Wentide Zhenglun ji qi Yingxiang" (The Inner Party Debate in the Summer of 1955 on the Question of Agricultural Collectivization and Its Influence), *Lilun Yuekan* (Theory Monthly), 1986, no. 8, pp. 30–33. For English-language analysis, see Shue, 1980, and Walker, 1966.

7. Mao, 1977, pp. 281–83, and MacFarquhar, 1974, pp. 19–25.

8. On the National Agricultural Program, see Mao, 1977, pp. 277–80; *Communist China, 1955–1959*, 1971, pp. 119–26; Chang, 1975, ch. 1; MacFarquhar, 1974, pp. 27–29; and Klatt, 1965. In particular, the Forty Points avoided the issue of the proper sequencing of a number of the measures it recommended; some of its regional targets were unrealistic; and the question of how to fund the program was largely ignored. Klatt is particularly good on problems of the Forty Points.

question of the relationship of the supreme leader of the Party to Party institutions and the relationship of the Party to the people. It would not have been hard for disgruntled Party members to liken Mao's arbitrary interventions to accelerate the pace of collectivization and socialist transformation to those of Stalin.[9] Even before Khrushchev's secret speech, however, Chinese leaders had already reached the conclusion that the relationship between the Party and the populace, and in particular the question of the role of intellectuals in the political system, deserved greater attention. The Chinese leadership authorized a degree of societal liberalization and viewed intellectuals as increasingly critical to the success of China's drive toward industrialization.[10] Of perhaps greater import was the Chinese claim that "certain systems" would be established in China to insure that a Stalin could not emerge there.[11] After Khrushchev's speech, Mao may have been more careful about unleashing personal initiatives. But he was also at the forefront of efforts to liberalize society.[12] At the very least, in 1956 he grudgingly supported most elements of Khrushchev's analysis of Stalin.

In September 1956, the CCP leadership faced a number of important political issues. None was critical or posed the threat of a crisis in the short term, but they all raised difficult questions for which existing Party experience and ideology had few ready answers. These included the roles and prerogatives of the top leader in the political system and his relationship to other top figures; the mission of the CCP now that socialism, at least as defined by ownership relations, was established in China; the state's relationship to the people; and how the state was to stimulate the creative energy of the people. Mao and other leaders spent the next year attempting to address this agenda.[13]

B. Economic problems and policies before September 1956

When the CCP took power in 1949, its ideas on how to develop agriculture were fairly well developed. These included land redistribution and collective cultivation. Patterns of agricultural landholding and the organization of

9. MacFarquhar, 1974, pp. 39–56.
10. In particular, Zhou Enlai, "On the Question of Intellectuals," in *Communist China, 1955–1959*, 1971, pp. 128–44.
11. "On the Historical Experience of the Dictatorship of the Proletariat," in *Communist China, 1955–1959*, 1971, pp. 144–51; see p. 149.
12. Lu Dingyi, "Let a Hundred Flowers Bloom, Let a Hundred Schools of Thought Contend," *Communist China, 1955–1959*, 1971, pp. 151–63, and MacFarquhar, 1974, who minutely chronicles Mao's interventions in 1956–1957.
13. The most complete discussion of the leadership and these questions is MacFarquhar, 1974, passim; see also Teiwes, 1979a, chs. 6 and 7; Harding, 1981, chs. 4 and 5; and Kraus, 1981. Because these questions have been so thoroughly treated, they will not receive major attention here.

productive activities went through a series of changes from 1949 to 1956. These stages were land reform; the formation of, first seasonal and then permanent, Mutual Aid Teams, where small groups of peasants cooperated to carry out major agricultural tasks; the establishment of cooperatives; and finally, the development of fully collectivized rural units of one hundred to two hundred households. Chinese leaders saw several advantages in larger units of production. First, they felt that the pooling of land and labor would unify fields, allowing the cultivation of more land, and promote a more even (and intensive) allocation of resources to the fields. Second, they recognized that the larger units created economies of scale. Third, they believed that planning (and tax collection) was also easier when collectives rather than individual households were the units of organization. Finally, ideology convinced them that the larger the unit, the better. The larger the unit, the more socialist principles could be used in management and distribution.

Chinese leaders did not favor large-scale investment in agriculture. During the FFYP only about 7 percent of all invested funds went to agriculture, and most of this went to a few large water-conservancy and hydroelectric projects. This meant that peasants would have to invest their own savings in order to increase production substantially. Party leaders felt that collectives could better mobilize and more efficiently use peasant resources than could individual peasants.

Before the launching of the collectivization movement, the CCP had instituted a policy of unified purchase and supply of grain. This policy served several functions, the most important of which forced peasants to deliver a fixed quota of grain to state purchasing agents at prices set by the government. These prices were well below the market price. In this way, not only was the state assured of an adequate supply of grain, but the combination of the low price paid to peasants and the high price of industrial products was a major source of funds for the industrialization of China. A second major reason for this policy was that it cut the more speculatively inclined of China's peasants off from access to the market.[14] In the first winter this policy was applied, an excess of 3.5 million tons of grain was collected by the state (or more than 10 percent above normal levels, despite a poor harvest). This led to severe problems in the rural areas and may have caused some high-ranking CCP leaders to reconsider a harsh extractive strategy in the countryside.[15]

The policy of industrialization, with overwhelming priority to heavy industry, was uncontroversial. Chinese leaders lacked experience in industry,

14. See Shue, 1980. ch. 5.
15. On excessive procurement and the political tensions this caused, see Bernstein, 1969.

and disputes were usually results not of conflicting ideological positions but of differing perceptions of a strange new area of activity.

The Chinese copied the Soviet model of development very literally. In this they were aided extensively by Soviet advisers. Soviet-supplied factories were the core projects of industrialization, and Soviet procedures guided Chinese planning and management practices. Central to planning was the use of material balances to formulate the plan, and "one-man management" in the factory to run the plant.[16]

By 1956, however, Chinese leaders came to realize that there were serious problems in the Chinese economy. Some leaders, particularly Mao Zedong, focused on the general problems associated with the Soviet model. Other leaders focused on the consequences of the small leap forward of 1956.

In April 1956, after thorough discussions with thirty-four ministers and other concerned officials, Mao Zedong summarized their findings in his famous speech "On the Ten Major Relationships."[17] In this address, Mao stressed problems associated with the Soviet model but advocated only incremental changes – moving in the direction of greater balance – in the allocation of resources dictated by the model. He argued that too much investment and concern went to heavy industry and not enough to agriculture and light industry. He suggested that the ratio of light industrial investment to heavy industrial investment should change from 1:8 (as it was in the FFYP) to 1:7. He failed to mention how much more investment agriculture should receive. His views suggested the development of dangerous disproportions in the economy. The growth of agricultural production was falling behind the needs of the growing population, the need for light industrial raw materials, and export demands. Without major increases in farm output, the rate of overall growth in China would decelerate. By 1956 it was becoming increasingly clear that the rural sector would have trouble fulfilling its targets in the FFYP (targets were not reached in 1953, 1954, and 1956). Mao argued that slightly more current investment in agriculture and light industry would allow for faster heavy industrial growth in the future. He upheld the priority of heavy industry but advocated slightly less emphasis on heavy industrial

16. One-man management, except in the Northeast, was one of two areas where the Chinese did not blindly copy Soviet practice. (The other was piece rates. The Chinese never used piece rates as extensively as the Soviets, and seemed to resist the expansion of their use beyond about 40 percent of the industrial work force. See Charles Hoffman, 1967.) One-man management weakened the authority of the Party committee in enterprises, and a new system under which the manager handled affairs under the unified leadership of the Party committee became policy at the Eighth Party Congress. On one-man management, see Schurmann, 1968, pt. IV; Brugger, 1976; and Andors, 1977, ch. 3.

17. Mao, 1977, pp. 284–307.

production. His redistribution of investment funds was probably not enough to relieve the agricultural bottleneck.

A second major issue Mao raised was the centralization of administration associated with the Soviet model. Local authorities had little say about economic activities in their areas. Moreover, they had few resources to develop local projects. Central ministries in Beijing exerted direct control over the activities of enterprises, and enterprises required central approval to increase fixed assets by as little as 200 yuan, or about $100.[18] There was a tremendous amount of red tape and buck passing, and a slow response time in many matters.[19]

Along with these general problems, the political agenda in 1956 contained a number of more recent problems spawned by the small leap – the adventuristic increase in industrial production and investment in the first half of 1956. First, there was the question of the leap itself. By May–June 1956 it was becoming unsustainable, and Zhou Enlai, Chen Yun, and others gradually introduced policies of economic retrenchment. Mao was displeased by such policies, but he did not actively oppose them. Second, many problems existed in the newly formed collectives. Management systems were crude; rural cadres simply espoused a "commandist" work style of ordering peasants about; they concentrated only on principal crops and paid little attention to subsidiary crops and sideline production. Incentive systems were weak in the new collectives: Private plots were abolished (briefly); privately owned draft animals were confiscated and given to the collective; and too large a percentage of collective funds was used to expand production and pay administrative expenses, and not enough funds were distributed to the peasants. All of these problems harmed production and the enthusiasm of the peasants for the new institutions. Party leaders spent a great deal of time from late 1956 to late 1957 trying to iron out the many problems of the collectives.[20]

A third problem spawned by the small leap was its impact on industry and consumers. In 1956, investment increased by 62 percent over the figure for 1955. This greatly exceeded the supply of raw materials, and enterprises engaged in bargaining, payoffs, and other illegal maneuvers to obtain materials, giving rise to inflationary pressures. The crash campaign associated with the small leap led to excessive attention to the quantity of output at the expense of quality, variety, and workers' safety. Poor quality meant that

18. See Donnithorne, 1967, p. 473.

19. The Soviets were not unaware of this and launched their own decentralization in 1957, something the Chinese undoubtedly observed with great interest. On Soviet decentralization, see Breslauer, 1982; Katz, 1972, esp. chs. 5 and 6; and Nove, 1968, chs. 2 and 7.

20. An excellent short discussion of problems in the collectives is Walker, 1965.

many new products had to be remade or that consumers had to bear the burden of buying virtually useless items. In either case, the end users were dissatisfied.

Negative financial effects constituted a fourth problem. The state ran a budget deficit of around 2 billion yuan, or more than 6 percent of government revenues. This was the product of a number of factors. About 1.4 million more industrial workers than planned were hired in 1956 (or more than 10 percent of the number of industrial workers in 1955), greatly enlarging the wage bill. In addition, there was a wage increase totalling about 2 billion yuan for those workers who had been hired several years earlier. Agricultural loans were also increased by more than 2 billion yuan. The budget deficit and all the extra currency in circulation contributed to inflation as increases in production failed to keep up with consumer spending power. Similarly, taxes and the profits of enterprises (the principal sources of state revenue) did not increase as fast as did state expenditures.

Moreover, because most consumer goods were ultimately dependent on agricultural raw materials and the rate of agriculture growth was slowing, this situation of shortages (or "tenseness," as the Chinese described it) in the market would be prolonged. A shortage of consumer goods undermined the policy of industrial incentives, which was based on material interests. What good were bonuses and steep wage gradations if there were no goods to buy?[21]

Socialist transformation also created severe difficulties for the newly socialized industrial, commercial, and handicraft enterprises. They suffered from many of the same problems as agricultural collectives: They were too large; incentives were destroyed when individual craft workers or traders were brought together in one organization; the variety and quality of goods produced fell; and management was chaotic.[22]

Socialist transformation brought about another problem. Previously, capitalist enterprises had been controlled through the state's monopoly in the supply of raw materials. Yet with socialist transformation, these enterprises, referred to as joint public-private and collective enterprises, while nominally different from state-owned enterprises, functioned exactly as state enterprises did. New mechanisms of control and planning were required if they were to be fully integrated into the national economy. In 1957, joint public-

21. The problems discussed in these three paragraphs are examined in Bo Yibo, "Report on the Working of the National Economic Plan for 1956 and the Draft National Plan for 1957," *Current Background*, no. 465 (July 9, 1957), and Li Xiannian, "Report on Final Accounts for 1956 and the 1957 Budget," *Current Background*, no. 464 (July 5, 1957).

22. Chen Yun, "On the Socialist Transformation of Private Industry and Commerce," in *New China Advances to Socialism*, 1956, pp. 102–17.

private and collective enterprises numbered 112,000. State-owned enterprises totaled 58,000.[23] Thus, the state now supervised the affairs of almost 200 percent more enterprises than it had in 1955. This undoubtedly severely strained the managerial capacity of economic departments.

The leap of 1956 caused one final problem. Many peasants seeking work migrated to the urban areas in 1956, swelling urban population by 6.3 million, for the largest yearly increase in the FFYP period.[24] The state was forced to draw more than three million tons of grain from state reserves to feed the urban population. This amounted to about one-seventh of the total grain reserve, and demonstrated the state's need to extract more resources from the slow-growing rural sector.[25]

In 1955–1956, the leading economic officials were Chen Yun, China's top-ranking vice-premier and general economic overseer, and Li Fuchun, chairman of the State Planning Commission, with Premier Zhou Enlai effectively working with both of them. Chen and Li had worked closely together formulating the FFYP, and through mid 1955 held very similar views on economic construction.[26] But beginning in late 1955 their views began to diverge. Before socialist transformation, Chen Yun affirmed the general view that all elements of the Chinese economy needed to be planned, not just state-owned industrial enterprises.[27] But as he directly supervised the process of socialist transformation of capitalist industry and commerce, he began to doubt the utility of bringing these enterprises under planning.[28] Indeed, at the Eighth Party Congress, Chen called for market relations to guide the activities of these enterprises. In the same forum, Li Fuchun continued to support the idea of incorporating all elements of the economy under planning.[29] Li objected to a number of the points Mao made in his speech on the Ten Major Relationships, while Chen Yun supported Mao's calls for more balanced development.[30] In short, as embodied in the two top economic officials of the PRC, ideas about economic development and management

23. State Statistical Bureau, 1982, p. 207. This source does not give figures before 1957. Perkins, 1966, p. 109, has a slightly different set of figures, with data for 1955. In that year, there were a few more than 15,000 socialist industrial enterprises out of a total of 125,000 industrial firms.

24. Cited in Orleans, 1982; see p. 284.

25. Chen Yun, 1981, p. 122.

26. Bo Yibo, "Comrade Fuchun Will Always Be with Us," in Foreign Broadcast Information Service, *Daily Report, China,* January 11, 1980, L 11–L 17; see L 13.

27. Chen Yun, 1982, p. 242.

28. Ibid., pp. 271–309.

29. These views are discussed in Chapters 4 and 5.

30. See Li Fuchun, "Progress of the First Five Year Plan for Developing the National Economy," in *New China Advances to Socialism,* 1956, pp. 79–102; for analysis, see MacFarquhar, 1974, ch. 5.

began to diverge. Chen Yun increasingly favored balanced, stable growth. Li Fuchun championed rapid growth, particularly in heavy industry. And Mao Zedong favored rapid but more balanced growth.

Leaders not directly responsible for the functioning of the Chinese economy could claim tremendous economic achievements in the 1949–1956 period, in 1956 in particular, but officials charged with running the economy were well aware that the economic system was rife with problems. How could the budget deficit and inflation be cured? What could be done to raise agricultural output? What was the best administrative system for running the economy? What were the most appropriate allocations of investment funds? These and other questions weighed heavily on the minds of China's decision makers at the Eighth Party Congress. The answers to these questions presented by leading officials depended on the coalition of which they were a part.

When the leadership assembled for the Eighth Party Congress in September 1956, it was thus confronted with a host of problems, issues, and dilemmas. Of most immediate concern were problems caused by the small leap of 1956. The economy needed to be cooled down, and basic structures in the countryside required consolidation. Party leaders also had to decide what was the best economic system for China and what was the appropriate allocation of resources to each economic sector. Answers to these larger questions were considerably harder to formulate, and there was significantly less agreement on how to respond to these long-term issues than there was on how to solve immediate economic problems. The Party also faced crucial questions of social policy. China's development efforts required intellectuals to play a greater role in economic construction. But how could the Party insure the political loyalty of the intellectuals? How was the contradiction between professionalism and politics to be resolved? Most fundamental, Party leaders confronted the relationship between the Party and society now that socialism was established in the People's Republic. In other words, how was the transition from revolutionary transformation to problem management to be carried out?

C. Preview: politics and economics, September 1956 – October 1957

At the Eighth Party Congress in September 1956, the CCP affirmed that the key contradiction in Chinese society was that of an advanced superstructure and a backward economic base. Economic development, or "the development of the productive forces," officially became the highest priority. The congress also endorsed ideas about improving the functioning of the CCP and the state apparatus, decentralizing authority, and expanding the role of Chinese citizens in political life. Proposals to modify or reform the economic system were also presented. Few concrete resolutions emerged from the congress on the economy and political issues. Yet the speeches of leading figures defined the subsequent policy debates.

The following year of policy contention can be divided into three periods. The first, from October 1956 to the end of February 1957, marked the high point of the influence of the financial coalition led by Chen Yun and Li Xiannian. During this period, Mao Zedong devoted himself to questions about the nature of socialist society and more particularly to how contradictions in Chinese society could be resolved. Financial officials, especially Chen Yun, dominated economic decision making, introducing market elements to the economy and carrying out other policies that undercut the position of the planning and heavy industry coalition. The second period lasted from March 1957 to mid June 1957. In these months, Mao and the Party were preoccupied with Party rectification and with encouraging intellectuals to speak out freely to air their views and to let "one hundred flowers bloom and . . . one hundred schools of thought contend." In other words, academic, if not intellectual, freedom was official policy. At the same time, the planning and heavy industry coalition responded to the challenge emanating from the financial coalition, and leading planners presented an innovative program that addressed the problems of the Chinese economy while protecting their bureaucratic interests. Finally, the third period, from the second half of June to mid October 1957, saw the reintegration of the Chinese political agenda and the beginning of a new line of development – the Great Leap Forward. During this period, Mao and the Party suppressed the critics of the Party and moved to adopt the planners' program.

The two main themes of the first period (October 1956 to the end of February 1957) were Mao Zedong's drive to rectify the Party, expand the role of the people in criticizing the Party, and include non-Party elements of the population in the affairs of the state, and Chen Yun's assertion of the interests of the financial coalition.

Foreign-policy issues (Polish nationalism and the Hungarian uprising)[31] and the economy were the main items on the agenda of the Second Plenum of the Eighth Central Committee, which met on November 10–15, 1956. Zhou Enlai announced a 20 percent reduction in the investment budget for 1957 (compared with 1956) and stressed the need for a thorough consolida-

31. On these events in general, see Brzezinski, 1966, ch. 10. On the Chinese role in these events and their impact in China, see Friedman, 1965; Gittings, 1968, ch. 6; MacFarquhar, 1974, ch. 12; and Radvanyi, 1970.

tion of the newly socialized economy. The commercial network was a particularly troublesome area; Chen Yun assumed the portfolio of minister of commerce. After the plenum, Zhou Enlai departed on a diplomatic tour of Asia and Eastern Europe that kept him out of China from late November to early February 1957, leaving Chen Yun as acting premier.

In December 1956, the Politburo met to reevaluate the Stalin question and the uprisings in Eastern Europe. Two decisions emerged from this meeting. One was the document "More on the Historical Experience of the Dictatorship of the Proletariat." The other was the apparent decision to launch a Party rectification campaign in 1958.[32]

In January 1957, opposition to Mao's Hundred Flowers policy was voiced, especially by the General Political Department of the People's Liberation Army.[33] Also in January, Mao called a meeting of provincial Party secretaries where he lobbied for the Hundred Flowers and the opening up of the political system to intellectuals and other Chinese citizens. At the same meeting, Chen Yun put forward the programmatic position of the financial coalition, centering on the three balances – in budgets, in loans and loan repayments, and in supply and demand – and appeared to secure the support of at least Mao and the Party secretaries for the financial coalition's platform for guiding economic developments in 1957.

By February 1957 Mao was convinced that Party opposition to his Hundred Flowers policy was sufficiently widespread to require him to seek a forum for his message more amenable to his control. To that end, he exercised his prerogative as head of state and convened a meeting of the Supreme State Conference. There, on February 27, 1957, he gave his famous speech on contradictions among the people. Mao's address so changed the political situation that he and other generalist political leaders devoted no attention to economic affairs for the next three months, leaving the budgeteers and planners to manage the economy and debate their two policy proposals.

Despite Mao's speech on the correct handling of contradictions among the people, it required almost two more months of lobbying by the Chairman to convince the Party that it should allow "blooming and contending" and to persuade intellectuals to take his calls seriously. Once under way, the Hundred Flowers Campaign became one of the few occasions when the leaders permitted the populace to present their views in a fairly direct and free way.

32. Text of "More . . ." is in *Communist China, 1955–1959*, 1971, pp. 257–72. For analysis, see MacFarquhar, 1974, pp. 172–78. In general, the documentation for other statements made in this chapter is fully presented in Chapters 4–8.
33. See Chen Qitong, Ma Hanbing, Chen Yading, and Lu Le, "Women dui Muqian Wenyi Gongzuode Jige Yijian" (Several of Our Opinions on Current Literary and Art Work), *Renmin Ribao* (People's Daily), January 7, 1957.

This resulted in such an outpouring of criticism of the regime, by intellectuals and students in particular, that the leaders quickly reversed their decision to allow citizens to speak in uncontrolled situations. The details of the criticisms and the dynamics of this extraordinary event have been widely discussed.[34] Suffice it to say that intellectuals and students charged the Party with grossly mismanaging the affairs of state, becoming a new class of rulers divorced from the people, and managing things about which the Party knew nothing.

On April 27, 1957, the CCP Central Committee announced the inauguration of a rectification campaign. The rectification directive allowed non-Party members to participate in the rectification of Party cadres, but did not require them to do so. Nonetheless, Mao and the United Front Work Department encouraged intellectuals to criticize the Party, which they did. But as the criticisms mounted, Mao began to have second thoughts. On June 8, 1957, an editorial in *Renmin Ribao* (People's Daily) announced the end of the Hundred Flowers, and on June 18, 1957, a revised text of Mao's contradictions speech was published with insertions that greatly narrowed the scope of legitimate criticism ex post facto. These postdated standards were then used to send hundreds of thousands of intellectuals, capitalists, and others to "labor reform," "labor education," or prison. Many of these people remained incarcerated until early 1979. This routing of the Party's critics, most of whom had rather loyally followed the Party's call to express their opinions, was called the Anti-Rightist Campaign.

Compared with the turbulence in the political system, the economy and economic issues seemed to be isles in the lee of the storm. This was partly illusory. The leaders of the financial coalition continued to push for the three balances, though Chen Yun appears to have been much less vigorous in personally propagating his opinions during this period. The leaders of the planning coalition, Bo Yibo and Li Fuchun, embarked on an inspection trip that took them to Sichuan and Shaanxi in April and May. On their trip, and in the newspapers during this time, they redefined the fundamental interests of the planning coalition in a way that at once invalidated many of Chen Yun's criticisms and was more appealing to the Party. They called for self-reliance, emphasis on building medium-sized and small factories, decentralization, and industry aiding agriculture. The development of the refined policy platform of the planners is the major theme of this second period, March 1957 to mid June 1957.

The campaign to repress and purge the Party's critics was launched in

---

34. Among the many sources on this period, see T.H.E. Chen, 1960; Doolin, 1964; Rene Goldman, 1962; MacFarquhar, 1960; Nieh, 1981; and Spence, 1981, ch. 12.

earnest in late June and July. All Chinese periodicals devoted extensive coverage to disproving the charges made against the Party during the Hundred Flowers. The entire line of policy development since the Party's conference on intellectuals in January 1956 was found unsound. The Party and its leaders concluded that intellectuals were unreliable and, by a rather contorted logic, came to believe that the voices of the Hundred Flowers reflected the views of only a rotten handful who created problems because the Party had been less assertive in exercising the dictatorship of the proletariat than it had been in earlier periods. The lesson of the Hundred Flowers was thus obvious. The Party had actively to lead all aspects of Chinese life. The Hundred Flowers revealed that there were enemies or potential enemies lurking, awaiting the opportunity to strike out at the Party. Class struggle still existed, and it was much more intense than Mao and other CCP leaders had thought in late 1956 and early 1957. These conclusions of the Party and the leadership greatly reinforced the reemergence of the platform of the Party as an agent of social transformation.

Failure of the Hundred Flowers and the actual content of the criticisms of the Party undermined the prestige and power of Mao and the CCP. In the short run, the loss of prestige could be handled by denying that there was a problem and crushing all those who had spoken out. The lesson of this purge would not be lost on others who might have felt betrayed by the abrupt change of political course. Heightened political tension (and terror) would silence opposition and doubts. But how could the Party's image be restored to a more positive footing? The answer was for the CCP to do those things that it did best and to try to avoid those things in which it was inexperienced. In other words, the Party would employ social transformation policies and mobilization campaigns in all areas rather than have the Party and the state develop along more rational legal lines. By denying the differences between the present and the Yanan days of the early 1940s, the Party revived styles of work that had fallen increasingly out of favor.

Developments in the economy contributed to reevaluation of the Party's role. All economic policy in 1957 was based on the belief that a bumper harvest could be obtained in the summer and fall. After the extensive flooding of 1956, it was hoped that the weather would be milder in 1957. With a year's consolidation, it was also hoped that the collectives would be stronger and that higher prices for subsidiary agricultural products would stimulate production. These expectations were dashed. The harvest of 1957 was poor, increasing only about 2 percent over the preceding year. Its failure to keep up with population growth undercut a strategy of development based on light industry and agriculture. Moreover, it created a perceived grain crisis in the summer and fall of 1957. The prospect of even more stringent supplies of food and consumer goods no doubt increased the sullenness of the urban population. Once again, agricultural production was a pressing problem. An incentivist policy to deal with agriculture was ruled out as politically unacceptable and not very effective in practice, or so critics could claim from the experience of 1957.

Given the changed political environment, Chen Yun and his allies were not likely to fare well. While Chen attempted to defend most elements of the financial coalition's program, he was not effective in stopping the momentum building up behind the planning coalition's program and the increased emphasis on mass mobilization. The free market was closed down in August, and the Party launched a rural socialist education campaign that imposed much greater political control on the collectives.

The planners quickly took advantage of the budgeteers' weakened position. Other planning leaders amplified Bo Yibo's ideas about developing agriculture through the application of heavy industrial inputs. The planning coalition's proposals were so persuasive that political leaders accepted them with increasing enthusiasm, in particular at the Third Plenum of the Eighth Central Committee.

The Third Plenum began on September 20, 1957, with a report by Deng Xiaoping on the rectification campaign. Deng tried to devise a weak compromise of criticizing the rightists but continuing to employ intellectuals. Reports were also made by Zhou Enlai, Chen Yun, and Deng Zihui. Chen and Deng Zihui attempted to cool the flames of Party mobilization, but their efforts were symbolically rejected when the Central Committee issued a directive on developing a mass campaign to build water conservancy projects in the winter of 1957 and spring of 1958. On October 4, the Soviet Union launched the first sputnik. Sputnik had a profound effect on Mao, convincing him that the socialist camp was now superior to the capitalist world. The Chairman, who had been in semiseclusion from late July until the Third Plenum, in his concluding speech adopted the planners' program, injected his own concerns of even faster rates of advance and renewed mass mobilization, and launched the Great Leap Forward.

Why did the Great Leap Forward unfold in this manner? The following chapters examine the developments of 1956 and 1957 in much greater depth. But to understand where the coalitions came from, it is necessary to explicate the nature of coalitions and state economic action in China.

3

Institutions and policy in China

This chapter presents a broad framework for analyzing institutional and leadership interactions in China. As noted in Chapter 1, this framework is heavily influenced by the "new institutionalism" literature. Much of this recent literature, however, focuses on democratic or authoritarian political systems with market economies and therefore cannot be applied easily to the study of communist nations with planned economies. The lines of cleavage in communist societies are different from those in democratic or authoritarian systems, and the all-encompassing nature of the state apparatus in a communist country makes moot much of the debate about the role of the state (versus societal influences). Yet despite these differences, there are still significant insights to be gained from this approach.

The following thirteen propositions about organizations, institutional alignments, the nature of the Chinese state, and the relationships among institutions and leaders in China should *not* be seen as deductive axioms on which the remainder of the chapter expands. They reflect basic steps in the argument that are developed in the course of the study and are offered to make the logic of the analytical framework as explicit as possible. These statements are phrased quite generally, and most are China-specific, although they may apply to other states as well.

1. For a modern state and the regime ruling it to progress from poverty to relative prosperity and to survive when confronted by severe international threats, at least four functional imperatives must be met: resource extraction, security, economic development, and national integration. In addition, a revolutionary state explicitly adopts a fifth function, social transformation. All the functions of the state are indispensable, given the assumptions of international conflict and a quest for broad material improvement. Each is at least partially in conflict with the others.

2. Institutional and organizational structures are created to manage these

functions. In the case of a regime that comes to power through a revolutionary process, these organizational structures are consciously created.

3. The interplay of structures and functions gives rise to tendencies of articulation, or broad policy programs. Individuals within each structure are assigned responsibility for administering policy in one key area. Shared perspectives and the operation of the personnel system lead to a fairly widespread consensus within each institution on just what policies should be adopted. This in turn leads to a broad overall view of which state goals should be emphasized.

4. A bureaucracy has four sets of interests: the personal goals of its staff; the corporate interests of the agency – those policies that facilitate the effective performance of the bureau's major mission(s); the programmatic interests of the organization – a broader range of policies or a policy program that facilitates the pursuit of corporate interests, not necessarily closely related to the unit's functional responsibilities; and the bureau's leadership interests – its choices of who is to lead the country or hold other key posts (because those individuals will look sympathetically on the bureau). In most cases, individuals outside a bureaucracy determine how well it fulfills its corporate goals.

5. An agency's programmatic and leadership interests are more likely to be pursued successfully when the leaders judge that the agency's corporate goals have been achieved. Individuals may have means of achieving their personal interests other than loyal service to their bureau. The better the unit pursues its corporate, programmatic, and leadership interests, however, the easier it will be generally for individuals within the unit to attain personal goals.

6. Central leaders in charge of the affairs of one area of state policy tend to change from being statesmen to being advocates. In other words, a process of "reverse cooptation" (or cooptation from below) takes place.

7. In order to bolster their claims on state resources, bureaucracies form coalitions. Coalitions tend to develop along "system," or *xitong*, lines.

8. Bureaucratic ideologies and cultures, while important in protecting the routines of bureaus and asserting the importance of the mission performed by the bureau for the state, are too narrow and particularistic to form the contact points on which bureaucratic coalitions can be built. Bureaucratic coalitions require the formation of broader ideological or policy frameworks on which separate bureaucratic ideologies are hung. A framework is the least common denominator of the interests of the organizations in the coalition and becomes the general tendency associated with it.

9. A coalition may be offensive or defensive in nature. An offensive coali-

tion implies a greater degree of interaction and a more active program of action (to alter the status quo) than does a defensive coalition.

10. The more a coalition controls its procedures for personnel management, the less likely it is that alternatives to the general tendency of that coalition will appear.

11. Because the functions of the state change slowly and because of the costs sunk in organizations, the tendencies associated with each coalition also change slowly. This is why the same policy options keep recurring in the political histories of socialist states.

12. The leaders of the state are constrained significantly by the choices presented to them by the coalitions. This does not prevent the leaders from developing new policy initiatives, but it does make bold new initiatives less likely.

13. The tendencies and policy packages of each coalition are comprehensive. The individual planks of these platforms are interdependent. Coalition leaders push hard for the complete policy packages they prefer. Central leaders, on the other hand, must ensure that all requirements for effective state action are at least minimally satisfied with the resources available. The leaders attempt to pick and choose, try to develop viable, integrated plans, or, if need be, compromise when clashing system views are presented. Compromise solutions undermine the coherence of coalition programs and lead to suboptimal performance. This in turn leads to renewed claims by each coalition for the dominance of its comprehensive platform. Leaders may then elect to adopt one coalition's overall perspective. When this occurs, the other functions of the state tend to be slighted, raising the prospect that necessary minimum levels of performance will not be maintained and triggering another round of policy debate. This dynamic helps to explain why there has been so much policy instability in China.

This chapter will expand on and support these points. The basic argument is that the functions of the state, or the requirements of effective state action, and the organizations designed to manage these functions give rise to various tendencies within the political system. These tendencies at least partially conflict, limit the choices available to leaders, and structure the decision-making environment, but do not preclude the ability of elites, on occasion, to formulate innovative policies. This argument will be developed as follows. (1) The functions of the state will be introduced briefly; (2) the politics of functionally oriented systems (coalitions) will then be presented in a general way; (3) the analysis will be made more concrete and applied to the Chinese political system in an analysis of leadership and policy making; (4) the specific characteristics and platforms of the coalitions of the Chinese political system will be presented summarily; and finally, (5) some of the conceptual and empirical difficulties of such an approach to Chinese politics will be raised.

A. *The functions of the state*

The emergence of the European nation-state over the last three or four centuries has been one of the epochal developments in human history. The state appeared in an "international" context, characterized by anarchy.[1] This self-help system placed certain requirements on political entities if they were to survive. Geography, resource distribution, and other factors may have mitigated the imperatives facing the nascent states of Europe, but in the final analysis they all faced the same choice. In a nutshell, they could develop armed forces, extract more resources from society to pay for these forces, create a bureaucracy to administer the military and to collect taxes, become increasingly involved with the domestic economy as technology developed in order to guarantee availability to the military of sufficient munitions, provide internal security forces to deal with resistance to greater resource extraction, and finally institute new forms of state-society linkages to lessen resistance to the growth of the state and to mobilize the populace to serve state ends, or they would face the very likely prospect of being conquered or being absorbed into an emergent state that did fulfill these imperatives.[2] In short, there was a basic functionalist logic to the development of the modern state.[3] For a state to emerge and survive, it thus had to fulfill four major functions: resource extraction and mobilization; maintenance of order, both internally and in the international arena; economic development; and national integration. The means by which these functions were accomplished varied, but certain minimal levels of successful task performance were essential.[4]

1. As used here, "anarchy" does not mean the absence of rules, but rather the absence of hierarchical authority. The importance of anarchy in the study of international relations has been a hallmark of the work of Kenneth Waltz. See Waltz, 1954 and 1979.
2. These points are developed in much greater detail in many sources. Some of the most important are Bendix, 1978; Giddens, 1985; Gilbert, 1975; Skocpol, 1979; Tilly, 1975 and 1985; and of course Weber, 1978, esp. chs. 9 and 13.
3. A number of authors in the new institutionalism school deny that there is a functionalist logic to institutions. See March and Olsen, 1984, esp. p. 737, and Ikenberry, 1988, esp. p. 226. In the context of the development of the European state, I think these views are incorrect.
4. The functionalist logic to state development has relaxed, if not disappeared totally, over the last several decades, particularly in Africa and possibly in Latin America. For a critique of the Weberian notion of state development, especially applicable to Africa, see Jackson and Rosberg, 1982. I am grateful to Henry Bienen for calling their argument to my attention. Nonetheless, the Chinese experience is closer to European state building than to the experience in sub-Saharan Africa because of the severe international pressures felt by China since 1840 and

A fifth state function has come into prominence more recently. As previous regimes failed to satisfy the minimum requirements for effective state action (the four functions just discussed),[5] socially transformative revolutionary movements arose in the twentieth century, best exemplified by the Bolsheviks and the Chinese Communist Party (CCP). Class and other social relationships were radically altered once these revolutionary movements seized power and began to consolidate their rule. Often social transformation was combined with economic transformation in order to increase the state's ability to survive. Indeed, the coming to power of a consciously revolutionary regime within a state often provoked increased international pressures. Thus, in addition to the four previously named functions of the state, the modern revolutionary state has a fifth function – social transformation.

The leadership of a revolutionary state constructs structures, or systems of organizations, to manage or carry out the five functions. A complex apparatus of administration is built to direct economic processes, to manage the extraction and mobilization of resources, and to foster economic and social development. Military and police forces, if they do not already exist, are created to serve the security functions of the state. A variety of united-front, mass-organization, and pseudo-democratic bodies are established to reintegrate the newly restructured polity. The raison d'être of the Communist Party, in addition to assuming the mantle of leadership generally, is to transform the old society.

A revolutionary regime creates these systems to manage the functions of the state somewhat more consciously than do states that have evolved over longer historical periods. Even in nonrevolutionary states, however, the growth of organizations (structures) has been a major part of the history of the modern state. As Weber argues, without either structures with greater capacity than feudal or patriarchal networks or the possibility of charismatic leadership to deal with routine affairs of state, political entities could not become modern nation-states. Only organizational networks provide the sovereign with the capacity to meet the requisites of state building and survival.

As fundamental state tasks interact with the structures designed to carry them out, organizational routines develop. These routines are ways of looking at the problems associated with a function and at how that function relates to the operation of the state as a whole.[6] These organizational views, in

the belief of almost all leaders and intellectuals that such pressure was a matter of life and death for the nation. See Bedeski, 1975 and 1981.

   5. This is one of Skocpol's (1979) main points.

   6. In addition to a number of the sources cited in n. 2, these statements draw on Wilson, 1973; Pfeffer, 1981; Selznick, 1984; Stinchcombe, 1965; Downs, 1967; Douglas, 1986; and Kaufman, 1975.

turn, develop into specific "tendencies" – alternative directions or value allocations preferred by leaders associated with the different functions.[7] In other words, functions give rise to structures, or systems, which give rise to tendencies. Tendencies develop because organizations create methods to manage the tasks they are assigned. Over time, organizations learn under what conditions they can best meet their responsibilities and under what conditions they will have trouble fulfilling their assigned duties. Since leaders and the members of an organization are rewarded largely on the basis of how their unit performs, they advocate policy positions that increase the likelihood that the organization will fulfill its tasks. Because organizational missions are largely fixed, the tendencies of bureaucratic organizations exhibit great stability. Since the functions of the state usually change only slowly, the tendencies associated with those functions also change only slightly over time.[8]

B. The politics of functionally oriented systems

The five functions of a revolutionary regime introduced above (resource extraction, resource mobilization, security, national integration, and social transformation) may not be an exhaustive list of the basic tasks of a socialist state. For example, education and culture are not fully accounted for.[9] For purposes of this study, however, discussion of additional systems is not necessary.

The five systems to be examined in this work will be called the Extraction and Allocation System (EAS); the Economic Transformation System (ETS); the Integrative System (IS); the Social Transformation System (STS); and the Security System (SS). These names and the initials associated with them can be quite confusing. For the sake of readability and clarity, the EAS will most often be labeled the budgeteers, the financial coalition, or the budget group; the ETS will be the planners or the planning and heavy industry coalition; the IS will be referred to as the integrators; the STS will be called the mobilizers or the Party; and the SS will most often be referred to simply as the military and the police. This association of systems with particular name tags

7. The classic discussion of tendency analysis is Griffiths, 1971.

8. Kaufman, 1975, is an excellent brief discussion of why institutions are resistant to change. The association of function and tendency helps to explain why many discussions of economic reform in China and the Soviet Union today sound very similar to proposals made decades ago. There is a recurring pattern to policy arguments because of the continuing linkages of functions, structures, and tendencies in these political systems.

9. "Culture" is used here to mean an intellectual pursuit, not the basic traditions and fabric of society. Elements of both education and culture fall under several systems, but there would appear to be room for the development of another system incorporating these two elements. Perhaps other systems and functions as well might be identified by other analysts.

foreshadows later sections of the analysis. At this point, the focus is on organizations, bureaucracies, systems, and the individuals staffing them more generally. These organizations are particularly important in China because of the lack of representative and democratic institutions.

The concept "system" means the sum total of organizational activities that can be characterized as attempts to satisfy one of the five functional demands. Using this definition, a system is merely an aggregate of activities, an analytical construct. This definition says nothing about the interconnectedness of institutions within each system. In contrast, a coalition is a real network of organizations that coordinate their activities to carry out one of the functions of the state despite the separate responsibilities and tasks of the organizations.

Bureaucracies and offices within bureaucracies are the basic components of systems. A "bureaucracy" as the word is used here means any organization that fulfills four conditions: It is large; most of its employees work for it full time and receive most of their income from working for it; its personnel system is largely merit-based rather than based on ascriptive characteristics of its workers or on elections; and most of its output is not evaluated by markets.[10]

A bureaucracy has four sets of interests or goals: the personal goals of its members; its corporate interests; its programmatic interests; and its leadership goals.[11] The personal interests of the membership reflect the sum of the individual interests of the staff. These interests are often summed up as concerns with status, salary, security, job satisfaction, and promotion. Most of the time, satisfactory (or better) levels of bureaucratic performance promote the attainment of individual interests, but in a number of cases institutional performance and goals are undermined by individual aims.[12] The personal goals of the members of the organization are the set of organizational interests of least importance to the discussion here.

The corporate interests of an organization concern its ability to perform

10. Downs, 1967, pp. 24–25. Downs defines an organization as a "system of consciously coordinated activities of forces of two or more persons explicitly created to achieve specific ends." Note that the Weberian definition of "bureaucracy" is not used here; it is an ideal type useful for comparison but not for analyzing intra- and interbureaucratic dynamics. It might be argued that in the Chinese case there is no such thing as a bureaucracy, because organizations are staffed ascriptively. This may be true of top leaders, but I do not think that ascriptive characteristics explain rank-and-file staffing of Chinese organizations. On this point, see Vogel, 1967. This means not that appointments to state organizations are necessarily based on merit but that the overall staffing procedures are closer to being merit-based than under any other system.

11. These goals are discussed in Harding, 1987, esp. pp. 225–37.

12. This point is a commonplace in the literature on bureaucracy; the interplay of self-interest and bureaucratic dynamics is developed systematically in Downs, 1967. See also Harding, 1981, pp. 2–17; Merton, 1952; and Crozier, 1964.

its assigned tasks. Some of the corporate interests of an organization involve the resources it has at its disposal to fulfill its mandated functions, such as budget levels, skill of its personnel, and number of personnel. Another major aspect of the corporate interests of an organization involves the tasks it is assigned. Are the tasks important and likely to increase the power of the organization? How is the performance of the organization measured? Who evaluates its performance? An overburdened, underfunded, and largely unskilled bureaucracy will find it extremely difficult to achieve its corporate interests and will face the threat of declining power, leadership replacement, encroachment on its turf by other organizations, and, in the worst case, organizational death.

The programmatic interests of an institution reflect broad policy perspectives that facilitate the fulfillment of corporate goals. In other words, programmatic interests refer to an overall policy environment that allows the bureaucracy the best chance of achieving its other interests. Programmatic goals make up the tendencies associated with each system. For example, the military of a state faced with a threat from either or both superpowers would probably have programmatic interests in the development of the state's heavy industrial and electronics industries to provide weapons needed to stand up to the superpower (or it might have programmatic interests in maintaining and developing commercial ties with a state that can provide such weapons).

Finally, bureaucracies have leadership interests. Certain leaders, on the basis of prior experience and behavior or because of their association with one organization, may be more sympathetic to some organizations and their missions than they are to others. Organizations hope to influence the selection and appointment of leaders who are inclined to favor their interests, and they work against the promotion of leaders less considerate of their position and views.

In addition to these different types of interests, organizations themselves have subdivisions with their own sets of interests, which may be significantly at variance with the larger interests of the organization as a whole. This is perhaps easiest to see in the case of the Chinese military. The People's Liberation Army (PLA) is a unified military organization, but the three service branches have different and, to varying degrees, competing interests. Within production ministries, such as the Ministry of Metallurgical Industries, there are financial departments that may have a more bottom-line approach than does the overall ministry, with its concern for meeting the physical production target.

It should be clear that there is no one constant interest attached to a bureaucracy. The political context, the type of policy issue, the overall degree

of conflict within the political system, and other factors all affect the articulation and pursuit of bureaucratic interests in China and other nations. But
although the preceding discussion suggests we should not impute an a priori
interest to Chinese bureaucracies, or to bureaucracies in general, there are
good reasons for concentrating on the programmatic interests of various institutions, which are a product of organizational leadership and the personnel system.

Leaders of the state recognize the importance of the state's functions and
closely follow the activities of bureaucracies designed to fulfill those functions. Some of the highest-ranking leaders are charged with leading some of
the most important bureaucracies. In addition, some leaders are charged
with overseeing general developments in an area of key importance. This
area need not be coterminous with a system.

Central leaders who have oversight responsibilities are expected to act, in
Downs's terms, as "statesmen." They are supposed to see both that organizations in a major area perform their tasks effectively and that overall goals
of the leadership are furthered. Often a central leader is "captured" by the
bureaucracies he is supposed to be supervising; in other words, a process of
"reverse cooptation," or cooptation from below, takes place.[13] The leader
becomes closely involved in the affairs of the area he is charged with supervising. He cannot adequately evaluate developments in this area if he does
not know many of the details of the operation of the bureaucracies in the
field. Leaders of the bureaucracies under the general control of the central
leader pursue activities that further enmesh him in the affairs of the area.
Bureaucratic leaders realize that their work can be facilitated if they can
obtain aid from the central leader. In addition, the bureaucratic leaders,
eager for promotion to higher levels, do their best to impress and flatter the
central leader by seeking his counsel and by deferring to him, thus further
drawing him into the affairs of this area. When their bureaus come under
criticism, bureaucratic leaders may turn to the central leader for support.
For his part, the central leader may believe that if he steps in and handles

13. On reverse cooptation in China, see Dittmer, 1987, p. 25, where he notes "a process of
reverse cooptation: those Party leaders sent to manage a bureaucratic organ tended to adopt
the organizational interests of that organ as their own, and to represent those interests in Party
policy-making councils." This began to take place in the mid 1950s. The classic discussion of
cooptation is Selznick, 1980. Two prominent examples of reverse cooptation in China are Chen
Zhengren and Luo Ruiqing. On Chen, see MacFarquhar, 1974, pp. 18, 142–43, 325, and Stavis,
1978. Surprisingly, Stavis fails to mention Chen, despite his appointment in 1959 as head of the
Ministry of Agricultural Machinery. Nonetheless, the ministry's position in the 1960s was increasingly at odds with Mao's position, suggesting that Chen's views had changed. On Luo
Ruiqing, see Harding and Gurtov, 1971, esp. pp. 7–11.

I use the masculine pronoun in the text because in China all leaders of the major state systems
were men. I do not mean to imply that leaders must necessarily be male.

this one field of endeavor very well, it will strengthen his position in the leadership by confirming his competence to manage the affairs of the state. Or he might believe that only his interventions prevent the total breakdown of work in this area. Thus central leaders may be entwined in the affairs of the bureaucracies they are supposed to be overseeing from an Olympian perspective, and in the process may change from "statesmen" to "advocates."

Besides the involvement of top leaders in the operations of important bureaucracies, the standard operating procedures of bureaus themselves further link leaders and organizations and lay the groundwork for the formation of bureaucratic coalitions. Every organization or bureaucracy creates standard operating procedures, or routines, to manage the tasks assigned to it. Indeed, it is the development of these procedures (and the mobilization of expertise) that accounts for the efficiency of bureaucracy in the Weberian sense.[14] Routines simplify choices about how the organization is to carry out its tasks, reduce ambiguity, increase efficiency, and lower costs. By reducing choices available to decision makers and presenting them with a predefined menu of alternatives or potential solutions to problems, standard operating procedures make a bureaucratic organization a viable entity.

In addition, routines convey the impression that the same rule is applied to all cases and all individuals. The bureaucracy thereby avoids the stigma of seemingly arbitrary behavior, which can undermine support for the bureau or even the regime as a whole. Standard procedures thus serve political purposes as well as efficiency.

When new bureaus are formed to manage tasks, they must go through an initial period of developing routines. Bureaucracies pay a high price in their early lives developing such procedures. In economic terms, this is when "sunk costs" are incurred. Once the routines have developed, costs drop dramatically, and a learning effect is observed.

Costs as well as gains are associated with standard operating procedures. In many ways, costs are the converse of the advantages of developing these routines. The existence of routines may inhibit the development of new ways of dealing with a problem or analyzing a situation. The established procedures for acquiring information and processing it may bias the presentation of issues or lead to the overlooking of vital data. The cost involved in developing routines in the first place and the cost of formulating alternative procedures and routines are so high that few leaders are willing to jettison established routines. The costs of transition to improved procedures may exact

14. Weber, 1978, pp. 956–1005.

a higher price than leaving the old, if less effective, mechanisms in place. In this way, bureaucracies become resistant to change.[15]

Constant involvement in activities for which bureaucracies have developed routines leads the heads of bureaus and their staffs to believe that they are the ones best equipped to deal with that activity. They see participation in such activities by outsiders as interference in their internal affairs. Bureaucracies will resist this interference by attempting to carve out spheres of autonomy. In this way, they try to reduce outside supervision to a minimum.

In any political system there are many organizations, all of which are in competition with each other. They compete, for example, for budgetary resources, qualified personnel, and support from the leadership. All organizations perform what are perceived to be necessary services, so all have valid claims to some degree. They are also in contention with the central leadership to expand the scope of their autonomy. But resources are finite, and choices must be made by the central leadership. Since bureaucratic performance is often difficult, if not impossible, to measure objectively, leaders must make political choices about the allocation of resources. Whenever bureaus (or subsections of a bureau) are competing against each other for funds, it is relatively easy for political leaders to exert control over the allocation process. Leaders can divide and ally with some organizations to deflect the demands of other organizations. To counter this, bureaucracies form their own coalitions in attempts to bolster their claims to the resources of the state.

On what basis can bureaucracies form coalitions? Coalitions can exist when certain groups of bureaucracies serve the same set of larger goals or system concerns. The relationship between bureaus is often interdependent, as seems to be the case particularly in economic affairs. The leaders of bureaucracies with strong support from the central leadership may realize that achievement of their functional goals requires inputs from other units. Even with strong central support, bureaus may still be vulnerable to the opposition of all other bureaus. Members of weak bureaus in the same system may realize that one way to strengthen their position is to enter into a coalition with the strong bureau. This may net them fewer resources than they might wish, but it probably assures them of a more stable supply of resources than if they acted independently. For the strong bureau, the logic of such a coalition is essentially defensive. If it is isolated, it may not be able to withstand the force of a grouping of other bureaus, and consequently its share of resources

15. In addition to the sources cited in n. 6, this section draws on Allison, 1971; March and Simon, 1958; Sharkansky, 1970; and Steinbruner, 1974.

may diminish. Forming coalitions forestalls isolation and can further reinforce ties within a bureau's supply line. It also gives the strong bureau an
even greater base of power.

Other bureaucracies or systems may have to form a coalition in an attempt
to counter the original coalition. Although it may be possible for all other
organs to band together to oppose the budgetary requests of a coalition, this
does not enable the opposing coalition to argue for its own needs. Whereas
an offensive coalition is based on a positive similarity of interests and concerns, a defensive coalition is marked by less intensive interactions, fewer
points of contact, and, often, a purpose more akin to preserving the status
quo. For bureaucracies to form offensive coalitions, a smaller, more mutually agreeable common denominator must be found. It is here that the
personnel factors mentioned earlier come into play. The central leader assigned to supervise the affairs of an area of policy or a system may play a key
catalytic role in the ironing out of a bureaucratic coalition and in helping to
formulate the overall tendency associated with it.

Earlier it was suggested that system tendencies result from efforts by organizations to perform their functions. While partially true, that formulation
is simplistic. It is true that bureaucracies develop standard operating procedures to carry out their tasks and that they resist attempts to change those
procedures. In addition to defending their routines on grounds of efficiency,
bureaucracies often develop ideologies that not only defend the routines and
the basic mission of the organization but also attempt to convince outsiders
of the crucial importance of the institution to the overall working of the state.
Within a bureaucracy, distinct corporate cultures emerge that help to unify
the thinking of the members of the bureau and increase organizational élan.[16]

But these ideologies are likely to be too particularistic to draw widespread
support from outside the units promoting them. For a coalition of bureaucracies to form and remain fairly stable, a common ideological framework
must develop that reflects the general tendency of the system. Individual
bureaucratic ideologies are then hung on this broad framework, which is the
least common denominator for the organizations in the system. Usually, the
central leader assigned to the affairs of the system plays a key (if backstage)
role in the development of the ideological framework of the coalition. This
framework is likely to justify the importance of the basic function of the state
for which each bureau in the coalition is at least partially responsible. By
asserting that this function is the most important, or at least more important

16. On corporate cultures generally, see Deal and Kennedy, 1982. For evidence of their
existence in China, see Oksenberg, 1982, esp. pp. 181–82, and Shirk, 1986?.

than other functions, the coalition lays claim to requisite resources and expansion of its role in the political system, justifies the accrual of more resources to the coalition generally, and provides a platform for each of its members to make claims for the redistribution of the budgetary pie. Often, however, it is not enough to assert the importance of the coalition's function. All functions are indispensable. Claims for the preeminence of one coalition are not very convincing, and may sound so particularistic to the central leadership as to engender a backlash. Accordingly, coalition tendencies must present a picture of the positive effects that will flow from following the general interests of the system in question. This picture of the general good may be essential if the coalition is to win support from the central leadership and other coalitions. The inability to provide a convincing and desirable picture of the future under the tendency's policies may be critical to the failure of the coalition to promote its position in the political system.

While one general coalition tendency might develop, this does not mean that other tendencies or dissenting views might not emerge from within each grouping. Each coalition, as noted, is divided into bureaus and subbureaus. Some of these bodies have different views of their importance and their role in the coalition and the state in general. They may be dissatisfied with their role in the coalition and may seek to create an alternative to the given tendency and try to win others over to their viewpoint. The emergence of such a dissenting tendency within the coalition may also signal to other groupings the desire of the dissenting unit to defect to another coalition more amenable to the dissenter's interests.

The degree to which the personnel procedures of the coalition and the bureaucracies within in it are autonomous is another key factor in determining whether dissenting tendencies will arise within a coalition. If the coalition controls its own promotion procedures and decisions (its *nomenklatura*), individuals within the coalition have very little incentive for bucking the system and formulating dissenting views. If there are multiple channels for personnel advancement and the coalition in question is not in control of all of them, some individuals within each system will appeal to the leaders who control the alternative channels.[17]

This section has analyzed the general process by which coalitions and their tendencies can come into being. This abstract formulation provides the background necessary for understanding many of the key aspects of the Chinese political system in the mid 1950s, which is the subject of the next section.

17. On the Chinese personnel system, see Barnett, 1967, esp, pp. 48–63; Manion, 1985; and Burns, 1987.

C. The Chinese political system

This section has two aims. One is to expand on the analysis presented in the preceding section and put meat on the bones of the general framework presented there by applying it to the specifics of the Chinese political system. The other is to introduce background material about the Chinese political system so that many of the peculiarities of Chinese politics do not have to be presented when I consider the origins of the Great Leap Forward. The section has three parts: a discussion of leadership in China, an examination of the coalitions in China, and an investigation of the dynamics of coalitions and their effects on politics in China.

C.1. The leadership and policy making

In the mid 1950s, the top leadership in the People's Republic of China (PRC) was made up of the members of the Politburo and Secretariat of the CCP and the premier and vice-premiers of the State Council. Altogether, this group comprised about thirty individuals, many of whom occupied multiple positions.

Mao Zedong, as chairman of both Party and state, was the top-ranking Chinese leader. Between May 1945 and September 1956, the Thought of Mao Zedong was enshrined in the Party constitution as the summarization of Marxism-Leninism as applied in China. This privileged position for Mao's views was just one source of his unique power in the Chinese political system. In addition, his record of guiding the Party from victory to victory from the mid 1930s through the mid 1950s, his unparalleled network of connections with all other major figures in all fields of Party work, and the institutionalization of his role as China's top leader – he had the right to overturn Central Committee decisions, elevating him above the rules of democratic centralism – made his position all but impregnable.[18] Moreover, it is clear that Mao's skills at political maneuver and plotting were far and away superior to those of his colleagues. He had a coterie of followers who were politically loyal solely to him. He had special contacts with the military and used the security detail assigned to protect the central leadership as a personal intelligence service. In addition to all these sources of power, Mao was a transformative type of leader – he sought to alter preferences fundamentally

18. On Mao's ability to overturn Central Committee decisions, see Tan Zongji, "Yijiusisan Nian Sanyue Zhongyang Zhengzhiju Huiyi" (The March 1943 Meeting of the Central Politburo), *Dangshi Yanjiu* (Research on Party History), 1980, no. 2, pp. 77–78, and Mao, 1977, p. 92.

or change the nature of politics in China, and was often successful. He did
not take reality as a given and often acted counter to reality. His ability to
continue to do this throughout his career was a measure of his power, and
was often the source of immense sorrow for the Chinese people. In contrast,
his Politburo colleagues were much more broker types – generally working
within the confines of existing material conditions and institutional patterns
of politics. Even after reference to the Thought of Mao Zedong was deleted
from the Party constitution (in 1956, largely out of deference to de-Stalini-
zation in the Soviet Union), Mao remained the key ideological arbiter of
Chinese Marxism.[19] Nonetheless, as will be argued throughout this work, in
economic affairs Mao's power was constrained, narrowed, or channeled by
the workings of the bureaucracy.

Other top leaders who held key positions as policy generalists were Liu
Shaoqi, the number-two man in the Party and key manager of CCP organizational affairs; Zhou Enlai, premier of the PRC and China's leading admin-
istrator; and Deng Xiaoping, head of the CCP Secretariat, which was in
charge of the day-to-day functioning of the CCP. Both Liu and Zhou were
intensely loyal to Mao and the functioning of the CCP. Even when they
disagreed with Mao, both followed his ideas as best they could. Given his
relative youth, Deng, who seems to have had few differences with the Chairman in the 1950s, probably had ideas about succeeding to the top leadership
post after Mao's passing. In the early 1950s, Deng's career skyrocketed, moving
him from the leadership of one of China's most backward regions to the
pinnacle of power. Nonetheless, his experience at the center was still limited
in the mid 1950s, especially when it is compared with that of the other half-
dozen most important CCP leaders.[20]

Mao's role in the political system was not as arbitrary and despotic as it
was to become in the 1960s. Since he first ascended to the top position in
the Party (in a de facto if not a de jure sense) in the mid 1930s, the Party had
laboriously built up the system of Leninist norms about inner Party decision
making and dissent. These norms provided for relatively free and open debate on an issue before a decision was made; no punishment for those who
had disagreed with an option once that option became policy; and a willingness to reconsider a policy already adopted if it appeared that the policy was

19. On Mao's sources of power and sources of power more generally in China, see Teiwes,
1984, esp. ch. 1; Dittmer, 1978; Oksenberg, 1977. On the distinction between transformative
and broker leaders, see March and Olsen, 1984, p. 739. Also useful for understanding leadership are Riker, 1986; Schattschneider, 1960; and Nordlinger, 1981, esp. pp. 92–94. The biographical and philosophical literature on Mao is also helpful. See Schram, 1967 and 1983; Terrill, 1980; Starr, 1979; Wylie, 1980; and Liao Kai-lung (Liao Gailong), 1980.

20. On Liu, Zhou, and Deng, see Dittmer, 1974 and 1977; MacFarquhar 1974 and 1983;
Harding, 1981; and Khrushchev, 1974, p. 288.

not working well. Although these rules were sometimes violated, all Chinese leaders believed that they were valid in the mid 1950s and generally behaved as if these rules were binding on them.[21]

In addition to Mao, Liu, Zhou, and Deng, other central leaders, one of whom ranked higher than Deng, must also be considered. But most of the other top leaders, regardless of rank, were assigned to manage the affairs of a particular ministry or group of ministries (*xitong* in Chinese, usually translated "system"). Politburo members Chen Yun, Li Xiannian, Li Fuchun, Bo Yibo, and Peng Dehuai and some others were key functional leaders. Despite long and sometimes complicated interpersonal relations, these leaders took on the perspectives of the ministerial system they headed. They were supposed to be generalists, or "statesmen," but they often became "advocates," even "zealots." Yet these leaders were not punished for becoming spokesmen for the organizations they supervised and for losing their generalist perspective. Policy debates seem to have generated little personal animosity, even when leaders aggressively pursued and defended their units' interests. Perhaps all leaders realized that by becoming heads of bureaucracies some could not help becoming advocates.

Some observers, particularly those who use factional models, deny that leaders take on the perspective of bureaucracies or that bureaucratic organizations pursue their own interests.[22] Yet Andrew Nathan, in the most rigorous factionalism model, concedes that bureaucratic organizations provide the "trellis" on which factions can develop.[23] This means that factions might also be seen as groups presenting their bureaucratic interests. As Tang Tsou brilliantly argues, if factions grow out of bureaucracies,

> [this] increases the probability . . . that in fact these informal groups also share at least some elements of the specialized ideology of that organization, as well as some of the components of the general ideology of the system of which that organization is a part; [and] that these organizational goals do not consist solely of the aggrandizement of power and material interests of the informal groups, but are also shaped by the formal goals of the organization.[24]

As later chapters will show, organizational interests profoundly colored leadership behavior in China, and while fundamental considerations of political power were involved in the origins of the Great Leap Forward, these considerations had much less to do with personal aggrandizement than with the power of coalitions. The leadership of some of the coalitions under discussion

21. Teiwes, 1979a and b.
22. For example, Domes, 1974, and Pye, 1981, ch. 3.
23. Nathan, 1973, p. 65.
24. Tsou, 1975, p. 100. This section also draws heavily on Harding, 1984.

here changed during the period of Mao's rule, but basic institutional and coalitional interests did not (with the planning coalition serving as the best example). Organizational interests were more important than factional interests in the making of economic policy.

In the Chinese political system under Mao, two very broad patterns of policy making within the elite were common. One was from the top down and the other from the bottom up (bottom seen in relative terms). In the top-down approach, the central leadership decided on such crucial issues as the "nature of the present era," the pace of advance, and key allocational priorities. General policy guidelines were formulated and sanctified by the elite. These guidelines were sent down to the bureaucracies for refinement and specification and were translated into concrete policies. This represented a relatively synoptic pattern of policy development.

The bottom-up policy-making pattern constituted a more ad hoc style of decision making. In the course of their activities, ministries or other units frequently ran into unexpected problems or conflicts with other units. Those problems that could be handled within the ministry were taken to the minister or other high-ranking officials in the bureau. In the case of conflicts with other agencies, disputes were passed to higher levels. If the disputes concerned agencies within the same xitong, the head of the xitong played a decisive role in dispute resolution. The same may also be true of intersystem disputes. Policy emerged from the bottom up when conflict involved units from different systems and could be resolved only by the top leaders.[25]

To aid it in its efforts to lead the Chinese polity, the CCP used a number of devices to enhance its ability to control and coordinate policy developments. One such mechanism, shrouded in mystery, is the personal staffs of leaders. Other, even more ad hoc devices available to top leaders included the dispatch of personal guards to investigate the situation in their hometowns and other places.[26] The central leadership also established organs to help coordinate affairs. In the Party structure, these were called departments or commissions. In the state structure, these were called xitong, or systems. (To avoid confusion, the Chinese term will be used to refer to the actual Chinese staff offices.) These were networks of bureaucratic agencies

25. This is well described in Kenneth Lieberthal and Oksenberg, 1988, esp. chs. 2 and 4.
26. The most famous example is found in Zhonggong Zhongyang Bangongting Lilun Xuexi Xiaozu (The Theoretical Study Small Group of the General Office of the Central Committee of the Chinese Communist Party), "Yongyuan Mingji Mao Zhuxide Lingdao Jianchi Wuchan Jieji Zhuanzhengxia Jixu Geming" (We Will Always Remember Chairman Mao's Leadership in Upholding Continuing the Revolution Under the Dictatorship of the Proletariat), *Renmin Ribao* (People's Daily), September 8, 1977.

with responsibilities in the same general area. These xitong form the starting point for bureaucratic coalitions in China.[27]

The number and the responsibilities of xitong have varied. In the mid 1950s, there were eight: (1) internal affairs and public security; (2) education and culture; (3) heavy industry, planning, and construction; (4) light industry; (5) finance and trade; (6) communications and transportation; (7) agriculture; and (8) united front. Some of these xitong figure prominently in the systems discussed in Section B of this chapter. The planning group, or economic transformation system, is composed of the third and sixth xitong. The budget group, or economic allocation system, comprises the fourth, fifth, and seventh xitong. But some xitong, particularly the second and part of the first, do not fit the more general conceptual framework we used. Nor do the xitong include the military and the social transformation systems – the mobilizers. Despite these difficulties, these xitong and other organizational structures form the basis for the structural, systemic analysis that will follow.

Another important control and coordination mechanism was "dual rule." All units and groups in China are under dual rule. This means that in addition to the normal hierarchy of command in a bureaucracy, there is also a CCP organization (a branch or fraction) in every unit. It has been argued that even in specifically state organs, the Party branch is the key locus of decision making. In addition, the branch is largely responsible for personnel, propaganda, and security matters in the ministry. Although the minister and the head of the Party fraction in a ministry may be one and the same person, it is argued that the minister exerts his authority under his Party hat. The existence of dual chains of command in every non-Party organization has implications for the development of dissenting tendencies within a coalition. As mentioned earlier, when alternative channels of advancement exist, or when units do not control their personnel procedures, challenges to the existing tendency may arise. Through control of organizations, the CCP attempts to check excessive commitment to coalitional tendencies, and to replace zealots with leaders more loyal, at least temporarily, to the Party's more general policies. Dual rule, it might be argued, weakens the autonomy of coalitions.[28] Cooptation from below, however, plus the likelihood that Politburo members who head coalitions control the *nomenklatura* of that system, militates against this view.

The effectiveness of dual rule was enhanced by the fact that by the mid

27. On xitong and central departments, see Barnett, 1967, pp. 5–9 and 21–23; Donnithorne, 1967, pp. 18–20; and Oksenberg, 1982, pp. 178–80.
28. This paragraph draws very heavily on Barnett, 1967. See also Schurmann, 1968.

1950s, personal mobility within the state administration was slowing down dramatically. When the CCP came to power in 1949, the bureaucracy was staffed largely by personnel recruited by the old regime. By the mid 1950s these people had largely been replaced. The early 1950s also saw the establishment of many new bureaus, most of which had been fully staffed by the mid 1950s. Finally, in the mid 1950s, the leaders and most members of the CCP were still fairly young, suggesting that generational succession would not really begin until the mid 1960s. Thus, chances for rapid upward mobility were small, strengthening the control of the Party group in each organization.[29]

Often the central leadership was constrained in its ability to formulate policy by several factors. In addition to the usual time and information constraints, certain issues became increasingly complex and technical as the economy developed, and required expert formulation of policy options. The emerging operational procedures of the bureaucracy further preempted or reinforced certain lines of policy development. This does not mean that the central leadership was precluded from launching bold new departures, but it does suggest that policy making was increasingly circumscribed by the options presented or made available to the leadership by the bureaucratic coalitions. To a great extent, leaders balanced, mediated, coopted, altered, transformed, or selectively combined the policy programs of the various coalitions. Even Mao could rarely break out from the net of policies woven by the economic bureaucracies.[30]

Given the growing influence of the coalitions on the formulation of policy options, much of Chinese politics revolved around questions of which coalition's view of the world would dominate the decision-making agenda of the top leaders. No one coalition was powerful enough to insure that its views always effectively dominated the presentation and definition of issues. Thus, the leaders of the various coalitions and their staffs were constantly involved in efforts to bargain with the leaders of the state and other coalitions, and in efforts to redefine (or repackage) their own interests and functions in ways that leaders of other groups or policy generalists might be able to support.

29. Important studies on the Chinese bureaucracy include Barnett, 1967; Harding, 1981; Kau, 1971 and 1969; Lampton, 1977; Oksenberg, 1974b; Vogel, 1967 and 1970.

30. Testimony to the power of the bureaucracy is found in the writings of the top leaders. See, for example, Mao, 1977, pp. 292–95, 334–36, and 407–8; 1969b, pp. 154–59, 161–65; and Zhou Enlai, 1984b, pp. 418–22. This last article was so antibureaucratic that during the Cultural Revolution it was attributed to Mao. Cf. Joint Publications Research Service, no. 49826, *Translations on Communist China*, no. 90 (February 12, 1970), pp. 40–43.

C.2. The coalitions and the Chinese political system

By the time the CCP came to power it had already established, or planned to establish in the near future, institutions responsible for the five functions discussed in Section A.[31] The CCP had been established in 1921 and had directly concerned itself with social transformation. Shortly thereafter, it became concerned with questions of the united front, and institutions within and outside the Party were established to manage this aspect of social integration. These organs and the CCP's class policy in general were the main tools with which the CCP dealt with the issue of integration.[32] In 1927, what later became the People's Liberation Army (PLA) was founded, and after the CCP set up relatively stable base areas, internal security forces were established to manage the order, or security, function.[33] As the base areas and the PLA expanded, the need for funds and supplies increased. By the early 1930s the Commissariat of Finance was responsible for the extraction and mobilization of resources.[34] While no true planning apparatus to manage economic development was established until 1952, Chinese leaders did not hide their intention of developing a planned economy and state ownership of key economic institutions after they came to power.[35] By 1956 standard operating procedures and the perspectives of each system had matured and crystalized as the entire political system became consolidated. Indeed, there was surprising continuity in the staff of certain organs. Many planning commission staff hired in the early 1950s still serve in that body today.[36]

Who were the leaders and what were the components of each coalition? The principal leaders of the Extraction and Allocation System (the budgeteers, or financial coalition) were Chen Yun, member of the Standing Committee of the Politburo, first vice-premier of the PRC, and in late 1956 minister of commerce; Li Xiannian, member of the Politburo, vice-premier, minister of finance and head of the finance and trade xitong; Deng Zihui,

31. Moreover, there are parallels to some of the bureaucratic organizations and conflicts in the late imperial and Republican period. Suggestive evidence for this is found in Paul A. Cohen and Schrecker, 1976; Eastman, 1984; and Chi, 1982. William Kirby of Washington University, St. Louis, is currently working on planning under the Kuomintang.

32. On integration in general, see Binder, 1964, and Geertz, 1973, pp. 255–310. On the united front, see Van Slyke, 1967; Seymour, 1987; and Li Weihan, 1987.

33. On the early origins and development of the PLA, see Griffith, 1967; Whitson with Chenhsia Huang, 1973; and Jencks, 1982. On internal security, Griffin, 1976; Lotveit, 1973, chs. 4 and 5; Zhong Kan, 1982; and Hu Yaobang, 1980. One of the anonymous referees of this work states that the last source is a Taiwan forgery.

34. Lotveit, 1973, ch. 7.

35. For example, see Mao's speech "On New Democracy" (January 1940) in Mao, 1986, esp. pp. 365–66. See also Schran, 1976.

36. Kenneth Lieberthal and Oksenberg, 1988, pp. 153–55.

vice-premier, Central Committee member, head of the agricultural xitong, and head of the Party's Rural Work Department; and Jia Tuofu, head of the light industry xitong and member of the Central Committee. Other leaders in the budget group were Liao Luyan, minister of agriculture, and Yao Yilin, vice-minister of commerce. The principal units in this coalition were the Ministries of Finance, Commerce, Agriculture, Light Industry, and Textiles and the People's Bank of China. This grouping is discussed fully in Chapter 4.

The Economic Transformation System (the planners, or planning and heavy industry coalition) was led by Li Fuchun, member of the Politburo, vice-premier of the State Council, and chairman of the State Planning Commission (SPC); Bo Yibo, alternate member of the Politburo, vice-premier, chairman of the State Economic Commission (SEC), and head of the heavy industry xitong; Wang Heshou, member of the Central Committee, minister of metallurgical industries, and head of the State Construction Commission (SCC); Huang Jing, member of the Central Committee, minister of the First Ministry of Machine Building, and somewhat later chairman of the State Science and Technology Commission; and Zhao Erlu, member of the Central Committee and minister of the Second Ministry of Machine Building. The principal components of the planning coalition were the planning agencies (the SPC, the SEC, and the SCC) and the various ministries involved in heavy industrial production and the production of raw materials necessary for heavy industrial production, such as ministries concerned with energy production. This grouping is examined in Chapter 5.

The Integrative System was considerably more amorphous than the budget and planning groups. The main leaders of this group were Li Weihan, Central Committee member and head of both the Party's United Front Work Department and the united front xitong in the state structure; Dong Biwu, member of the Politburo and president of the Supreme Court; and Lai Ruoyu, member of the Central Committee and head of the All-China Federation of Trade Unions. Major institutions associated with this grouping were the two offices Li Weihan headed, the courts and the legal system, and such non-Party institutions as the labor unions, the National People's Congress, and the Chinese People's Political Consultative Conference. This group played a critical role in the political development of the Hundred Flowers Campaign, but it was not very important in economic discussions, and it does not receive much attention in this study.

The key unit in the Social Transformation System is the CCP. As noted earlier, the CCP had other and more general functions, such as leadership and coordination. In other words, social transformation was only one task of the CCP, albeit a vital, perhaps even a defining, one. The leaders of the CCP were Mao, Liu, Deng, other members of the Politburo; the heads of the Party work departments; and the provincial Party secretaries. This system is discussed in Chapter 6. The top leaders of the Party also had special leadership responsibilities, and they are therefore treated separately in Chapter 7.

Finally, the leaders of the Security System (the military and the police) were Peng Dehuai, member of the Politburo, vice-premier, and minister of national defense; Lin Biao, member of the Politburo and vice-premier; Luo Ruiqing, member of the Central Committee, head of the internal affairs xitong, and minister of public security; and Kang Sheng, alternate member of the Politburo. The key institutions in this system were the PLA and the Ministry of Public Security. In addition, there were probably more informal security organs in the Party under Kang Sheng's charge. The economic views of this group are hard to determine; important new information on the military and the economy is just beginning to appear. Consequently, this system does not receive significant attention, although Chapter 6 includes brief comments on it.[37]

Since this book focuses on economic questions, it concentrates on the views of the budget group, the planners, and the Party. The specific tendencies associated with each coalition are discussed in detail. In order to provide the reader with a preview of the analysis, Table 2 presents a summary of the major issues on which these three systems held differing views. These issues might be seen as points of contact and conflict among the tendencies of the three systems. Like any brief summary, the chart exaggerates the clarity of each tendency and the degree of conflict among the tendencies.

The three coalitions and their tendencies are perhaps best summarized by the ethos that guided each one. For the budget coalition, this was balanced, relatively slow, stable growth based on material incentives and the market. For the planners, it was mobilization of the majority, even the vast majority, of state resources to build a heavy industrial base very quickly, or forced draft industrialization. For the Party, it was a concern with maintaining close contact with the people and a firm belief in the efficacy of mass mobilization as an instrument of both economic development and political awakening.

---

37. On the informal security organs in the Party, see Zhong Kan, 1982, and, if credible, Hu Yaobang, 1980. On the military and the economy, an early and still very suggestive work is Hsieh, 1962. Much more recent information on this key issue is found in Lewis and Xue, 1988, but the subject remains obscure, particularly in regard to the 1950s.

Table 2. *Economic positions of the three coalitions*

Issue	Budget group	Planners	Party
Amount of extraction	Moderate	High	High
Favored sector(s)	Agriculture; light industry	Heavy industry	Heavy industry; agriculture
Laws governing economic development	"The three balances" (budgets, loans, materials)	"Law of Planned, Proportionate Development"	No laws binding
Strictness with which laws are applied	Very strict	Not very strict	Not applicable
Method of distributing final product	State commerce plus markets	Planned allocation of heavy industrial products	Opposition to markets
Method of developing agriculture	Price and incentive policy; smaller units of production	More industrial inputs; collectivized agriculture	Social mobilization and reorganization
System of ownership (excluding agriculture)	State plus some individual and collective	State	State
Incentives	Remunerative	Remunerative, normative, coercive	Normative, coercive
Staffing	Employ former (capitalist) managers	Employ bureaucratic and technical experts	Employ politically loyal
Control mechanism	Finance	Planning	Ideology
Ethos	Balance	"Big push" for heavy industry	Yanan-style mobilization

C.3. The coalitions and Chinese politics

The functions of the state must be minimally fulfilled if the state (and the regime in power) is to sustain itself, given whatever international threat exists and the state's desire for material improvement. In the long run, survival requires that each system produce sufficient outputs in its functional area. (In the short run it might be possible to increase greatly the coercive nature of the state so that defective performance in any one area does not necessarily lead to the state's collapse. But this does not appear to be a viable long-term option.) Thus, in a simple though basic way, the systems are linked because they are essential, and better functioning in one area cannot truly compensate for poor performance in another. The leadership must pay constant attention to each area.

The key task of a coalition is to formulate and implement a linked package of policies that satisfies the functional requirements established for that system. In Table 2, the differences among the three coalitions on economic questions are totalistic in nature. This means not so much that the budget, planning, and Party groups differ on specific issues, such as allocation of resources, but that they differ in such a variety of crucial dimensions. On some issues, the differences are not great. It is the reinforcing nature of each area of difference that is particularly significant. What is vital is that the sum total of each coalition's position reflects a coherent policy program, one that each group believes must be implemented in toto. Otherwise, the individual policies will not have the desired payoff.

The coalitions, as can be inferred from their names, overlap to some degree. In economic affairs, these areas of overlap can be quite substantial. However, there are strong political motives for the leaders of coalitions to defend the comprehensive nature of their system's policy platforms rather than gladly accept compromises dictated by the central leadership. If coalition leaders did accept compromises, the relative unity and strength of the coalition would be undermined. This would undercut the basis of power of the coalition leader himself. Leaders no doubt believe, probably rightly, that mixes of policy platforms from different coalitions will not produce the desired results. There is a logical consistency to the positions associated with each system as well as a political and bureaucratic basis. Mixing different options destroys the reinforcing effects of the various planks in a coalition's platform. This suggests that when compromises or mixes are imposed on the coalitions by the central leadership, an unstable situation results. No coalition can prove its superiority, and all argue that if more of their policies are adopted, results will be much better. Since a compromise solution is bound to bring about less than optimal outcomes for the coalitions, the issue of which coalition's views should predominate in economic affairs will continually reappear on the political agenda for as long as economic results are defined as unsatisfactory by the central leadership.

The ability of a coalition to present a forceful and compelling argument to the central leadership is affected by many factors. Certainly the cogency and attractiveness of the main tendency of the coalition are a key consideration. Another is the skill with which the coalition's leader and some of the other major figures in the grouping argue for their point of view. Personal relations among leaders of various sorts are also a factor. Moreover, the interplay of coalitions is conditioned by the environment and other developments. For example, the degree of international tension strongly affects the force of arguments associated with the security system. If the international environment is not threatening to China, it is hard for the PLA leadership to argue for a rapid military buildup. Similarly, poor or deteriorating economic conditions may strengthen the hand of the budget group at the expense of the mobilizers within the Party. Overall levels of economic and organizational development may also affect the position of each coalition. One of the reasons the PLA could not argue compellingly for rapid military modernization in the 1950s was that Chinese industry was so backward that it could not serially produce advanced munitions. Finally, every state is occasionally confronted with new or unexpected problems. The degree to which a coalition presents innovative and persuasive proposals to deal with those problems (and the degree to which others do not) affects its standing.

Central leaders have to decide how much of each coalition's output they need. The work of each coalition consumes significant resources, and consumption in one area precludes using the resources elsewhere. The central leadership confronts two more or less conflicting imperatives. The first is that each function of the state has to be at least partially satisfied. The other is that as good communists they seek to bring about the good (i.e., socialist, then communist) society. Devoting too many resources to some of the functions of the state may hinder advancement to the good society. Insufficient resources in another area may have the same effect. These conflicting sets of concerns lead to an uneasy dynamic. To build the good society (to the extent that the good society is not coexistent with any one coalition) leaders adopt policies that are compromises among the policy platforms of the various coalitions. They concentrate resources in areas where they might be most beneficial in promoting desired developments, and allocate as few as possible to those areas where they might hinder movement toward the desired goal. But as has just been argued, such compromises are unstable and tend to inhibit development. The leadership is ultimately forced to side with one or several coalitions at the expense of others. Such decisions undercut the other coalitions and raise the likelihood that some of the vital functions of the state will receive insufficient attention, weakening the position of the regime. This necessitates the striking of a new compromise or the wholehearted adoption of another tendency. The interplay of these considerations is a critical element in explaining the dynamics of Chinese politics.

D. Conceptual and empirical difficulties

In lieu of a conclusion, this section addresses a number of possible conceptual or empirical difficulties with the approach developed here. These considerations include the basically structural-functional nature of this approach; the possibility that the argument is circular; the possibility that it is leaders who shape coalitions, rather than coalitions that shape leadership choice; data limitations; and the problem of the single-case study.

My analytical framework clearly has strong structural-functional elements. The key questions are of whether such elements are warranted and, more important, whether the structural functionalism used here shares the defects associated with earlier structural-functional approaches. Such approaches have been termed conservative (supporting the status quo), ideological, and teleological. In addition, the assumption of functional patterns of development in state evolution has been called into question by some empirical studies.[38]

In response, it should be noted that the use of "functionalism" in this chapter is different from its use in the early literature on comparative politics. Functionalism here suggests imperatives that must be met if the state is to survive. It makes no assumption about what the exact response to these imperatives might be in a given situation, or about what is the "best" response. Moreover, given the exigencies of international competition, even what seems like appropriate forms of dealing with functional imperatives might not survive a test of arms. One plausible hypothesis is that the more severe the threats to the security of a state, the more functional (and uniform) the state's response.[39] Faced with profound international threats over many years, both the CCP and the Kuomintang (the leading party in Repub-

---

38. On structural functionalism in political science, see Almond, 1960, and Almond and Powell, 1978. An overview of the criticisms of Almond's work is found in Chilcote, 1981, pp. 178–82. On the critique of functionalism and the state, see Badie and Birnbaum, 1983; March and Olsen, 1984; Ikenberry, 1988; Skowronek, 1982; and Jackson and Rosberg, 1982. Almond addresses some of these criticisms in his 1973, esp. pp. 3–8. One particularly detailed analysis of Almond's writings is Rothman, 1971.

39. It is interesting to note that Skowronek's 1982 discussion, cited by many as proof of the limits to functionalism in state development, concerns a state not facing severe international pressures.

lican China, 1912–1949) drew lessons from the Chinese empire's failure to build a strong state, and the two parties articulated a number of common policies on state building.[40] Thus, because functionalism is used in the sense of general imperatives and not as a specific set of policy responses, and because of the historical evidence of the case at hand, a functional starting point for the approach used here is justifiable.

The same can be said about the creation of structures to manage functions. The framework used here does not address how a structure should meet functional demands, or whether some types of structures are better than others. The argument is simply that state structures are consciously created to fulfill some fairly explicit purposes, although they need not necessarily fulfill the designed purposes or accomplish the assigned tasks very well.

The differences between the approach used here and prior structural functionalism can also be used to rebut criticisms that the approach used here is ideological, conservative, and teleological. This framework is designed to explain change, not to justify the status quo by denying the utility or desirability of change. Similarly, criticism of this approach as teleological or ideological seems misplaced, since this framework contains no assumptions about what constitutes the best or most desirable state.

The problem of circularity is more troublesome. Although the analytical framework used here is developed on the basis of one case and then used to explain that same case, the conclusion will consider briefly several other cases, which may help allay concerns about circularity. Moreover, I hope that the propositions and the framework developed here will be applied in the future to other cases and that such testing will confirm the significance of this approach for the study of Chinese politics over an extended period. The framework presented in this chapter has both broadly analytical and more narrowly empirical components. The utility of analytical frameworks lies in their ability to provide new insights or a fresh perspective on empirical material. Models do not need to show that individuals acting in the historical situation under discussion actually perceived reality in the terms the model or framework stipulates. Reliable historical data of this sort are difficult to come by for most political analysis, and are particularly difficult in the Chinese case. I believe this framework and the case at hand generate new understandings of the nature of Chinese politics and of one turning point in Chinese history. I cannot prove that political actors actually understood their activities in the terms this framework sets out. (For what it is worth, I believe they did.)

A third concern is that an important part of the framework is perhaps

40. Bedeski, 1975 and 1981.

inverted. Specifically, the concern is that it is not coalitions and tendencies that constrain and alter the perceptions of leaders but, rather, leaders who continually press their preferences on the bureaucracy. Some leaders from the 1950s, in particular most of the leaders of the financial coalition, are still living and playing important roles in Chinese politics. There is a real question about who is doing what to whom. In some areas, however, there has been a fair amount of turnover in the leadership (this is especially true among the planners), yet many of the same policy options keep reappearing on the political agenda. In addition, instances have already been cited – and more will be presented later – of cooptation from below and of top leaders feeling that their options were controlled by the bureaucracy or that the bureaucracy was not responsive to their input. The true test of whether the system-tendency view influences leadership options is whether the system tendencies persist despite elite turnover. (Unfortunately, such a test requires the persistence of a similar policy environment over a prolonged period. The fundamental changes that have occurred in the post-Mao era limit the utility of this test in this case; the Chinese state is still redefining its relationship with society and the economy.)

The problem of circularity is exacerbated by data limitations. In general, sources and information concerning the leadership (from the rank of vice-minister up) are much better and more extensive than with rank-and-file staff members of a bureaucracy. Interviews are one way to get around this, but memories fade after thirty years, and access to people in the know remains quite limited. Although I have consulted as wide a range of sources as possible, the voices of the elite will probably be heard to a disproportionate degree.

Some comparativists might object that this is a single study of one dramatic incident. The applicability of the framework and the findings of this book to other cases remains undemonstrated. In a narrow sense, this criticism is correct. I believe, however, this is not just any case study, but a critical case. The standard view of the Great Leap is of ideology (or Mao) run amok. Under such circumstances, the pursuit of economic and bureaucratic interests would not be expected. If I can show that even in what is regarded as an extreme period of mass mobilization and ideological leadership, institutional interests were well represented in economic policies, one should expect that they are even more active in more ordinary times.

No doubt more conceptual and empirical problems could be raised. In the end, the best rejoinder to all criticism lies in the degree to which this study enhances our understanding of Chinese politics and China's political economy.

Part II

*The institutional origins of
the Great Leap Forward*

4

The financial coalition

The center of economic reform proposals in 1956–1957 was the coalition of interests associated with the Ministry of Finance, the Ministry of Commerce, and the Ministry of Agriculture. The leaders of these and other bureaucracies articulated a series of policies from late 1956 into 1957 that if sustained over time (and implemented reasonably effectively) would have changed China from a centrally planned, Soviet-style economy to one that combined market and planned elements. The priority for heavy industry and the high levels of investment in metallurgical and machine building industries associated with centrally planned economies would have been lessened, and more attention would have been devoted to consumer goods, agriculture, and consumption levels. It is not possible to determine whether a true market socialist economy would have developed in China as a result of these reforms. Yet this was the direction in which Chen Yun, Li Xiannian, and other ranking figures were pushing China's political economy.

The financial, or budgeteer, coalition sought both to circumscribe and to undermine the power of planning and heavy industry in the Chinese economy, and to constrain the ability of political generalists to intervene in economic decision making. Changes in rules, procedures, and patterns of policy making were all part of the financial coalition's reform proposals. In its efforts to limit interventions by nonspecialists, this group received support from the planning coalition and from a number of top leaders. Moreover, larger trends, especially those stemming from Mao Zedong's efforts to incorporate broader elements of Chinese society into the political system, facilitated the expression of reformist ideas.

Ultimately, reform efforts failed. When the overall political climate became inhospitable after June 1957, the case for reform was doomed. Yet even if the Anti-Rightist Campaign had not been as extreme as it was, it is quite clear that the reform program would have been in serious trouble. First, the planners and heavy industry were unhappy with many of the reforms, and they devised an alternative path of development that appeared to be more responsive to political and economic concerns than was the program of the financial coalition. Second, Mao was unwilling to allow the rules, procedures, and institutions championed by this coalition to constrain his preferences. In this he was joined by a number of other prominent Party figures and by Party activists of all sorts. Finally, the contradictions and demands inherent in the reform program itself undermined its viability.

This chapter and the two that follow share a common organizational framework. Each chapter first presents the interests, policies, and ideology of the coalition under consideration. This is followed by a summary of the views of key leaders of the group in question, as presented at the Eighth Party Congress in September 1956. This summary provides an empirical referent to link the more abstract discussion of coalition interests and policies with the specific terms of debate in mid to late 1956. Each chapter then discusses the development of the policy arguments and proposals of the relevant grouping as they appeared from October 1956 to October 1957. The analysis of the financial coalition in this chapter concludes with an evaluation of both the economic and political achievements and the failures of the coalition.

A. The financial coalition as a system

In 1956–1957, the main institutions in the financial coalition were the Ministries of Finance, Agriculture, Light Industry, Textiles, and Commerce and the People's Bank of China. The Ministry of Foreign Trade, the Ministry of Grain, and other organizations were part of this grouping. Chen Yun, Li Xiannian, Deng Zihui, Jia Tuofu, Liao Luyan, and Yao Yilin were the coalition's principal spokesmen and leaders.[1]

The financial coalition was charged with the responsibilities of providing revenue and grain to the state to be used for state building and preserving activities and for distributing grain, goods, and monies once central leaders decided on key priorities. In an agrarian socialist society, the extractive function is most closely associated with acquiring grain from the peasantry. Once taxes and grain requisitions were collected, the budgeteers, under the guid-

---

1. There is an extensive literature on the workings of elements of this coalition. Sources in Chinese include Zuo Chuntai and Song Xinzhong, 1988; Shangye Bu Jingji Yanjiusuo, 1984; Zhou Taihe, 1984, pt. 2, chs. 5–8; Xing Hua, " 'Yi Wu' Shiqi Shixing Jizhong Tongyi yu Fenji Guanli Xiang Jiehe, Zezhongde Caizheng Tizhi" (The Financial System of the "First Five-Year Plan" Period, Which, While Combining Centralization and Division of Management Responsibility by Levels, Emphasized Centralization), *Caizheng* (Finance), 1983, no. 2, pp. 13–15; Chen Xin, 1956; Ge Zhida, 1957; Wang Jingzhi, 1956; and Yang Bo, 1956. Major secondary statements include Oksenberg and Tong, 1987; Lardy, 1978b and 1983; Kenneth Lieberthal and Oksenberg, 1988, esp. pp. 106–13; Solinger, 1984; and Walter, 1981.

ance of the central leadership and in line with the plans set by the planning coalition, were responsible for formulating a budget based on these taxes and other government receipts. Moreover, since the financial coalition requisitioned grain (and stored it in granaries and warehouses belonging to units in its grouping), it was also responsible for grain distribution and, by extension, the distribution of all consumer goods.

Because China was a densely populated country with a well-developed traditional agricultural base, there were strict limits on how much grain could be extracted and how easily it could be requisitioned. These facts colored all aspects of the policies put forward by the budgeteers. The profound difficulty of greatly expanding the extraction of surplus from society ("primitive socialist accumulation") provided the general context for the interplay of organizational tasks and procedures that generated the basic tendency associated with this group.

All Chinese leaders realized that agricultural growth was essential for the success of China's development efforts. Agriculture provided food, raw materials for light industry, and exports that paid for the import of complete plants and high technology. Overall economic performance was closely linked with agricultural performance, especially with the portion of rural production that entered state channels. Agricultural production and agricultural procurement were necessarily closely related.[2] A vital issue in this linkage is peasant incentives: incentives to produce and incentives to market grain and other agricultural crops. Leaders of the financial coalition were well aware from their experience in 1954–1955 that excessive extraction had a detrimental effect on incentives and production – indeed, on all work in the countryside.[3] From these circumstances, the leaders of this grouping gradually developed key policies on economic issues.

The coalition confronted the actual tasks of obtaining taxes and grain and distributing consumer goods. It quickly became apparent that these tasks were extremely arduous. To carry them out, the leaders sought to ease the demands placed upon them in a number of ways. They argued for lower rates of accumulation (or investment). Less investment meant that the state did not need to extract as much grain and tax revenue. They favored balancing the budget, the state credit plan, and supply of materials. Budget deficits, too great a supply of credit, and shortages of materials lead to inflation

2. The connection between agricultural production and resource extraction is the reason for linking the Ministry of Agriculture and related organizations with the Ministry of Finance and other units. In Chinese bureaucratic terms, the agricultural system (xitong) was allied with the finance and trade system (and also the light industry system).

3. Chen Yun, 1981, p. 122; 1984, pp. 272–79; 1986, pp. 60–65, 76–77; Li Xiannian, 1989, pp. 228–29. For background, see Bernstein, 1969.

in either overt or disguised form. The leaders of the CCP were well aware of the effect that the hyperinflation of the last years of the Kuomintang government had had in undermining support for that regime and retained a healthy fear of almost any type of price increase.[4]

Leaders of the financial group became extremely zealous in arguing for balanced budgets, and they believed that the "three balances" (of budgetary revenues and expenditures, of credit disbursements and receipts, and of material supply and demand) would act as a mutually reinforcing check on economic imbalances that would cause inflation, undermine the effectiveness of incentives, and disrupt the normal functioning of the economy. These balances had to be enforced very strictly and constantly if the undesirable side effects of imbalance were to be avoided.

In addition, the coalition proposed a number of other coping mechanisms to ease the demands placed on its units. Foremost among these was an expanded role for the market. The commercial bureaucracy simply lacked the resources to control all market transactions and to replace all merchants and peddlers with state trading units. A limited role for the market would allow relief from the impossible burden of trying to distribute all consumer goods throughout the country. But the extent to which the market would be allowed to work and the degree to which the state sector and the market would be in competition with each other remained controversial even within the coalition.

The financial coalition also favored elevating the growth of agricultural production to a high place on the national political agenda. One way to increase agricultural output was to increase investment in the rural sector. Given the budgeteers' concerns with balanced budgets, increases in agricultural investment required cuts in funds earmarked for other uses. Another method to stimulate agricultural production was to increase incentives, using markets and prices to encourage peasant diligence. Coupled with the market were calls to increase light industrial output. Plentiful consumer goods stimulated urban-rural exchanges, facilitating resource extraction. And light industry had other advantages, from the coalition's perspective. It produced large profits quickly. The profits from, and the taxes assessed on, light industrial output were also much easier to collect than was the agricultural tax.

In short, the leaders of this group supported policies that reduced the amount of funds and grain to be extracted and lowered the demands placed on their organizations to distribute commodities. These leaders had a much less all-embracing vision of the state than did other coalitions of organiza-

4. A good short account of the political costs of Kuomintang economic mismanagement is Pepper, 1980, ch. 4. On the CCP's fear of inflation, see Eckstein, 1977, ch. 5.

tions in the Chinese state. To phrase the point differently, this coalition was perhaps the one most heavily influenced by society.

The preceding account does not clearly convey the centrality of the Ministry of Finance in the coalition. First, unlike any other element of the coalition, the Ministry of Finance is a relatively comprehensive organ. Charged with the task of financial allocation, it has some authority to involve itself in the affairs of all other organizations with regard to their use of funds.[5] Second, the minister of finance, Li Xiannian, was usually the highest-ranking minister in the coalition. (Chen Yun has often ranked higher than Li, but it was only between late 1956 and early 1958 that Chen served as a minister in the coalition.) Deng Zihui, head of the Party's Rural Work Department, had differed substantially with Mao Zedong on the pace of agricultural collectivization in 1955 and was in relative disfavor.[6] Jia Tuofu, Liao Luyan, and others were too junior in rank to serve as chief spokesmen for the group. Therefore, leadership of the coalition fell to Chen Yun and Li Xiannian. Chen, a member of the Politburo Standing Committee, was the regime's chief economic troubleshooter and was more of a generalist than Li Xiannian.[7]

In contrast to the Ministry of Finance, the ministries of agriculture and commerce faced severe limitations on their ability to guide the financial coalition. The agriculture ministry was not particularly autonomous. In agriculture, there was a great deal of redundancy in the Chinese political system. The CCP apparat often controlled agricultural policy implementation, and with their long experience in rural base areas, most CCP leaders felt they understood agricultural policy questions and did not need to defer to agricultural specialists. Nor was the Ministry of Commerce a strong organization. The range of Commerce's responsibilities was extremely wide, and they were, to be realistic, heavy beyond the capacity of the units in the commercial system. A great deal of time, therefore, was spent trying to solve

5. Kenneth Lieberthal and Oksenberg, 1988, pp. 63, 106–11.

6. Deng Zihui, "Zai Quanguo Disanci Nongcun Gongzuo Huiyishangde Kaimuce" (Opening Address to the Third National Rural Work Conference), *Dangshi Yanjiu* (Research on Party History; hereafter *DSYJ*), 1981, no. 1, pp. 2–9; Mao Zedong, "Summing-up Speech at the 6th Expanded Plenum of the 7th CCP Central Committee," in Joint Publications Research Service (hereafter JPRS), *Miscellany of Mao Tse-tung Thought* (hereafter *MMTTT*) (Arlington, Va.: JPRS no. 61269-1, February 20, 1974), pp. 14–26, esp. p. 20; Mao, 1977, pp. 211–34, esp. pp. 224–25. For analysis of this well-known dispute, see Qiang Yuangan and Lin Bangguang, "Shilun Yijiuwuwu Nian Dangnei Guanyu Nongye Hezuohua Wentide Zhenglun" (A Preliminary Discussion of the Internal Party Debate on the Question of Agricultural Cooperation in 1955), *DSYJ*, 1981, no. 1, pp. 10–17. Deng Zihui was the most outspoken of Mao Zedong's lieutenants, the only one who stood up to Mao directly on several occasions. See Teiwes, 1988, esp. pp. 13–15.

7. The most complete biography of Chen Yun is Bachman, 1985b.

insoluable problems. The commercial network was more internally oriented than were other units in the coalition. Commerce was also a field that carried a great deal of Marxist-Leninist-Maoist ideological baggage. (Nevertheless, Mao would note in 1958 that commerce and light industry were much less dogmatic in copying the Soviet Union than were planning and heavy industry in the period 1950–1957.)[8] Capitalist commerce was seen as corrupting and as a threat to socialist institutions. Those who came into contact with commerce were tainted by this association, even if they were trying to manage socialist commerce.[9]

Finally, both the Ministry of Commerce and the Ministry of Agriculture were facing a newly restructured environment in the mid 1950s. By mid 1956, Chinese agriculture was almost completely collectivized. Less than a year earlier, most of the Chinese peasantry had not even been organized into semicollectivized units. A dramatic change in rural social organization took place in an exceptionally short time. The Ministry of Agriculture found it impossible to keep up with the shifting environment. Much the same thing happened with the socialist transformation of capitalist commercial organizations in late 1955 and 1956. The Ministry of Commerce suddenly faced a great increase in the number of units for which it bore direct responsibility. This further strained already fragile institutional control over the commercial network.

In contrast to Commerce and Agriculture, Finance faced no such great change in the nature and scope of its duties in the mid 1950s. Its environment was largely stable. Consequently, the staff of the ministry was not engaged in the frantic process of developing new standard operating procedures to cope with new or expanded duties.

Membership of light industry in this coalition is debatable, but several facts justify its inclusion. First, the vast majority of raw materials for light industry came from agriculture; for example, cotton for textiles, forestry products for paper making. In contrast, most raw materials for the planning and heavy industry coalition came from within that group. Second, light industry suffered from the emphasis placed on heavy industry under the Soviet model of development that the Chinese leadership took over in the early to mid 1950s. The dominant goal in economic policy making at that time was development of the productive forces of society. This left little room for channeling more resources into light industry. Because light industry was so dependent on agricultural inputs, it was hard for leaders of ministries involved in consumer goods production to argue for expanded invest-

8. Schram, 1974, p. 98.
9. See Solinger, 1984, esp. ch. 1; Shue, 1980, chs. 5 and 6; and Bennett, 1978, pt. II.

ment in light industry when there was a pervasive shortage of raw materials. Therefore, light industrial leaders had no real choice but to attach themselves to the budgeteers if their interests were to be pursued.

Thus, the Ministry of Finance led the budgeteer coalition because the ministry's leader was one of the two top leaders in the grouping, because the ministry was actively involved in basic state activities that affected all other actors in the political system, and because it lacked some of the weaknesses associated with other members of the coalition. A final key element of the Ministry of Finance's power was its relative autonomy. The technical nature of its work made supervision by outsiders very difficult. Apparently the ministry and its leaders were well aware of this and often failed to consult with top leaders (or at least Mao Zedong) until after drafts of the budget had been completed. [10]

B. The financial coalition at the Eighth Party Congress

For two reasons, this section deals with the views of leaders of the financial coalition at the landmark Eighth National Congress of the Chinese Communist Party. First, the speeches of these leaders provide detailed content for the more general statement of the interests and policies presented in Section A. The speeches illustrate the actual terms of debate on policy issues, and not the more subterranean or abstract principles that lurked beneath the surface of policy discussions in the mid to late 1950s. Second, the speeches constituted the first attempt by the financial coalition to alter the prevailing pattern of resource allocation and procedures governing the administration of China's economy. These speeches represented the starting point for reform efforts in 1956; in fact, they provided justification for many of the early reforms of the late 1970s and early 1980s.

At the congress, there were four keynote and seven other major speeches on questions relating to the financial coalition. [11] The four principal speakers were Chen Yun, Li Xiannian, Deng Zihui, and Jia Tuofu. Other speeches were given by the ministers of commerce and foreign trade; the director of the Central Handicrafts Administrative Bureau; the vice-ministers of com-

10. On several occasions, Mao complained that the Ministry of Finance was monopolizing financial affairs and that the political generalists (meaning Mao, no doubt) were unable to influence budget making. The extent to which Mao was engaging in deliberate political maneuver and hyperbole is unclear. Probably his comments in 1956 were less motivated by political concerns than those of 1958. See Mao, 1977, pp. 334–35, and *MMTTT*, pp. 77–84. For more details, see the Appendix to the present volume.

11. A major speech means a speech by a cadre at the provincial (ministerial) level or higher. There were many speeches by subprovincial officials and "models" – exemplary workers, peasants, managers, and others, none of which will be discussed here.

merce, textiles, and light industry; and the director of the Planning Bureau for Light Industry and Textiles of the State Planning Commission.

The focus of Chen Yun's speech to the Eighth Party Congress was on problems caused by the "socialist transformation" of capitalist industry, commerce, and handicrafts, but his speech touched on many other themes too. No speech or document by a top Party leader in the twenty years following Chen's address would make more controversial and important arguments about market-oriented reforms.

Chen's speech was in five parts.[12] First, he argued that factories (the newly socialized enterprises and other plants in the light industrial sector) themselves should purchase raw materials and market their products rather than have the commercial departments supply them and tell them what to produce. In other words, factories should not be fully integrated into the planning system. Second, and related, he struck out at the tendency toward blind amalgamation in industry, agriculture, commerce, and handicrafts. Mergers harmed incentives by placing additional layers of administration between producers and consumers. Chen wanted previous patterns of organization restored. This led into the third point. All old regulations governing capitalist industry and commerce should be rescinded. These measures, designed to restrict such enterprises, had created state bureaucracies with effective monopolies over trade and material supply. Since the capitalist enterprises were now essentially state-owned, there was no need to restrict them. In fact, Chen pressed for competition between these enterprises and many of the state monopolies in order to promote economic flexibility.

Fourth, he called for changes in price policy, arguing that the prices of some classes of goods should be unfrozen and allowed to fluctuate with market demand. He calculated that the changes associated with these four policies would affect about a quarter of all commodity sales in China.

Finally, Chen advocated "suitable changes . . . in the state's control over certain products." The changes he sought meant a drastic reduction in attempts to plan light industrial production. Instead, Chen felt most such production could be guided by consumer demand. He concluded his call for reform by saying, "In industrial and agricultural production, planned production will be the mainstay, to be supplemented by free production carried on within the scope prescribed by the state plan and in accordance with market fluctuations."[13]

The entire thrust of Chen's speech was toward improving incentives, gear-

12. "Speech by Comrade Chen Yun," in *Eighth National Congress of the Communist Party of China*, vol. 2: *Speeches* (hereafter *8PC/S*), 1956, pp. 157–76.
13. Ibid., p. 176.

ing production to market needs, reducing bureaucratic interference in economic activity, and improving the quality of consumer goods. The measures he favored included greatly expanding the role of the market, promoting competition between enterprises and bureaucracies, and allowing different forms of ownership to coexist. Taken individually, many of these measures were not great departures from current policies. Taken together, however, they foreshadowed a basic change in the nature of the Chinese economic system. Chen's remarks were couched in limited, cautionary terms, but they marked a break with the process of extreme etatization that had characterized the Chinese political economy since 1949, and left room for the reemergence of a civil society out of which further economic reform could grow.

In two elliptical passages in his speech, Chen hinted at a radical redefinition of direction for the Chinese economy. One proposal concerned foreign trade. He called for improvement in the work of import shops and cooperatives. This was to be made by the Ministry of Foreign Trade, which was to rehire "professional personnel who did various kinds of import work in concerns run by foreign merchants in the past. . . . The few state import corporations which monopolize the whole import business at present and still have a low level of professional skill cannot meet the demands of society." [14] This not only hinted at a role for the national bourgeoisie, a suspect political class, but also implied a role for the compradore bourgeoisie (seen as class enemies). The compradores were precisely the people who had done professional work for firms in foreign trade before the revolution.

Even more interesting is why Chen might have raised this issue in the first place. Since most Chinese imports came from the Soviet Union and Eastern Europe, and were more bartered than traded, why was the skill level of import shops an issue for discussion? It might become an issue if, Chen and other Chinese leaders were suggesting, the direction of Chinese foreign trade were to change. Import personnel with greater skills would matter if imports were to increase or more imports were to come from capitalist economies. [15]

14. Ibid., pp. 167–68.
15. The possibility of such a shift in trade patterns had been raised earlier in 1956. In June 1956, at the Third Session of the First National People's Congress, Zhang Bojun, the noncommunist minister of communications, proposed that the port of Zhanjiang in Guangdong province be developed so that Chinese trade with overseas Chinese in Southeast Asia could be expanded. See "Jiaotongbu Zhang Bojun Buzhangde Fayan" (Speech by Minister of Communications Zhang Bojun), in *Zhonghua Renmin Gongheguo Diyijie Quanguo Renmin Daibiao Dahui Disanci Huiyi Huikan*, 1956, pp. 162–68. To maximize China's foreign exchange reserves (small at the time) and obtain the most beneficial terms, a high skill level among import personnel was crucial. In addition, payment for increased imports from capitalist countries demanded increased exports

The other radical suggestion in Chen's speech undermined the justifica-tion for a planned economy. He argued that most plans for light industry were based on estimates. Because of his insistence that light industrial pro-duction should reflect market needs, and because plans were largely esti-mates, Chen concluded there was no need for rigid planning in much of light industry. He stated:

> Since there is no need for the state plan to set rigid targets for many of the factories and commercial departments, we should not waste more money and labor in collect-ing much statistical information that has turned out to be useless. Thus, the number of statisticians can be drastically reduced. At present, many statisticians in commer-cial departments are working on figures that are not of much use.[16]

Chen implicitly argued that it was impossible to plan consumer-goods pro-duction and sales fully (or even largely). Statistical information was either unavailable or unreliable. In what was still the largest component of Chinese industry at the time, planning could be applied only to the most common and essential consumer goods. Implicitly, Chen raised the question of whether the situation in heavy industry was any better. The answer provided by other speakers at the congress was "Not much,"[17] thus casting doubt on the basic premises of planning in China. Chen stated that other methods, particularly the market, must supplement planning.

In addition to undercutting the rationale for planning, Chen also attacked some of the planners, at least indirectly. His statements undermined the justification for expanding the statistical system. This was an implied criti-cism of the head of the State Statistical Bureau, Xue Muqiao. Not coinciden-tally, Xue was also a vice-chairman of the State Planning Commission.[18]

Chen's suggestions for radical reform should be seen as a partial rejection of the Soviet model of development. The Soviet model was central to the interests of the planning and heavy industry coalition. Attacking the model indirectly threatened the interests of the planners. (Indeed, it appears that the Ministry of Finance had compiled a report before January 1957 conclud-ing that the Soviets obtained greater advantage from Sino-Soviet relations

to the West. Chen's brief and ambiguous remarks on this subject can be read as an implied criticism of Sino-Soviet trade relations and the Soviet model of development. With exports to the West expanding, more emphasis would be placed on light industry to supply the exports, and with the diversion of exports from the Soviet Union to the West, fewer pieces of equip-ment – or even whole plants destined for heavy industry – would need to be imported from the USSR. In 1956–1957, interest in trade with capitalist economies, especially Britain and Japan, expanded. See Cheng, 1986, pp. 235–37, and Wang Heying et al., 1987, esp. pp. 83–86 and 278–79.

16. Chen, *8PC/S*, p. 174.

17. "Speech by Comrade Li Fuchun" (chairman of the State Planning Commission), *8PC/S*, pp. 288–303.

18. On Xue, See Klein and Clark, 1971, pp. 370–72, and Choh-ming Li, 1962.

than the Chinese did.)[19] In short, Chen Yun advocated a major revision of the assumptions and procedures that underlay the Chinese economy in the 1950s along lines that were congenial to the interests of the financial coalition.

Li Xiannian spoke to the Eighth Party Congress on price questions. But the implications of the price reforms he proposed touched on basic allocational issues.[20] To a certain extent, Li differed with Chen Yun on price questions. Although they agreed that prices should be used to stimulate production, Chen proposed that the prices for some goods be allowed to float. Li, on the other hand, favored the deliberate control of price increases, decreases, and differentials to regulate production. In Li's view, price changes should be administered by the government. Nonetheless, he favored a thorough revamping of prices, particularly as a tool for promoting the development of subsidiary agricultural products.

Li noted that the proposed price changes would cause an immediate loss of state revenue and an increase in expenditures. The state would have 1 billion to 2 billion yuan less to use. The price changes would ultimately serve to increase production and hence revenues, but to begin with, the state would have to spend more on higher procurement prices. Consequently,

a reduction in revenue would necessitate a *corresponding* reduction in expenditure. Under *the principle of balancing the budget,* there are few ways to get around this. . . . This will in various ways affect relations between industry and agriculture, between heavy and light industry, and between the needs of national construction and the people's needs in the way of consumer goods. . . . The income of the peasants will be increased and their purchasing power raised. . . . Consequently, the share of total investment on light industry has to be raised and a suitable revision will have to be made in the proportion of investments in heavy industry and other fields. Under the condition of ensuring a *fairly* high rate of industrial development it is proper to make necessary changes in keeping with the changing situation.[21]

Li Xiannian's speech addressed the issues of balance and proportion in the economy. He favored giving agriculture and light industry more importance. Implicit in his discussion was the view that planning and budgetary allocation should flow from consumer purchasing power and not from plans fixed without any reference to the needs and requirements of the people. The implications of his remarks were that he was willing to see a slower rate of growth and that the rate of economic growth was at least partially determined by a balanced budget and the distribution of budgetary expenditures. In short, his opinions on proportionate relations in the economy, the rules

19. Deng Xiaoping, 1967, p. 62.
20. "Speech by Comrade Li Hsien-nien [Li Xiannian]," *8PC/S,* pp. 206–24.
21. Ibid., p. 220. Emphasis added.

governing economic activity, and how strictly those rules should be applied were significantly different from those of the top planners.

Deng Zihui, the head of the CCP's Rural Work Department, expanded on Chen Yun's remarks on promoting subsidiary agricultural production by peasant households.[22] He held that "agriculture is the basic factor for the growth of industry." If the CCP wanted industry to expand, agriculture must grow. Deng did not shy away from indicating how this was to be accomplished: "We [the CCP] must resolutely stand for the fundamental interests of the peasants and we must know how to meet the *immediate* demands of the peasants' *personal interests*" (emphasis added). In other words, he called for more and better incentives to increase production.

Deng agreed with the principle of priority for industry but felt that agriculture absolutely could not be neglected. Heavy industry should be developed in order to provide the advanced inputs to the rural sector that would greatly increase agricultural productivity. Light industry should expand to meet the increasing demands of peasants for consumer goods.[23] He did not want other Party leaders to push industry too far, however.

But the development of industry requires a *corresponding* development of agriculture. Should agricultural production fall behind the demands of industrial development, that is, should it fail to meet the requirements of a developing industry in respect to foodstuffs, raw materials, accumulation of funds and an expanding market for its manufactures, then the result would be a slowdown in the pace of development, and possibly even give rise to a tension in the relations between the workers and the peasants. . . . Therefore, we must draw up a correct plan, *throw in the necessary investments* and make vigorous efforts to ensure that our relatively backward agriculture will *keep in step* with the development of industry.[24]

Deng stated that the relationship between industry and agriculture was correctly handled in the First Five-Year Plan (FFYP) and in the draft proposals for the Second Five-Year Plan (SFYP). It would have been impolitic for him to say otherwise. Yet he called for more investment in water conservancy. He also favored price reforms, backing Li Xiannian's proposals; better commercial work in the countryside; better (less rigid) planning of agricultural production; and allowing peasants to take their products to the free market once they had fulfilled the state purchasing quota. In sum, the policies advocated by Deng Zihui were highly congruous with Chen Yun's and Li Xiannian's speeches.

The last major leader of the financial coalition to speak at the Eighth Party

22. "Speech by Comrade Teng Tzu-hui [Deng Zihui]," *8PC/S*, pp. 177–98.
23. Ibid., p. 187.
24. Ibid., pp. 187–88. Emphasis added.

Congress was Jia Tuofu, head of the Fourth Staff Office (responsible for light industry) under the State Council.[25] Jia reviewed the course of development in light industry. He enunciated a series of policies that would make light industry less subservient to the interests of heavy industry.

Jia made the case for increased investments and new construction in light industry. First, he pointed out that if light industry failed to meet the needs of the peasantry, the state would find it difficult to procure grain and industrial crops. Therefore light industrial output was to increase by 60 percent during the course of the SFYP. (In supplying this figure, Jia was far more specific than were Zhou Enlai and official proposals for the SFYP.) He noted that 90 percent of light industrial output came from enterprises already existing at the start of the FFYP. About 60 percent of these factories had originally been capitalist or handicraft enterprises. According to Jia, there was little potential left for developing production there. Consequently, significant increases in renovation, reconstruction, and new construction were required. In the SFYP, light industrial investment as a percentage of total industrial investment must exceed the figure of approximately 12 percent in the FFYP, Jia argued.

Second, Jia favored a continuation of the existing pattern of economic administration. About 80 percent of all light industrial production came from factories under the control of the localities. Jia thought this pattern of decentralized small plants was better than a centralized light industrial system with big plants at the core. Small enterprises repaid investment very quickly, earned high profits, and were more apt to be responsive to local consumer demand. He called for unified central planning and aid in developing the technical level of these enterprises and the educational level of their workers and staff, but he opposed central administration of light industry itself.

Third, Jia discussed problems in building enterprises and supplying new equipment. He stated that the machine-building industries ignored the needs of light industry for equipment. He argued that light industry should therefore create its own machine-building capability. He also advocated the establishment of specialized secondary schools and universities to provide more technical personnel for the light industrial system. Previously, almost all technicians had been channeled into heavy industry.

On questions of price, agriculture, and commerce, he echoed the views of Chen, Li, and Deng. More emphasis on agriculture, higher crop prices,

25. Jia Tuofu, "Guanyu Fazhan Qinggongyede Jige Wenti" (Several Problems in the Development of Light Industry), *Xinhua Banyuekan* (New China Semimonthly; hereafter *XHBYK*), 1956, no. 21, pp. 100–102.

fewer bureaucratic links between producer and consumer, higher prices for better products, and light industrial production in line with consumer demands were all central to his views.

Jia Tuofu supported the relevant financial coalition positions on commercial and light industrial issues. Moreover, he strongly disagreed with the planners about how to develop industry. The planners were unresponsive to the demands of units under Jia's supervision. He implied that the planners prevented sufficient investment funds from flowing to light industry, and stated that the planners had been allotted too many technical personnel. In effect, he argued that a larger share of the pie should go to light industry.

Lower-ranking officials in the financial coalition endorsed and supplemented the speeches of their leaders. Ye Jizhuang, the minister of foreign trade, noted that great attention was paid to imports (which went to heavy industry), but little concern was shown for exports. He outlined a series of steps to expand exports and called on China to become a net exporter.[26] The minister of commerce, Zeng Shan, and a vice-minister of commerce, Yao Yilin, also echoed Chen Yun's demands for change in commerce.[27] The director of the Central Handicrafts Administrative Bureau, Bai Rubing, reiterated many of Chen Yun's ideas on handicrafts. Unlike everyone else in the coalition, however, he explicitly called for better local Party leadership in handicrafts.[28] Three cadres at the vice-ministerial level supported Jia Tuofu and Chen Yun on light industry.[29]

The speeches by these Party officials show a consistent line of argument.

26. Ye Jizhuang, "Gaijin Wo Guo Chukou, Baozheng Guojia Gongye Jianshe" (Improve Our Country's Export Work, Guarantee National Economic Construction), *XHBYK*, 1956, no. 21, pp. 155–56.

27. Zeng Shan, "Gaijin Riyonggongyepinde Shengchan he Fenpei Gongzuo" (Improve the Work of the Production and Distribution of Daily Use Industrial Products), *XHBYK*, 1956, no. 21, pp. 165–67, and Yao Yilin, "Caiqu Youxiao Cuoshi Jiejue Zhurou he Shengcai Gongying Wenti" (Adopt Effective Measures to Resolve Pork and Vegetable Supply Problems), *XHBYK*, 1956, no. 21, pp. 214–15. Yao's speech (presented to the congress in written form) was so in keeping with Chen's ideas that a 1981 internal version of Chen's speeches attributes Yao's speech at the congress to him. (See Chen Yun, 1981, pp. 14–19.) According to several sources, Chen did give a speech on this topic on September 7, 1956. See Fang Weizhong, 1984, p. 177, and *Zhonghua Renmin Gongheguo Jingji Guanli Dashiji*, 1986, p. 88. No such speech appears in the two openly published volumes of Chen's works (Chen 1984 and 1986), although he returned to the subject in November 1956 (1986, pp. 15–27).

28. Bai Rubing, "Shougongye Neibu he Waibu Guanxishangde Xin Wenti" (New Questions in Handicrafts' Internal and External Relations), *XHBYK*, 1956, no. 21, pp. 147–48.

29. Hu Ming (head of the light industrial and textile planning bureau of the State Planning Commission), "Jin Yibu Tigao he Fazhan Wo Guo Liangpin Gongye" (Progressively Raise and Develop Our Country's Food Products Industry), *XHBYK*, 1956, no. 21, pp. 205–6; Qian Zhiguang (vice-minister of textiles), "Fazhan Fangzhi Gongye, Manzu Renmin Xuyao" (Develop the Textile Industry, Satisfy the People's Needs), *XHBYK*, 1956, no. 21, pp. 158–60; and Song Naide (vice-minister of light industry), "Tigao Wo Guo Riyonggongyepinde Zhiliang" (Raise the Quality of Our Country's Daily Use Industrial Products), *XHBYK*, 1956, no. 21, pp. 210–11.

Key elements of their discussions included more investment in light industry and agriculture, a greater concern for balance in the economy, greater
reliance on material incentives, use of the market, and less bureaucratic
(implicitly, less political) interference in economic processes. These speeches
seemed aimed at a common external enemy or a prevailing pattern of policies. The differences among speakers within this system were minor compared with their overwhelming areas of agreement. In short, the speeches
provide a solid base line from which to measure developments in the position of the financial coalition up to late 1957.

C. The financial coalition, October 1956 – October 1957

Effective politicians in any system attempt to use problems appearing on the
political agenda to further their interests and policy views. They do not merely
respond to the press of events, but use the interplay of problems and issues
to shape the larger policy environment. This is precisely what the leaders of
the financial coalition did in the period from October 1956 to October 1957,
but with diminishing effectiveness after early 1957. The reasons are multiple; they include the change in the political climate after June 1957, when
the Hundred Flowers Campaign of liberalization gave way to the Anti-
Rightist crackdown; assertive leadership and advocacy by the planning coalition; irresolvable contradictions within the program of the financial coalition; and the seeming withdrawal of top budgeteers from policy advocacy.

In late 1956 and most of 1957, the leadership of the financial coalition was
preoccupied by four closely connected issues: drafting and implementing
economic plans for 1957, drafting the Second Five-Year Plan, reforming the
system of economic administration (especially in the fields of industry, commerce, and finance), and dealing with agricultural and commercial problems.

The coalition took steps to bolster its strength for policy advocacy. Most
important, the journal of the Ministry of Finance, *Caizheng* (Finance) was
established in October 1956. Until then, items on financial matters had been
discussed in newspapers and in the planning journal *Jihua Jingji* (Planned
Economy), and more theoretical articles had been published in the journal
of the Institute of Economics of the Chinese Academy of Sciences, *Jingji
Yanjiu* (Economic Research). While most of the articles in *Caizheng* touched
on items of interest only to those engaged in financial matters, a number of
articles also had implications that clearly affected relations among the coalitions. In the inaugural issue, for example, Jin Ming, a vice-minister of finance, argued that the Ministry of Finance did not pay enough attention to

financial supervision. He conceded that finance was subordinate to the economy (meaning physical production) but pointed out that the economy was also promoted by finance. He called for more attention to the people's livelihood and not just to economic development.[30] And the finance and trade bureaucracies were in the forefront of efforts to establish research institutions to study concrete and theoretical problems in their areas of responsibility.[31] *Caizheng* and these institutes served as platforms for the circulation of ideas and as institutional bases for the development of expertise.

C.1. The economic plans for 1957

The formulation of economic plans is a central political activity in all planned economies. Fundamental questions of resource distribution are embedded in all such discussions, even if the plan does not control economic processes. The deliberations over the 1957 economic plan in China were particularly arduous and full of conflict. The year 1956 had seen unprecedented advance, but too much had been undertaken. Investment in capital construction increased by more than 60 percent over 1955, but supplies of raw materials and budgetary revenue could not keep pace with the small leap forward. By the second half of 1956 most Chinese leaders were well aware of growing imbalance in the economy, and the depth of their understanding of these problems increased over time.

Primier Zhou Enlai proposed that work on the 1957 plan begin earlier than usual. On the eve of the Eighth Party Congress (September 15–27, 1956), the newly formed State Economic Commission (SEC; charged with drawing up annual plans)[32] presented, after many revisions, a preliminary draft of the 1957 plan. But this draft was not in keeping with the policies enunciated at the congress. The draft was based on the production figures of 1956, which many felt could not be sustained. Moreover, the production targets of the SEC could not be reconciled with financial plans. Zhou called a meeting of State Council vice-premiers and the heads and vice-heads of the eight staff offices under the State Council. They were in conference for three straight weeks but failed to reach a consensus: Some wanted to quicken the pace of development; others wanted a slower rate of advance. Immedi-

30. Jin Ming, "Jin Yibu Fahui Caizheng Gongzuo zai Shehuizhuyi Jianshezhongde Zuoyong" (Progressively Develop the Utility of Finance in Socialist Construction), *Caizheng*, 1956, no. 1 (October), pp. 1–4.

31. See Halpern, 1985, pp. 84–85.

32. On the early organizational history of the SEC, see *Zhonghua Renmin Gongheguo Jingji Guanli Dashiji*, 1986, pp. 82–83, 85–86, and 91. The SEC was authorized to employ 1,300 staff members, but by June 30, 1956, it had only half that number (p. 86).

ately before the Second Plenum of the Eighth Central Committee (November 10–15, 1956), and after repeated discussions with the party fractions of State Council organizations and the Politburo, Zhou opted for a policy of retrenchment in the 1957 plan: Capital construction would be cut by 20 percent from 1956 levels. The decision was announced at the Second Plenum.[33] The communiqué of the plenum stated in summing up Zhou's speech: "Because there are certain items that are not satisfactory and there is over-spending on certain items in the current year's plan, there must be suitable retrenchment in certain fields in the coming year's plan, within the framework of continued progress, and there must be an energetic economy campaign in government organizations."[34] Immediately after the plenum, Zhou Enlai left to make official visits to a number of Asian and European nations. He was away from November 18, 1956, to February 6, 1957.[35] In his absence, Chen Yun, ranking vice-premier, served as acting premier.

The communiqué issued by the plenum indicated that the Central Committee had determined that a "small part" of the capital construction budget and other items were not correct (Mao was to say 10 percent).[36] There was recognition that increases in wages had been excessive in 1956 and that all future wage increases must be gradual. The plenum unanimously adopted the call to launch a movement to increase production and practice economy – standard for the Party when it faced economic difficulties. But the financial coalition had a strong influence on how this movement was to be developed: "Production should be increased only where supplies of raw materials were definite and the increase was needed by the community. Irrespective of increased production or economy, quality of work must be guaranteed and attention given to safety."[37] For the first time in PRC history, a decrease in investment for capital construction was authorized. Since large-scale capital-construction projects were usually undertaken over several years and many

33. This paragraph is based on Chen Xuewei, "Tansuo Woguo Shehuizhuyi Jingji Jianshe Guilude Zhongyao Chengguo" (An Investigation of an Important Achievement of Our Country's Laws of Socialist Economic Construction), *DSYJ*, 1985, no. 2, pp. 64–68, esp. p. 64. The 20 percent reduction figure is found in Qiang Yuangan and Chen Xuewei, "Zhongping 1956 Niande 'Fan Maojin' " (Reevaluate the "Opposition to Rash Advance" of 1956), *DSYJ*, 1980, no. 6, pp. 34–41 (see p. 38); see also Zhou Enlai, 1984b, pp. 229–38. Indeed, planning was so disrupted by the high tide of 1956 that the State Planning Commission's control figures for the 1956 plan were not approved by the Party center until October 1956. (Control figures are supposed to be the basis for the year's plan.) See *Zhonghua Renmin Gongheguo Jingji Guanli Dashiji*, 1986, p. 89.
34. "Communique of the 2nd Plenary Session of the CCP 8th Central Committee," in *Documents of the Chinese Communist Party Central Committee, September 1956–April 1969*, vol. 1 (hereafter *Documents*), 1971, pp. 105–7.
35. Huai En, 1986, pp. 391–94.
36. Mao, 1977, p. 335.
37. "Communique," p. 105.

projects had been started in 1956, the leadership had to devise some criteria on which to base its retrenchment. The ones they chose – raw material supply and community needed – were highly compatible with the views of the budgeteers.

The budget figures and planned targets adopted at this meeting controlled the development of economic activity in 1957 (the SEC presented control figures for the 1957 plan on November 28, 1956).[38] Most economic policy discussions in 1957 revolved around the issue of whether these targets were a temporary and expedient response to imbalance or symbolized the beginning of a different approach to economic development. The financial coalition would spend most of the first months of 1957 articulating a new development strategy.

An editorial in the January 1957 issue of *Caizheng* argued that in 1956 a number of cadres forgot the phrase "more economical results" in the four-character phrase *duo, kuai, hao, sheng* – more, faster, better, more economical results – and that they forgot the state's financial, material, and technical condition in arranging capital construction. It noted that many believed strict financial supervision hindered work. But with the reform of the financial management system, financial supervision should be strengthened to insure that imbalances and waste did not appear in economic development. The 1957 plan would be completely reliable, at least in part because it had the benefit of the errors of 1956.[39]

Another article in the same issue directly attacked the planners. Wang Ziying argued that the problems in the 1956 budget were not on the revenue side but on the expenditure side of the ledger, which he detailed. He criticized "many people" who still did not recognize these problems and felt that all pre-1956 budgets had been conservative. These people pointed to budget surpluses and raw material reserves as illustrations of conservatism and felt that great increases in capital construction sped up socialist development. Less stringent financial supervision promoted enterprise activism, they said. Wang rebutted these views and advocated that all plans be drawn up in accord with financial, material, and technical abilities. When plans exceeded

38. "A Review of the 1956 Economic Plan and an Explanation of the Draft Plan for 1957" (an uncleared version of a speech by Jia Tuofu, who was by that time also vice-chairman of the State Economic Commission), *Jihua Jingji* (Planned Economy; hereafter *JHJJ*), 1957, no. 4, in *Extracts from China Mainland Magazines* (hereafter *ECMM*), no. 90 (July 15, 1957), pp. 17–31 (see p. 21); "An Outline of a Speech by Li Xiannian at the National Conference of Finance Directors," *Caizheng*, 1957, no. 11, in *ECMM*, no. 117 (February 3, 1958), pp. 10–14 (see p. 10); *Zhonghua Renmin Gongheguo Jingji Guanli Dashiji*, 1986, pp. 91–92.

39. "Kaiyuan Jieliu Chongfen Kekaode Fazhan Shehuizhuyi Jianshe" (Broaden Sources of Income and Reduce Expenditures, Completely and Reliably Develop Socialist Construction), *Caizheng*, 1957, no. 1 (January), pp. 1–2, 7.

these abilities, economic disorder resulted. He argued that devoting about 40 percent of the budget, or a little more, to capital construction was too much, and that a figure of 35–38 percent was more appropriate. This was a direct criticism of Bo Yibo, the head of the SEC (who had proposed the 40 percent–plus figure to the Eighth Party Congress).[40] Wang closed by demanding that financial supervision play a much larger role in economic management.[41]

The boldest statement by the financial coalition on reforming the macro-economic patterns of the Chinese economy was presented on January 18, 1957. On that date, Chen Yun made perhaps the most important speech of his career to a conference of provincial Party secretaries, presenting the three balances (budgets, credit, and materials). He outlined principles and policies both to cope with the overheated economy created by the small leap forward of 1956 and to establish a more stable foundation for economic development. Most fundamentally, he argued that the scale of capital construction should correspond to national strength, defined in terms of the state's financial, credit, and material resources. According to Chen, if the scale of capital construction exceeded the state's resources, economic dislocations would result, and the more construction exceeded the state's capacity, the more severe the dislocation. From this general principle, he presented five specific ways to ensure that the scale of construction did in fact correspond to China's strength. First, it was necessary to balance financial revenues and expenditures and bank loans and receipts – ideally, to have a slight surplus in revenues and receipts. Second, top priority in the allocation of materials was to go to guaranteeing basic living standards, particularly in urban areas. Current minimum production needs would rank second on the priority list. Finally, remaining raw materials would be allocated to capital construction. This marked a complete reversal of previous allocational rules. Third, the supply of consumer goods must correspond to social purchasing power. Fourth, plans should dovetail. This meant that not only should national strength and capital construction be balanced in any one year, but current capital construction plans should be based on the previous year's plan and give due consideration to the following year's plan. Finally, the pace of agricultural development would be slow for a considerable period. This meant a deceleration of the overall pace of construction, since agriculture supplied a large percentage of the state's financial revenue (directly through taxes and req-

40. "Speech by Comrade Po Yi-po [Bo Yibo]," *8PC/S*, pp. 45–62. This will be discussed in more detail in the next chapter.
41. Wang Ziying, "Yijiuwuliu Nian Guojia Yusuan Bianzao he Zhixingzhong Youxie Shenma Jingyan Jiaoxun" (Some Lessons and Experiences in Drawing Up and Implementing the National Budget for 1956), *Caizheng*, 1957, no. 1 (January), pp. 3–7.

uisitions, indirectly through the profits and taxes of light industrial enterprises) plus the raw materials for light industry and the exports to pay for
imports of technology for heavy industry.

A number of Chen's remarks directly attacked the planners or undermined a number of their key interests. He argued that 1957 construction
figures would be even less than the control figures for 1957 and that a number of key capital construction projects would have to be stopped or post-
poned. This directly contradicted Bo Yibo's assertion at the Eighth Party
Congress that key construction projects should not be cut for the sake of
economy. Chen also took up the three ratios presented by Bo at the Eighth
Party Congress. He felt that Bo's efforts were laudable but that his figures
were off. In their stead, he presented the three balances. He also noted that
in working on the plan for 1958 the State Economic Commission (headed by
Bo) had projected a capital construction budget of 16.2 to 18.1 billion yuan.
This would be a 33–50 percent increase over the figure for 1957. These
figures were unreasonable, Chen argued; the state could not provide the
materials necessary for such plans.[42]

Chen's speech (and additional speeches by Li Xiannian and possibly Chen
Yun to the same group later in the month)[43] suggested a thorough revamping
of economic planning and management procedures. First of all, the three
balances would decisively shift significant planning responsibilities to financial officials. Specifically, the Ministry of Finance would control two of the
three critical balances: financial balances and banking balances. (The People's Bank of China was under the supervision of the Ministry of Finance.)
At the very least, Chen argued, budgets should not be formulated after the
plan had been drawn up, as they had been before. By demanding that plans
dovetail, Chen attempted to lock planners and central officials into a steady
pattern of economic development without surges or retreats. Finally, he
advocated a decisive role for agricultural production in determining economic activities. This, taken together with his support for supplying livelihood needs first, indicated that he favored the allocation of more resources
to light industry and agriculture. In sum, Chen's proposals called for a fundamental restructuring of the management of the Chinese economic system.

Chen's efforts were at least partially successful. Many top leaders were
influenced by his remarks, as will be seen in Chapter 7. The Party's theoretical journal ran an article entitled "Why Do We Say Waste Caused by Plan-

42. Chen Yun, 1981, pp. 34–43. This version of the speech does not give its exact date.
Chen, 1986, does (p. 40).
43. Li Xiannian, 1989, pp. 221–27, and Chen Xuewei, "Bajie Sanzhong Quanhui Shuping"
(An Evaluation of the Third Plenum of the Eighth Central Committee), *DSYJ*, 1986, no. 2, pp.
9–10. No text is available for Chen's January 27, 1957, speech.

ning Is the Greatest Waste?"[44] The March 1957 issue of *Jihua Jingji*, the journal of the planning units, announced that the capital construction target for 1957 had recently been further reduced and that the target for 1958 would be only about the same as the amount invested in 1956 (14.5 billion yuan). This article was an attempt to convince opponents of the need to implement additional retrenchment.[45] Articles in *Caizheng* in March 1957 developed the themes of Chen's January address.[46] Even an article on material supplies in *Jihua Jingji* agreed that materials should be allocated according to the priority Chen had laid down in January; namely, living standards should be considered first, then the needs of current production, and only after these had been fulfilled should resources be devoted to capital construction.[47]

Chen Yun continued his criticisms of the planners and of the SEC in particular at the Third Session of the Second Chinese People's Political Consultative Congress in March 1957.[48] In his speech, Chen argued that construction projects should be arranged solely on the basis of the state's financial strength. In discussing how long it would take to modernize China, he was very pessimistic. He also revealed that current tenseness in market supply was not likely to be alleviated in the near future. People would have to acclimatize themselves to "tense balance." Chen offered little to alleviate this glum evaluation of the situation except to note that by carrying out the campaign to increase production and practice economy, the worst of the shortages could be eased.

At the Conference of Financial Bureau and Department Heads, which ran from February 20 to March 11, Chen Yun's three balances were featured prominently. Rely on the three balances (budgets, banking activity, and materials) to make the budget (and implicitly, the plan) completely reliable, the conferees were told. Increases and decreases in income and expenditures would be strictly controlled. The 1957 budget could be balanced, but it would

44. Fang Fa, "Weishenma Shuo Jihua Suo Zaochengde Langfei Shi Zuidade Langfei?" *Xuexi* (Study), 1957, no. 2, pp. 7–8.

45. Li Qian, "Genju Guojiade Caili, Wuli Toushande Anpai 1957 Nian Jiben Jianshe Jihua" (Appropriately Arrange the Capital Construction Plan for 1957 on the Basis of the State's Financial and Material Strength), *JHJJ*, 1957, no. 3 (March), pp. 4–5, 13.

46. Wang Wen, "Lixing Zengchan Jieyue Chongfen Fahui Guojia Caizhengde Jiandu Zuoyong" (Strictly Increase Production and Practice Economy, Thoroughly Develop the Supervisory Function of State Finance), and Shen Jingnong, "Lun Caizheng he Jingjide Xianghu Yicun Guanxi" (On the Interdependent Relations of Finance and Economics), *Caizheng*, 1957, no. 3 (March), pp. 1–2, 13, and 6–11, respectively.

47. Men Zuomin, "Xiqu 1956 Nian Wuzi Gongying Gongzuode Jiaoxun" (Assimilate the Lessons of Material Supply Work in 1956), *JHJJ*, 1957, no. 2 (February), pp. 8–11.

48. Chen Yun, "Lun Zengchan Jieyue Wenti" (On Questions of Increasing Production and Practicing Economy), *XHBYK*, 1957, no. 7, pp. 15–17. Surprisingly, this speech does not appear in any of the post-1980 collections of Chen's speeches.

be a "tight balance," one involving sharply reduced expenditures. Because of the mediocre harvest in 1956, revenue in 1957 would be limited.[49] The Ministry of Finance promised to work closely with other ministries in carrying out the campaign to increase production and practice economy. The ministry's contribution would be to strengthen financial supervision.[50]

In June 1957, Rong Zihe, a vice-minister of finance, discussed the three balances and in particular the role of credit in the national economy. He noted that the question of equilibrium among the budget, credit, and materials had been broached as early as 1950 by the Finance and Economy Commission of the People's Republic of China (which Chen Yun headed) and argued that this was the best way to manage the economy. The amount of money in circulation mirrors commodity production, he stated. This made it impossible for the Ministry of Finance to paper over financial deficits by printing more currency. Only strict control over finances, credit, and supply and demand for raw materials could provide for economic stability in China.[51]

At the Fourth Session of the First National People's Congress in late June 1957, Li Xiannian attempted to reassert the primacy of the financial coalition (which had come under assault by the planners). Li reviewed the well-known conditions caused by the upsurge in the first half of 1956. He noted that "many plans, already bold enough, were surpassed, resulting in the spending of more money than was originally intended." He argued that "in handling financial problems, not only must we consider expenditure and revenue, but also the relationship between finance and economy." To any who misunderstood his point, he explained that the economic problems of 1956–1957 were much more severe than the 1956 budget deficit by itself might indicate.[52]

Many of Li's criticisms were, however, muted by the Anti-Rightist Campaign that was emerging as the Party's response to the Hundred Flowers criticism. Li stated, "In financial work, too, achievements were fundamental, and the shortcomings and mistakes of a secondary character." Directly confronting the Party's critics, he asked whether this was a proper assess-

49. Agriculture accounted for a large percentage of state revenues through the profits and taxes that were earned on light industrial products.

50. Xinhua News Agency, "Quanguo Caizheng Ting, Juzhang Huiyi" (National Meeting of Financial Bureau and Department Heads) (March 12, 1957), *XHBYK*, 1957, no. 8, pp. 98–99, and editorial, "Chongfen Kekaode Anpai he Zhixing 1957 Niande Guojia Yusuan" (Arrange and Carry Out the 1957 State Budget on a Completely Reliable Basis), *Caizheng*, 1957, no. 4 (April), pp. 1–3.

51. Rong Zihe, "The Question of Equilibrium for the State Budget, the State Credit Plan, and the Supply and Demand of Raw Materials," *Caizheng*, 1957, no. 6, trans. in *ECMM*, no. 87 (June 17, 1957), pp. 15–22.

52. Li Xiannian, "Final Accounts for 1956 and the 1957 State Budget," trans. in *Current Background*, no. 464 (July 5, 1957), pp. 4, 9.

ment, and proceeded to justify his answer that it was. He did this through a long discussion of the three balances as a key lesson learned from the experiences of 1956. In what was at least a partial concession to Party opponents, and was no doubt reflective of his personal beliefs, he noted:

Had we been a bit conservative last year and thus saved some raw materials and commodities, it would be helpful in working out the plan for 1957. . . . We should gradually expand our material reserves . . . and thus ensure the *even, smooth* progress of our national construction, thereby further exploiting the superiority of the planned economy.[53]

Provocatively, Li accorded doctrinal status to the three balances by stating that they were an objective economic law that officials must strive to grasp. While he conceded that balance was relative, his tolerance of imbalance was quite a bit lower than either Li Fuchun's or Mao Zedong's: "Our task lies in strengthening the organizational work and examination in connection with implementation of the plan and budget, and in constantly overcoming any imbalanced situation that may arise, thus enabling ourselves to push forward our national construction."[54]

Li reiterated that "state finances are the concentrated expression of the various economic activities of the state and its work in all fields" and discussed strengthening financial supervision as one good way to carry out the campaign to increase production and practice economy:

It should be pointed out that the strengthening of financial administration and supervision is aimed, not at interfering with, but at promoting, the development of our work. Strict financial supervision and the mechanical financial viewpoint are two different things. It is incorrect if administration is too strict, or carried to excess [and] it is just as incorrect if we relax administration and control so as to cause a diffusion and waste of the resources of the state.[55]

Thus, despite the changed political atmosphere, Li attempted to consolidate and advance the three balances put forward by Chen Yun in January 1957. But the difficulties the budgeteers would have in consolidating the positions articulated since early 1957 are symbolized in the editorial in *Caizheng* discussing Li's speech. To refute the "rightists," it spent a great deal of time defending the view that the problems of 1956 were secondary to the achievements scored in that year. Discussion of the three balances was buried in the third-to-last paragraph, and concern with financial supervision was relegated to the next-to-last paragraph.[56]

53. Ibid., p. 7; long quotation, p. 11. Emphasis added.
54. Ibid., p. 15. Recall that Li had just emphasized smooth, even growth.
55. Ibid., p. 22; long quotation, p. 29.
56. "Wei Wanmande Shixian 1957 Nian Guojia Yusuan er Nuli" (Strive to Carry Out the 1957 Budget Completely) *Caizheng*, 1957, no. 7 (July 15, 1957), pp. 14–15. This issue of *Caizheng* was published later than usual, thereby allowing it to include Li's speech but also requiring it to reflect the increasingly repressive political environment; see p. 15.

After Li Xiannian's June 1957 speech on the budget, it became increasingly clear that the financial coalition had lost control of the 1957 economic plan and of economic management generally as China's leaders found its views increasingly unpalatable. Nonetheless, those views continued to appear in the press, albeit with rapidly diminishing frequency. In October, in a special issue of the journal *Jingji Yanjiu* (Economic Research), Yang Peixin, an official in the banking system, defended the three balances. The economists who criticized the Party during the Hundred Flowers Campaign claimed that the Party ignored balance in the economy and that the budget deficit of 1956 was an extremely serious problem that the CCP had largely ignored. Yang's article, originally written in April, was an attempt to show that the CCP had been concerned with the three balances since 1950. Yang tried to promote the interests of the budgeteers, but it is doubtful that his article helped them. By late 1957 the Party had branded the "bourgeois economists" with the label "proponents of balance." Defending balance, as Yang did, only served further to link the financial coalition with the Party's critics.[57]

It was left to Li Xiannian to do what he could to salvage the budgeteers' position at the National Finance Conference in September. On September 3, he briefed other financial officials on the work of the Ministry of Finance in 1957 and on the drawing up of the budget for 1958. Agriculture had become a striking problem, he noted, and it was essential to continue to implement the three balances. There was still a little too much capital construction in 1957. The work of carrying out the three balances had not been fully developed.

The equilibrium between finance, credit loans and commodities should be given attention. Not only that, attention should also be paid to the equilibrium between commodities of the first category [capital goods] and commodities of the second category [consumer goods]. If commodities of these two categories are not balanced, purchasing power and supply of consumer goods cannot be balanced. If consumer goods are in short supply, capital construction will be hindered and the growth of commodities of the first category will be adversely affected.[58]

Therefore, light industry had to advance almost as quickly as heavy industry if workers were to be provided with incentives. Li was still committed to the ideas put forward by Chen Yun in January 1957.

57. Yang Peixin, "Guanyu Caizheng Shouzhi, Xianjin Shouzhi, Wuzi Gongqiu Pingheng Wentide Yanjiu" (A Study of Questions of Balance of Financial Revenues and Expenditures, Credit Inflows and Outflows, and Material Supply and Demand), *Jingji Yanjiu*, 1957, no. 5 (October), pp. 50–63. Other criticisms of the "bourgeois economists" can be found in the same issue, pp. 26–49 and 64–122. The views of the economists who criticized the Party are found on pp. 123–33.

58. "An Outline of Speech by Li Xiannian at the National Conference of Financial Directors," *Caizheng*, 1957, no. 11, in *ECMM*, no. 117 (February 3, 1958), pp. 10–14; see p. 12.

But Li's speech also revealed how the agenda was slipping out of the control of the financial coalition. In outlining measures to develop agriculture, Li mentioned fertilizer, water conservancy, and technical measures, but not his own preference for price incentives. He also noted that the key to accelerating socialist development and the people's standard of living was increased investment. Nevertheless, the summing-up article on the Ministry of Finance meeting emphasized the three balances and balance between production and consumer goods.[59]

The financial coalition would make one last effort to hold off the oncoming Great Leap Forward at the expanded Third Plenum of the Eighth Central Committee in September–October 1957. But it was decisively defeated by the coalition of Party and planning interests (discussed fully in Chapter 8).

C.2. The Second Five-Year Plan

The concrete work of drawing up the Second Five-Year Plan (SFYP) was the responsibility of the State Planning Commission (discussed in more detail in Chapter 5). Although evidence of interventions by the financial coalition in the drafting process is both sparse and circumstantial, it is clear that the budgeteers attempted to influence the outlines of the plan profoundly.

The proposals for the SFYP were formulated by Zhou Enlai, with significant assistance from Chen Yun, in the summer of 1956. The chairman of the State Planning Commission, Li Fuchun, and his principal deputy, Zhang Xi, were in Moscow, apparently negotiating with the Soviets on economic assistance and technology transfers. Zhou presented the outlines of the SFYP to the Eighth Party Congress, along with the draft proposals for the plan. Perhaps reflecting Zhou's personality, his speech and the proposals carefully balanced the perspectives of the financial and planning coalitions.[60]

The planners appear to have undertaken a number of preparations to finalize the plan, but curious delays appeared in transmitting the proposals to

59. Xinhua News Agency, "Ministry of Finance Convenes Conference of Department and Bureau Chiefs to Examine the Implementation of the 1957 State Budget and to Work Out the 1958 Local Budget," October 6, 1957, trans. in *Survey of China Mainland Press*, no. 1631 (October 15, 1957), pp. 13–14.

60. On the drafting process, see Xue Muqiao, "Zai Zhou Enlai Tongzhi Lingdaoxia Gongzuode Huiyi" (Reminiscences of Working Under Comrade Zhou Enlai), and Wang Guangwei, "Zhou Zongli yu Diyi, Er Wunian Jihuade Bianzhi" (Premier Zhou and the Drawing Up of the First and Second Five-Year Plans), in *Huainian Zhou Enlai*, 1986, pp. 31–41 and 42–45, respectively; Wang Yaping, "Dierge Wunian Jihuade Huigu" (The Second Five-Year Plan in Retrospect), *DSYJ*, 1987, no. 4, pp. 64–69. Zhou Enlai's speech and the proposals for the SFYP are found in *Eighth National Congress of the Communist Party of China (Documents)*, 1981 (reprint of the original 1956 edition, with slightly different pagination; hereafter *8PC/D*), pp. 279–348 and 245–76, respectively. Zhou's balancing of perspectives is discussed in Chapter 7.

planners. The SFYP proposals were adopted by the Eighth Party Congress on September 27, 1956, but the Central Committee of the CCP did not formally submit the proposals to the State Council for discussion until December 13, 1956. The delay may be explained by a revision in the plan targets. Perhaps more surprising, the State Council did not discuss the proposals until its February 7, 1957, meeting. This was after Chen Yun's landmark January 18 speech on readjustment and while Chen was still acting premier. (Zhou had just returned from his foreign travels but was in South China.) Only after this State Council meeting did the planners officially receive the proposals.[61]

Sometime in late 1956 or early 1957, those who favored "criticizing rash advance" in 1956 reduced the target for capital construction investment in the SFYP from 100 billion yuan to 90 billion.[62] In early 1958, Mao identified Chen Yun and Zhou Enlai as those who had spearheaded the drive against rash advance, and he also hit out at the Ministry of Finance under Li Xiannian.[63]

The financial coalition no doubt continued to discuss the emerging SFYP with the planners. Certainly many of the points the budgeteers made about the 1957 plan were equally applicable to the SFYP. But there is nothing to indicate definitively what the terms of the debate were.

C.3. Decentralization

Since April 1956, if not earlier, the central leadership had been discussing the proper mix of centralization and decentralization in the system of economic administration. Mao Zedong's views in his famous speech "On the Ten Major Relations," with its call to expand the powers of lower levels of the administrative system, set the groundwork for policy developments. Between May and August 1956 the State Council met repeatedly to discuss how to decentralize authority, but, as the speeches by Liu Shaoqi and Zhou Enlai at the Eighth Party Congress revealed, no consensus had been reached by September 1956. Decentralization was still an important issue on the agenda, but it remained a vague and elusive goal.[64] Apparently as a result of

61. On the chronology, see *JHJJ*, 1957, no. 3 (March), p. 1. Zhou did not return to Beijing until February 12. See Huai En, 1986, p. 394.

62. Xue Muqiao, 1979; see p. 3.

63. On the criticism of Chen and Zhou, see Bo Yibo, "Respect and Remembrance – Marking the 60th Anniversary of the Founding of the CCP," *Hongqi* (Red Flag), 1981, no. 13, trans. in Foreign Broadcast Information Service, *Daily Report, China*, July 29, 1981, K 26–36; see K 33. On the criticism of the Ministry of Finance, see *MMTTT*, pp. 77–84.

64. Mao, 1977, esp. pp. 289–95; Fan Shouxin, "Bada Guanyu Jingji Tizhi Gaigede Sixiang Jiqi Shixian" (The Thought and Practice of the Reform of the Economic System of the Eighth

Zhou Enlai's foreign travels in late 1956 and early 1957, Chen Yun took charge of drafting specific policies on decentralization.

On January 10, 1957, the Party center established a "five-man small group on economic work." Composed of Chen Yun, Li Xiannian, Li Fuchun, Bo Yibo, and Huang Kecheng, its responsibilities were to provide unified leadership over economic work under the guidance of the Politburo. Chen Yun headed the group, which balanced the interests of various coalitions. Chen and Li Xiannian represented the financial coalition; Li Fuchun and Bo Yibo were the leading planners; and Huang Kecheng was one of the two military representatives in the Party Secretariat and until December 1956 was director of the military's rear services (logistics) department. The activities of this group were rarely discussed, but recent accounts reveal that it handled the issue of decentralization.[65]

At the Meeting of Provincial Party Secretaries (January 18–27, 1957, where Chen made his major speech on readjustment), Mao directed the five-man small group to study questions of decentralization involving industry, commerce, finance, agriculture, communications, and education. After the meeting, the State Council, central ministries and commissions, and various provincial leaders discussed these points and concluded that the issues of industry, commerce, and finance were the most urgent. The five-man small group presented drafts of its regulations to the Party's central leaders, who gave their approval on July 25, 1957. Chen Yun, who was in charge of drafting, then presented the draft documents on reforms in these areas to the Third Plenum in September and October; they were formally approved in November 1957.[66]

No further details are available on the inner workings of the five-man small group on decentralization. In ministerial journals, however, there was a broad-ranging discussion of aspects of decentralization. Worth noting in particular are several articles by people in the Ministry of Finance who actually argued for greater financial centralization. Wang Ziying, who wrote the January 1957 article that implicitly criticized Bo Yibo, published another controversial article in April 1957. In contrast to many who called for decentralization, he called for increased centralization. He was particularly con-

Party Congress), *DSYJ*, 1985, no. 5, pp. 60–63; Fang Weizhong, 1984, p. 172; Zhou Enlai, "Report on Proposals," and Liu Shaoqi, "The Political Report of the Central Committee of the Communist Party of China to the Eighth National Congress of the Party," both in *8PC/D*, pp. 279–348 and 9–115, respectively.

65. *Zhonggong Dangshi Dashi Nianbiao*, 1987, p. 280; Chen Yun, 1986, p. 353 n. 35; Chen Xuewei, "Bajie Sanzhong" (n. 43); *Zhonghua Renmin Gongheguo Jingji Guanli Dashiji*, 1986, p. 99. On Huang Kecheng's background, see Klein and Clark, 1971, pp. 397–401.

66. Chen Xuewei, "Bajie Sanzhong"; *Zhonghua Renmin Gongheguo Jingji Guanli Dashiji*, 1986, p. 99; Chen Yun, 1986, pp. 66–68, 78–95.

cerned about the growth of extrabudgetary funds since 1954. Since the state budget was based on the state plan, there was a certain fit between the budget and the plan. There was no such connection with extrabudgetary expenditures, and this was harmful, Wang asserted. He favored strict control of such funds and strict financial centralization. He argued that local tax surcharges should be remitted to the state treasury and not retained locally. (These issues were important in the 1980s as well.) As he had earlier, Wang said that financial supervision and control should play an extremely large role in economic management. He was concerned with the relationship between the state and the enterprise but not with the relationship between the local levels and the enterprise. He all but ignored the role of the provinces in financial management, and thus de facto opposed expanding financial authority at that level of government. In short, Wang appeared to favor giving the Ministry of Finance absolute control over every penny of government revenue and expenditure.[67] While others were in sympathy with Wang, the overall tenor of the discussion favored decentralization.[68] The Ministry of Finance was still reluctant to decentralize significant financial authority, and central leaders eventually had to order it to carry out decentralization.[69]

As in the drafting of the Second Five-Year Plan, evidence for the involvement and views of the financial coalition in the decentralization decrees of late 1957 is sporadic. Yet the information available does suggest that the Ministry of Finance in particular was opposed to financial decentralization, taking a position that was congruous with the interests central to the coalition it led.

---

67. Wang Ziying, "Improve the Fiscal System and Strengthen Financial Discipline," *Caizheng*, 1957, no. 4, in *ECMM*, no. 87 (June 17, 1957), pp. 15–22.

68. On opposition to decentralization, see Yu Weixin, "Difang Yusuan he Guomin Jingji Jihuade Guanxi Wenti" (On the Relationship Between National Economic Plans and Local Budgets), *Caizheng*, 1957, no. 3 (March), p. 14.

69. Halpern (1985, pp. 110–33, esp. pp. 119–20) sheds important light on these developments, relying on an informant in the Ministry of Finance. The informant's views cannot be corroborated by documentary evidence at this time, but they fit the arguments of this chapter well. Writing before the publication of Chen Yun, 1986, which contains a draft of the financial reform document stating that Chen drafted the document, Halpern argues on the basis of her informant and Chen Yun, 1981, that Chen drafted only the commercial and industrial regulations. The two views are not as incompatible as they seem. Chen no doubt played the decisive role in the commercial reforms (in addition to his other responsibilities, he was minister of commerce from late 1956 to early 1958). He would have supervised the financial decentralization as well, and was no doubt unhappy about it. Excerpts from his speech to the Third Plenum focus on the financial reform and how carefully it had to be implemented (Chen Yun, 1986, pp. 66–68). Yet as both economic specialist and central leader he probably was pressured to authorize financial decentralization.

C.4. Agricultural and commercial problems

In the aftermath of the small leap forward of late 1955 and early 1956, the Party repeatedly stressed that achievements were fundamental and undeniable but that there were many problems. This rhetorical device obscured the true severity of the problems. Enormous amounts of bureaucratic·manpower went into dealing with problems of agriculture and commerce and with the organizational difficulties of newly socialized industry and handicrafts. In the half-yearly official compilations of laws and regulations of the PRC from the second half of 1956 through 1957, 27 percent of all published regulations were in these areas, with 30 percent of the first half of the 1957 volume devoted to these questions.[70] The problems were complex and tedious to deal with, and Chen Yun, Deng Zihui, and other financial coalition officials devoted vast amounts of time to them. The situation was apparently so bad that Chen gave a long speech to the Second Plenum of the Eighth Central Committee in November 1956 on pork production and subsidiary agricultural products.[71] Conditions must have been truly bad for the fifth-ranking Party leader to concern himself with these details in such depth. Indeed, immediately after the plenum, Chen was named minister of commerce on top of his other assignments. (Simultaneously, Jia Tuofu, director of the State Council's light industry staff office, was named a vice-chairman of the State Economic Commission – presumably strengthening the position of light industry in the planning process.)

Central to all problems in agriculture and commerce was the issue of grain procurement. Simply put, the state was finding it increasingly difficult to obtain enough grain to meet the demands of urban consumers, light industry, exports, and disaster relief. Five days after the conclusion of the Second Plenum, a joint directive of the CCP Central Committee and the State Council stated that urban food consumption must be cut because agriculture could not support existing levels.[72]

A policy of reducing urban food supplies could only be a desperate measure. It all but guaranteed urban unrest at a time when the Chinese working class was already dissatisfied.[73] Chen and others attempted to use the grain

70. Calculated from *Zhonghua Renmin Gongheguo Fagui Huibian*, vols. 4–6 (July–December 1956; January–June 1957; July–December 1957), 1981 (reprints of volumes issued in 1957 and 1958).

71. Chen Yun, 1986, pp. 15–27. A note states that this is only a portion of Chen's talk to the plenum. The excerpt is longer than his landmark January 1957 speech, and the whole speech was probably longer than his other major speech at the Eighth Party Congress.

72. "Directive of the CCP Central Committee and the State Council on Present Grain Work," in *Documents*, pp. 437–40.

73. A number of industrial and student strikes and other disturbances took place between

problem to spur reforms in the agricultural and commercial realms, speaking on this and related topics on many occasions.[74]

A number of Chen's many ideas on commerce, agriculture, and the operation of the recently transformed capitalist industries and commercial outlets were implemented during this period, and points he made at internal meetings of the Ministry of Commerce were discussed in public.[75] (Unfortunately, the ministerial journal of the Ministry of Commerce is not available.) Chen and his allies saw the market playing a larger role in allocation, called on bourgeois professional managers to assume a leading role in economic administration, and promoted the reduction in size of some enterprises to improve incentives.

But these policies were fraught with problems. Many staff members in the Ministry of Commerce were unhappy about the increased competition Chen's reforms would cause.[76] Often the price incentives Chen and others advocated had an inflationary impact. The onset of price incentives and price increases was delayed. Hence the financial coalition could not quickly solve the problems of slow growth in living standards and agricultural output. For example, in early 1957 the prices of a number of commodities increased, and this sparked concern and anger on the part of consumers. Reviewing this situation, Chen Yun noted that many of the price increases resulted from deliberate government moves undertaken to stimulate production. Some of the increased procurement prices for agricultural commodities had to be passed on to consumers, because if the state did not increase selling prices,

September 1956 and the spring of 1957. More than ten thousand workers engaged in strikes, and similar numbers of students also protested, affecting eleven provinces and two cities. See Hao Mengbi and Duan Haoran, 1984, p. 483.

74. Chen Yun, 1986, pp. 28–35, 50–54, 55–58, 60–65, and 69–77; 1981, pp. 20–26 and 27–33; Li Xiannian, 1989, pp. 228–29.

75. For example, at the end of November 1956 an article in *Renmin Ribao* criticized the excessive bureaucratization of the commercial system. Presumably the author drew his inspiration from Chen's speeches (Lin Shu, "Shangye Jigou Yingdang Jingjian" [Commerical Organs Should Be Simplified], repr. in *XHBYK*, 1957, no. 2, pp. 84–86); an article in late December analyzed for several industries in Shanghai the progress of the reforms Chen had proposed at the Eighth Party Congress for consumer-goods industries. These reforms had begun even before the congress (Ji Yin, "Gongyepinde Zichan Zixiaode Yige Chenggongde Changshi" [A Successful Attempt to Produce and Market Industrial Products by Oneself], repr. in *XHBYK*, 1957, no. 2, pp. 82–84). Many other articles supporting Chen's economic views were reported in the Chinese press in late 1956 and early 1957. *Da Gong Bao* (The Impartial Daily) was particularly active in supporting Chen, especially his view that former capitalists had a leading role to play in the new joint enterprises (the ones recently nationalized) (see the *Da Gong Bao* articles reprinted in *XHBYK*, 1957, no. 3, pp. 42–44, 48–51, 55–56; no. 4, pp. 76–78; and no. 5, pp. 83–86). This idea was to come under attack from the mobilizers in the Party.

76. Deng Liqun, 1981, p. 107, notes opposition to Chen's policies from the Ministries of Commerce and Foreign Trade (which Chen argued at the Eighth Party Congress should be reformed). Downs, 1967, pp. 208–10, argues that bureaucratic restructuring always provokes opposition from within the affected bureaucracy.

financial balance and balance between the supply of consumer goods and social purchasing power could not be achieved. He asserted that chaos in the market would result if these balances were not maintained. He also said that one of the reasons for price increases was that the free market had been in operation for only six months and, whereas the price effects of the market became apparent immediately, there was a time lag before peasants could respond to price incentives.[77]

Chen Yun's ideas were firmly endorsed at meetings of the Ministries of Commerce and Finance in February and March 1957. Vice-Minister of Commerce Zeng Chuanliu called on the Ministry of Commerce to expand the sources of materials and insure the supply of key commodities in accord with market demands. He wanted the cost of transporting commercial goods and organizational overhead pared, the commercial network simplified, the number of levels in the commercial system reduced, and personnel in the commercial network cut.[78] Vice-Minister Yao Yilin spoke on work in joint commercial enterprises and small shops. The important thing, Yao stated, was for the former capitalists to be enthusiastic and take an active part in enterprise management. Collective enterprises resulting from excessive mergers were to be broken up into smaller units.[79]

The overall precariousness of the economic situation was hinted at by Rong Zihe in his speech to the Financial Conference.[80] He noted that preliminary estimates for the past several years revealed that the average yearly increase in consumer goods provided by industry and agriculture was about 7 percent. Subtracting reserves and increased population from this amount (but apparently not subtracting exports) left only a 4 percent per capita yearly improvement. But a number of Chinese leaders seemed to think that this rate of increase could not be continued. A high-ranking French politician who toured China in May 1957 and was received at the highest levels stated:

But even if there has been progress (which, I repeat, seems to me incontestable even if the figures themselves must be treated with reserve) in total production and living standards, it is no less certain that the rate of progress is decreasing from both of these points of view. This has been confirmed to me personally by the Minister of Agriculture [Liao Luyan].[81]

77. Chen Yun, 1986, pp. 50–54.
78. Zeng Chuanliu, "Guoying Shangye Xitong Zengchan Jieyue Mubiao" (The Target for the State-Run Commercial System in Increasing Production and Practicing Economy), repr. in *XHBYK*, 1957, no. 7, pp. 65–66. See also *XHBYK*, 1957, no. 6, p. 44.
79. "Shangye Bu Fubuzhang Yao Yilin Tan Jinnian (1957) Gongsi Heying Shangdian he Xiao Shangfang Gaizaode Renwu" (Vice-Minister of Commerce Yao Yilin Talks About This Year's Tasks in Transforming Joint Public-Private Commercial Enterprises, Small Shops, and Peddlers), *XHBYK*, 1957, no. 7, pp. 89–90.
80. See n. 49.
81. Faure, 1958, pp. 182–83.

In recognition of these developing trends, some cadres responsible for agricultural affairs may have suggested a large increase in the procurement price of agricultural commodities. A writer in the Party theoretical journal *Xuexi* (Study) noted that "some peasants" wanted the purchase price of grain to rise by 30–50 percent. A 30 percent increase would cost the state 1.3 billion yuan a year and would necessitate raising the procurement prices for other crops as well. The total amount spent to purchase agricultural commodities would be equivalent to one-half to two-thirds of the capital construction fund. The Party obviously rejected such an idea.[82] It seems unlikely that these requests stemmed purely from peasants. No doubt some officials were echoing, or in fact making, these proposals in an effort to provide the peasantry with more incentives. The financial coalition cadres may have felt that only such incentives could stimulate production as much as they wanted.

Deng Zihui, director of the Party's Rural Work Department, and his colleagues worked quietly behind the scenes to rectify and improve the newly formed higher-stage agricultural producers cooperatives, or collectives. Many of the collectives were in disarray. Mao Zedong noted:

Minister of Agriculture Liao Luyan, who is concurrently Deputy Director of the Rural Work Department of the Party Central Committee, says in effect that he himself feels discouraged and so do the responsible cadres under him, and that the cooperatives won't work anyway and the forty-article Program for Agricultural Development is no longer valid.[83]

After the Eighth Party Congress, Deng undertook a series of rural investigations and instituted advanced methods to rectify the co-ops. By the end of 1956 he was advocating "big collective, small freedom," meaning, as he would explain in June 1957, that "the major productive material – land – should be under collective ownership; with all other productive materials, ownership should depend on conditions; it is not necessary for 100% of them to be owned by collectives."[84] He repeatedly criticized cadres for their "mechanical" viewpoints: for wanting only concentration of power and ownership, not decentralization; for wanting only large collectives, not small ones; and for thinking of only higher-stage collectives as socialist. Many rural cadres were dogmatic. In response to the near-crisis of rural organization, Deng advocated responsibility systems and rural contracts. Agricultural work was divided into tasks, with groups, households, or individuals responsible for

82. He Wei, "Tantan Guojia Tong Nongmin zai Jingji Fangmiande Maodun" (Discussing Economic Contradictions Between the State and the Peasantry), *Xuexi*, 1957, no. 12 (June 18), pp. 22–25.

83. Mao, 1977, p. 351.

84. Deng Zihui, quoted in Lin Bangguang and Deng Yun, "Deng Zihui Shehuizhuyi Nongye Hezuoshe Jingji Tizhi Chutan" (A Preliminary Exploration of Deng Zihui's Thought on the Socialist Collective Economic System), *DSYJ*, 1987, no. 1, pp. 37–42, 47; see p. 38.

carrying these out. If they exceeded their quotas, or contracts, the surplus went to the contractor. Deng favored the promotion of individual subsidiary economic activities as vital to the overall well-being of collectives as well as that of individual peasants. He stated that up to 10 percent of all peasants could farm independently without harming socialism.[85] Thus, Deng and his colleagues were attempting to implement policies that enhanced the flexibility of collectives, expanded the role of individual activities within the collective framework, clearly specified tasks and responsibilities within collectives, and improved incentives for members.[86]

It is impossible to say how extensively Deng's policies were implemented, but by the summer of 1957 they had become less sustainable. First, the improvements and reforms in agriculture and commerce had not altered the problems of extracting surplus from the countryside.[87] Critics could claim that the policies of the financial coalition did not work. Agricultural production, despite price incentives and markets, grew by only 2 percent in 1957. Second, and more important, the emerging Anti-Rightist Campaign, beginning in June 1957, undermined many of the tenets of the financial coalition. Markets came under ideological attack and were effectively closed in August 1957. Many peasants who engaged in rural commerce were arrested. The theme of class struggle reappeared throughout China, and individual activities by peasants and others were criticized and punished. In other words, the overall political atmosphere became hostile to the policies of the financial

85. If Deng took this to be the upper limit for individual farming, then he marginally differed with other top leaders, who were prepared to see a couple of percent of the peasantry go it alone. I believe, however, that Deng saw this as a starting point, an attempt to set a floor, so that individual farming might gradually be expanded.

86. Deng's publicly available speeches, in addition to his report to the Eighth Party Congress, are "Lun Nongye Hezuoshe Neibu Maodun yu Minzhu Ban She" (On the Internal Contradictions and Democratic Management of Agricultural Collectives), *Renmin Ribao* (People's Daily), May 7, 1957, and "Guanyu Nongye Hezuoshe Kuoda Zaishengchan ji Qita Jige Wenti" (On Expanded Reproduction in Agricultural Collectives and Several Other Questions) (portions of a speech to the Third Plenum), in *Renmin Shouce 1958*, 1958, pp. 520–24. Because Deng's policies influenced the post-Mao agricultural reforms, there is an extensive literature on his career. This paragraph draws heavily on the following: Jiang Boying, 1986; Yu Zhan, "Deng Zihui Lun Nongmin Jiqi Huxiang Hezuo" (Deng Zihui on Peasants and Mutual Cooperation), *Dangshi Tongxun* (Communications on Party History), 1987, no. 2, pp. 22–27; Lin Bangguang and Deng Yun (n. 84); Dai Qingqi and Yu Zhan, "Xuexi Deng Zihui Tongzhi Guanyu Shixing Nongye Shengchan Zerenzhide Guandian" (Study Comrade Deng Zihui's Ideas on Implementing the Agricultural Responsibility System), *Xinhua Wenzhai* (New China Digest), 1982, no. 4 (April), pp. 50–51; "Shenqie Huainian Deng Zihui Tongzhi" (Deeply Cherish the Memory of Comrade Deng Zihui), *Nongye Gongzuo Tongxun* (Agricultural Work Bulletin), 1981, no. 5, pp. 7–9; and Wang Guanlan et al., "Deng Zihui Tongzhi yu Wo Guode Nongye Hezuohua Yundong" (Comrade Deng Zihui and Our Country's Agricultural Cooperativization Movement), *Nongye Gongzuo Tongxun*, 1981, no. 6, pp. 2–5. Li Xiannian also supported paying more attention to grain and other agricultural work (see 1989, pp. 228–29).

87. For example, see Chen Yun, 1986, pp. 60–65. For a detailed secondary analysis, see Walker, 1984.

coalition.[88] All Party officials and organizations of the state were required to refute every criticism made by those who had spoken out during the Hundred Flowers period. This was particularly disadvantageous for the financial coalition, because many of the criticisms made by non-Party figures were exactly the same as those made by Chen Yun, Li Xiannian, and other leaders of the budgeteers. The situation required them to undermine the strength of their own reform proposals.[89] If the financial coalition did not counter the perceived attacks on the Party, then those in charge of Party discipline and the Ministry of Public Security might accuse members of the coalition of being themselves rightists. The coalition members were caught in the position of being damned if they did counter the Party's critics (thereby undermining their own proposals) and damned if they did not (thereby risking jail or purge).

Chen Yun and other leaders of the financial coalition did not immediately give way to the political currents undermining their position. At the National Vegetable Conference in July, for example, Chen asserted.

In the past, we paid attention to factory buildings and machines, to the neglect of the daily needs of the workers and staff, and the supply of vegetables and other nonstaple food has not been handled effectively. I believe that the supply of these things is of no less significance than the construction of factories, and it should be considered as important as factory construction.[90]

In contrast, Bo Yibo, head of the State Economic Commission, stated in June 1957 that capital construction was a central task for both economics and politics.[91]

Chen and others attempted to defend the policies they had propounded since September 1956; they made a final stand at the Party's Third Plenum in September–October (see Chapter 8), but their efforts were too little too late. The first attempt to combine plan and market in China's socialist economy had come to naught, but the legacy of the effort would live on to legitimize future attempts at reform.

88. On closing markets, see "Provisions of the State Council Prohibiting the Entry Into the Free Market of Agricultural Products and Other Materials Planned by the State for Purchase and Unified Purchase," *Zhonghua Renmin Gongheguo Fagui Huibian, 1957, 7 Yue – 12 Yue* (July–December 1957), 1981 (repr. of 1958 ed.), pp. 366–69. On peasant arrests, see Lai Ying, 1969.

89. Brief summaries of the criticisms concerning CCP economic mismanagement are found in Zhou Enlai's "Report on the Work of the Government," in *Communist China, 1955–1959,* 1971, pp. 299–329.

90. Chen Yun, 1981, p. 49.

91. Bo Yibo, "Working of the National Economic Plan for 1956 and the Draft National Plan for 1957," in *Current Background,* no. 465 (July 9, 1957), p. 21.

D. Conclusion

From September 1956 to October 1957, leaders of China's financial, commercial, agricultural, and light industrial bureaucracies created an innovative program to develop China's economy. This program paid more attention to agriculture and light industry, emphasized material incentives, encouraged the use of markets in conjunction with plans, and saw financial indicators as key tools for bringing about macroeconomic balance. The program was a response to both the general environment in which these organizations functioned – most important, a densely populated agrarian country with little easily extractable surplus – and the specific situation of too rapid growth and institutional change that had characterized the last half of 1955 and early 1956.

The financial coalition's break with a traditional Soviet model of development should not be overstated. The budgeteers wanted the market to remain subordinate to the plan, *relatively* more resources to be devoted to light industry and agriculture, and continued significant investment in heavy industry. Budgeteers never denied the importance of Party leadership. Moreover, the true complexities of the financial coalition's program were only beginning to be seen when the reforms of 1956–1957 were canceled. What structure of property rights should exist? How could market and state prices coexist? How could inflation be prevented?

Neither should the significance of the 1956–1957 reforms be denied. They legitimized organizing concepts and institutions that offered alternatives to existing patterns of growth and administration. They were the beginning of a process of reform that, if allowed to continue, might have led to a fundamental break with the Soviet model. If given time to work, the reforms would have won broad social support that would have created the possibility for a very different pattern of economic development. Finally, the reforms served as model and inspiration when China's leadership addressed the issue of reform more fundamentally in the late 1970s and early 1980s.[92]

Four things account for the failure of the financial coalition to prevail. The first, and most important, was the changed political atmosphere after the onset of the Anti-Rightist Campaign. Simply put, an emphasis on markets, material incentives, reliance on middle-income and rich peasants and former capitalists, and slower growth could not survive in an environment that emphasized class struggle, ideological education, and the need for rapid eco-

---

92. This view is forcefully argued in Solinger, 1981.

nomic development. It was Mao Zedong's prerogative as China's dominant leader to determine the overall tenor of political and economic debate. Whereas the financial coalition had some support from Mao in early 1957, Mao's views had shifted by the summer, and there was nothing the financial coalition could do to change his mind.

The budgeteers did what they could to affect the overall atmosphere and policy-making environment in late 1956 and early 1957. Their programs unfolded as a major debate was under way among Chinese economists about the role of the Marxist "law of value" in socialist economies, and they drew the support of important noncommunist economists and industrial figures.[93] But such efforts were not uncontested and, more important, not very significant compared with Mao's ability to set the tone of all policy discussions.

A second cause of the failure of the financial coalition to institutionalize its programs was trouble with the policies themselves. In the short run (1957), they failed to work. A period of under one year was not enough time to assess the efficacy of budgeteer policies; nonetheless, that was the time given to the coalition. Price incentives and markets spurred only small increases in agricultural production, and critics could argue that the financial coalition's policies would not solve the problem of agricultural production shortages. How could a series of economic policies predicated on the idea of increasing production through the operation of material incentives work if the goods that served as the material rewards for increased output could not be provided? Critics could claim that the policies had been tried and found wanting. Moreover, the slow, stable growth promised by the financial coalition was not something that excited the passions of the Party or many of the people. Living standards would not rise rapidly; China would not become a major economic and military power quickly. Incremental improvement was insufficient for many key elements of Chinese society and the polity.

Third, the leaders of the financial coalition were partly to blame for the failure of their programs to take root. Available evidence shows them to have been not very active in the promotion of their policies after February 1957. Chen Yun made few public statements of any kind after that time, and the

93. On the "law of value" debate, see Lin, 1981, esp. pp. 5–29; *Jianguo Yilai Zhengzhi Jingjixue Zhongyao Wenti Zhenglun (1949–1980)*, 1981, pp. 88–92, 110–31, 165–69; and for the most controversial statements, Sun Yefang, 1979, pp. 1–14, 24–41 (reprinting articles from 1956–1957). Ma Yinqu, a Columbia University Ph.D. in economics and the noncommunist president of Beijing University, supported balanced growth in 1956–1957. See Ma Yinqu, 1981, pp. 120–69, reprinting articles from 1956–1957. Huang Yanpei, a leading noncommunist industrialist, also publicly supported financial coalition positions. See Huang Yanpei, "Dajia Dou lai Canjia Zengchan Jieyue Yundong" (Everyone Should Participate in the Movement to Increase Production and Practice Economy), *XHBYK*, 1957, no. 8, pp. 39–42. Both Ma and Huang had worked with Chen Yun on economic questions in the early 1950s.

same can be said for the other top leaders. They did not entirely vacate the political stage, but they did not travel around the country promulgating their views as the leaders of the planning coalition did. As a whole, the leaders of the financial coalition were less active than were other leaders.

This lack of aggressive leadership should not be overstated. The drafting of internal regulations and plans and the formulation of laws and regulations probably took up most of the budgeteers' time. Moreover, it is doubtful that Chen Yun, Deng Zihui, Li Xiannian, and their colleagues could have done anything to alter the situation after the liberal Hundred Flowers gave way to the extremist Anti-Rightist Campaign. Mao had already defeated an activist Deng Zihui in 1955, and there was no reason to think that the financial coalition would have fared any better even if it had mobilized support to try to block the Great Leap Forward.

Finally, the program of the financial coalition proved less responsive to the needs of key constituencies in the Chinese political system than did an alternative program formulated by the planning and heavy industry coalition. The planners' program emerged as their response to the budgeteers' proposals. The planners met the bureaucratic and economic challenges, Party leaders would decide, better than the financial officials did. This result is the subject of the next chapter.

5

The planning and heavy industry coalition

The coalition of planning and heavy industrial organizations and leaders was on the political defensive in the fall of 1956. Overinvestment in capital construction was most pronounced in the heavy industrial sector. The small leap of 1956 served the interests of heavy industry by adding new fixed assets to that sector but also resulted in planners' losing control of economic activity. Since the small leap could not be sustained, planners felt it was imperative to restore order to economic processes. How, then, could they serve the interests of this coalition while responding effectively to the difficult economic environment of late 1956 and early 1957? Precisely at this time, the financial coalition was pressing its agenda of reform and financial control. This posed an additional challenge to the leaders of the planning coalition. Faced with the financial coalition's innovative program of economic change, incorporating the market and increased priority for financial indicators as methods of macroeconomic management, what was the planning coalition to do in order to regain its position at the center of state economic administration?

The answers to these questions formulated by the two top planners, Li Fuchun and Bo Yibo, and their associates would be both profound and disastrous. They too developed an innovative program, but it was based on self-reliance, industry aiding agriculture, emphasis on building more small and medium-size factories, and decentralization. This program offered an alternative method of dealing with critical agricultural bottlenecks, the political challenge posed by the financial coalition's slower rate of growth and reliance on suspect political classes and groups, and declining Soviet support for China's industrialization. The planners were the first to revive the Yanan slogan of *ziligengsheng* – self-reliance. They argued that an economic slowdown was unnecessary. China could build most of its industrial requirements itself, and industry could provide the technical inputs needed to escape the constraints imposed by declining agricultural performance. The answer was not to reduce investment or to reallocate investment funds from heavy industry to agriculture and light industry, but to spend more on the construction of heavy industry. The planning coalition promised to do more with less, to do it faster, and to do it better. In effect, this coalition denied that trade-offs on economic questions existed. If the leaders of chief state economic control organizations could deny such limitations, it is not surprising that generalist leaders were even less skeptical of the planners' program. When Mao and other political leaders took the planners at their word and injected a desire for even more rapid development, these policies became central economic planks of the Great Leap Forward program. The result was an economic disaster, not dynamic growth.

The coalition's political achievements should not be gainsaid. It managed to reverse economic policies detrimental to its interests in a short period of time, and to win acceptance for a program protective of many of the fundamental values associated with the coalition. It appealed to the desire for rapid advancement felt by many in and out of the Party, and seemed to promise the leadership a relatively easy solution to China's economic woes. This was brilliant politics if dubious economics.

This does not mean, of course, that the Great Leap was purely the product of the planners, or that Mao's and others' interventions were not crucial. But ultimately the economic innovations of the Leap, with the exception of rural people's communes, had their roots in the planning coalition's advocacy in early to mid 1957.

A. The planning and heavy industry coalition as a system

Since the mid nineteenth century, Chinese intellectuals and leaders had been concerned with building a wealthy and strong nation. By the time the Chinese Communist Party (CCP) came to power, the goal became the transformation of China from a poor agrarian society with no modern industry into a powerful socialist industrialized society in a very short time. To achieve rapid economic development, China adopted the Soviet development model.[1] With the help of Soviet advisers, the Chinese established institutions and

1. Less work has been done on the politics of heavy industry and planning in China than on the politics of finance. This does not mean that important work is lacking, however. See, inter alia, Chao Kuo-chun, 1959; Donnithorne, 1967; Perkins, 1968 and 1966; Rawski, 1975; Kenneth Lieberthal and Oksenberg, 1988; and K. C. Yeh, 1967. There are also a number of industry-specific studies, often of a largely quantitative nature, which will not be cited here. Major statements in Chinese include Zhao Yiwen, 1957; *Jingji Jianshe Changshi Duben*, 1956; He Jianzhang and Wang Jiye, 1984; Wang Haibo, 1986; Liu Suinian and Wu Qungan, 1986; Zhou Taihe, 1984; *Zhongguo Shehuizhuyi Jingji Jianshe Wenxian Ziliao Xuanbian*, 1984; and Hu Hua, 1985.

procedures that were copied from the Soviet Union.[2] By the mid 1950s, the State Planning Commission (SPC), the State Economic Commission (SEC), and the State Construction Commission (SCC; later known as the State Capital Construction Commission) were established. Specific functional ministries were formed and charged with the tasks of supervising productive activities and running major enterprises in their areas of jurisdiction. In the planning coalition, these ministries included the Ministry of Metallurgical Industry, the various Ministries of Machine Building (the number has varied over time), the Ministry of Coal, and the Ministry of Petroleum. The coalition's principal leaders in the mid 1950s were Li Fuchun, chairman of the SPC; Bo Yibo, chairman of the SEC; Wang Heshou, minister of metallurgical industries and concurrently chairman of the SCC; Huang Jing, minister of the First Ministry of Machine Building and concurrently chairman of the State Science and Technology Commission (he also was the first husband of Jiang Qing, or Madame Mao); and Zhao Erlu, minister of the Second Ministry of Machine Building.[3]

Central to an understanding of this grouping is the Soviet model of development. According to one scholar of the Soviet Union, the basic features of the Soviet model, or the "command economy," were:

(1) a high degree of centralization of economic decision making and planning [with centrally determined wages and prices]; (2) comprehensive . . . planning [with incentives heavily weighted to the fulfillment of plans]; (3) preference for physical units as instruments in accounting; (4) the use of "material balances" for obtaining internal consistency of the plans; (5) a centralized administration for material supplies, which operated as a rationing system; (6) imperative [i.e., legally binding] and detailed plans; (7) a hierarchically organized administration within factories; (8) the relegation of market categories and mechanisms to a secondary role, mainly to the sphere, albeit important, of personal consumption and labor; and (9) coercion by the state, as direct organizer of the economy with its ubiquitous controls and etatization not only of the economy but of the other spheres of life as well.[4]

While other characterizations of the Soviet model may differ slightly as to the exact components of the system, there is a high degree of consensus about what constitutes its core elements.[5]

2. On the Soviet role, see Borisov and Kolosov, 1975, esp. pp. 47–51, 61–64, and 85–92; "Sulian Jihua Zhuanjia Baogao Jianyi Huibian Kaishi Faxing" (Collections of Soviet Planning Experts' Reports and Suggestions Have Started Publication), *Jihua Jingji* (Planned Economy; hereafter *JHJJ*), 1958, no. 9 (September), p. 15; Gu Zhuoxin, "The Development of Planning and Industrial Construction in the Past Decade," *Jihua yu Tongji* (Planning and Statistics), 1959, no. 13, trans. in *Extracts from China Mainland Magazines* (hereafter *ECMM*), no. 204 (March 14, 1960), pp. 19–29; and Lardy, 1978a, p. viii.

3. For biographical information on these figures, see Klein and Clark, 1971, pp. 494–98, 738–42, 906–7, 390–93, and 82–84, respectively.

4. Lewin, 1974, pp. 113–14, as quoted in Erik P. Hoffman and Laird, 1982, p. 38. Bracketed information provided by Hoffman and Laird.

5. Other versions of the Soviet model are to be found in Katz, 1972, ch. 2, and in Magdoff,

However the Soviet model is defined, it is clear that the Chinese quickly installed its central features. Not until 1956 would leaders begin to question whether the Soviet model was fully applicable to China. Until that time, the Chinese devoted more funds (on a percentage basis) to heavy industry than the Soviets did during their First and Second Five-Year Plans.[6] Indeed, Mao noted that the planning and heavy industrial sectors were particularly dogmatic in their copying from the Soviet Union in 1950–1957, but he partially excused this because of the CCP's lack of experience in industrial management.[7] Even after doubts arose about the Soviet model, no major cuts were made in the share of funds allocated to heavy industry until the economic collapse in the early 1960s following the Great Leap Forward.

Once the leadership committed itself to Soviet-style industrialization, the general position of the planning coalition was essentially conservative. Even though the forced-draft industrialization of China would be revolutionary in its effects, once the basic decision was made to launch the industrialization drive the planning coalition sought to defend its control over capital construction, industrial planning, general investment decisions, and macroeconomic ratios; its management of key enterprises; and its distribution of heavy industrial products. By opting for the Soviet model, Chinese leaders were handing over the running of the economy (or at least industry) to the planners and the industrial ministers. The fact that members of the coalition monopolized the standard operating procedures associated with planning and industrialization gave them considerable power over the economic decision-making agenda.

Granting this authority to the planners was not unreasonable. In the early 1950s, Chinese leaders believed that the Soviet model worked and that it was the only practical way to develop the economy. The centerpiece of the industrialization drive was the complete installations the Soviet Union exported to China. Soviet advisers and experts were part of the package deal that sent the plants to China. It was a constant refrain (present even today) that the Chinese leadership was well aware that it and the Chinese people "lacked experience in economic construction." Whom else could the Chinese turn to but the Soviets? The United States and the United Nations were at war with China in Korea until the middle of 1953, and the United States maintained pressure on its allies not to trade with China after the cease-fire. An export-oriented light industrial strategy of development was therefore

1975, esp. pp. 18–29. On the Soviet model as applied in China, see Dernberger, 1981, esp. pp. 44–46, and Ward, 1980.
    6. On Chinese doubts, see Mao, 1977, pp. 284–307. On China's giving even greater priority than the Soviets to heavy industry, see Yeh, 1967.
    7. Schram, 1974, p. 98.

not feasible. The leadership's perception of a continuing threat posed by American imperialism dictated priority for heavy industry so that China could create an arms industry, and the decision to develop nuclear weapons in January 1955 only reinforced the need to develop heavy industry rapidly.[8] The Chinese leadership really saw no alternative to adopting the Soviet model and Russian technology.

In China, as in the Soviet Union, a large portion of the budget was channeled into investment, particularly in heavy industry. Within heavy industry, the steel and machine-building sectors were the most favored. The output of the heavy industrial sector was largely redirected into new projects in heavy industry[9] through allocational methods controlled by the planning agencies and the ministries themselves. Since these organizations largely governed the distribution of their own products, their most basic interest was in maintaining high rates of investment in, and high targets for, heavy industry. This would at once make China a powerful country and strengthen the bureaucratic interests of this sector.

It could be argued, as Chen Yun did argue,[10] that the planning coalition was analogous to a system of ownership, with control over the products it produced and with a seemingly boundless enthusiasm for new investment in heavy industry. The planners would provide the funds and the targets for heavy industrial projects and plants. Through the distribution system run by the planning bodies and the ministries, the coalition controlled who received the output of enterprises under its control. Since most heavy industrial products went to other heavy industrial projects, the coalition was largely closed to the outside, with little trickle down or spillover. In short, the planners and leaders of heavy industry created a system that produced and disposed of heavy industrial products in ways that maintained their dominance and impenetrability. Moreover, their insatiable demand for investment meant that light industry and agriculture were squeezed ever more tightly.

These facts explain why the planning coalition advocated the views attributed to it in Table 2 (Chapter 3). The most basic interest of this grouping was the call for high investment, with most investment allocated to heavy

8. On the nuclear weapons decision, see Lewis and Xue, 1988, pp. 35–39.

9. Perkins (1968, pp. 601–8) demonstrates that in the Soviet Union the vast majority of heavy industrial products stay within that sector and that in at least the two key areas of heavy industry, steel and machine building, most output returns to those sectors. The steel industry is the largest consumer of finished steel products, and the machine building industry is the largest consumer of machines. While the Soviet economy was considerably more planned than the Chinese in the 1950s (Perkins notes that the Soviets were planning about 1,500 products; the Chinese, only about 20–25 percent of that number), Perkins believes that the relationship presented above holds in China as well.

10. Chen Yun, 1981, p. 179.

industry. Coalition leaders argued that without this priority, China could never develop into a strong industrial power. To guide planning efforts, the coalition subscribed to the "law of planned, proportionate development." This "law," for which a long history exists in both Soviet and Chinese planning, means that the economy should be planned and that plans should fix basic ratios of investment in the heavy industrial, light industrial, and agricultural sectors, with heavy industry receiving the bulk of funds and material. Also inherent in this approach to development and planning was the use of "material balances," the basic tools of planning. The state would determine how much of each kind of good it needed and assign production targets on the basis. All this would be done in quantitative, not monetary, terms. Both the use of material balances and the law of planned, proportionate development implied that laws and balance would be less strictly enforced under the planners than under the budgeteers. Changes in the economic or political environment might suggest minor modifications in the sectoral investment ratios. The inability to predict fully how much of each kind of commodity was needed also required that material balances be fairly rough.[11] Since heavy industry was highly interdependent and its output largely reinvested in new heavy industrial projects, naturally the planning coalition would attempt to retain control over the distribution of heavy industrial products. Because agricultural products and consumer goods were not of great concern to them, they did not much care how these were distributed.

The Soviet model was predicated on the ability of the state to extract surplus from the peasantry or, at the very least, to ensure that the rural sector did not take more resources from the industrialization drive than it supplied to the state. As agricultural performance lagged, the planners' strategy was to advocate the modernization of agriculture through the introduction of industrial inputs. In this way, new monies were not invested in agriculture directly; instead more funds flowed to heavy industry. Given the high ratio of peasants to arable land in China, planners believed the effective use of industrial inputs required collective agricultural organizations. (Individual peasants could not afford chemical fertilizer or mechanized equipment. Collectives were better able to purchase such items.)

Excluding the rural sector (under collective ownership after 1956), the planning group favored state ownership of all production units. A unified ownership system facilitated planning and control, thereby ensuring that there were no leakages from the state sector to the collective or the individual. The planners, however, were not much concerned about the issue of

11. The most elaborate demonstration of the coarseness of Chinese planning is Lyons, 1987, pt. 2.

ownership in some sectors. The key factor was whether heavy industrial enterprises were state-owned. Only these enterprises were the true objects of planning.

Following the Soviet model, the planners favored all types of incentives. If quotas were met and overfulfilled, workers and managers would receive bonuses. If quotas were not met, workers and managers were punished. Workers and staff were also frequently told that they were in the forefront of building industry and were therefore the builders of socialism. In this way, nationalism and socialist spirit were tapped.

Effective planning required technical expertise. Planning was also a form of economic coordination, which demanded bureaucratic skills. Accordingly, the planners advocated employing bureaucratic and technical experts in positions of management responsibility.

As noted, once the Chinese leadership embraced the Soviet model, the position of the planning coalition was essentially defensive. The overall tendency of this grouping followed naturally from the perceived imperatives of the Soviet model. That this system of economic administration was not native to China is not critical. Once the central leadership committed China to emulating the Soviet experience, the planning coalition became the dominant group in the management of the Chinese economy because of Soviet assistance to China and because the leadership saw the goals of the Soviet model as central.

Yet while the planning coalition organized the most powerful interests involved in the functioning of the Chinese economy, its power and scope should not be overemphasized. Perhaps because of the coalition's dominant position, the production ministries felt less constrained than the group's leaders to support overall goals and instead argued for narrower ministerial interests. In particular, there was an intense rivalry between the metallurgical (steel) and machine-building branches of heavy industry.

The central planning organs in China were also considerably less than omnipotent. The experience and skill of the planners were quite limited. By 1952, when the State Planning Commission was established, 28 items were under national distribution (meaning subject to national planning and allocation). This figure rose to 96 in 1953, 134 in 1954, 163 in 1955, and 235 in 1956.[12] While these numbers reflect steady growth, they demonstrate only limited planning capacity. Even in an underdeveloped economy, 235 products do not account for many of the components required for plan fulfill-

12. "A Brief Description of the State Distribution of Commodities in the Past Year," *Tongji Gongzuo* (Statistical Work), 1957, no. 13, in *ECMM*, no. 97 (September 3, 1957), pp. 21–27; see p. 21.

ment. Moreover, until 1956 the SPC was charged with both long-term and yearly plans. Formation in 1956 of the State Economic Commission, with responsibility for yearly plans, was a rational decision that would have strengthened planning capacity in the long run, but in that year it probably meant that the few skilled personnel in the planning organs were divided up.[13]

It would be a fundamental error to dismiss planning in China because of these signs of weakness. Even if the capacity of the planners and the scope of planning were limited, the SPC and SEC played essential coordinating and political roles. Like the Ministry of Finance, the planning organs were at the very center of the economic decision-making process in China. Although the planners may not have been able to say exactly how much of one type of product was needed, by 1956 they had a fair idea of some of the current linkages in the production process. If the output of steel was to increase by a million tons, the planners knew roughly how much more coal this demanded. With this knowledge, they could enforce a certain amount of discipline on the ministries that were overzealously pursuing their own interests. Similarly, the planners used their knowledge to force ministries to produce products essential to the fulfillment of another ministry's targets. Thus, while they may not have been able to plan in a true sense, they knew how to control the economy generally. This did not mean that they always did so, but they did have the ability.

The SPC, because of its key role in economic decision making, often acted arrogantly. A 1980 eulogy on Li Fuchun stated:

As a comprehensive branch of the national economy, the State Planning Commission has close business relations with all ministries and commissions of the State Council. Comrade Fuchun demanded that in making contacts with other ministries and departments, all comrades of the State Planning Commission must avoid troubling comrades of other ministries and departments, try as far as possible to visit other ministries on their own initiative when problems crop up and have more consultations with comrades of other ministries and departments. The State Planning Commission must not take upon itself the affairs that should be handled by other ministries and departments.[14]

The fact that Li issued injunctions of this sort suggests that acting high-handedly was part of the SPC work style and was a serious problem.

In addition to their coordinating and facilitating role, the other resource that the planners had in the 1950s was political clout. Li Fuchun and Bo

13. See Chapter 4, n. 30.
14. Gu Zhuoxin et al., "Comrade Li Fuchun's Important Contributions to Economic Planning Work," *Renmin Ribao* (People's Daily; hereafter *RMRB*), May 22, 1980, trans. in Joint Publications Research Service, no. 75888, *China Report, Economic Affairs*, no. 64 (June 12, 1980), pp. 73–82 (quotation, p. 81).

Yibo were Politburo members, although Bo was only an alternate member. Li Fuchun had close relations with Mao Zedong (his wife was an old friend of Mao's) and with Zhou Enlai and Deng Xiaoping, stretching back to Li, Zhou, and Deng's joint work in Europe in the early 1920s. Moreover, no CCP leader had more experience than Li in negotiating with the Soviet Union. He had spent August 1952 to May 1953 in the Soviet Union hammering out the details of the 156 Soviet-supplied projects that formed the centerpiece of the First Five-Year Plan (FFYP), and he undertook a similar mission in the summer of 1956 in preparation for the drafting of the Second Five-Year Plan (SFYP).[15]

Bo Yibo lacked Li's depth of contacts and experience, but he too was a considerable figure in CCP leadership circles. Bo's career after 1949 provides a fine example of bureaucratic cooptation. In 1952–1953, when he was minister of finance, he favored tax policies that were relatively lenient toward private enterprises, a policy associated with Chen Yun.[16] Yet, as will be shown, he became an ardent proponent of heavy industrialization.

Compared with the planning apparatus, the production ministries within the coalition had leaders of low rank. There were several Central Committee members among the vice-chairmen of the planning commissions, but no ministry had more than one member of the Central Committee. Wang Heshou of Metallurgical Industries, for example, was only an alternate member of the Central Committee. Thus, despite technical limitations on their abilities, Li Fuchun and Bo Yibo, as the leaders of the planning and heavy industry group, could ensure that they retained ultimate control over their sometimes unruly compatriots in the production ministries.

B. The planning and heavy industry coalition at the Eighth Party Congress

Speeches by the leaders of the planning coalition at the Eighth Party Congress reflected defensiveness because of many disruptions and serious problems in the economy. The planners were not in control of the planning process in 1956. The effect of the "high tide of socialist transformation" had been felt in all areas. Mao was unwilling to see cadres lag behind; consequently,

15. On Li's trips to the Soviet Union, see Klein and Clark, 1971, p. 496; Duan Junyi et al., "Ta Yongyuan Shi Womende Bangyang" (He Was Always Our Model for Study), *RMRB*, June 2, 1985, repr. in *Xinhua Yuebao* (New China Monthly), 1985, no. 7 (July), pp. 60–64 (see p. 62); Xue Muqiao, "Zai Zhou Enlai Tongzhi Lingdao xia Gongzuode Huiyi" (Recollections of Working Under the Leadership of Comrade Zhou Enlai), and Wang Guangwei, "Zhou Zongli yu Di Yi, Er ge Wu Nian Jihuade Zhiding," (Premier Zhou and the Drawing Up of the First and Second Five-Year Plans), both in *Huainian Zhou Enlai*, 1986, pp. 36 and 43, respectively.
16. For a stinging rebuke of Bo's views in 1953, see Mao, 1977, pp. 103–11.

all plans were adventuristic. Moreover, Mao and others were beginning to question the Soviet model. In June 1956, Li Fuchun had attempted to refute several of the points in Mao's Ten Major Relationships.[17] Coalition leaders appeared to be worried in September 1956 that the political mandate bestowed upon them was weakening. Li and Bo Yibo tried to defuse some of the problems with planning and reassert its primacy. Li Fuchun discussed the means by which planning could be improved, and Bo Yibo suggested a system whereby surges in investment, like that in 1956, could be avoided. The other thirteen coalition leaders who spoke at the congress focused less on the general interests of the group and more on ministerial goals.[18]

Li Fuchun, despite a fairly self-critical tone, continued to uphold many of the fundamental beliefs of the planning coalition.[19] He argued that the greater the degree of state ownership, the better the economy could be planned. He noted that the key factor in strengthening the planned nature of the economy was not socialist industrial development but socialist transformation of agriculture, industry, and handicrafts. He equated socialist transformation with the process of bringing agriculture and the other areas "into the orbit of planning." Here Li rebutted Chen Yun and others who were arguing for the disaggregation of hastily formed and overcentralized collectives and for a reduction in the scope of planning.

Li noted that the planning organs had concerned themselves with direct planning of socialist enterprises and had allowed the State Council offices responsible for agriculture and commerce to handle affairs in those sectors by means of indirect planning. This, Li thought, was an appropriate division of labor. Apparently he was not eager to have the SPC acquire responsibility for areas peripheral to the interests of the coalition.

Li revealed that there were fundamental difficulties in planning work: The SPC had not grasped objective economic laws sufficiently and had performed its balancing work poorly. He noted that the SPC had not paid enough attention to agriculture, coastal industry, light industry, wages, and productivity – seemingly everything except adding new heavy industrial capacity. Particularly striking in Li's speech was his use of the past tense to describe this lack of attention, clearly implying that the SPC had corrected these errors.

17. See MacFarquhar, 1974, pp. 61–67.

18. For background on the period leading up to the Eighth Party Congress, see MacFarquhar, 1974, esp. pp. 15–32, 57–74, and 86–91. See also Mao, 1977, pp. 284–307, and Li Fuchun, "Progress of the First Five Year Plan for the Development of the National Economy," in *New China Advances to Socialism*, 1956, pp. 79–101.

19. "Speech by Comrade Li Fu-chun," in *Eighth National Congress of the Communist Party of China*, vol. 2: *Speeches* (hereafter *8PC/S*), 1956, pp. 288–303.

Li saw the current situation as without serious problems. He felt that establishment of the State Economic Commission would improve the planners' ability to grasp economic affairs. He also believed that directives issued by the Central Committee and the State Council had already solved the difficulties of early 1956 and that balance was being restored.

Li's commitment to balance and proportion was relative. In a passage reminiscent of Mao Zedong, he said:

> Proportions are governed by their own laws and must be planned in accordance with the specific conditions of our country. But proportions that have been laid down are *not rigid formulae*. . . .
>
> We must set about the work with a forward looking viewpoint and always bear future developments in mind. *Balance in economic life is relative.* When old imbalances are rectified, new ones emerge. . . . Our responsibility is to proceed from a forward looking viewpoint and take positive measures to continuously detect and eliminate weak links, rectify new imbalances, and thus ensure that the national economy as a whole will advance step by step towards a *new upsurge.*[20]

Li concluded by remarking that Chinese planners had not studied the Soviet experience in planning sufficiently, and presented his own ideas on reform. He first suggested the use of a level-to-level system of planning. Important national products would be planned and balanced by the center; important local products would be planned and balanced by the localities and their plans reported to the center; and subsidiary local products would be left to the localities and the "primary units" to manage. In addition, targets in the state plan were to be divided into mandatory targets, targets subject to adjustment, and reference targets. With mandatory targets, the plan, as sent down, had to be fulfilled. With targets subject to adjustment, a range of fluctuation was allowed between the planned target and actual output. Finally, reference targets had no binding effect on production units.

These planning reforms continued to ignore the non–heavy industrial sectors of the economy. Li was willing to allow prices, taxes, and commercial policies to control subsidiary production. He gave lower levels somewhat greater planning responsibility, and allowed non-key sectors to go their own way (implicitly, as long as they continued to provide plentiful levels of extractable resources for use by heavy industry). No fundamental change was inherent in his remarks. He attempted to protect the basic interests of the planning coalition despite problems with planning work and growing demands for decentralization.

Bo Yibo's speech to the congress put forward several key ratios designed to insure smoother development of the national economy.[21] He argued that

20. Li, pp. 288–89. Emphasis added.
21. "Speech by Comrade Po I-po [Bo Yibo, hereafter referred to as Bo]," *8PC/S*, pp. 45–62.

at least 20 percent of national income should be devoted to accumulation (roughly equivalent to investment). State revenue should not be less than 30 percent of national income. Finally, allocations for capital construction in the budget should not be less than 40 percent of budgetary expenditures. These percentages were higher than the average figures for the entire FFYP but lower than the projected figures for 1956. Bo thus proposed a check on the pattern of mobilization of resources often associated with Mao Zedong – Bo favored slightly lower levels and a more stable process. Bo's ratios placed the budget in the service of investment. The budget was subordinate to the needs of construction, which Bo made clear would emphasize industry. Moreover, by not linking state revenues in his second ratio (state revenue 30 percent of national income) and state expenditures in the third (capital construction 40 percent of expenditures), he may have implied that a balanced budget was not essential.

Bo's real purpose was to defend the dominance of the planning coalition. For example, in discussing the correct ratio between accumulation and consumption of national income, he noted that in the FFYP peasant income per household was increasing 2.6 percent per year in real terms. The peasant population, however, was probably growing faster than the number of households, suggesting lower per capita increases in rural consumption. Bo implied that this was a satisfactory rate of advance. He seemed unperturbed by the agricultural bottleneck that would be created if this trend continued. He was more interested in the fact that industrial construction was increasing at a 43 percent annual rate, and heavy industrial construction at a rate of 51.5 percent per year.[22]

Elsewhere in his speech, Bo said:

Our state budget is based on the principle of "taking from the people and spending on the people." If we lower the said [necessary?] level, there would be less taken from the people and consequently less spent on the people. In that case, the country's needs . . . will not be satisfied, and the people's . . . interests will also be impaired. Therefore . . . it is necessary to maintain the said level.[23]

This was certainly a criticism of those who argued for reducing accumulation, and may have been aimed specifically at Li Xiannian.

Bo emphasized the "looseness" of his percentages, noting that they would evolve as the economy developed. Moreover, they might be changed appropriately depending on the specific conditions encountered, such as the weather. He noted, "In drawing up our annual or long-range plans for development of the national economy, we *may* take these percentage figures

22. Bo, p. 48.
23. Bo, pp. 56–57.

[the three ratios above] for reference."[24] In short, the balances Bo put forward remained flexible.

Bo closed with a criticism of the budget balancing of Li Xiannian: "It is clear that no problem can be solved with such a conservative attitude as neglecting the growth of production and opening up new financial resources while attempting to solve financial difficulties by *cutting indispensable construction funds* or retrenching on indispensable living expenses."[25] Bo's comments here paraphrase remarks made by Mao Zedong in 1942, which asserted the primacy of production over finance and which may have been criticism of Chen Yun.[26]

Bo thus tried to guard the planning coalition from a two-pronged attack. His general percentages were designed, at least partly, to insulate heavy industry from the demands made by Mao and others to increase investment too rapidly. Bo and the planners disliked the turbulent fluctuations Mao's policy preferences created. At the same time, Bo attempted to preempt plans by Li Xiannian and Chen Yun to reduce expenditures on construction.

The other speakers associated with the planning coalition at the Eighth Party Congress were less concerned with taking the high ground of defending the policies and power of the entire group. Most either defended or promoted the interests of the individual ministries they led. The speeches by these leaders can be divided into two categories. The first was the debate between the Ministry of Metallurgical Industries and the First Ministry of Machine Building over which sector, steel or machine building, should be the most important sphere of productive activity in the planning and heavy industry group. The second comprised speeches by the leaders of the remaining components of the coalition. These leaders suggested that the growth of the processing industries in heavy industry (steel and machine building) was increasingly outstripping the capacity of the raw materials sector (particularly fuels) and the transportation system.

The proponents in the debate between steel and machine building were the heads of the Ministry of Metallurgical Industries, Wang Heshou (who concurrently chaired the State Construction Commission), and of the First Ministry of Machine Building, Huang Jing (concurrently head of the State Technological Commission).[27] Huang argued for the priority of the machine-

24. Bo, p. 61. Emphasis added.
25. Bo, p. 62. Emphasis added.
26. Watson, 1980, p. 59. On the possible criticism of Chen Yun, see Bachman, 1985b, pp. 18–20.
27. Neither the minister of the Second Ministry of Machine Building, Zhao Erlu, nor any other major figure from the Second Ministry spoke at the Eighth Party Congress. Most likely this was because the Second Ministry was concerned with the defense industry and the CCP did not want public discussion of issues related to defense.

building sector.[28] Because machine tools were vital for all economic activity and the foundation of the machine-building industry was weak, he asserted that machine building should be the top priority within heavy industry and consequently receive substantially increased resources. He presented a series of measures to transform existing machine-building enterprises from repair shops to plants serially producing standardized machines.[29] He also called for the development of an independent design capacity in line with China's actual conditions. Technical personnel should be awarded higher status and be used better; technical education should be expanded and further developed. Nevertheless, he concluded his remarks by stating that the success or failure of the machine-building industry would be determined by the style of thought and political work within the sector. Huang requested Party committees at all levels to give more supervision and direction to the activities of machine-building enterprises.

Wang Heshou attempted to defend the interests of the metallurgical industries from the encroachments of both the Ministry of Machine Building and the financial coalition,[30] although most of his remarks were aimed at Huang Jing. As Huang had with machine tools, Wang noted the linkages between the steel industry and all other sectors of economic activity. He argued that steel was the basis of all other industries. In other words, steel was a prerequisite for the development of the machine-building industry. In addition, he pointed out the political significance and national-security aspects of steel development, arguing that China could not really be considered a strong country until its steel production caught up with that of advanced capitalist economies. He then outlined policies to increase the self-reliance of the steel industry and to improve its organization and efficiency.

Wang noted that some people felt there was a constraint on how much money could be invested in the steel sector. He conceded that new steel mills were indeed expensive. He argued, however, that steel production was very profitable and that, *if steel profits were retained within the metallurgical sector*, steel could be largely self-financed. Wang refuted those who argued for more investment in light industry because light industry accumulated funds quickly. He implied that steel could accumulate funds just as quickly.

---

28. Huang Jing, "Shi Jixie Gongye xiang Wanzheng Tixi he Zixing Shejide Fangxian Fazhan" (Cause the Machine Building Industry to Develop in the Direction of a Complete System with an Independent Design Capacity), *Xinhua Banyuekan* (New China Semimonthly; hereafter *XHBYK*), 1956, no. 21, pp. 133–35.
29. On this process in China's industrial development, see Rawski, 1980, ch. 1.
30. Wang Heshou, "Gao Sudu Fazhan Wo Guode Gangtie Gongye" (Develop Our Country's Iron and Steel Industry at High Speed), *XHBYK*, 1956, no. 21, pp. 142–44.

Again paralleling Huang Jing, Wang Heshou closed his speech with a call for more Party leadership over the metallurgical industries. Unfortunately for Wang, he also had to offer self-criticism for his former strong support of one-man management. Under this scheme, repudiated at the Eighth Party Congress, factory managers had extensive control over all facets of activities in enterprises, and Party committees became mere appendages of management. [31]

The remaining ministries in the planning coalition wanted to have the importance of their work upgraded so that more resources could be allocated to them. In particular, the leaders of the transportation and energy sectors were outspoken in their calls for more investment.

For example, the minister of petroleum noted that not only was oil production not keeping up with demand, it was not even keeping up with the targets in the FFYP, and the difficulties of oil exploration and production had been underestimated. [32] The minister of coal also pointed out supply

31. For analysis of this issue, see Schurmann, 1968, pt. IV; Brugger, 1976; and Andors, 1977, ch. 3. For a discussion in Chinese, see Pang Song, "Xin Zhongguo Qiye Lingdao Zhidude Lishi Kaocha" (A Historical Investigation of New China's Enterprise Management System), *Dangshi Tongxun* (Communications on Party History), 1987, no. 6 (June), pp. 9–15.

Since one-man management had been government policy in 1953 and after, Wang was certainly not alone in promoting its implementation. And the call for strengthened Party leadership, particularly in enterprises, became policy at the Eighth Congress. Why were leaders like Huang Jing and Wang Heshou championing Party control when most of the leaders of the financial coalition were not?

A number of reasons suggest themselves. First, a strengthened Party role was policy. Having once endorsed one-man management, Huang and Wang now sought to demonstrate their commitment to the new policy. Second, there were more political explanations. By calling for increased Party input in management, they may have been trying to coopt the Party into becoming responsible for heavy industry. Thus, interests of the planning coalition and the Party might become fused. This, in turn, would create an alliance that could resist demands emanating from the financial system to redistribute investment and to reform and restructure basic aspects of the economic system. In a more positive sense, Huang and Wang, aware of the Party's having apparently fulfilled its mission of socialist transformation, were trying to supply a new organizational purpose: the industrialization of China. And indeed, this is largely what the Party itself concluded at the congress.

But why were budgeteers less eager to invoke strengthened Party leadership in their endeavors? Leaders of the financial coalition may have felt that it was precisely the defects of Party leadership that had led to the problems of 1956 that they were trying to solve. Second, the measures they advocated were largely mechanical (i.e., adjusting prices) or spontaneous (allowing the market to function). There was little for the Party to do. Finally, financial coalition leaders argued for a slower, more balanced, and more controlled style of economic development. This ran counter to basic Party tendencies associated with "campaigning." Efforts to incorporate direct, active Party leadership into financial-coalition policies would have been destabilizing and most likely would have led to the suppression of budgeteer interest and reform proposals.

The call for more Party leadership in the other branches of heavy industry was more muted than was the case in the two privileged sectors. But heavy industrial leaders still devoted more attention to Party leadership than did the leaders of the financial coalition.

32. Li Jukui, "Shiyou Gongye Mianqian Zhongda Renwu" (The Great Tasks Before the Petroleum Industry), *XHBYK*, 1956, no. 21, pp. 203–4.

shortages and said that the coal industry would probably not be able to meet its targets in the Second Five-Year Plan. Unless drastic measures, such as large increases in investment, were taken, coal production in 1962 would be about 20 million tons below the projected demand. In addition to increasing investment, the minister, Chen Yu, called for the development of local coal mines to supply local needs. These mines would be financed largely by the localities. Nonetheless, Chen argued that local coal production was to enter the national plan.[33] In contrast to many calls for decentralization at the Eighth Party Congress,[34] this was actually a call for centralization.

Leaders in the transportation departments echoed the demands of energy-producing ministries. They pointed out that transport capacity was increasingly falling behind the volume of goods requiring transport, and they called for more investment in this sector. Most of these leaders also argued for organizational restructuring, with local Party committees playing an expanded role.[35] Presumably, they desired increased Party participation in management in order to ensure that their concerns received an adequate hearing and because the Party might quickly resolve jurisdictional and other bureaucratic problems.

At the very least, the leaders of units in the planning and heavy industry coalition were concerned with defending their slice of the investment pie. Most were, in fact, trying to increase their share. In their individual efforts to increase investment, they advocated rather narrow organizational interests. They also argued against claims made by other sectors, notably the financial coalition, on state resources. Not only did leaders of the planning coalition assert the strategic importance, and hence the need for more investment, of their bailiwicks, but they also tried to coopt and entrap Party committees at various levels into supporting the perspectives, both general and particular, associated with the coalition.

What justification is there for claiming that the planning coalition had overall interests when its components were largely pursuing bureaucratic interests?

33. Chen Yu, "Jiaqiang Meitan Gongye Jianshe, Manzu Guomin Jingji Xuyao" (Strengthen Construction of the Coal Industry, Satisfy the Needs of the National Economy), *XHBYK*, 1956, no. 21, pp. 206–8.

34. Many of these are discussed in Harding, 1981, pp. 109–10, 120–21, and 126–29; Lardy, 1978b, pp. 30–31; MacFarquhar, 1974, ch. 10; and Prybyla, 1970, ch. 7.

35. Wang Shoudao (head of the Sixth [Transportation] Staff Office), "Fazhan he Gaizao Wo Guode Yunshu he Youdianye" (Develop and Transform Our Country's Transportation and Tele-communications Industries), *XHBYK*, 1956, no. 21, pp. 131–33; Teng Daiying (minister of railroads), "Tigao Tielude Yunshu Nengli he Xin Jian Tielude Zhiliang" (Raise the Capacity of Railway Transport and the Quality of Newly Built Railways), *XHBYK*, 1956, no. 21, pp. 134–35; Li Yunchang (vice-minister of communications), "Xunsu Jiejue Gonglu, Shuiyun Yunshude Zuse Wenti" (Speedily Resolve Problems of Obstructions in Road and Water Transportation), *XHBYK*, 1956, no. 21, pp. 199–201.

First, the most basic interests of the coalition were not directly challenged at the Eighth Party Congress. No one at the congress suggested that heavy industry should not be the priority sector. In September 1956, no one questioned the primacy of material balances in industrial development. No one disagreed with the system of allowing heavy industry to distribute its final product. No sense of crisis confronted the coalition. Because the criticisms were aimed at the coalition's more peripheral interests, individual ministries did not have to band together to face a basic threat to their common modus operandi. In the context of a shared set of beliefs within the planning coalition and a leadership that still accepted the premises underlying planning and heavy industry, there was little reason for components of the coalition not to argue for narrow bureaucratic interests. The financial coalition would later challenge many of the investment patterns associated with the planners. As of September 1956, however, the budgeteers still accepted as legitimate most of the mechanisms by which the planners controlled the economy.

Moreover, it was not clear that the planning coalition's pursuit of individual interests was harmful to overall goals. If each ministry made a legitimate claim for expanding the resources devoted to it, this only strengthened the overall power of the coalition, particularly if the individual ministries were pressing their claims for more resources on the larger political system rather than calling for a redistribution of funds within the coalition itself. But demands for resource redistribution within the coalition raised fundamental managerial and political challenges for coalition leaders.

Thus, the pursuit of bureaucratic interests favored overall goals. The individual interests articulated by the constituent members of the coalition aggregated into key tenets of the grouping's ideology – more investment and more technical personnel for heavy industry and continued hegemony for the planners over economic decision making. This last goal was to be achieved through an expanded role for the Party in supervising heavy industry. Planning leaders apparently hoped that the Party's interests would overlap with their coalition's.

C. The planning and heavy industry coalition, October 1956 – October 1957

Central to the political and economic agenda of the planning coalition from October 1956 to October 1957 was rectifying the problems of 1956, drawing up and implementing the annual plan for 1957, and completing the draft of the SFYP. The plan for 1957 had to be formulated, and the proposals for the

SFYP had to be transformed from a list of targets in only a few areas to a fairly concrete plan of action. Closely related to planning activities in 1957 was a growing recognition of increasingly severe shortages of critical raw materials and economic imbalance. These problems were addressed first by the financial coalition, which seized control of the economic decision-making agenda when Party leaders became preoccupied with the issues of the Hundred Flowers Campaign and Party rectification. The budgeteers' threat to the dominant position of the planning coalition first induced defensiveness, because in the difficult economic circumstances of early 1957 planners lacked obvious counters to a challenge. But by the spring and summer of 1957 top planners had developed a devastatingly persuasive alternative to the financial coalition's program, one that would supply most of the elements of the economic policies of the Great Leap Forward.

During the fall of 1956 and the winter of 1957, the planning coalition did little of special importance. Its principal leaders were not particularly visible, absorbed as they were in problems caused by the overheated economy of 1956. Moreover, given these problems, the planners were not in a strong position to counter Chen Yun and the other budgeteers with the planners' standard policy program.

Immediately after the Eighth Party Congress, the State Planning Commission started refining the SFYP. An editorial in *Jihua Jingji* (Planned Economy) warned that the proposals for the SFYP were not a plan and that much hard work was required to develop a real plan. It urged planners to absorb the lessons of the FFYP, to seek truth from facts, to carry out more investigation, to understand economic laws, and only then to draw up the SFYP.[36] Another article on the SFYP revealed the growing concern of the planners with insuring that the SFYP was reliable and active. The plan would be constrained by the financial, material, and personnel weaknesses of the Chinese state. While raw material shortages were seen as a major problem, wishful thinking still characterized the planners' ideas about agricultural development. The essay stated that agriculture was to grow by 6.3 percent a year in the SFYP (the figure for the FFYP was 4.3 percent). This was a high rate of growth, but the projected increases for grain and cotton strained credulity. The draft figures for the plan called for grain to increase by 38 percent over the entire plan period, more than double the rate for the FFYP, and cotton to increase by a whopping 47 percent – 25 percent was the comparable figure for the FFYP. Although the targets for the FFYP in agricul-

36. "Jin Yibu Fazhan Wo Guo Shehuizhuyi Shiyede Weida Gangling" (The Great Plan for Progressively Developing Our Country's Socialist Cause), *JHJJ*, 1956, no. 10 (October), pp. 1–3.

ture had just barely been attained, the planners felt that through collectives, increased irrigation, and improved technology and tools these new targets would be fulfilled.[37]

As further preparation for drawing up the SFYP, a vice-chairman of the State Planning Commission described in detail the Soviet experience in drawing up five-year plans. His emphasis was all on material balances and on a thorough consideration of forward and backward linkages in the production process, with priority for the metallurgical and machine-building sectors. The emerging Soviet decentralization experiments, *sovnarkhozy*, were introduced, and the Chinese were encouraged to study them seriously and critically.[38]

Despite all the apparent preparation by the planners, formulation of the SFYP was delayed, as discussed in Chapter 4. Whereas the SFYP proposals were adopted on September 27, 1956, the Central Committee of the CCP did not submit them to the State Council until December 13, 1956, and the State Council did not discuss them until February 7, 1957.[39] The delay suggests that a number of basic targets were still under debate.

While work on the SFYP was stalled in early 1957, work on the 1957 annual plan proceeded. On November 28, 1956, the SEC convened a planning conference to draw up the control figures for 1957. In light of the cutbacks ordered by the Second Plenum of the Eighth Central Committee (November 10–15, 1956), the planners faced a taut economic environment. Investment would not increase in 1957, shortages of key materials were critical, and foreign exchange for imports was severely limited.[40] Several articles drawing on discussions at the planning conference presented lessons to be learned from 1956 in drawing up the 1957 plan. An editorial in the December issue of *Jihua Jingji*, noting that while social purchasing power in 1956 went up by 14 percent, consumer goods increased by only 7 percent, drew the conclusion that planners should match purchasing power and the supply of consumer goods more carefully. The editorial noted that targets for 1957 included an increase in industrial output by 15 percent and an increase in agricultural production by 8 percent, including a 7 percent increase in grain and a 13 percent rise in cotton output.

Increasing quality and tapping potentials were keys to expanding indus-

37. Jia Chuan, "Guanyu Dierge Wunian Jihua Shiqi Guomin Jingjide Fazhan Sudu" (On the Rate of National Economic Advance During the Period of the Second Five-Year Plan), *JHJJ*, 1956, no. 10 (October), pp. 4–7.

38. Yang Yingjie, "Jieshao Sulian Bianzhi Wunian Jihuade Chengce he Fangfa" (An Introduction to the Procedures and Methods Used by the Soviet Union in Drawing Up Five-Year Plans), *JHJJ*, 1956, no. 11 (November), pp. 1–8.

39. See *JHJJ*, 1957, no. 3 (March), p. 1.

40. *Zhonghua Renmin Gongheguo Jingji Guanli Dashiji*, 1986, pp. 91–92.

trial output, it stated. Lack of raw materials forced a reduction of capital construction. It said that with the exception of industry (which would receive slightly more investment in 1957 than in 1956), all capital construction would be sharply curtailed. Within industry, investment was to be concentrated on the weak links – steel, coal, electrical generation, petroleum, wood, building materials, textiles, and paper. The raw materials sector was held up for special attention.[41] This list omitted machine tools as a priority sector for 1957. Concomitantly, construction of the No. 1 Tractor Factory, China's first factory to produce agricultural machinery, was delayed. Increasing technical inputs to the rural sector was a lower priority than other demands on the machine-building industry.[42]

By early January 1957 raw-material shortages were even worse than feared. Coal miners were ordered to give up two of the three days of the lunar New Year, the most important Chinese holiday. The planning agencies also discovered that many of the raw-material shortages could be blamed at least in part on poor enterprise management and the lack of a thorough system of raw-material accounting and supervision. Targets for construction in 1957 were further lowered in early 1957.[43]

Yet elements of the planning coalition persevered in the naked pursuit of core interests without reflecting the austere environment of early 1957. An editorial in the January 1957 issue of *Jihua Jingji* argued that it was still necessary to struggle against conservatism in production. It stated that with two exceptions, no aspect of industrial production was characterized by rash advance. All industrial targets, it said, were both active and reliable. While conceding the need to cut capital construction, the editorial noted that some

41. "Bian Hao 1957 Niandu Guomin Jingji Jihua" (Formulate the Yearly National Economic Plan for 1957 Well), *JHJJ*, 1956, no. 12 (December), pp. 1–4, 29. See also Hebei Sheng Jihua Weiyuanhui (Economic Planning Committee of Hebei Province), "Bianzhi 1957 Nian Jihua Yao Jieshou Guoqude Jingyan Jiaoxun" (In Drawing Up the Plan for 1957 We Should Learn the Lessons of Previous Experience), *JHJJ*, 1956, no. 11 (November), pp. 15–16, and *RMRB* editorial, "Toushan Anpai Jiben Jianshe Xiangmu" (Appropriately Arrange Capital Construction Items, February 13, 1957, repr. in *XHBYK*, 1957, no. 5, pp. 56–57.

42. "Jiqi Zhizao Gongye Tiaozheng Jianshe Jihua Baozheng Guojia Zui Xuyaode Zhongdian Jianshe" (The Machine Building Industry Readjusts Construction Plans to Guarantee the State's Most Necessary Key Construction Projects), *XHBYK*, 1957, no. 6, pp. 40–41.

43. For some of the many articles on these themes in early 1957, see *RMRB* editorial, "Dajia Dou lai Jieyue Meitan" (Everyone Must Save Coal), January 13, 1957, in *XHBYK*, 1957, no. 3, pp. 41–42; *RMRB* editorial, "Meikuang Zhigongde Guangrong Renwu" (The Glorious Task of Coal Miners and Staff), January 27, 1957, in *XHBYK*, 1957, no. 4, p. 70; and Song Shaowen (Vice-chairman of the SEC), "Guanyu Gongye Qiye Kaizhan Zengchan Jieyue Yundongde Jige Wenti" (Several Problems in the Movement to Increase Production and Practice Economy), *Gongren Ribao* (Workers' Daily), February 26, 1957, in *XHBYK*, 1957, no. 6, pp. 34–36. On the further reduction in capital construction, see Li Qian, "Genju Guojiade Caili, Wuli Toushan Anpai 1957 Nian Jiben Jianshe Jihua" (Appropriately Arrange the Capital Construction Plan for 1957), *JHJJ*, 1957, no. 3 (March), pp. 4–5, 13.

people were using the problems in capital construction as an excuse to lower production quotas, overreacting to the campaign to oppose rashness. The editorial called for emphasis on continued opposition to conservatism.[44] This editorial ran directly counter to the direction of policy development in late 1956 and early 1957;[45] perhaps not coincidentally, the next issue of *Jihua Jingji* announced that the SPC and SEC had reorganized the journal's editorial board.[46]

The composition of the new editorial board is important because *Jihua Jingji* was to play a major role in the reformulation of the planning coalition's program. It included Song Ping, Ma Hong, Yang Yingjie, Luo Gengmo, Xue Muqiao, and ten others, with Xue Muqiao as chairman and Yang Yingjie, Luo Gengmo, and Ma Hong as vice-chairmen. Xue, Yang, Luo, and Song Ping were all vice-chairmen of the State Planning Commission, and Ma Hong had been secretary-general of the State Planning Commission until he was purged with Gao Gang in 1953. This appointment to the board marked his rehabilitation. Other members of the board were leading writers on economic issues. The original editorial board's members are not known, but it would appear, first, that a rectification of the old board had occurred; second, that the clout of the new editorial board was greatly strengthened; and, third, that the planning bodies would exercise more direct control over *Jihua Jingji*.

While the planners readjusted the leadership of their house organ, *Renmin Ribao* hinted at the direction planning officials should follow to counter Chen Yun's control of economic decision making in 1957. An article pointed out that China must develop an independant capacity for the design of industrial equipment. According to the article, the most important task in improving design was to "gradually shake off the condition where we solely rely on foreign blueprints in production design work and copy backward foreign products, and develop the independent ability to design equipment." In other words, China's heavy industrial sector had to be more self-reliant.[47]

The defensiveness of the planning coalition was exemplified by Bo Yibo's

44. "Chongfen Liyong Xianyou Gongye Qiyede Shengchan Nengli" (Fully Utilize the Production Capacity of Existing Industrial Enterprises), *JHJJ*, 1957, no. 1 (January), pp. 5–6.

45. For an overview of opposition to rashness, see Qiang Yuangan and Chen Xuewei, "Zhongping 1956 Niande 'Fan Maojin' " (A Reevaluation of the "Opposition to Rash Advance" of 1956), *Dangshi Yanjiu* (Research on Party History), 1980, no. 6, pp. 34–41.

46. "Guanyu Jiaqiang *Jihua Jingji* Zazhide Bianqi Gongzuode Jueding" (Decision on Strengthening the Editorial Work of *Planned Economy* Magazine), *JHJJ*, 1957, no. 2 (February), pp. 1–2.

47. Ji Yin, "Gaijin Chanpin Sheji Shi Zengchan Jueyue Yige Zhongyao Tujing" (Improving Product Design Is an Important Way to Increase Production and Practice Economy), *RMRB*, February 14, 1957, in *XHBYK*, 1957, no. 5, pp. 51–52.

one major speech at this time, delivered to the National Model Agricultural Workers Conference in late February 1957. He endorsed the view of Chen Yun (and as will be shown, Mao) on the importance of agriculture in the entire economy. He came closer than any other planning coalition leader in the 1956–1957 period to even voicing support for the three balances. Bo stated that capital construction in 1957 had to proceed on the basis of the state's financial and material strength and that there had to be a balance of production materials, livelihood materials, finances, and foreign exchange.

Yet several phrases in Bo Yibo's speech suggest continued differences with the budgeteers. He again denounced a one-sided financial or technical viewpoint in carrying out the campaign to increase production and practice economy. He attempted to show that the growth of rural income was keeping pace with income growth in the urban areas, hence denying the need to redistribute budgetary expenditures and cut capital construction to aid the peasants, as Li Xiannian and Deng Zihui had advocated at the Eighth Party Congress.

Bo's terms of discourse were more political than those used by financial coalition spokesmen in their major speeches at this time. Perhaps this was because Bo spoke to a more "politically conscious" audience. Still, he argued that the campaign to increase production and practice economy was an effective measure taken by the working class to ensure the defeat of capitalism, and that the campaign was "a form of a great rectification movement to oppose bureaucratism and subjectivism." In this regard, Bo was well ahead of many members of the Politburo in calling for a rectification campaign and focusing on bureaucracy as the primary target. He also frequently praised the CCP and Mao.[48]

Bo's speech marked the nadir of the planning coalition's position in 1957. After almost endorsing the financial coalition's views in late February, this coalition embarked on a major rethinking of its policies. In a remarkably short period of time, its program was not only reformulated but also disseminated throughout China, attracting growing, soon to be irreversible, support. The basic interests of the planning coalition were presented in a way that was simultaneously attractive to elements outside the coalition and fully defensive of its core beliefs.

A planning conference in March 1957 announced a decision to devote more effort to developing medium-size and small – and locally administered – collieries, iron mines, and blast furnaces in order to help overcome pro-

48. "Guowuyuan Fuzongli Bo Yibode Baogao" (Report of State Council Vice-Premier Bo Yibo), *XHBYK*, 1957, no. 6, pp. 57–59. On rectification and bureaucratism, see MacFarquhar, 1974, pp. 179–249; Harding, 1981, pp. 116–52; and Teiwes, 1979a, pp. 211–74.

duction bottlenecks.[49] This became one of the distinctive features of the so-called Chinese model of development. Until now, all emphasis on small and medium-size enterprises had been confined to the light industrial sector. This meeting marked a major change: The focus shifted to producer goods industries. In addition to the production effects, this policy had an even more profound impact: It increased local self-reliance (and de facto decentralization), thereby partially insulating large heavy industrial plants from demands that they devote their production to local needs. In short, a policy of stressing local industry actually preserved heavy industry's hegemony in economic affairs.

Articles in March and early April indicate that the planning coalition was beginning to shake off the passivity of late 1956 and early 1957. The Party's theoretical journal asserted that China needed "several dozen million tons, [even] several hundred million tons of steel."[50] A late-March article discussed the capital construction plan for 1957. Despite the overall decline in investment expenditures in 1957, investment in industry would actually increase over the figures for 1956. The SEC's plan provided for a certain amount of redistribution of investment funds. Machine-building industry funds were cut, but the coal, power-generation, metallurgical, and other raw-materials industries received increased resources. The chemical industry was a major beneficiary, receiving 13 percent more funds, the bulk of which went to chemical fertilizers.[51] Although light industry was also supposed to expand, the planners were able to protect the interests of heavy industry quite well despite economic strains.

In April, *Jihua Jingji* published a report on the plan for 1957 by Jia Tuofu, vice-chairman of the State Economic Commission and head of the Light Industry Staff Office of the State Council. He attempted to balance the pressures he faced from conflicting roles (he was a member of both the planning and budgeteer coalitions). For example, he announced that the 15 percent increase in the gross value of industrial production forecast in December 1956 was now reduced to 6.2 percent. He also stated that capital construction in 1958 would not greatly exceed the 1957 figure and still might not

49. Liu Hongsheng, "Disici Quanguo Sheng, Qu, Shi, Jihua Huiyi Guanche Zengchan Jieyue Jingshen Toshan Anpai Jinnian Difang Jihua" (The Fourth National Conference of Provincial, Prefectural, and Municipal Planners on Using the Spirit of Increasing Production and Practicing Economy to Arrange This Year's Local Plans Properly), *XHBYK*, 1957, no. 8, p. 43. Riskin, 1971, provides an overview of the issue of small-scale industry in the 1950s.

50. Chen Daoyuan, "Women Xuyao Ji Qian Wan Dun, Ji Wanwan Dun Gang" (We Need Several Dozen Million Tons, Several Hundred Million Tons of Steel), *Xuexi* (Study), 1957, no. 6, pp. 17–18.

51. "Jinnian (1957) Wo Guo Jiang Xingjian Sibai Bashiqi Xiang Da Chang Guang" (This Year Our Country Will Build 487 Large Factories and Mines), *XHBYK*, 1957, no. 8, pp. 50–51.

reach the 1956 level. Jia said nothing, however, to suggest greater concern for light industry and agriculture (which he had advocated at the Eighth Party Congress). He repeated calls for increased investment in coal, electric power, chemicals, and other sectors facing major production shortages that would limit the overall economy. In a policy that was to develop in mid 1957, he argued that design standards were too high and should be lowered appropriately. Not all construction projects needed to be supplied with the largest, most sophisticated equipment. Investment in nonproductive projects was to be greatly reduced.[52] Jia's inability or unwillingness to press demands for increased light industrial and agricultural development should be seen as a symbolic turning point in the reassertion of planning coalition dominance.

In early April, the policy of developing small and medium-size plants in the metallurgical and coal sectors took off. A study of problems to be confronted in the SFYP emphasized the need for smaller enterprises and more self-reliant industrial development, and envisioned that the same construction projects in the SFYP would cost about 10 percent less than comparable plants in the First Five-Year Plan.[53] A *Renmin Ribao* editorial argued that many more smaller plants in the metallurgical sector must be built. One 1.5 million–ton steel mill took nine years to build and cost 1.2 billion to 1.5 billion yuan, whereas the same amount of money could fund eleven to thirteen 160,000-ton plants and would require only four years for construction. Managers of capital construction projects and factories were urged to shed their desire for the most advanced equipment and technology in the projects under their supervision. China could not produce advanced machines, but if the country built more small plants more productive capacity could be added and foreign exchange could be saved.[54] No big plants should be constructed for a while. The construction of many additional smaller plants would help promote the machine-building industry.[55] On April 12, the State Council issued a directive on developing local coal mines. The emerging spirit of the time was summed up in an editorial entitled "To Spend Less and Do More Is Possible."[56]

52. "A Review of the 1956 Economic Plan and an Explanation of the Draft Plan for 1957," *JHJJ*, 1957, no. 4, trans. in *ECMM*, no. 90 (July 15, 1957), pp. 17–31.

53. "Jieshao Guojia Jihua Weiyuanhui Chubu Yanjiude Guanyu Dierge Wunian Jihua Ruogan Wenti" (Introducing Some Preliminary Studies of the State Planning Commission on Certain Problems in the Second Five-Year Plan), *JHJJ*, 1957, no. 4 (April), pp. 10–12.

54. *RMRB* editorial, "Guanche Yejin Gongye Jianshe Fangjian" (Carry Out Construction Policy in the Metallurgical Industry), April 4, 1957, in *XHBYK*, 1957, no. 9, pp. 70–71.

55. Li Feng, "Geng Duo Caiyong Yibande Jishu Shebei, Jiakuai Wo Guo Gongye Jianshe Sudu" (Use Even More Ordinary Technical Equipment, Increase the Speed of National Industrial Construction), *XHBYK*, 1957, no. 9, pp. 71–72.

56. "Guowuyuan Guanyu Fazhan Xiao Meiyaode Zhishi" (Directive of the State Council on

Some officials in the machine-building sector argued against smaller enterprises, however, noting that one 64,000-ton casting factory was about 25 percent cheaper than eight 8,000-ton factories, and more efficient too.[57] This may have been a rearguard action by the machine tool industry to fight off smaller budgets. The machine-building sector gave further evidence of its lack of political sensitivity in April, when an article on agricultural mechanization asserted that the development of heavy industry was a prerequisite for successful mechanization. According to the article, only after twenty-seven years would there be enough tractors for 1 billion mu of land, or about half of China's sown land in 1957.[58] The author feared that mechanization would take jobs away from the peasants, and he called for a solution to this problem before mechanization was carried out. Mechanization should not be a major task in the SFYP.[59]

Given the production and investment cutbacks the machine-building industry faced in 1957 and the growing perception that agriculture was a bottleneck squeezing overall growth, it seems odd that agricultural mechanization did not receive the attention that for sound economic (and political, bureaucratic) reasons it might have had. The minister of the First Ministry of Machine Building would shortly reverse this denigration of agricultural mechanization.

Views such as those expressed by the machine building industry were very much in the minority. Overall, spokesmen for the planning coalition kept the pressure on those who questioned the primacy of the planning and heavy industry nexus. Xue Muqiao, vice-chairman of the State Planning Commission and director of the State Statistical Bureau, rebutted ideas associated with Chen Yun and others. In an article expounding the law of value, he criticized those who

thought that socialist states should not "interfere" with economic activity, that state-owned enterprises should be completely handed over to their workers and staff to manage for themselves, allowing them to freely produce and freely develop according to market needs. In reality, acting in this way completely abandons the leading role of state planning.[60]

Developing Small Coal Mines), *XHBYK*, 1957, no. 9, pp. 72–73; see also "Shidang Fazhan Xiao Meiyao" (Appropriately Develop Small Coal Mines), *RMRB*, April 14, 1957, in *XHBYK*, 1957, no. 9, pp. 64–65. The editorial is "Shao Huaqian Duo Banshi Shi Kenengde," *RMRB*, April 11, 1957, in *XHBYK*, 1957, no. 9, pp. 73–74.

57. "Guojia Jingji Jianshe Youguan Bumen Fuzeren Tan Xiezuo Jianchangde Zhongda Yiyi" (Responsible Personnel from Units Concerned with the State's Economic Construction Discuss the Great Significance of Coordinating the Construction of Factories), *XHBYK*, 1957, no. 9, pp. 67–68.

58. State Statistical Bureau, 1982, p. 140. One mu equals 0.0667 hectare.

59. Zhao Xue, "The Problem of Agricultural Mechanization in China," *JHJJ*, 1957, no. 4, trans. in *ECMM*, no. 87 (June 17, 1957), pp. 10–14.

60. Xue Muqiao, "Shehuizhuyi Shengchan Guanxide Neibu Maodun" (Internal Contradictions in Socialist Relations of Production), *Xuexi*, 1957, no. 9, pp. 2–5; quotation, pp. 4–5.

This was a direct attack on Yugoslavia, but in September 1956 Chen Yun criticized the statistical departments for doing a great deal of useless work and proposed that many light industrial enterprises should in fact produce for the market, and in November 1956 he supported aspects of Yugoslavia-style worker management.[61] For the sake of political argument, Chen's remarks could be distorted to fit Xue's criticisms. How was Xue, not a member of the Central Committee, able to criticize implicitly the fifth-ranking Party leader? He must have had a strong patron to protect him, most likely Bo Yibo.[62] Other rebuttals of attacks on the reputation of heavy industry and planning and of attempts to erode the group's position appeared with regularity.[63]

All these articles and statements pale in light of the blitz launched by Bo Yibo and Li Fuchun from May to August 1957. On an inspection tour of Xian and Chengdu in May, Bo and Li pulled together the various elements of the reformulated planning-coalition position, and they hammered away repeatedly until their ideas became policy. In Chengdu, Bo argued that if survey, design, and processing work in construction was done well, about 25 percent of the total investment cost could be saved. In April, the State Planning Commission had estimated that only 10 percent could be saved. Bo conceded Mao's February 1957 criticism that the planners had ignored the interests of the 600 million Chinese (Chapter 7). Planners and industrial officials one-sidedly stressed the large, the modern, the automated, and the capital-intensive (i.e., the very expensive). Bo consequently argued that many

61. See "Speech by Comrade Chen Yun," *8PC/S*, p. 174, and Chen Yun, 1981, p. 24.

62. A well-placed informant suggests that Xue was one of Bo's secretaries in the 1950s. Xue had many contacts with Chen Yun as well, but Chen had criticized Xue's work unit, as noted in Chapter 4. It is possible that Xue's criticisms were an answer to Wang Ziying's attack on Bo Yibo's speech to the Eighth Party Congress. See Chapter 4, n. 41.

63. For example, an article in June by another vice-chairman of the State Planning Commission strongly opposed Sun Yefang's understanding of the law of value. In July, a *JHJJ* article explicitly repudiated Sun's idea that all planning and statistics should be based on the law of value. See Yang Yijie, "Dui Jihua Jingji he Jiazhi Guilude Yanjiu" (Research on the Planned Economy and the Law of Value), *JHJJ*, 1957, no. 6, pp. 1–4, and He Wei and Liu Guoyu, "Bu Neng ba Jihua Fangzai Jiazhi Guilude Jichushang" (Planning Cannot Be Based on the Law of Value), *JHJJ*, 1957, no. 7, pp. 9–11, 30.

The planning coalition left no stone unturned in its efforts to make sure that the budgeteers did not expand the bridgeheads they had gained in early 1957. In February 1957, an article noted that priority for expansion of the means of production was not the same as priority for heavy industry. While the author did not spell out the implications of this distinction, he implied that light industry and agriculture could be expanded at the expense of heavy industry (Zi Si, "Shengchan Ziliao he Zhonggongye Chanpin zhei Liangge Guannian bu Ying Huntong" [The Two Concepts of Production Materials and Heavy Industrial Products Should Not Be Confused], *Xuexi*, 1957, no. 3, p. 23). In May, a defender of the planning coalition conceded that there was a difference between heavy industrial products and the means of production but stated that in actual economic work priority for heavy industry was the way to realize priority for the means of production. See Ju Nong, "Guanyu Youxian Fazhan Zhong Gongyede Lilun Genju Wenti" (On Basic Theoretical Questions on Giving Priority to the Development of Heavy Industry), *Xuexi*, 1957, no. 9, pp. 8–9.

more small and medium-size enterprises should be built. Lowered building standards (cheaper buildings), more labor-intensive enterprises, and dispersed construction were now key policies. This avoided the problem of excessive urban construction, which increased rural migration and brought new demands for the construction of urban amenities. Self-reliance as the base, foreign assistance as secondary (*zili gengsheng weizhu, zhengqu waiyuan weifu*) became policy.[64] This was the first time the politically charged phrase *zili gengsheng*, associated with the Yanan years, was revived after 1949.[65] Bo's speech implied that China could do more with its limited investment funds; investment funds could also be saved by lowering standards and carrying out other measures; smaller factories could enter production faster than large ones could. From the famous slogan associated with all economic upsurges in China, "more, faster, better, more economic results," Bo omitted only "better." That lacuna would be filled shortly.

A week later, Li Fuchun and Bo Yibo spoke in Chongqing. On this occasion, Li was the featured speaker, but his remarks were practically identical to Bo's words of the week before. Li called for the center and the localities to take medium-size and small enterprises as the base and build large enterprises only when necessary. He noted that China could equip many plants and mines through its own efforts and that it should strive to supply 70–80 percent of all equipment to new industrial and mining projects. He wanted the localities to play the leading role in developing light industry, and implied that the growth rate of light industry should be a little lower.[66] A day later, the Party center approved and circulated a report by Li and Bo on these and other issues.[67]

Li and Bo returned to Beijing at the end of May, just in time to address the National Design Conference. Again they spread the gospel of more, faster, and more economical results – and now they added "better." Li's long speech to the conference focused on how design could be made better to allow faster construction. Excessively high safety and health standards were a target for attack. In the SFYP, he advocated a 20 percent reduction in the cost of industrial construction and a 30 percent reduction for nonproductive construction, such as housing. In all their speeches during this time, Li and Bo

64. "Bo Yibo Fuzongli zai Jiben Jianshe Gongzuozhong Ruhe Jinxing Zhengfeng" (Vice-Premier Bo Yibo Talks About How to Carry Out Rectification in Capital Construction), *RMRB*, May 11, 1957, in *XHBYK*, 1957, no. 11, pp. 90–91.

65. Oksenberg, 1970, esp. pp. 20–31.

66. "Li Fuchun, Bo Yibo zai Chongqing Tan Guanche Qinjian Jianguo Fangzhenzhongde Wenti" (In Chongqing, Li Fuchun and Bo Yibo Discuss the Question of Carrying Out the Policy of Building the Country Through Industry and Thrift) (May 18, 1957), *XHBYK*, 1957, no. 12, pp. 104–5.

67. *Zhonghua Renmin Gongheguo Jingji Guanli Dashiji*, 1986, p. 97.

implied that such savings were to be reinvested in new construction. Li also stated that there should be little growth in the machine-building industry in the SFYP.[68] If that industry wanted to maintain its priority status, it would have to develop new organizational missions.

Bo's speech to the conference emphasized decentralization, the lack of coordination between the center and the localities, and frequent disputes between ministries over trifles. The conference suggested that a specialized unit headed by a vice-premier should be established to resolve arguments quickly.[69] No doubt, the conferees felt Vice-Premiers Li Fuchun and Bo Yibo were the obvious candidates for the job. This appointment would strengthen Bo's or Li's ability to defend and promote the interests of the planning coalition and unify the bureaucratic interests within the coalition.

Many articles quickly embraced Li's and Bo's ideas.[70] Bo's report to the Fourth Session of the First National People's Congress in June 1957 codified the tenets of the planners' new program. The now familiar litany of measures was once again presented, but Bo added one new element to the discussion. He noted, "The development of our agriculture lags far behind the demand of the people's livelihood and behind the demand of the development of light industry." Because of this, "the Draft National Program for Agriculture must be continually carried out; . . . special care should be taken to develop the chemical fertilizer industry."[71] Bo became the first Politburo member to mention the Draft Agricultural Program (the Forty Points on Agriculture) publicly since January 1957. He thereby suggested a revival of the mobilization style of rural development that had for decades been associated with the Party. Mobilization might enable agricultural production to grow with-

68. "Comrade Li Fuchun's Report to the National Design Conference," *Jianshe Yuekan* (Construction Monthly), 1957, no. 8, trans. in *Union Research Service* 8, no. 25 (September 24, 1957), pp. 433–55.

69. "Quanguo Sheji Huiyi" (National Design Conference) (June 8, 1957), *XHBYK*, 1957, no. 13, pp. 134–35.

70. For example, "Dierge Wunian Jihua Jue Da Bufen Jianshe Xiangmu Women Neng Ziji Sheji" (We Can Design the Vast Majority of Items in the SFYP Ourselves), *XHBYK*, 1957, no. 13, pp. 135–36; Zhang Xiangbo, "Gengduode Caiyong Guonei Zhizaode Jiqi" (Use Even More Machinery Built in China), *XHBYK*, 1957, no. 13, pp. 136–37; *RMRB* editorial, "Duo Jian Zhong Xiao Xing Qiye" (Build More Medium-size and Small Enterprises), in *XHBYK*, 1957, no. 16, pp. 188–89; Song Shaowen (vice-chairman of the SEC), "Jiben Jianshe Bixu Guanche Qinjian Jianguode Fangzhen" (Capital Construction Must Carry Out the Policy of Building the Country with Industry and Thrift), *Xuexi*, 1957, no. 11, pp. 22–24; Yi Lin, "Guanyu zai Gongye Jianshezhong Chongfen Fahui Touzi Xiaoguode Jige Wenti" (Several Problems in Fully Developing Investment Efficiency in Industrial Construction), *JHJJ*, 1957, no. 6 (June), pp. 5–7, 15; and Wu Liyong, "Fazhan Difang Liantie Gongye Shi Jiejue Shengtie Buzude Zhongyao Banfa Zhiyi" (Developing Local Iron-making Industries Is One of the Major Methods of Resolving the Shortage of Pig Iron), *JHJJ*, 1957, no. 6 (June), pp. 10–11.

71. Bo Yibo, "Working of the National Economic Plan for 1956 and Draft National Plan for 1957," *Current Background*, no. 465 (July 9, 1957), p. 10.

out requiring additional investment funds, likely to be taken from heavy industry. To hedge his bets, however, Bo advocated increased investment in chemical fertilizers. If the mobilization strategy did not work or was not adopted as policy, the state would be locked into a path of development relying on greatly increased inputs of heavy industrial products to boost agriculture. This "heavy industrial supply model" was in opposition to a market-oriented approach. A market strategy would require increased investment in light industry in order to supply consumer goods the state could sell to the peasants in exchange for their crops. The heavy industry approach was not incompatible with a mobilizational style, and if technical inputs were to flow to the countryside in large number (as they must), then investment in heavy industry must increase. In mid 1957, the leaders of the planning coalition convinced the general leadership of the wisdom of combining the mobilizational and heavy industrial approaches to increasing agricultural output.

Bo was forced to announce the further lowering – to 4.5 percent – of the targeted growth rate for the gross value of industrial output. Nonetheless, in "the 1957 plan for industrial production we continued to adhere to the principle of priority development of capital goods." In fact, 1957 was the first year when the value of heavy industrial output exceeded that of light industrial output. The 1957 plan evaded the investment priorities laid down in Mao's Ten Major Relationships in April 1956. Despite Bo's apparent concern for agriculture, state investment in agriculture was actually cut by 200 million yuan, or about 18 percent. Light industrial investment was also reduced because of agricultural shortages. While there was a certain amount of rationality in reducing light industrial expenditures, Bo's version of the 1957 plan marked a movement away from the sectoral balances put forward by Mao and endorsed by the financial coalition.

Within heavy industry itself, priorities were shifted. In 1956, 50 percent of all industrial investment went to coal, electric power, metallurgy, chemicals, and forestry.[72] In 1957, these five lines of production received 59.1 percent of all industrial investment. Investment cuts were made in the textile industry, food processing, and machine building. Bo asserted that "capital construction is a question of first-rate importance in our economic life and political life at the present stage."

Bo also noted that consumer purchasing power would increase by 1.8 percent in 1957, but consumer-goods production would go up only by 1.1 per-

---

72. In the 1950s, forestry and wood production were frequently treated as part of heavy industry. This was probably because lumber was a building material used in capital construction.

cent. This was in addition to the more than 1 billion yuan surplus in purchasing power carried over from the previous year. Despite this, Bo opposed expanding light industrial production. He apparently took a much more sanguine view of the gap between purchasing power and the supply of consumer goods than Chen Yun did.

Bo closed by reiterating all the points he had made with Li Fuchun in May 1957. Lower building standards; do more with less money; build more small and medium-size plants capable of entering production quickly; rely on China's own industrial base to supply the requirements for capital construction; give more play to the local areas to develop industry; and so on – this was China's new path to development.[73]

With this speech, the basic interests of the planners were repackaged in a form fully palatable to the central leadership and virtually immune to criticism by the budgeteers. This effort demonstrated a remarkable exercise of leadership by Li Fuchun and Bo Yibo. Facing political challenges to planning-coalition primacy and difficult objective economic conditions, which weakened the coalition's voice in policy deliberations, Li and Bo developed a program that repulsed the political challenges (in this they were serendipitously aided by the collapse of the Hundred Flowers) and promised to solve many of China's economic problems. They did this without any fundamental shift in the basic positions of the coalition. Heavy industry was protected from demands that more funds be devoted to light industry and agriculture. In fact, more funds would be allocated to heavy industry because technical inputs from heavy industry would become the engine of agricultural growth. True, there were some cutbacks in the machine-building industry, but these could be made up as the policy of industry aiding agriculture was refined. Planners and ministerial officials did not give up their control over large enterprises; they envisioned small and medium-size plants being built and run by the localities to meet local needs. In some ways, this further insulated modern heavy industry from the demands of the localities. (The rhetorical dimension of the planners' program should not be ignored. Plant and technology transfers from the Soviet Union increased during the Great Leap Forward, despite the rhetoric of self-reliance.)

Altogether, Li and Bo's program was a brilliant political achievement and a great victory for the planning coalition. Whether it was a good economic policy for China in 1957 is another matter. Nonetheless, by mid 1957, the emerging watchwords of China's economic strategy were self-reliance, industry aiding agriculture, more medium-size and small enterprises, and de-

73. Bo, "Working of the National Economic Plan."

centralization. Basic directions for the Great Leap Forward were now established.

In July, August, and September 1957, the planning coalition expanded on the themes of May–June, beginning with the National Planning Conference, convened from July 25 to August 22 to draft the control figures for the plan for 1958. On the first day of the conference, Bo Yibo conceded that in previous years the annual plans had often been drawn up late, a situation the State Planning and State Economic commissions resolved to change; this meeting in the summer of 1957 would make a good start on the 1958 plan. He emphasized the simultaneous development of industry and agriculture. Industries that provided technical inputs to agriculture, particularly chemical fertilizers, would receive increased investment. A second major area of attention was the raw-materials sector. Since production of raw materials was falling behind the needs of processing industries, increased output was required. Bo also made a detailed report (never published) on the targets for 1958.[74]

Even while the planning meeting was in session, Bo traveled to Tianjin to discuss the control figures with more than a thousand cadres in that city. Here again he stressed simultaneous development of industry and agriculture and increased output in the raw-materials industries. More medium-size and small industrial enterprises were top priorities. Administrative and military expenditures were cut further, and investment and construction standards for nonproductive construction were also reduced. In discussing the development of agriculture, Bo clearly implied that the peasants themselves would finance much of the water conservancy works and other measures required to raise yields. State investment would increase only in such areas as chemical fertilizers and a few very large water-control projects. He noted that because of the shortage of raw materials, light industrial investment would again be lowered in 1958. Light industrial investment would increase only when more agricultural raw materials were available.[75]

By the end of August, draft targets were agreed upon, and Jia Tuofu presented a summary of the planning conference. He noted that, "according to preliminary decisions," investment in 1958 would be slightly higher than in 1957. More investment would be allocated to agriculture, coal, and other raw material–producing industries. Investment in machine building and tex-

74. "Guojia Jihua Huiyi" (National Planning Meeting), *XHBYK*, 1957, no. 18, pp. 206–7.

75. "Bo Yibo xiang Tianjin Ganbu Baogao Bianzhi Yijiuwuba Nian Jihua Kongzhi Shuzi Wenti" (Bo Yibo Reports on Problems of Formulating the Control Figures for the 1958 Plan to Tianjin Cadres), *XHBYK*, 1957, no. 17, pp. 206–8.

tiles would be cut. Jia called on light industrial enterprises to increase production, but promised no new investments. Jia's summarization and the other materials discussing the content of the planning meeting reflect the near-total domination of the line of development put forward by Bo Yibo and Li Fuchun.[76] Perhaps the only area where the planning coalition was not wholly successful was in significantly raising investment totals. But that too would change in a few months.

Shortly after the planning conference, the SEC under Bo Yibo issued the first, and least noticed, of the decentralization decisions in the second half of 1957. It was that a somewhat different allocation method would be used in the coming year for goods subject to distribution by the State Council, the planning agencies, and the ministries themselves. The State Council departments in industry and communications would continue to requisition needed materials from the central government. However, ministries not engaged in production would apply to local governments for building and raw materials. Organizations under the Ministry of Commerce, the ministry itself, and the Ministry of Finance were explicitly included in this provision. This notice served a dual purpose for the planning coalition. It protected the central allocation system for industrial production and investment. The center would continue to see that heavy industrial output provided inputs to other capital goods projects. The regulation maintained heavy industry's separation from the rest of the economy. Second, it weakened the position of non–planning coalition ministries in requesting materials for capital construction. Local authorities were more likely to use whatever construction materials they could get to build local industry, not to build new warehouses for the commercial departments. It may also have stripped away some of the Ministry of Commerce's control over allocation.[77]

Throughout the summer and early fall, the planners' journal expanded on the views presented at the planning conference. In August, in addition to

76. "Guojia Jihua Huiyi" (n. 74); "National Planning Conference Closes," trans. in *Survey of China Mainland Press* (hereafter *SCMP*), no. 1602 (September 3, 1957), p. 18; "Jia Tuofu Summarizes Planning Conference," *SCMP*, no. 1607 (September 11, 1957), pp. 34–36; *RMRB* editorial, "Draw Up Well the Economic Plan for 1958" (September 7, 1957), in *SCMP*, no. 1612 (September 18, 1957), pp. 13–18; and editorial, "Bianhao 1958 Niandu Jihua Zhengque Jiejue Dangqian Guomin Jingjizhongde Zhuyao Maodun" (Draw Up the 1958 Annual Plan Well, Correctly Solve Current Major Contradictions in the National Economy), *JHJJ*, 1957, no. 9 (September), pp. 1–4.

77. See "Notification on the Drawing Up of the 1958 Commodity Supply Plans" and "Why Are Supply Plans for Certain Commodities Under Unified Distribution and Ministry Control to Be Placed in the Hands of Provincial and Municipal Governments?" *Shangye Gongye* (Commercial Industry), no. 37 (September 12, 1957), trans. in *ECMM*, no. 118 (February 10, 1958), pp. 32 and 44–46, respectively.

refuting the rightists' claims that the Party could not run a planned economy,[78] several of the main second-level figures in the planning apparatus
discussed relations between industry and agriculture. Liao Jili, a member of
the editorial board of *Jihua Jingji*, wrote an article entitled "The Only Way
to Accelerate the Development of Heavy Industry Is to Accelerate the Development of Agriculture" that was actually a defense of the position that the
way to increase agricultural development was to invest more money in heavy
industry, particularly fertilizer.[79] Wang Guangwei, vice-chairman of the State
Planning Commission, argued in several articles that there was a great deal
of labor in the countryside and that this was the advantage of China's large
population. Labor power should be organized on the basis of low investment, quick returns, and greater economic results to carry out rural capital
construction, open up waste land, and promote the development of multiple
cropping. Proper arrangement of China's rural population was the key to
developing agriculture.[80] The point of these articles was either to insulate
heavy industry from agricultural problems, by arguing like Wang that agriculture could really take care of itself with some mobilization, or to show
like Liao that accelerated heavy industrial development would solve agricultural problems. Many other articles echoed this view of the planning coalition.[81]

In September, Xue Muqiao presented ideas about how to reform the planning and management system in China. He claimed that his views drew on
Chen Yun's idea that large matters should be planned but details should be
free for production units to decide. Nonetheless, the actual suggestions that
Xue made on reforming the planning system were generally congruous with
the proposals in Li Fuchun's speech to the Eighth Party Congress – mandatory targets that had to be fulfilled; targets subject to adjustment, where
producers had a certain amount of latitude to change targets; and reference
targets, which were to inform but not control production. Xue, like Li, also
suggested that the center should manage only those items that were important throughout the country. Localities should have a greater role in plan-

78. Editorial, "Jitu Youpai Fenzi dui Jihua Jingji Zhidude Changwang Jingong" (Repulse the
Savage Attacks of Rightist Elements on the Planned Economic System), *JHJJ*, 1957, no. 8, pp.
1–3.
79. Liao Jili, "Jiakuai Nongyede Fazhan Cai Neng Jiakuai Zhong Gongyede Fazhan," *JHJJ*,
1957, no. 8, pp. 4–6.
80. Wang Guangwei, "Duiyu Anpai Nongye Laodonglide Yijian" (Opinions on Arranging
Agricultural Labor Power), *JHJJ*, 1957, no. 8 (August), pp. 6–9, and "Fazhan Nongyede Jige
Wenti" (Several Problems in Developing Agriculture), *Xuexi*, 1957, no. 17, pp. 25–28.
81. For example, Xiao Yu, "Nongye Touzi Ruhe Anpai" (How to Arrange Agricultural Investment), and Gu Wenshu, "Dui Wo Guo Dangqian Fanghong Jianshede Yijian" (Opinions on
Current Flood-Control Construction in Our Country), *JHJJ*, 1957, no. 9 (September), pp. 5–8
and 8–10, respectively.

ning items important to them, and production of many commodities should be controlled only indirectly through the state's price and tax policies. Xue, however, added a few points that might be seen as supportive of the financial coalition's position. He called for a larger role for the market. This was no minor statement in September 1957. The free market for agricultural commodities had effectively been closed down in August, and the market was increasingly seen as part and parcel of capitalism.[82]

It is hard to know what to make of Xue's proposals. Others have seen Xue as a spokesman for Chen Yun's views (reflecting their long working relationship),[83] but Xue was a vice-chairman of the State Planning Commission and chairman of the State Statistical Bureau and, as I suggested, personally close to Bo Yibo. Was Xue trying to strike some compromise between the budgeteers and the planners? Why was he willing to take the politically risky position of endorsing a wide role for the market? Whatever the reason for Xue's proposals (which were given rather insignificant treatment in *Jihua Jingji*), it is hard to show that they had much effect on the decentralization documents then under consideration.[84] While thought-provoking, Xue's article remains obscure in significance.

The drumbeat of publicity for the planning coalition continued. A number of articles explained that the simultaneous development of industry and agriculture meant both increased investment in heavy industry to supply more technical inputs to agriculture and mobilization of the peasants.[85] An essay on the chemical-fertilizer industry called for doubling the production target for this sector in proposals for the Second Five-Year Plan. Many of these articles suggested not just that the chemical fertilizer industry should be developed, but also that agricultural mechanization should receive more attention. In short, the planning coalition attempted to capture the agricul-

---

82. Xue Muqiao, "Dui Xianxing Jihua Guanli Zhidude Chubu Yijian" (Preliminary Opinions on the Current Planned Management System), *JHJJ*, 1957, no. 9 (September), pp. 20–24. In fact, it was not Chen Yun who first discussed planning large items and leaving it to local units to work out the details; it was Mao. See Schram, 1989, pp. 102–3.

83. See Chang, 1975, p. 55, and Schurmann, 1968, p. 197. For other analysis, see Harding, 1981, pp. 109–13.

84. Nina Halpern notes that because there are significant differences between Xue's ideas and the actual decentralization decrees, written by Chen Yun, "it is difficult to use this comparison even as an indicator of Xue Muqiao's influence" (much less Chen Yun's, if Xue was his stand-in). See Halpern, 1985, p. 124.

85. Editorial, "Fazhan Gongye Bixu he Fazhan Nongye Tongshi Bingju" (The Development of Industry Must Proceed Simultaneously with the Development of Agriculture); Ji Chongwei, "Gongye Yingdang Jiji Zhiyuan Nongyede Fazhan" (Industry Should Actively Aid the Development of Agriculture); Wang Xingfu and Lan Jianzhao, "Dali Fazhan Huaxue Feiliaode Gongye" (Greatly Develop the Chemical Fertilizer Industry); and Luo Wen and Shangguan Zhangyin, "Guanyu Fazhan Nongtian Guan'gai Wenti" (On Questions of Developing Farmland Irrigation), all in *JHJJ*, 1957, no. 10 (October), pp. 1–4, 7–10, 11–15, and 15–17, respectively.

tural issue as its own, so that the solutions proposed by the planners would preserve their control over economic resources.

Jihua Jingji was not the only place where articles expounding views of the planning coalition were published. After the National Planning Conference in July–August 1957, many of the individual components of the coalition held planning conferences. In August the Ministry of Metallurgical Industries announced a plan whereby it would begin to construct eighteen medium-size and small iron and steel mills in eighteen provinces. The combined output of these plants would be greater than that of one large mill. Moreover, they would cost considerably less, would go into production much faster, and would be geared to meeting local demands.[86] A National Chemical Planning Conference concluded that by the end of the Second Five-Year Plan China would be self-sufficient in all chemicals except rubber. A big push to develop chemical fertilizers was envisioned.[87] China's designers proclaimed that they could design almost every type of project to be included in the Second Five-Year Plan. Self-reliance was possible.[88] The machine-building ministries foresaw that by the end of 1962 they would be able to provide 80 percent of the machines and equipment required in the SFYP.[89] This exceeded the 70 percent self-sufficiency figure put forward by Zhou Enlai in the proposals for that plan. Plans were beginning to escalate, and this phenomenon would become almost infinitely worse in 1958.

Thus, by the middle of October 1957 the members of the planning coalition were vigorously pressing for the program first enunciated by Li Fuchun and Bo Yibo in May and June. They promised to do more, better, faster, and more economically. This was to be achieved by self-reliance, industry aiding agriculture, emphasis on medium- and small-scale industry, and decentralization. The planning coalition had seized control of the economic agenda.

D. Conclusion

The leaders of China's planning and heavy industry coalition, like the leaders of the financial coalition, developed an innovative program to fit the chal-

86. "Medium and Small Iron and Steel Plants to Be Built," *SCMP*, no. 1602 (September 3, 1957), p. 17.

87. "Chemical Planning Conference Closes," *SCMP*, no. 1616 (September 24, 1957), p. 18. See also Gao Jian, "China's Chemical Fertilizer Industry," *Da Gong Bao* (The Impartial Daily) October 9, 1957, in *SCMP*, no. 1642 (October 31, 1957), pp. 19–20.

88. "Chinese Designers Will Map Next Five Year Plan," *SCMP*, no. 1621 (October 1, 1957), pp. 2–3.

89. "China Makes Two-Thirds of Machinery Needs," *SCMP*, no. 1622 (October 22, 1957), pp. 2–3.

lenging economic and political environment they faced from October 1956 through October 1957. The planning coalition was on the political defensive during roughly the first half of this period. As the costs and defects of the small leap forward of late 1955 and early 1956 became increasingly obvious, it was clear that some economic readjustment was necessary. The budgeteers used that opportunity to push their reforms.

The planning coalition had to respond to this challenge if it wanted to preserve its integrity, core values, and political and economic power. Beginning in March, and accelerating rapidly thereafter, it altered a number of the elements of its key programs without fundamentally transforming them. It shifted, rhetorically at least, from a strategy that relied on imports of technology from the Soviet Union, large modern factories as the centerpiece of industrialization, centralized planning and management, and insulation from the rest of the economy to one that emphasized self-reliance, medium-size and small factories, some decentralization, and industry aiding agriculture. Almost every one of these new strains in its program actually required increased inputs for the heavy industrial departments. Decentralization, at least as envisioned by the planners, was supposed to keep heavy industry insulated from demands by other sectors. Only nonpriority fields were to be handed over to lower levels. Instead of heeding the calls of Mao and many other Chinese leaders for increased investment in light industry and agriculture and marginally reduced funds for heavy industry, the planning coalition quietly, and effectively, increased its share of investment.

The coalition presented China's leaders with the possibility of rapid development despite problems in the agricultural sector. The revised program of the planning coalition called for more, faster, and cheaper production – as it said, "To do more with less is possible." For a party and leadership reeling from criticisms articulated during the Hundred Flowers, rapid growth was a political necessity. Moreover, the planners thought they were providing an answer to agricultural problems through the introduction of heavy industrial inputs to the countryside coupled with rural mobilization.

Many of these policies may have been the product of wishful thinking; nonetheless, they were politically and economically compelling. A market-oriented, more balanced strategy of growth had apparently been tried by the financial coalition and found wanting. Giving more play to China's intellectuals to stimulate growth had only ended with the intellectuals criticizing the Party – they were seen to be unreliable. What other choice did Chinese leaders have but to adopt the planning coalition's program as their own? What other program could speak to the leadership's and the Party's political and economic concerns? Only the planning coalition under the brilliant leadership of the peripatetic Li Fuchun and Bo Yibo could respond to the crisis of 1957, thereby setting the economic agenda for the Great Leap Forward while at the same time preserving and furthering the interests of the coalition.

6

The Party as agent of social transformation

In contrast to the coalitions examined in the two preceding chapters, the Chinese Communist Party (CCP), as the agent of social transformation, is not predominantly concerned with economic issues. The function of social transformation is to restructure and reform society and social relations. In most revolutionary societies in the twentieth century, and certainly in China, the Communist Party is the special institution of social transformation. The Communist Party, once it seizes power, also provides overall leadership in the political system and mediates the relationships among the other intra-state coalitions. The Communist Party, then, is both above the other coalitions (this is particularly true of the central leadership) and the embodiment of one particular coalition. In its capacity as the organization charged with social transformation, the Communist Party is different from other ruling parties in one-party states. In Benjamin Schwartz's elegant characterization,

the mystique of the Communist Party lies not in its organizational structure but in its transcendent status as the incarnation of the will of History and in its universal, messianistic, "proletarian" mission. From this stems its claim of infallibility and utter disinterestedness. It was this that provided the sanction for totalitarian intervention in every corner of life.[1]

After completion of the "Socialist Transformation of Capitalist Industry, Handicrafts and Commerce" and the collectivization of agriculture, the CCP had apparently completed its mission. Following the Soviet model, there was nothing left to be transformed – China had arrived at socialism (state ownership). Although many processes (industrialization, urbanization, expanding education, etc.) required continued management and supervision, undertaking these tasks was not the same as revolutionary social transformative leadership. Party leaders would later argue that although the "relations of production" had been transformed, the "superstructure," particu-

1. Schwartz, 1970, pp. 25–26. Schwartz's views are a criticism of Huntington's (1968, pp. 334–43 and passim) and others' views about Leninist political parties.

larly in the realm of the Chinese people's worldview, had not been fully remolded. This view would have increasingly ominous and deleterious effects in China, but the Eighth Party Congress in September 1956 specifically rejected the idea that the "superstructure" was backward. On the contrary, the CCP asserted that the "productive forces" were lagging behind the "superstructure." The Party was thus faced in late 1956 with a profound question of which it was only partially aware: What was the role of the Party now that China was a socialist society? Party leaders could address such a major issue only indirectly at the Eighth Party Congress.

The Party itself was a conglomeration of people in diverse roles, ranging from provincial party secretaries to rural activists to propagandists and ideologists. These various roles imposed different demands on, and helped to instill divergent perspectives among, Party members. Nonetheless, all had an underlying commitment to social transformation and, by 1956, the maintenance of Party rule. Moreover, the membership of this coalition included more than the formal membership of the CCP: It took in many youth-league members and activists in Chinese society who aspired to CCP membership.

This chapter provides a brief overview of the Party as the agent of social transformation. The Party explored various paths to redefine its mission after the formal establishment of socialism in China; these had little to do with the kinds of questions in which the financial and planning coalitions were involved. The chapter also includes a short appendix discussing the views and positions of the Chinese military and the Ministry of Public Security. They are brought in here because, like the CCP's, their views were not well articulated during 1956–1957.

A. The Party as a system

How the CCP grew from a tiny group of intellectuals in 1921 to a mammoth mass organization of westernized and native intellectuals, peasants, soldiers, patriotic youth, and a smattering of workers in 1949 is a remarkable saga.[2] All the experiences of the CCP on its path to power were in some ways formative, but scholars agree that the Yanan period of the late 1930s and early 1940s was the most decisive. It was then that the CCP systematized and codified its basic approach to organizational affairs, its ideology, and its views on Party-populace relations.[3]

2. There is a vast literature on the CCP and its experiences on the path to power. Particularly useful are Ladany, 1988; Chen Yung-fa, 1986; and Harrison, 1972.
3. On the Yanan period (in addition to the sources in n. 2), see Compton, 1966; Reardon-Anderson, 1980; Schran, 1976; Johnson, 1962; Selden, 1971; Womack, 1987; and Wylie, 1980.

One principal lesson the CCP learned during its struggle to power, and in particular during the Yanan period, concerned how to develop Marxism in China. The Stalinist phrase "there is no fortress that socialism cannot storm" aptly captured the experience of the CCP. The Party's history argued persuasively for a voluntaristic interpretation of Marxism-Leninism, namely Mao Zedong Thought, in which political expertise and commitment were more important than technical knowledge. By putting politics in command, a dedicated and determined CCP, apparently unconstrained by objective laws, successfully overcame long odds to win power. Closely allied to this voluntaristic aspect of Chinese Marxism was the idea that ideological and collective incentives should outweigh remunerative and individual incentives.

With the Party occupying precarious and isolated geographical bases during the Yanan period, CCP survival demanded the development of mechanisms and programs to ensure popular, particularly peasant, support. To meet this need, the CCP developed the "mass line" style of close Party-mass relations, which required thorough Party penetration of society. In the context of civil war and invasion, the CCP not only had to penetrate society and promote good relations with the populace, it needed to mobilize the people to support its aims. While the specific policies the CCP used during this time are not crucial here, it is important to note that it developed the mechanism of the mobilizational campaign to channel the aroused energies of the populace to support Party objectives. Campaigns were profoundly antithetical to the style of policy implementation associated with Weberian bureaucracies.[4]

Additional aspects of the CCP experience that related to voluntarism, the mass line, and campaigns were self-reliance and egalitarianism. The CCP's bases were economically backward, often sparsely populated areas whose economies could not sustain large, bureaucratic administrations. Moreover, the CCP received very little outside aid in its wars. Thus, the Party was forced to rely on the resources available locally and those it could develop. Military units and administrative organs planted fields, set up factories to supply materials, and attempted to be as self-sufficient as possible. Local areas were encouraged to maximize self-sufficiency and to employ all available resources. The poverty of these areas enforced a regime of relative egalitarianism on CCP members.[5] First, there were simply too few goods to

---

4. On the Maoist conception of bureaucracy and how it should work, see Whyte, 1973 and 1974.

5. The relative nature of this egalitarianism must be stressed. A number of Party intellectuals were disillusioned by the inequalities they found in Yanan. See Merle Goldman, 1971, ch. 2.

allow some to receive tremendously more than others. Second, CCP leaders were well aware of how destructive the appearance of special privileges and a soft life for the leadership would be to the morale of ordinary CCP cadres and the peasants.

Thus, as with all good political programs, the tenets of the "Yanan way" were interrelated. Voluntarism provided a theoretical underpinning for self-reliance, and successes in self-reliant development further proved the correctness of voluntarism. The mass line and campaigns also reinforced egalitarianism. It is impossible for cadres to lead campaigns and make the mass line work if there was too great a social distance between masses and officials. In short, the CCP developed a simple, yet comprehensive program during the Yanan period that was both extremely effective in terms of Party survival and growth and compelling to the membership.[6]

The top CCP leadership and many cadres who staffed the higher levels of the Chinese bureaucracy in the 1950s had been recruited before or during the period when these beliefs were most forcefully expressed. Many had in fact helped to formulate and solidify the commitment to voluntarism, the mass line, and self-reliance. For many leaders, then, this "Yanan syndrome"[7] of values formed the basis of their greatest triumphs. In later years, these values came to embody the "good old days" for many, and the influence of the Yanan syndrome persisted throughout the Maoist era. In part, this was because this pattern of values was Party doctrine at the time when upper-echelon cadres were first recruited into the CCP and began to climb the ladder of power and prestige. Probably more important, however, was Mao's continuing commitment to these ideas.

Although these values represented the dominant Yanan syndrome, this does not mean that no other patterns of Party activity influenced Party doctrine.[8] Moreover, all Party leaders recognized in 1949 that the patterns of rule and beliefs that had served the CCP so well in the struggle for power might not be particularly well suited to the tasks of national integration and economic construction. In Mao Zedong's words, "We shall soon put aside

6. This grossly oversimplifies a complex situation. The various base areas had different experiences and learned different lessons about how to carry out the struggle against the Japanese and the Kuomintang. Regular army units behaved differently than guerrilla forces did; underground forces in Japanese-occupied areas had little in common with Yanan; and the CCP's diplomatic outpost in Chongqing under Zhou Enlai faced yet another set of unique circumstances. All of these (and other) experiences are part of the CCP's legacy. Nonetheless, voluntarism, self-reliance, egalitarianism, the mass line, and campaigns became the key organizing myths for Party development.

7. The phrase is Peter Schran's. See Schran, 1975.

8. For a discussion, see Lewis, 1968.

some of the things we know well and be compelled to do things we don't know well."[9]

With the assumption of power, the CCP was forced to expand dramatically. The Party grew from about 4.5 million in 1949 to more than 10.7 million in 1956.[10] Along with the Party's size, the social background of its membership changed as well. Before 1949 the Party was overwhelmingly composed of peasants and a few intellectuals. By 1956 almost 70 percent of its members were peasants. Intellectuals accounted for 11.7 percent, and members with a worker background made up 14 percent.[11] With the transformation of the Party from an organization fighting to seize power to one responsible for governing society, the Party and the state needed many people with skills quite different from those possessed by most revolutionary cadres. Many intellectuals and workers were inducted into the Party very quickly, sometimes with suspect political credentials. In a saying reflective of the cleavages in the Party caused by fundamental changes in recruitment patterns, some cadres argued, "Old revolutionaries aren't treated as well as new ones, new revolutionaries aren't treated as well as non-revolutionaries, and non-revolutionaries aren't treated as well as counter-revolutionaries."[12]

The revolutionary vitality of the CCP also began to dissipate after it assumed power. The great mobilization campaigns of the early 1950s[13] undoubtedly helped to sustain revolutionary élan. But after the successful completion for socialist transformation, there were indications that the CCP was succumbing to the pressures of routinization and completion of its basic mission. The time appeared to be at hand for it to move on to another stage of development.[14] Loss of fervor, creeping bureaucratism, and complacency were becoming widespread problems in Party and state organs.[15]

9. Mao, 1969a, p. 422.
10. Lewis, 1963, p. 110, and Martin, 1981, p. 13.
11. The background of 5.2 percent of the membership is described as "other." See Lewis, 1963, p. 108, and Martin, 1981, p. 39.
12. *Xuexi* (Study), 1951, no. 1, cited in Vogel, 1967, p. 39.
13. These were identified by Zhou Enlai as land reform; resist America, aid Korea (the Korean War); the suppression of counterrevolutionaries; the Three-Anti, Five-Anti Campaign; and ideological remolding. To these the collectivization of agriculture and the socialist transformation of capitalist industry, commerce, and handicrafts should be added. See Zhou Enlai, "Report on the Work of the Government" (June 26, 1957), in *Communist China, 1955–1959*, 1971, pp. 300–329; see p. 302.
14. Discussions of stages of development of a socialist or authoritarian regime are found in Huntington, 1970; Jowitt, 1977; and Lowenthal, 1970.
15. These phenomena are acutely captured in Wang Meng's short story "A Young Man Arrives at the Organization Department." He describes how an idealistic young Party member coming to the local Party Organization Department expects the Party to be the true vanguard of the people. Yet everywhere he turns he encounters apathy, laziness, and people merely

By the time of the Eighth Party Congress the general tendency of the CCP was an amalgam of diverse strands. Certainly many of the elements of the Yanan syndrome were still present, but the environment was so different that many of these values were seen as old-fashioned and inappropriate. The general tendency of the Party also incorporated aspects of a more Leninist version of what a Communist Party should be. This was, first, because of the more normal and stable situation in which the CCP found itself after coming to power. It was no longer dispersed and fighting for survival; the center really did have the potential to oversee affairs in all areas. Second, the Chinese were copying the Soviet model extensively in the early to mid 1950s. The Chinese view of the role of the Party was heavily influenced by Soviet theory (if not by practice under Stalin). Finally, the prerequisites of the Soviet model of economic development influenced the Party's conception of its role vis-à-vis society.

These different sources of the Party's core positions combined to form the views presented in Table 2 (Chapter 3). The Party was committed to change China in a short period of time from a backward agricultural nation to one with an advanced industrial base. The CCP fully endorsed a high rate of accumulation and a great deal of investment in heavy industry. With its long history of close relations with the peasantry, however, it was more concerned about conditions in the countryside than the planning and heavy industry coalition was. This concern of the Party was reflected in its willingness to devote more attention and resources to the rural areas than the planners did. Even though the CCP was determined to follow the Soviet pattern of development, the Party's experience made it hard for it to accept the notion that the success of China's developmental efforts would be determined by objective laws. The spirit of voluntarism remained central to its view of the world. Following Marx and a traditional Chinese disdain for merchants, the CCP was opposed to the operation of free markets and favored state control of commerce.[16] Marxism also gave rise to a distrust of forms of ownership of industry other than state ownership, and to a preference for rural collective ownership over private farming. Though the CCP was willing to spend more on the rural areas, central investment was not the key element for the development of China's agriculture. Mass mobilization, based on perceived rural class cleavages, was the real motor of rural change. The CCP believed that the elimination of the "irrational" aspects of individ-

going through the motions. The atmosphere of despair is so omnipresent that by the time the story ends the young man is in danger of losing his ideals (Wang Meng, 1981; originally published in 1956).

16. The Marxist and Chinese disdain for commerce is brought out nicely in Solinger, 1983, esp. pp. 195–203.

ual farming, the economies of scale introduced by larger units of production, and the growth of collective consciousness would all contribute to the expansion of agricultural output.[17] The Party favored ideological incentives as positive inducements, and coercion, particularly aimed at those who ideology predicted would oppose socialism. Finally, the CCP favored hiring the politically loyal in preference to bureaucratic or technical experts. The Party did not disdain expertise, but political criteria remained the most important factor in personnel management.

Although these positions constitute the general tendency associated with the Party as agent of transformation, many individual positions were confronted with opposing viewpoints or were called into question by the apparent completion of socialist transformation. Significant tension existed between the view that no laws bound the CCP and the idea that economic planning and a planned economy were run by set rules and procedures. Belief in the efficacy of mass mobilization for transforming society was challenged by the fact that, according to CCP ideology, all objects of transformation had been completed by 1956. Finally, some in the Party argued that economic or technical expertise should be as important as political virtue. Without qualified leadership in the increasingly complex processes under CCP jurisdiction, the rate of advance would slow.

Thus, on the eve of the Eighth Party Congress, the Chinese Communist Party, as the principal agent of social transformation, was confronted with many serious problems. The Party's general tendency and the tasks it faced were increasingly disconnected. As a result, debates surfaced about how to modify the core values and policies of the Party to suit the changed environment. Indiscipline, loss of morale, and apathy were growing. Finally, the Party faced the questions of what its role should be and of how it could maintain its revolutionary purity now that social transformation was apparently over.

B. The Party at the Eighth Party Congress

At the Eighth Party Congress, three groups of speakers addressed Party questions. These groups were the provincial Party secretaries (or their equivalents for centrally administered cities and autonomous regions), leaders of the specialized departments under the Central Committee, and several senior Party leaders and Party elder statesmen without specific functional tasks. I shall discuss each group briefly.

17. On linking class struggle with mass mobilization and with larger rural production units, see Shue, 1980.

Twenty-two first Party secretaries of the then twenty-eight provincial-level units[18] addressed the Congress. With one exception, provincial-level units whose first secretaries did not speak were represented by other provincial secretaries.[19] The speeches of the provincial secretaries were wide-ranging and diverse. Apart from having to present information about their provinces, these officials seem to have had a fairly free hand in choosing topics to emphasize.

Five major themes emerged from the speeches (a speech may show more than one theme): (1) radical or original policy perspectives, (2) discussions centering on minority affairs, (3) calls for greater decentralization and increased investment in the provinces, (4) demands for a thoroughgoing rectification of the agricultural collectives, and (5) stress on Party leadership.[20]

In the first category, radical or original approaches, Zeng Xisheng of Anhui stood for the radical position, and Tao Lujia of Shanxi presented an innovative program for provincial development. Zeng's address was by far the most optimistic and forward-looking speech at the Congress.[21] He paid lip service to problems in policy implementation but extensively praised Party policies and Mao's leadership. Zeng's radicalism was demonstrated by his implicit calls for thought-reform campaigns in the countryside to eliminate the habits of traditional peasant cultivation (other secretaries endorsed traditional cultivation methods), by his defense of collectives larger than standard size;[22] and by his continued commitment to targets contained in the National Agricultural Program (the Forty Points on Agriculture). Zeng was, in fact, the only provincial Party first secretary who suggested that this document was still operative. In short, Zeng's speech marked a continued belief in the efficacy of the style of policy implementation associated with the "so-

18. Ningxia did not become an independent autonomous region until 1958.

19. The one exception is noteworthy, but it is difficult to determine what the absence of a provincial-level speaker from Liaoning meant. Liaoning was China's heavy industrial base in 1956 and was one of the handful of most important provinces. Because of this, it is odd that the only speaker from Liaoning was a model worker from Dalian. Another conspicuous absentee was Peng Zhen, the first secretary and mayor of Beijing. Indeed, Peng was the only nonmilitary full member of the Politburo who did not address the congress.

20. Other discussions of the speeches by provincial figures at the Eighth Party Congress are found in Goodman, 1984; Teiwes, 1971, esp. pp. 135–39; MacFarquhar, 1974, pp. 126–33; and Chang, 1975, passim.

21. Zeng Xisheng, "Wei Zhifu Ziran Zaihai Jianshe Zuguo er Fendou" (Struggle to Control Natural Disasters and Build the Motherland), *Xinhua Banyuekan* (New China Semimonthly; hereafter *XHBYK*), 1956, no. 20, pp. 60–62.

22. Zeng was speaking about water conservancy and was implicitly arguing that larger collectives with more labor power were needed to carry out the work. On the size of collectives and functional requirements for labor and other factors of production, see Oksenberg, 1969, esp. chs. 8, 10, 13–14. See also Jane Lieberthal, 1971.

cialist high tide," especially a willingness to employ mass campaigns to achieve desired ends.

Tao Lujia's speech was one of the most fascinating addresses delivered to the Eighth Party Congress.[23] Tao, who was not elected to the Central Committee until 1958, and then only as an alternate member, presented various ways to deal with the relationship between industry and agriculture in Shanxi. He noted that in principle many Party members recognized the need to develop industry and agriculture but that in reality most treated agriculture and industry as entirely different spheres of activity. He presented a plan to alter this situation.

Tao conceded that large-scale mechanization of agriculture was impossible until China's basic industries had developed to a much greater extent. This did not mean that interim steps could not be taken to transform agriculture technically. He noted that Shanxi had just drawn up a seven-year plan to guide the development of provincial industry (involving eighty-eight plants in all, including fertilizer plants and small steel mills) that would serve agriculture.

Tao also noted that light industry, especially agricultural processing industries, had been systematically ignored. He called for a tripling of 1955 light industrial output by 1962. In this way, industry would be developed, and peasants would have greater access to consumer goods and also higher incomes from their work in processing. He also argued that provinces should strive for basic self-sufficiency in the supply of consumer goods. Coastal areas should concentrate on high-quality goods needed throughout the nation. Provinces should satisfy the common needs of their populations.

Tao, like Chen Yun, felt that the commercial system was too restrictive, and he outlined a reform in commerce that had been under way in Taigu *xian* (county) since June 1956. There free markets under state supervision, state-owned commercial organs under county leadership, and a profit-retention system for the local organs were all part of the "Taigu experience," which received national attention in late 1956 and early 1957.

This summary makes clear that Tao was arguing for a substantial increase in provincial power. It is the programmatic nature of Tao's ideas, however, that distinguishes his speech from those of other leaders advocating increased provincial power. Nor was any other provincial leader as outspoken as Tao in pushing for local industry in order to promote agricultural produc-

23. Tao Lujia, "Zhengque Chuli Gongnongye Guanxi, Zujin Gongnongye Gongtong Gaozhang" (Correctly Handle the Relationship Between Industry and Agriculture, Promote a Joint Upsurge in Industry and Agriculture), *XHBYK*, 1956, no. 21, pp. 189–91.

tion. His emphasis on light, rather than heavy, industry was also unique. While parts of his program seem somewhat contradictory (for instance, the combined emphasis on the free market and provincial self-sufficiency in the supply of consumer goods), his speech suggests the emergence of new ideas about how to develop industry and agriculture. His program highlighted many policies that would receive widespread attention in the Great Leap Forward. Yet, given Tao's relatively low rank, it remains far from clear how much influence he had on the course of the policy debate from late 1956 until 1958.

The other topics discussed by provincial Party secretaries were less innovative and provocative. Nonetheless, they provide many insights into such issues as the nature of center-provincial relations, the process of collectivization in various provinces, and problems with local cadres. Because of their unsystematic character, and because of lack of space, I shall treat these speeches only briefly.

Many provincial leaders wanted the center to provide their provinces with more resources or give them greater control over decisions and finance at the provincial level. For example, Wang Enmao of Xinjiang told the Party center "not to be afraid" of investing more in Xinjiang. Li Jingquan of Sichuan called for the institution of a profit-retention system so that provinces could respond to local needs with their own monies. Zhang Zhongliang of Gansu felt there was a lack of central concern about developments in his province. And Liu Shunyuan of Jiangsu complained that in the first three years of the First Five-Year Plan (FFYP) the state allocated 38 million yuan to Jiangsu to invest in local industry – only 4.78 percent of the profits and taxes Jiangsu had remitted to the center.[24] Leaders from Beijing, Fujian, Guangdong, Jiangxi, Inner Mongolia, and other areas echoed these concerns.[25]

24. Wang Enmao, "Wei Xinjiang Weiwuer Zizhiqu Gezu Renmin he Quanguo Gezu Renmin Gongtong Guodudao Shehuizhuyi er Fendou" (Struggle So That the People of All Nationalities in the Xinjiang Uighur Autonomous Region and the People of All Nationalities Throughout China Can Together Make the Transition to Socialism), *XHBYK*, 1956, no. 21, pp. 150–51; Li Jingquan, "Buduan Gaijin Guojia he Nongminde Guanxi" (Continuously Improve Relations Between the State and the Peasantry), *XHBYK*, 1956, no. 20, pp. 52–54; Zhang Zhongliang, "Chongfen Liyong Shuili Ziyuan Fazhan Nongye Shengchan" (Thoroughly Utilize Water Conservancy Resources to Develop Agricultural Production), *XHBYK*, 1956, no. 21, pp. 162–64; Liu Shunyuan, "Chongfen Fahui Jiangsu Sheng Gongye he Ziyuande Qianli" (Fully Develop the Industrial and Resource Potential of Jiangsu Province), *XHBYK*, 1956, no. 21, pp. 137–38.

25. For Beijing, see Liu Ren in *XHBYK*, 1956, no. 21, pp. 55–57; for Fujian, Ye Fei, *XHBYK*, 1956, no. 21, pp. 201–3; for Guangdong, Tao Zhu, *XHBYK*, 1956, no. 21, pp. 68–70; for Jiangxi, Yang Shangkui, *XHBYK*, 1956, no. 21, pp. 198–99; and for Inner Mongolia, Kui Bi, *XHBYK*, 1956, no. 21, pp. 156–58.

Roderick MacFarquhar has neatly summarized the speeches given by provincial Party secretaries:

Reading the speeches of the provincial secretaries at the Congress one has an impression of impatience at the inability of the central authorities rapidly to satisfy local demands. Of course this is not a phenomenon peculiar to China, or even to developing nations where the acute shortages of national resources make allocation problems particularly severe. In a country as vast as China, all such problems would be compounded by the size of the bureaucracy and the slowness of its operations. [26]

Clearly, there were major tensions between the provinces and the center.

Another large group of provincial Party leaders focused on the question of Party rectification, especially in the rural areas. Many problems with the collectivization drive were revealed; a number of Party leaders felt that only a thorough housecleaning could turn the collectives into viable and stable units of production. Leaders from Guangdong, Hebei, Henan, Hunan, Jiangsu, Shaanxi, and Zhejiang all emphasized rural rectification and consolidation. In the area of rectification, one Shanghai leader favored supervision and criticism of the Party by the democratic parties in Shanghai. [27]

Finally, some provincial officials chose to emphasize the positive aspects of Party leadership. In contrast to those who discussed the negative (such as those who spoke on the need for rectification), this group argued that errors had developed because the Party had not done *enough*, and that the Party had failed to accept its appropriate share of the mantle of leadership. [28] Others merely described how important the Party had been in the past and implied that there was no reason why this should change. [29] While several of these speakers did not deny that the Party had problems, they did argue or hint that no other system could replace Party leadership.

A loose consensus seems to have marked the speeches of provincial leaders on the need for rural rectification and decentralization or more invest-

26. MacFarquhar, 1974, p. 133.
27. For Guangdong, see Tao Zhu in *XHBYK*, 1956, no. 21, pp. 68–70; for Hebei, Lin Tie, *XHBYK*, 1956, no. 20, pp. 64–66; for Henan, Wu Zhipu, *XHBYK*, 1956, no. 21, pp. 216–18; for Hunan, Zhou Xiaozhou, *XHBYK*, 1956, no. 21, pp. 174–76; for Jiangsu, Liu Shunyuan, *XHBYK*, 1956, no. 21, pp. 137–38; for Shaanxi, Zhang Desheng, *XHBYK*, 1956, no. 21, pp. 52–54; for Zhejiang, Jiang Hua, *XHBYK*, 1956, no. 21, pp. 102–4; and for Shanghai, Liu Shuzhou, *XHBYK*, 1956, no. 21, pp. 169–70. There were eight minor, or democratic, parties in China. They existed before the Communist takeover in 1949, and the CCP allowed them to continue to exist to serve united-front functions. They had no real role in government and did not compete with the CCP for power. For background, see Seymour, 1987.
28. See the speeches of Ouyang Qin (Heilongjiang), *XHBYK*, 1956, no. 20, pp. 85–87; Wang Renzhong (Hubei), *XHBYK*, no. 20, pp. 54–56; Tan Qilong (Shandong), *XHBYK*, 1956, no. 21, p. 183; and Chen Pixian (Shanghai), *XHBYK*, 1956, no. 21, pp. 169–70.
29. See "Speech by Comrade Ko Ching-shih [Ke Qingshi, Shanghai]," in *Eighth National Congress of the Communist Party of China, vol. 2: Speeches* (hereafter *8PC/S*), 1956, pp. 135–46, and the speech of Tianjin's Huang Huoqing, *XHBYK*, 1956, no. 21, pp. 192–94.

ment in the provinces. As the Great Leap Forward would reveal, when given the chance these leaders pushed decentralization to the maximum and attempted to build up the heavy industrial base of their provinces.[30] This consensus spoke to some of the concerns of the Party as agent of social transformation. Giving provinces more power over local affairs and rectifying the Party in the rural areas would strengthen the capabilities of local organs. Those leaders who spoke on the primacy of Party leadership would certainly not oppose policies designed to strengthen the "militant spirit and fighting abilities" of local Party organizations. Yet provincial Party secretaries presented no new ideas about exactly what this increase in capacity might be used for or what goals it might serve. Certainly the Party would be able to supervise and manage production tasks better after rectification. But there was no discussion of what role the Party should now play in the transformative sense. As with the Party center, in September 1956 provincial leaders could not present a vision of the role of or provide a clear mission for the Party.

Provincial leaders were important actors in the political system, but it is not at all clear how their influence was felt in political debates in 1956–1957. They did not share opinions about China's developmental course.[31] Moreover, all the currently available documentation on meetings between provincial leaders and central leaders from late 1956 to late 1957 suggests that central leaders were informing provincial figures of what to do; the speeches of the central leaders do not reflect provincial interests strongly, if at all.[32] To be sure, provincial leaders informed central leaders of their concerns, particularly during the latter's inspection trips, but the role of provincial leaders in national politics in this period remains enigmatic.

CCP functionaries who spoke at the Eighth Party Congress saw that Party leadership had been weakened. For Song Renqiong, deputy secretary-general of the Central Committee, the failure of inner Party democracy to take root caused errors and hurt the Party's fighting strength.[33] For Liu Lantao,

30. See Vogel, 1971, ch. 6; Goodman, 1986; and *Zhongguo Gongye Jingji Tongji Ziliao*, 1985, p. 19. David Lampton suggested to me that coastal provincial secretaries favored decentralization and light industrial development, and interior provincial secretaries favored heavy industry. I agree that coastal provinces desired decentralization in the 1950s, but not that they desired light industry. Light industry lacked raw materials and had few export markets. Coastal provinces desired heavy industrial development.

31. See esp. Goodman, 1984.

32. The major meetings were the Second Plenum of the Eighth Central Committee in November 1956, the Meeting of Provincial Party Secretaries in January 1957, various discussions with Mao during his tour of the provinces in March and April, the NPC session in June, and Mao's Qingdao meeting with provincial leaders in July. See Mao, 1977, pp. 332–83 and 473–82; MacFarquhar, Cheek, and Wu, 1989, pp. 275–362.

33. "Speech by Comrade Sung Jen-chiung [Song Renqiong]," *8PC/S*, pp. 147–56.

deputy secretary of the Central Control Commission, the increasing violation of Party discipline was the result of subjectivism and the breakdown of inner Party study procedures.[34] For Li Xuefeng, head of the CCP's Industrial and Communications Work Department, Party leadership was weakened by one-man management and implicitly by the strengthening of "administration" at the expense of politics.[35] Each proposed remedies that aimed to restore the Party to its former glory. Yet none of these leaders confronted the fact that the Party in the past had been a weapon in a revolutionary struggle. In a dialectical sense, the Party's identity and existence were inextricably linked with its opposite: the bourgeoisie and its political party, the Kuomintang. By 1956 the bourgeoisie had been dispossessed in China, and the KMT was in exile in Taiwan. In winning the civil war and seizing power, the CCP had created the conditions for its own transformation. Even if Party leaders took this dialectical view of the Party to heart, they still had no idea what the next stage in the development of the CCP would be.

Senior Party leaders and Party generalists all took up the theme of rectification in their speeches – generally brief – to the Eighth Party Congress. Concern with the Party's work style was highlighted by many leaders.[36] Lin Boqu, Party elder and Politburo member, called for the integration of Marxism-Leninism with China's actual conditions, and warned that without such integration, subjectivism might again develop in the Party. This could cause "serious reverses" in the "socialist revolution."[37] Zhu De, a member of the Politburo Standing Committee, argued that correct Party leadership would determine whether China became a powerful socialist country. He felt that the key to correct Party leadership was absorbing lessons from past mistakes and " adopting methods used in the rectification campaigns."[38] The need for thought reform and rectification was the theme of Li Lisan's address, based on his experience as errant leader of the Party from 1928 to 1931. The obvious lessons Li drew were that Party rectification and study must be ongoing and deeply rooted processes, or the Party (or at least some of its members) would continue to err.[39]

Finally, in his brief opening address to the congress, Mao Zedong warned:

34. Liu Lantao, "Zhengque Zhixing Dangde Jilu, Jiaqiang Dangde Jiancha Gongzuo" (Correctly Uphold Party Discipline, Strengthen Party Inspection Work), *XHBYK*, 1956, no. 21, pp. 171–74.

35. "Speech by Comrade Li Hsueh-feng [Li Xuefeng]," *8PC/S*, pp. 304–17.

36. For example, "Speech by Comrade Tsai Chang [Cai Chang]," *8PC/S*, pp. 279–87, and "Speech by Comrade Teng Ying-chao [Deng Yingchao]," *8PC/S*, pp. 225–35. These reports focused on ties between women and the CCP but also discussed the general issue of work style.

37. "Speech by Comrade Lin Bo-chu [Lin Boqu]," *8PC/S*, pp. 199–205.

38. "Speech by Comrade Chu Teh [Zhu De]," *8PC/S*, pp. 5–16; quotation, p. 13.

39. "Speech by Comrade Li Lisan," *8PC/S*, pp. 248–58.

"But we still have serious shortcomings. Among many of our comrades there are still standpoints and styles of work which are contrary to Marxism-Leninism, namely subjectivism in their way of thinking, bureaucracy in their way of work, and sectarianism in organizational questions."[40] Mao suggested the need for more ideological study within the Party and a possible move toward allowing non–Party members to criticize the CCP. But the most significant aspect of Mao's speech was its vagueness. He recognized the Party's organizational problems but proposed no real solutions. With regard to the larger questions of the Party's role in a socialist society, he was even less forthcoming.[41]

Various types of Party leaders (provincial leaders, central Party functionaries, and central leaders) presented a wide variety of views to the Party congress. The last two groups in particular, and a sizable number of the provincial speakers, endorsed improving Party procedures and performance, largely through intensified inner-Party study and rectification. But there was no clear consensus on the principal defects of the Party and the methods to be used to eradicate them. In a sense, these subjects symbolized the malaise of the Party as agent of transformation. The Party faced a fundamental, if little perceived, dilemma in 1956. The tasks it had been created for had been completed, and its new role was unclear. Most of its personnel were capable of functioning adequately only under conditions of revolutionary change, yet the slate of items making up revolutionary transformation had been wiped clean. The Party needed to redefine its role, but such a redefinition meant jettisoning many of those cadres who had brought it success. Needless to say, those cadres strongly resisted any situation in which they would lose status and perquisites. In light of this dilemma, it is not surprising that Party leaders approached this issue obliquely. The few who were willing to accept the psychic costs of even considering the total revamping of the Party and the discarding of so much of their own lives were well aware of the tremendous political costs this would entail.

C. The Party, October 1956 – October 1957

After the Eighth Party Congress, the Chinese political agenda was dominated by two issues. One, as discussed in Chapters 4 and 5, was economic

40. Mao Zedong, "Opening Address at the Eighth National Congress of the Communist Party of China," in *Eighth National Congress of the Communist Party of China (Documents)*, 1981, pp. 1–8; see p. 6.

41. For additional analysis of Mao's views, see MacFarquhar, 1974, pp. 110–12, and Harding, 1981, pp. 128–29. The development of Mao's thinking in 1956–1957 is a major theme of the next chapter of this volume.

policy. The other was Party-society relations, particularly Party rectification and the reshaping of the polity after the completion of socialist transformation. The Chinese Communist Party and most Party leaders devoted a great deal of attention to political questions and largely withdrew from playing an active role in economic decision making. The planning and finance coalitions had this arena to themselves and basically remained aloof from political deliberations. While it is something of an overstatement to say that the Chinese political system was bifurcated from late 1956 until mid 1957, the statement captures much of the reality of the Party's role in this period. But it was for Party leaders, especially Mao (as discussed separately in Chapter 7), to attempt to mark out a new trail for Party-society relations; that was not a task for the rank and file. Consequently, this section will be brief.

In economic issues, the only area that seemed to receive attention from the Party was enterprise management. In contrast to the financial coalition, which emphasized giving the capitalists a large role to play in joint public-private enterprises as a means of overcoming production problems, and the planning coalition, which favored adopting technical measures to meet production problems, the Party focused on mobilizing the masses and correctly leading them to solve whatever problems the enterprise faced. Enterprise production difficulties were therefore seen not as technical or staffing questions but as political questions that required Party leadership.[42] The Party was all but silent on other aspects of economic questions during the period from October 1956 to March 1957.

After the Eighth Party Congress, the Party's theoretical journal *Xuexi* (Study) concentrated on expanding on points made at the Congress and on raising the theoretical understanding of the membership. The focus of all work was to ameliorate the contradiction between the advanced superstructure and the backward economic base. Subjectivism, and after December 1956 revisionism, was criticized. Hints appeared that rectification was appropriate, but there was no linkage between rectification and the Hundred Flowers policy of allowing more intellectual freedom. *Xuexi* articles were largely of an exegetical nature.[43]

In late December 1956, in response to the uprisings in Eastern Europe and criticisms of the Soviet system created by Stalin, the CCP published

42. See, for example, Jiang Xueqing, "Shixing Minzhu Guanli You Si Da Haochu" (Carrying Out Democratic Management Has Four Big Advantages), *Da Gong Bao* (The Impartial Daily), December 19, 1956, in *XHBYK*, 1957, no. 3, pp. 56–57, and Su Ke, "Cong Wo Guo Gongren Qunzhong Canjia yu Qiye Guanlide Lishi Jingyan lai Kan Dangqian Heying Qiyede Minzhu Guanli Wenti" (Problems of Joint Enterprise Management in Light of the Historical Experience of Chinese Workers' Participation in Enterprise Management), *Gongren Ribao* (Workers' Daily), January 5, 1957, in *XHBYK*, 1957, no. 4, pp. 78–79.

43. See *Xuexi*, 1956, nos. 10–12, and 1957, nos. 1–5.

"More on the Historical Experience of the Dictatorship of the Proletariat." While many of the points in this document, which was twice as long as its April predecessor, "On the Historical Experience of the Dictatorship of the Proletariat" (China's response to Khrushchev's secret speech), were related to foreign policy and intrabloc relations, a number were also important domestically. In the April essay, the CCP had argued that "certain systems" needed to be created to ensure that the problems of Stalinism did not reappear. In December, however, it averred:

> No system, however excellent, is in itself a guarantee against serious mistakes in our work. Once we have the right system, the main question is whether we can make the right use of it; whether we have the right policies, the right methods and style of work. Without all this, it is still possible for people to commit serious mistakes and to use a good state apparatus to do evil things.[44]

The significance is that in the earlier essay structural remedies were seen as checks on the abuse of power. The December article also suggested that some of these structural remedies included more developed democracy, a fully developed socialist legal system, democratic methods of administration of the state apparat and enterprises owned by the state, and closer links between the Party and the people. These systems were important parts of Liu Shaoqi's report to the Eighth Party Congress. But the December essay suggested that these systems, though necessary, were insufficient to guarantee the "perfection" of the socialist system. It was also necessary to make sure that the leadership adopted the right policies, methods, and styles of work. Not surprisingly, the article was quite vague about how this would come about. It appeared that only when the leadership and the Party rank and file had been thoroughly imbued with Party doctrine could Stalin-type mistakes be avoided. This implied the need for a thorough rectification campaign.

The December essay also spoke of the existence of nonantagonistic contradictions in socialist countries. These occurred among the people (not between the enemy and the people) and included contradictions between different sectors of the population, between members of the Communist Party, and between the government and the people. This implied the need for new methods to resolve such contradictions. Because the contradictions were nonantagonistic, the people could play an active and largely autonomous role in their resolution. Nonantagonistic contradictions implied a more inclusivist

44. "More on the Historical Experience of the Dictatorship of the Proletariat," in *Communist China, 1955–1959*, 1971, pp. 257–72; quotation, p. 262. Cf. "On the Historical Experience of the Dictatorship of the Proletariat," in ibid., pp. 144–51.

cast to Party-society relations and the use of democratic procedures to resolve the problems of social pluralism that were the basis of such contradictions.

Finally, the article noted the need to guard against not just doctrinairism,
or dogmatism, but also revisionism. This meant that there were limits to
how much the basic system in China could change. Threats to the CCP's
dominant position in the polity and extensive use of markets would be viewed
very negatively from this ideological perspective. In the short term, this
criticism of revisionism was aimed at Yugoslavia and at Khrushchev's idea of
a peaceful transition from capitalism to socialism. In domestic affairs, the
most decisive effect of the criticism of revisionism would be felt from mid
1957 to 1976.

At the Politburo meeting where the basic points of "More on the Historical Experience" were discussed, the leadership probably decided to launch
a formal Party rectification campaign. If Mao was somewhat successful in
getting his colleagues to agree to rectification, his Hundred Flowers policy
was running into resistance. One of the deputy directors of the Political
Work Department of the People's Liberation Army and several other PLA
officials jointly published in *Renmin Ribao* an article that strongly criticized
the basic thrust of the Hundred Flowers in literature and art. This essay
garnered widespread support. Mao did his best to rebut the charges but had
made only slight headway by the time Zhou Enlai reported to him on his
trip to Eastern Europe in late 1956 and early 1957. Zhou reinforced Mao's
belief that only by fully exposing and redressing contradictions among the
people could future errors be avoided. Zhou's remarks precipitated Mao's
calling a meeting of the Supreme State Conference where he delivered the
speech on how to handle contradictions among the people.[45]

After this February 27 speech by Mao, the Party became overwhelmingly
concerned with the implications of handling contradictions among the people. At least three articles on handling contradictions appeared in each issue
of *Xuexi* from March until the termination of the Hundred Flowers Campaign on June 8. They emphasized the democratic side of democratic centralism and did not discuss class struggle. The Party and state's ills of bureaucratism, subjectivism, and sectarianism were to be checked by external

45. Chen Qitong, Ma Hanbing, Chen Yading, and Lu Le, "Women dui Muqian Wenyi Gongzuode Jige Yijian" (Several of Our Opinions on Current Literary and Art Work), *Renmin Ribao*
(People's Daily), January 7, 1957. For Mao's reactions and his view of the opposition to his
policy before his speech on contradictions, see MacFarquhar et al., 1989, pp. 113–27, esp. pp.
116–17. See MacFarquhar, 1974, pp. 175–83, for details. See also Mao, 1977, pp. 384–421; cf.
MacFarquhar et al., 1989, pp. 131–89.

criticism and a policy of "long-term coexistence and mutual supervision" by the bourgeois political parties and the CCP.[46]

In late April 1957, Mao finally won formal approval of the plan to launch a CCP rectification campaign aimed at the evils of bureaucratism, subjectivism, and sectarianism. With several notable exceptions, the rectification directive was similar to many previous such documents. First, the CCP was to take Mao's contradictions speech and a related March speech as the basis for discussion. Resolving contradictions among the people was a major theme of the campaign. Second, intellectual members of the Party were required to have contacts with the workers and peasants in order to help them overcome their tendencies toward individualism and liberalism. Third, all Party members who were physically fit were to engage in physical labor. This would help narrow the gap between leaders and led and give cadres a better feeling for how the people actually lived. Finally, "non-party people who wish to participate in the rectification campaign should be welcomed."[47] The Party thus invited non–Party members to attend Party meetings and voice their opinions, an unprecedented policy. After this directive was formulated on April 27, the Party was too busy to discuss any economic issues. Contradictions among the people and "blooming and contending" were the order of the day.

In advance of the formal launching of the rectification campaign, however, the Party evinced a certain concern with economic issues, or more precisely with questions of authority in industrial administration. The CCP was called on to pay greater attention to the political education of the workers.[48] Mass movements should still be carried out in industrial enterprises.[49] The Party was also concerned with the emergence of worker congresses and with other steps enterprises took to handle contradictions.[50] All these policies

46. See *Xuexi*, 1957, nos. 6–12; for an insider's account of developments in "blooming and contending," see Li Weihan, 1986, pp. 812–55. For some of the extensive secondary analysis of this period, see MacFarquhar, 1974, pp. 184–69; 1960; Kraus, 1981, ch. 3; and Teiwes, 1979a, chs. 6 and 7.
47. See "The CCP Central Committee's Directive on Rectification Campaign" (April 27, 1957) and "The CCP Central Committee's Directive on Leading Personnel at All Levels Taking Part in Physical Labor" (May 14, 1957), in *Documents of the Chinese Communist Party Central Committee*, vol. 1, 1971, pp. 253–57 and 259–63, respectively.
48. Wang Li and Cao Xingui, "Bixu Jingchang Zhongshi dui Gongrende Zhengzhi Jiaoyu" (We Must Regularly Stress the Political Education of Workers), *Xuexi*, 1957, no. 6, pp. 6–9.
49. Jiang Yiwei, "Qiye Gongzuozhongde Qunzhong Yundong Wenti" (Problems of Mass Movements in the Work of Enterprises), *Xuexi*, 1957, no. 8, pp. 14–16. Jiang was a prominent reform economist until June 4, 1989.
50. Cui Shaowu, "Zai Yuanliao Buzude Qingkuangxia, Women Zengchanle" (Under Conditions of Raw Material Shortage, We Increased Production), *Renmin Ribao*, March 3, 1957, in *XHBYK*, 1957, no. 7, pp. 67–68; Meng Fan, "Fangshou Fayang Minzhu, Zhihui ba Shi Ban Hao Buhui Ban Huai" (Go All Out to Promote Democracy; Only in That Way Will Things Be

reflected Party unease with a series of strikes in late 1956 and early 1957.[51]

Other than articles that repeated the priorities in Mao's Ten Major Relations, no discussions of economic questions appeared. The entire emphasis of the Party media was on handling contradictions, whether in agricultural collectives, industrial enterprises, schools, or the Party itself. The stress was on winning over the doubters; providing incentives for people, especially the peasants, to produce; and listening to the views of the people. In a sense, for practically the first time since 1949, the Party was voluntarily surrendering the initiative, or control over events, to society. This was codified by a Politburo decision, sponsored by Mao and Liu Shaoqi, on May 11 to encourage blooming and contending, and authorizing reporters to record exactly what people said, including cursing of the CCP.[52] This was a novel approach, and nobly inspired. Unfortunately for all China, when this effort was defined as a failure, the whole pattern of Party tolerance disappeared as well. The Party had had its fill of inclusivist policies in the spring of 1957 and decisively rejected them for at least the next twenty years.

It is hard to overstate just how virulently the Chinese Communist Party responded to the Hundred Flowers critics. Article after article hammered away at the newly designated rightists. The Party's reaction produced a result directly counter to the one intended by Mao. Instead of bringing about a more open political system, it exacerbated the CCP's intolerance. Instead of playing a larger role in economic construction and in the political sphere, intellectuals and non-CCP personnel suffered severe persecution; by 1958, 552,877 persons had been designated as rightists.[53] Instead of finding a new definition of the role of the Party, the CCP revived its focus on social transformation and class struggle, perhaps to the greatest extent since 1949. These developments have been well chronicled and need not be explored here.[54]

Managed Well and Not Badly), *Renmin Ribao*, April 25, 1957, in *XHBYK*, 1957, no. 10, pp. 85–87; *Renmin Ribao* editorial, "Zai Guoying Qiyezhong Zhubu Tuixing Zhaokai Zhigong Daibiao Dahuide Banfa" (In State-Owned Enterprises Gradually Promote the Method of Convening Worker Representative Congresses), May 29, 1957, in *XHBYK*, 1957, no. 12, pp. 108–9; "Shenyang Wuge Gongchang Zhaokai Zhigong Daibiao Dahuide Qubu Jingyan" (The Preliminary Experiences of Five Factories in Shenyang in Convening Worker Congresses), *Renmin Ribao*, May 29, 1957, in *XHBYK*, 1957, no. 12, pp. 109–12.

51. On the strikes, see Hao Mengbi and Duan Haoran, 1984, p. 483 n. 1. The strikes involved more than ten thousand workers.

The articles on worker congresses reflect different perspectives on how the interests of workers should be represented. Li Xuefeng, in his speech to the Eighth Party Congress (*8PC/S*, pp. 304–17), called for the Party to be the key articulator of worker interests through worker congresses. Lai Ruoyu, head of the trade unions, wanted the unions to be more aggressive in representing workers and less under the thumb of the CCP (*8PC/S*, pp. 236–47).

52. Ji Xichen, "Zai Fengkou Shang" (In the Draught), in *Renmin Ribao Huiyi Lu*, 1988, pp. 124–33; see pp. 124–25.

53. Hao Mengbi and Duan Haoran, 1984, p. 491.

54. See esp. MacFarquhar, 1974, pp. 261–310, and Teiwes, 1979a, ch. 7.

Not all criticisms leveled at the Party and the state were ignored. Party leaders agreed that bureaucratism was a serious problem and decided that many cadres at the center should be transferred to the lower levels of administration or should be returned to the "production front." In some ministries, up to 50 percent of the staff were "sent down" (*xiafang*). Intellectuals and younger Party members were especially likely candidates for sending down. Older leaders felt that these types of cadres could benefit especially from contact with the masses.[55]

Simultaneously, the Party formally authorized socialist education campaigns, both in the countryside and in the urban areas (in work units, particularly factories).[56] While the focus of Party activities was now on criticizing the rightists both outside the Party and within it, rectification continued.[57]

This combination of factors and policies – a highly charged political atmosphere, an ongoing purge, and the sending down of cadres to lower levels – bears a striking similarity to the situation that had prevailed in the period immediately before the High Tide of Agricultural Collectivization in the summer of 1955. At that time, too, many cadres were sent to the lower levels, a rectification campaign was under way, and Party cadres were much more likely to be punished if they were conservative than if they were aggressive in their commitment to fulfill and overfulfill targets.[58] Now upper-level cadres were not happy about being sent down to the basic levels to labor, for this lost them urban amenities and most of the perquisites of office. Agricultural labor was hard; cadres did all they could to return to their original units. The way to do this was to show their commitment to Party policy. As Lynn White notes, "One reason for the enthusiasm of the Leap may be found in the fact that many cadres, recently sent to the rural areas, would

55. On *xiafang*, see Harding, 1981, pp. 163–65, and Lee, 1966. Some of the many articles on *xiafang* include *Renmin Ribao* editorial, "Streamline Administrative Structures of Enterprises in Revolutionary Spirit," September 28, 1957, trans. in *Survey of China Mainland Press* (hereafter *SCMP*), no. 1628 (October 10, 1957), pp. 7–10; Mo Ai, "Beijing's Revolutionary Spirit," Xinhua News Agency (October 20, 1957), in *SCMP*, no. 1644 (November 4, 1957), pp. 14–17; and "Vigorous Retrenchment of Administrative Organs, Training, and Reformation of Cadres Through Labor," Xinhua News Agency (September 3, 1957), in *SCMP*, no. 1612 (September 18, 1957), pp. 1–2.

56. "Directive of the CCP Central Committee on Large-Scale Socialist Education Among All Rural People" (August 8, 1957) and "Directive of the CCP Central Committee on Rectification of Working Style and Socialist Education in Industrial Enterprises" (September 12, 1957), in *Documents of the Chinese Communist Party Central Committee*, vol. 1, 1971, pp. 271–73 and 275–77, respectively.

57. An excellent case study of how rectification was actually carried out during the Great Leap Forward is found in Teiwes, 1973.

58. Compare the situation in 1957 as described above with that portrayed by Vogel, 1971, ch. 4 (on 1955).

have had to do even more manual labor, if they had not instead spent their time mobilizing the people for the great new national movement."[59]

In short, the Party, whether consciously or not, had created an explosive situation, particularly in the countryside. Incentives were offered that encouraged local cadres to launch huge production drives. It was only a matter of lighting the fuse before a conflagration erupted. The Party lit the fuse with its directive of September 24, 1957, on launching a campaign to build water conservancy works.[60] This and the results of the Third Plenum were the sparks that set off the Great Leap Forward.

D. Conclusion

The Chinese Communist Party, as the organ of revolutionary transformation, was undergoing a crisis in 1956–1957.[61] It had completed all of its main fighting tasks with agricultural collectivization and the socialist transformation of privately owned enterprises. Apparently nothing was left on the agenda of revolutionary change. The Soviet experience had been replicated in China; any new endeavor at social transformation would have to be Chinese development.

Rather than searching for a new revolutionary mission, however, Party leaders, especially Mao, opted to redefine the nature of the Party and its relationship to society by opening it up to external criticism and recognizing the emerging pluralism of Chinese society. The aim was for the Party to incorporate broad segments of society into its membership and thus help resolve tensions between itself and society peacefully.

This attempt to redefine the Party's role failed. The leadership did not understand how critically China's intellectuals regarded the Party. More important, the CCP itself was not prepared for a change of mission. Too many cadres had devoted too much of their lives to winning the revolution; they were unwilling to listen to outsiders tell them what was wrong with them, what mistakes they had made, and how they should give up some, if not all, of their power and position. In particular, inclusivist policies threatened the status of peasant Party members with little education. Their skills lay in mobilizing people, not in administering an increasingly complex society. Once

59. White, 1978, p. 74.
60. "Decision of the CCP Central Committee and the State Council to Launch a Campaign for Building Irrigation Projects and Accumulating Manure in [the] Coming Winter and Next Spring" (September 24, 1957), in *Documents of the Chinese Communist Party Central Committee*, vol. 1, 1971, pp. 517–22. The fullest analysis of this campaign is Oksenberg, 1969.
61. For more details, see Harding, 1981, chs. 4 and 5.

the Hundred Flowers policies were deemed to have failed, these cadres took their revenge on their critics in the Anti-Rightist Campaign.

The failure of the Hundred Flowers led to reaffirmation of the transformative role of the Party. But it still left open the question of what remained to be transformed. Concrete goals and tasks were lacking in the summer of 1957. But by the time of the Third Plenum of the Eighth Central Committee, the acute problems of agriculture, the Soviet sputniks, and the seeming failure of ideological remolding to take hold among the Chinese people would suggest grand targets of revolutionary transformation. These targets were nature itself and the Chinese people.

E. Appendix:
Comments on the military and the Ministry of Public Security

The internal politics of the People's Liberation Army (PLA) focused on two interrelated issues. The first of these was the relevance within the PLA of past traditional leadership practices, associated with the war against Japan and the civil war, when there were close relations between officers and men. The second was how rapidly and how completely the Chinese military should modernize. All participants in the debate agreed that military modernization was essential, even the most ardent members of the General Political Department of the PLA, champions of the older leadership system.[62] But should military modernization take the form of a quick fix in order to meet the possibility of a surprise attack, or should military modernization be slower-paced, with reliance on the Soviet Union to deter potential attacks on China? The quick-fix option would take funds away from economic construction; more gradual modernization would limit military expenditures and make military development a product of overall economic and technical levels in China.[63]

The year 1955 was a highly contentious one in PLA politics. In mid January, Mao and the Politburo decided that China would develop nuclear weapons; they anticipated significant Soviet assistance in the effort. This decision was made in response to a series of veiled U.S. nuclear threats against China.[64] The nation began to mobilize its limited scientific and technical manpower to carry out this enormous undertaking.[65] Meanwhile, China continued its

62. See "Speech by Tan Cheng," *8PC/S*, pp. 259–78.
63. This presentation follows Hsieh, 1962.
64. Lewis and Xue, 1988, pp. 38–39.
65. An authoritative reminiscence of these developments is Nie Rongzhen, 1984, pp. 762–810.

ongoing confrontation with Taiwan and the United States over the islands off the coast controlled by the Kuomintang.

Shortly after the Offshore Islands crisis dissipated in the spring of 1955, a number of leading military figures, in particular Liu Bocheng and Ye Jianying, argued for a military quick fix. The Minister of National Defense, Peng Dehuai, though generally supportive of the desire for modernization, accepted the view of the Politburo that it would have to follow economic development.[66] Differences within the military were argued out at a March 1956 meeting of the Military Affairs Commission, where Peng made a keynote address that struck a balance between demands for rapid modernization and for maintaining key aspects of military tradition.[67] Differences still existed at the Eighth Party Congress, but they were minor.[68] By the time of the congress, China had decided to proceed with nuclear development and to undertake gradual military modernization in tandem with the expansion of industrial, scientific, and technical forces. It would rely on the Soviet Union to deter the United States from attacking. In addition, many of the political aspects of authority relations in the military, associated with the army in the 1930s and 1940s, were revived and incorporated into the modernization scheme. Military modernization and the nuclear-weapons program made the military look favorably on the planning coalition's views on economic questions, because only a modern heavy industry would create the conditions for improving China's military equipment.

If some general comments can be made about military issues and politics in the military, nothing can be said about the role of top military leaders in Chinese politics. Seven of the ten marshals of the PLA were named to the Politburo after the Eighth Party Congress, to make up more than 40 percent of all full Politburo members.[69] Despite this, their influence on national politics is at best obscure. They were involved in military and foreign policy questions, but evidence of their impact on other national policy questions is lacking.

The Ministry of Public Security was one of the tools of coercion in the hands of the Party. Probably staffed overwhelmingly by Party members, it was highly protective of the Party, as Luo Ruiqing, the minister of public security, stated at the Eighth Party Congress. The ministry often excessively

66. Hsieh, 1962, pp. 34–49; *Peng Dehuai Yuanshuai Fengbei Yongcun*, 1985, pp. 493–513.
67. *Peng Dehuai Yuanshuai Fengbei Yongcun*, 1985, pp. 514–25; *Zhongguo Renmin Jiefang Jun Dashiji, 1927–1982*, 1983, p. 351.
68. Compare "Speech by Comrade Peng Tehuai [Peng Dehuai]," *8PC/S*, pp. 17–44, and "Speech by Comrade Tan Cheng," *8PC/S*, pp. 259–78.
69. The marshals in the Politburo were Zhu De, Lin Biao, Luo Ronghuan, Chen Yi, Peng Dehuai, Liu Bocheng, and He Long. Marshals Ye Jianying, Nie Rongzhen, and Xu Xiangqian were members of the Central Committee.

expanded movements to attack counterrevolutionaries. Luo's views on class struggle were the most extreme of those voiced by any speaker at the Party congress, undoubtedly reflecting the view of the ministry; and although he did say that many unjust cases would be reevaluated, he did not apologize for anything, and he promised that the ministry would remain vigilant even after the completion of socialist transformation. The ministry also disliked mass involvement in public security. It seemed fond of campaigns but wished to be highly autonomous during them.[70] In general, it shared the perspective of the Party as agent of social transformation.

Like that of the military, the impact of the public-security departments on national political decision making is almost impossible to determine on the basis of currently available material. We do know that the éminence grise of the PRC's security departments, Kang Sheng, was intensely loyal to Mao. During the spring of 1957 he joined Mao in supporting the Hundred Flowers.[71]

70. "Speech by Comrade Lo Jui-ching [Luo Ruiqing]," *8PC/S*, pp. 98–124.

71. See MacFarquhar et al., 1989, pp. 210, 218, 246, 261, 264–65. On Kang more generally, see Hu Yaobang, 1980 (although this source may be a forgery – see Chapter 3, n. 33, in the present volume), and Zhong Kan, 1982.

7

The views of the top leadership

The ultimate power of decision in China in the mid 1950s lay in the hands of the half-dozen members of the Politburo Standing Committee, which, as determined at the Eighth Party Congress in September 1956, was composed of Mao Zedong, Liu Shaoqi, Zhou Enlai, Zhu De, Chen Yun, and Deng Xiaoping. Among these six leaders, Mao's position was supreme. He was not just first among equals; his power and position in the political system were unparalleled. He had unique ideological, experiential, and charismatic sources of authority. His political skills far surpassed those of his colleagues on the Standing Committee, and his determination to have his way was implacable.[1]

That Mao had these sources of power, however, does not mean he necessarily chose to use them. In the mid 1950s, he was relatively open to the ideas and suggestions of others. He had some sense of his own limitations and lack of knowledge, and he delegated authority to others to implement, and at times initiate, policy. Other Chinese leaders saw Mao's strength as his ability to set the major direction for policy, to formulate overall priorities, to identify and present general guidelines for solving the "principal contradiction." He was a "big-ideas man," not a master of details. His own ideology was undergoing change in the mid 1950s, and his views were not entirely consistent. He usually adhered to a collective, consultative style of decision making.

Mao's power was manifest in several areas in particular. He had the authority to make final decisions on the nature of class relations and class struggle in China. More broadly, he set the ideological tone for the regime, both internally and in China's relations with other communist parties. In domestic politics, he determined the pace of advance and could set broad overall

1. My views of Mao's role in the Chinese political system are heavily influenced by Frederick Teiwes, Roderick MacFarquhar, and Michel Oksenberg. Teiwes's relevant works include 1979a, 1984, and 1988. MacFarquhar's views of Mao are found throughout his 1974 and 1983 works. Oksenberg's views are found in 1971, 1974a, 1976, and 1977.

targets, but rarely did he champion particular detailed policies. In economic affairs in the 1950s, he paid special attention to the Chinese countryside.

Moreover, in the aftermath of Khrushchev's denunciation of Stalin in February 1956, Mao and other Chinese leaders were especially concerned to avoid being similarly criticized; and Mao was vulnerable to such charges. His intervention in July 1955 to accelerate the pace of agricultural collectivization without consulting other top leaders was precisely the type of rash behavior for which Khrushchev had denounced Stalin. The Chinese Communist Party had a stronger tradition of collective leadership than did the Communist Party of the Soviet Union; since the late 1930s, norms governing intra-CCP dissent, minority rights, and collective decision had evolved and in the main been followed.[2] One of the conclusions Mao and other CCP leaders drew from Stalin's mistakes was that these norms needed strengthening and revitalizing, and generally that democratic elements of the political system needed to be stronger. At the Eighth Party Congress, Mao agreed to a number of institutional arrangements that in the long run might have served to constrain his powers and also provide for his succession.

As a result, Mao played a minor public role at the congress. Major reports were delivered by Liu Shaoqi, Mao's heir apparent, Premier Zhou Enlai, and soon-to-be General Secretary Deng Xiaoping. Analysis of these reports and of the resolutions of the congress concerning them constitute the first part of this chapter, followed by treatment of the views of individuals in the top leadership. Despite good-faith efforts by Mao and his colleagues to temper his role in the policy process, 1956–1957 was a period of unusually heavy activity by the Chairman, and consequently I pay most attention to his views.

Most of the top leaders of the CCP held contradictory or superficial views about the Chinese economy. They appeared to be ignorant of key economic matters, or they avoided dealing with economic questions. This combination of ignorance, inattention, and lack of consistency of views on the economy created the need for economic specialists within the leadership to take on the bulk of decision making on economic issues. Inconsistency and "flexibility" on economic questions by the Politburo Standing Committee created opportunities for the economic coalitions to continue lobbying for their positions even when it appeared that a set line of development was in place. In other words, leadership inconsistency kept the pot of policy options presented by the coalitions boiling.

Although it can be argued that Mao's basic ignorance of economic ques-

2. Teiwes (1979a, pt. 1, and 1984, ch. 3) deals with this issue extensively.

tions and the inconsistencies in his policy positions elevated him above the constraints (or the limited options) presented by the economic bureaucracy, such a view is mistaken. It is true that Mao had a choice based on the options presented to him, and that at times he tried to tie incompatible elements of various options together. But he could not direct the bureaucracy to formulate new alternatives; consequently, the same options on economic affairs kept reappearing on the political agenda. Moreover, after the heyday of the Great Leap, even Mao concluded that he knew nothing about economics, and he largely avoided dealing with macroeconomic questions after the early 1960s. (We shall return to these points in Chapter 9 and in the Appendix.) His range of choice on economic policy questions was quite narrow, particularly as the economy grew increasingly complex.

A. Major reports to the Eighth Party Congress

The Eighth Party Congress was the first such convocation in eleven years. In the years since 1945, the Party had undergone fundamental changes and transitions. By 1956 it was the governing party in China, and it had carried out its agenda of socialist transformation. The Eighth Party Congress was thus a congress of victory, but it also provided an opportunity for the Party and the leadership to take stock, to summarize the positive experiences of the Party and to identify defects in the Party's work style. It was also incumbent on the leadership to present a new agenda of activity now that socialism was established in the PRC. The leadership put forward a line of economic development and modest political incorporation, encouraging a more active role for Chinese citizens in the administration of the state.

In their speeches to the Eighth Party Congress, Liu Shaoqi, Deng Xiaoping, and Zhou Enlai attempted to incorporate and synthesize the views of different coalitions within the Chinese state. Each leader tried to form a loose consensus about what sorts of policies should be adopted to achieve CCP goals and to meet the problems facing the leadership. Each took an Olympian perspective, largely standing above the intrastate coalitions. There were differences among their speeches, and the Party's guiding line emerged as an amalgam of their ideas.

Liu Shaoqi reported to the congress on the work of the Central Committee, Deng discussed the new Party constitution, and Zhou presented the proposals for the Second Five-Year Plan. In addition, the text of the new constitution and the proposals for the Second Five-Year Plan were circulated and adopted in the Resolution of the Eighth Party Congress. All of these speeches and documents were collectively examined and agreed upon by the Party center.[3] Nevertheless, the speakers no doubt had a greater role in preparing their reports than did others, and within the agreed-upon parameters of what should be in each speech the speakers could emphasize concerns that they felt should receive more attention. Hence it is reasonable to equate each speech loosely with the views of the individual who delivered it.

Liu Shaoqi's report on the work of the Central Committee was both the longest and the most general speech delivered to the Eighth Party Congress.[4] His remarks on the economy largely summarized Zhou Enlai's report on economic questions. Liu called for doubling of the gross value of industrial output by the end of the Second Five-Year Plan (SFYP) in 1962, a 35 percent increase in the gross value of agricultural output, and a 50 percent increase in national income. Heavy industry remained the key sector; within heavy industry, machine building and metallurgy would be the most important spheres of activity. Light industry should advance "appropriately." The keys to greater agricultural production were increases in both state investment, particularly in water conservancy, and in the efforts of the collectives themselves. Liu also suggested the need for commercial reforms. In addition, he demanded cuts in military and administrative expenditures in order to permit spending on production, education, and science to rise to about 70 percent of all expenditures in the SFYP. The comparable figure in the First Five-Year Plan was 58 percent.

Liu's section on the economy contained several controversial or contradictory aspects. First, in contrast to Mao Zedong's report on the Ten Major Relationships in April 1956,[5] Liu argued that the percentage of investment devoted to heavy industry should not be reduced. (He also opposed increasing the percentage.) Liu seemed only conditionally to endorse increasing light industrial investment. Second, his remarks on decentralization reflected a certain reluctance to allow the handing down of power to lower levels. When he did discuss decentralization, he emphasized increasing power

3. On the collective discussion of reports and documents, see "Speech by Comrade Sung Jen-chiung [Song Renqiong]," *Eighth National Congress of the Communist Party of China, vol. 2: Speeches* (hereafter *8PC/S*), 1956, pp. 147–56 (see pp. 153–54); Mao, 1977, pp. 312–23; and Teiwes, 1979a, p. 227. These sources refute MacFarquhar's 1974 view (p. 100 and passim) that featured speakers should be held personally and entirely accountable for the contents of their reports.
4. Liu Shaoqi, "The Political Report of the Central Committee of the Communist Party of China to the Eighth National Congress of the Party," *Eighth National Congress of the Communist Party of China (Documents)*, 1981 (reprint of 1956 original with slightly different pagination; hereafter *8PC/D*), pp. 9–115. In keeping with the rest of this study, the focus of analysis here will be on economic issues. Other aspects of these reports are thoroughly discussed in MacFarquhar, 1974, pp. 99–165; Teiwes, 1979a, pp. 226–30; and Harding, 1981, pp. 119–29.
5. Mao, 1977, pp. 284–307.

at the enterprise level, in contrast to Zhou Enlai, who focused on decentralization at the provincial level. In the segment of Liu's speech dealing with the political life of the state, he did advocate some decentralization to the lower levels of government, but here his aim was as much to check bureaucratism as to increase economic efficiency.

Liu favored strengthened Party leadership in the newly formed collectives, but for the somewhat incongruous reason that this would allow more attention to be paid to subsidiary agricultural production and the productive endeavors of individual peasant households within the collectives. (In fact, over the next year this strengthened Party leadership role in the collectives became increasingly incompatible with the requirements of subsidiary and individual production.)

Liu stated that in order to import necessary heavy industrial materials, complete plants, and technology (he and others envisioned that China's rate of self-sufficiency in the supply of machine tools would increase from 60 to 70 percent over the course of the SFYP), China needed to export more consumer goods. This policy also created conflicts. Here, export of consumer goods undercut policies designed to increase popular living standards. Zhou Enlai's report and the proposals for the SFYP revealed already serious contradictions on the question of living standards and growth rates. Increased exports of consumer goods and agricultural products would only complicate matters.

Finally, Liu did not use the phrase "the law of value"[6] in his discussion of commercial and price reforms, whereas Zhou did. Liu was perhaps less willing to allow a market to develop and was unenthusiastic about using price changes to promote production. His evaluation of the condition of the economy, far more optimistic than Zhou's,[7] may account for this. Palliatives such as the market might not be necessary, Liu thought.

In the section on the political life of the state, Liu focused on the state administrative system rather than on the Party. The consolidation of social order and the promotion of China's development required that the "broadest masses of people participate actively in state organs." The full mobilization of intellectuals to support national construction was particularly important, he argued. He saw improved cooperation between the CCP and intellectuals as essential; that interaction helped intellectuals remold themselves and struggle against their bourgeois nature. Liu's pronouncements on intellec-

6. For an overview of the law of value in China, see Lin, 1981, esp. pp. 11–19. On the contemporaneous Soviet discussions, see Nove, 1969, pp. 306–20. One particularly controversial discussion in Chinese is Sun Yefang, 1979, pp. 1–14 and passim (reprinting articles from the 1950s and 1960s), and Sun's retrospective view (1980).

7. On other differences between Liu and Zhou, see MacFarquhar, 1974, pp. 124–26.

tuals contradicted the position put forward by Li Weihan, head of the CCP's United Front Work Department, that intellectuals should remold themselves through their own actions.[8]

To deal with problems of Party sectarianism (Liu viewed Party discrimination against non-Party personnel in state organs as the Party's biggest shortcoming in state administration), Liu favored giving particular voice to the ideas of the bourgeoisie and the intellectuals to help the CCP to overcome its errors, encouraging "more vigorous self-criticism within the Party" and relying "on supervision by the masses of the working people as a whole." To cope with problems of bureaucratism and inefficiency in the state administrative system, he favored streamlining state organizations and enumeration of strict lines of bureaucratic responsibility; greater Party supervision over state affairs; a more active role for the National People's Congress and the local people's congresses in inspecting the bureaucracy; superiors and subordinates checking each other's bad habits; state supervisory organs carrying out their duties faithfully; people criticizing and exposing government errors; and a deconcentration of centralized administrative control, with more power going to the lower levels and a number of central cadres being transferred to the localities. Liu also firmly endorsed the establishment and development of the legal system, because "the period of revolutionary storm and stress is past."

In regard to the state (not the Party), Liu heartily endorsed the policies associated with social and political inclusion. His concern for the development of the legal system and his calls for mutual supervision by the democratic parties and the CCP and for an expanded role for the intellectuals all point to a narrowing of status differences between Party members and non-Party members. Liu identified bureaucratism as a defect of the state. He did not suggest that the Party suffered from the same fault. Bureaucratism was, at least in part, a structural defect in the state's organizational system. Consequently, it was appropriate to develop structural checks. Whereas he called for *criticism* of the state by the people, he called for the masses merely to *supervise* the CCP.

In the last section of his speech, on Party leadership, Liu asserted that CCP members had to gain technical expertise in their specialized fields. To eliminate defects in Party work, primarily subjectivism – the substituting of personal experience for objective knowledge – Liu favored intensified, systematic study of Marxism-Leninism by all cadres, especially high-ranking officials; increased teaching about the integration of theory and practice among

8. See "Speech by Comrade Li Weihan," *8PC/S*, pp. 348–68.

new Party members; more theoretical work by the Party as a whole; leading organs spending more time on investigation and research; and finally, strengthened collective leadership and inner Party democracy.

Thus, Liu Shaoqi perceived an entirely different set of problems affecting the Party from the ones afflicting the state. Because of this, he advocated different types of measures to reduce and eliminate defects in these two areas. Liu's opinions were in sharp contrast to the views of Deng Xiaoping, who delivered the report on the new Party constitution.

Deng's report on the constitution is an extraordinary document.[9] Of all the speeches at the Eighth Party Congress, his is the one that most directly confronted the role of the CCP now that the Party's agenda of social transformation was largely achieved. He argued for self-reliance by the populace, continued use of mass campaigns, and the mobilization of external criticism to correct Party errors (whose source he identified as bureaucratism). But he also advocated the elimination of most class categories in Chinese society and the "retooling"[10] of the CCP to equip it better to confront the tasks associated with socialist modernization. In short, Deng favored a unique blend of mobilization to promote democracy and professionalization to develop the economy. Neither Deng Xiaoping nor Mao Zedong, who also favored this position, believed that this combination was inherently impossible in late 1956 and early 1957.

In contrast to Liu Shaoqi, who saw Party errors as partial and not very severe, Deng felt that the danger of Party mistakes had increased now that the CCP was ensconced in power.[11] To Deng, these errors were primarily the result of bureaucratism, which he too saw as the source of subjectivism in the Party. He conceded the need for ideological education but said that "the Party has an even more important task, namely to strengthen the Party's leadership in various ways and to make appropriate provisions in both the state and Party systems for a strict supervision over our Party organizations and Party members."[12] Again, contra Liu, Deng called on the state to supervise the Party.

Deng also elaborated on the mass line. In addition to Mao's famous "from the masses, to the masses"[13] approach to leadership, he saw the mass line as the way to ensure that the CCP would continue to advance: "In one respect, it maintains that the *people must liberate themselves*, that the Party's entire

9. Deng Xiaoping, "Report on the Revision of the Constitution of the Communist Party of China," *8PC/D*, pp. 179–241.
10. On this word and its implications for politics in the Soviet Union, see Cocks, 1977.
11. For a similar analysis, see Harding, 1981, pp. 127–28.
12. Deng, "Report," p. 182.
13. Mao, 1965, pp. 117–22, esp. pp. 119–20.

task is to serve the people heart and soul, and that the Party's role in leading the masses lies in pointing out the correct path of struggle and helping them to struggle and build a happy life *by their own effort.*[14] This aspect of the mass line contained two related themes – self-reliance and populism. While the masses were to "liberate themselves," the Party's role was rather circumscribed: to point out the proper way for the people and to help them in their struggle. Deng's view reflected greater spontaneity and self-activation by the people than did Liu Shaoqi's.[15]

Deng detailed Party defects and identified their cause as bureaucratism, even though many of these defects had exactly the same symptoms Liu Shaoqi ascribed to subjectivism. The most significant structural remedy he prescribed for Party bureaucratism was criticism of the Party by outsiders. He argued that as many non-Party people as possible should be drawn into the struggle against bureaucracy. Although he conceded that some of their comments might be inappropriate and subject to criticism, he said, "The point is that these democratic personalities can provide a kind of supervision over the Party which cannot . . . easily be provided by Party members alone; they can discover mistakes and shortcomings in our work which may escape our notice, and render us valuable help in our work."[16]

Deng was ambivalent about bureaucracy and rational legal authority. He argued that in the 1945–1956 period the Party had scored its greatest triumphs when it had employed mass campaigns and used the mass line. Deng's belief in the continued efficacy and desirability of campaigns was a distinctly minority view at the Eighth Party Congress. He suggested, however, that future campaigns would be significantly different from previous movements – class would not be a major issue. Hence, "struggle campaigns"[17] would not reappear:

The former classification of social status has lost or is losing its original meaning. . . . The difference between workers and office employees [i.e., members of the bourgeoisie] is now only a matter of division of labor within the same class. . . . What is the point, then, of classifying these social strata into two different categories? And even if we were to try and devise a classification, how could we make it neat and clearcut?[18]

In other words, in light of changes in the ownership system and changing patterns of social mobility, Deng implied that class analysis was no longer

14. Deng, "Report," p. 185. Emphasis added.
15. On "populism" and "Leninism" in Chinese Marxism, see Meisner, 1971, and Schram, 1973.
16. Deng, "Report," p. 196.
17. On "struggle campaigns," see Cell, 1977, pp. 8–9 and passim. On the "displacement of class," see Kraus, 1981, ch. 3.
18. Deng, "Report," pp. 225–26.

useful. If class was not a key aspect in determining Party membership, what was? He argued that "one of the important tasks of the Party is to train and promote large members of new cadres." In case anyone missed the point, he stated that seniority was the chief defect in the selection and promotion of cadres, and he called on the Party to shift from recruiting of activists to recruiting of experts: "The Party must pay particular attention to its training of cadres to master production technique and various branches of professional knowledge *because cadres with such qualifications are the basic force for the building of socialism.*"[19]

Finally, of all the featured speakers at the congress, Deng praised Mao's leadership the most. His references to Mao were not cloying, but they were noticeable. The fact that among the top leadership Deng's views most nearly coincided with Mao's at this time undoubtedly had something to do with Deng's accolades.[20]

Zhou Enlai's report on the proposals for the SFYP reflected a central tenet of his personality: his ability to compromise and mediate.[21] In many parts of Zhou's speech, paragraphs supporting the position of the planning coalition were followed almost immediately by paragraphs reflecting the views of the financial coalition. As the head of the state apparatus, he stood above the leaders of the planning and financial coalitions, and his responsibilities required that he take the views of each position into account, balancing them as best he could.

However, Zhou's speech was more than just a composite of Li Fuchun's and Chen Yun's ideas. It contained a number of key points in addition to a carefully crafted compromise. First, like Deng Xiaoping, Zhou tended to place a slightly more negative emphasis on events than did Liu Shaoqi. Zhou was quick to assert that while achievements were tremendous, errors were extensive, including those associated with the "socialist high tide" of 1956. Liu had not added the qualifying phrase about errors and had ignored the problems of 1956.

On the issue of developing light industry, Zhou sided with heavy industrial officials by fudging light industrial questions. He waffled between saying 11.2 percent of industrial investment should go to light industry (this reflected the 1:8 ratio of light industry to heavy industry that in April 1956 Mao wanted changed to 1:7) and calling for a "suitable increase" in investment in this area. But he did not repeat Liu and others' arguments that light

19. Ibid., p. 234. Emphasis added.
20. For a similar conclusion, see Harding, 1981, p. 137.
21. Zhou Enlai, "Report on the Proposals for the Second Five Year Plan for the Development of the National Economy," *8PC/D*, pp. 279–348.

industry accumulated funds quickly; and immediately after his call for a suit-able increase in light industry, he mentioned a number of factors that un-dermined this position.

Zhou's most controversial proposals concerned the state administrative system. He noted that between May 1956 (i.e., immediately after Mao's speech on the Ten Major Relations) and the following August, the State Council had convened a series of meetings to discuss changing the adminis-trative system. A draft resolution was drawn up that was circulating in China at the time of the Party congress. Yet Zhou's discussion of the seven-point draft resolution was remarkably sketchy. First, an explicit demarcation of provincial jurisdictions over planning, finances, enterprises, materials, per-sonnel, and so forth, was essential. This gave the provinces a larger role in economic management. Second, localities had the right to manage all non-essential enterprises, all enterprises not having an effect on the overall econ-omy; in general, the enterprises' planning, finances, and personnel admin-istration were handed over as well. In enterprises, the institutionalization of dual rule, vertically from the ministry and horizontally from the local gov-ernment, was necessary. In some cases, the ministry would have more con-trol; in others, the locality would. Fourth, all units of the State Council needed to unify their plans and targets before sending them down to the local levels. This system would replace the one where each ministry issued targets to the localities without any coordination with other ministries. Fifth, the local authorities were allowed a certain range for adjusting targets handed down by the center. Specific arrangements would help develop minority areas. Finally, these reforms were to be instituted gradually.

As noted, Zhou's presentation of this reform was very vague, and he saw decentralization as very limited in scope. He omitted most of the key details, such as how much power was being given to the local levels. Zhou's decen-tralization was only down to the provincial level. In contrast, Liu Shaoqi had spoken of expanding the powers of enterprises. Zhou's proposals did not constitute a major change in the state administrative system. In fact, several of his points, such as the unified transmittal of targets from the center to the localities and the center's assuming responsibility for only those "enterprises and public institutions which are vital to the national economy as a whole and which are concentrated, of an overall nature, and of key importance," were more a form of rationalization of authority than a true delegation of powers to the lower levels.[22] All levers of control remained in the hands of

22. On rationalization of authority and administration, see Harding, 1981, pp. 28–30 and passim.

the center. Zhou evidently opposed a fundamental change in the nature of central-local relations.

Finally, in the section on "continuing to practice economy," Zhou talked about economic management and the quality of planning. Yet nowhere did he discuss the change in the management system (from one-man management to managerial authority under the enterprise Party committee) that figured in Liu's address and was the keynote of Li Xuefeng's speech.[23] Instead, Zhou emphasized enforcement of the "system of personal responsibility" and improvement of enterprise performance through technical upgrading. Again, Zhou favored centralization and no diminution of the vertical authority stemming from the State Council.

Zhou Enlai's report to the Eighth Party Congress on the proposals for the SFYP represented a composite of the views of the planners and those of the budgeteers. Moreover, he championed the interests of both coalitions against the growing demands of the CCP for change in the nature of central-local and interenterprise authority. According to Zhou, the SFYP would not be markedly different from the First Five-Year Plan (FFYP). Certainly there were few major policy shifts between the FFYP and the proposals for the SFYP: Most changes were marginal. Zhou recognized problems in the execution of the FFYP, but these were errors in implementation (most, implicitly, were caused by Party intervention). However, these problems did not necessitate major adjustments in the running of the economy. Rationalization of the command structure, strictly limited decentralization, and professionalization were all that was required to ensure that the SFYP would meet its targets. In short, Zhou called for incremental tinkering and limiting the Party's role in the economy.

The proposals for the SFYP[24] were not without inherent contradictions and problematical aspects. In addition, on the issue of decentralization, Zhou Enlai's discussion of the proposals did not tally with the content of the document itself.

Of the eleven heavy industry targets listed, five were to increase by a factor of four over the targets projected in the FFYP for 1957, and one of them by a factor of almost ten. Only two were not at least to double. Yet only two of the six light industrial products were to double. In agriculture, only the target for cotton was to increase by 50 percent. The target for grain was to increase by about 35 percent; for soybeans, only a 10 percent increase

23. "Speech by Comrade Li Hsueh-feng [Li Xuefeng]," *8PC/S*, pp. 304–17.
24. "Proposals of the Eighth National Congress of the Communist Party of China on the Second Five Year Plan for the Development of the National Economy," *8PC/D*, pp. 245–76.

was projected. Thus, despite slightly more investment in agriculture and perhaps light industry, the disproportion between heavy industry and the rest of the economy would continue to grow.

A second area of difficulty concerned commodity sales and living standards. Retail sales were to increase by 50 percent over the course of the plan. However, wages and income of workers and peasants were to increase by only 25–30 percent. How could commodity sales rise so much faster than income? A gap between social purchasing power and consumer goods available in 1957 (projected into the future) accounts for some of this discrepancy. Agriculture, however, was to grow by only 35 percent, and the targets for light industry were not particularly high (a 60 percent increase over the FFYP, according to Jia Tuofu; but no other leader would commit himself to that figure).[25] Would enough commodities be produced for a 50 percent increase in retail sales? It seemed unlikely. Light industry and agriculture were the principal exports financing advanced technology and imports of heavy industrial equipment. Therefore, not all of the increased amount produced in these areas would be consumed internally.

This led to another problem. While peasant income was to increase by 25–30 percent, the total output of agriculture was to increase by only 35 percent. This meant that the state would have only modest additional production to extract, and it is not clear that the SFYP proposals took population growth into account. Most likely, either peasant incomes would not rise so quickly or per capita food consumption would decline. In either case, worker and peasant incentives would not be as effective as hoped, because the material basis for those incentives was lacking.

The question of population raised an additional issue. Industry would create only 6 million to 7 million new jobs over the course of the entire SFYP. Urban population growth in the FFYP approached 6 million per *year*.[26] What would happen to people in the urban areas who could not find jobs?

In short, the proposals for the SFYP did not add up; they revealed basic contradictions between improved living standards and agricultural production. They ignored questions of population growth, the size of the labor pool, unemployment, and underemployment. If the SFYP had been formulated according to the proposals put forward at the Eighth Party Congress, it would have proved unworkable and would have generated many additional problems. The proposals for the SFYP were deeply flawed.

25. Jia Tuofu, "Guanyu Fazhan Qinggongyede Jige Wenti" (Several Problems in the Development of Light Industry), *Xinhua Banyuekan* (New China Semimonthly), 1956, no. 21, pp. 100–102.
26. State Statistical Bureau, 1982, p. 89. See also Rawski, 1979, p. 25.

If the proposals for the SFYP were so problematic, why were they adopted? Perhaps the leaders did not fully recognize the problems in the proposals or were negligent when they were being formulated. But another explanation must be considered. The leaders may have accepted the proposals because they reflected the distribution of power and influence in economic policy making. The planning coalition maintained its dominant role in the economy under the proposals. There were incremental increases in the shares of investment going to agriculture and light industry, but not enough to change the relationship between the planners and the budgeteers. Money for increased investment in light industry and agriculture came not from heavy industry but from reduced military spending. In short, the proposals were adopted because they reflected the existing configuration of institutional power arrangements in China.

A final aspect of the proposals deserving attention is the discussion of decentralization. The emphasis in the proposals was significantly different from Zhou Enlai's views. In contrast to Zhou's call to expand the jurisdiction of the provinces, the proposals favored expanding the jurisdictions of enterprises and institutions. More significant, the proposals stated that the localities should draw up development plans stressing agriculture. Under these plans, local industry and handicrafts were to receive attention so they could meet the needs of the local population, especially the peasants. But Zhou never called for local development planning. He conceded a need for provinces to have a "definite degree of jurisdiction over planning, finances, enterprises," and so on. But this stopped short of a full-blown plan. Moreover, the effect of Zhou's decentralization was to retain a unified economic system. The discussions in the proposals implied the beginnings of the development of a cellular economy[27] and provincial self-sufficiency.

Again, why were there differences between Zhou's discussion of decentralization and the examination of decentralization questions in the proposals (and differences between Zhou and Liu Shaoqi)? No conclusive answer is possible; arguably, Party discussions on decentralization were still at so high a level of generality that the coalitions of the Chinese state and Chinese leaders were unaware of how the distribution of power and authority would be affected by decentralization. Because the decentralization measures were still so general, differences in exposition among various speakers and documents should not be seen as very significant. The hard decisions about what kind of decentralization to launch were yet to be made.

"The Resolution of the Eighth Party Congress of the Communist Party of

---

27. Donnithorne, 1972, is most associated with the argument about the cellular nature of the Chinese economy.

China on the Political Report of the Central Committee"[28] summed up the congress. The resolution is best known for its controversial definition of the crux facing China and the CCP:

The major contradiction in our country is already that between the people's demand for the building of an advanced industrial country and the realities of a backward agricultural country, between the people's need for rapid economic development and the inability of our present economy and culture to meet that need. . . . This contradiction in essence is between the advanced socialist system and the backward productive forces of society. The chief task now facing the Party and the people is to concentrate all efforts on resolving this contradiction and transforming China as quickly as possible from a backward agricultural country into an advanced industrial one. . . . To fulfill this great mission, we must adopt correct policies in *economic, political, cultural* and other work.[29]

The key item on the agenda of the CCP was, therefore, economic development. Adoption of correct economic policies was ranked ahead of adoption of correct political policies. Indeed, most of the resolution was devoted to economic questions. It also discussed expanding democracy and opposing bureaucracy in the state and making the Party more democratic internally and more responsive to external suggestions. But it gave practically no attention to class struggle or the social-transformation role of the CCP.

The consensus announced, and the definition of the political agenda of the CCP presented, in the resolution was not likely to be long-lived. The proposals for the SFYP had impractical and unworkable elements. A growing divergence of views characterized the speeches of leaders charged with economic administration. A Communist Party that had spent most of its history mobilizing people to defeat its enemies was not likely to sit back quietly as the "productive forces" of the economy were developed. Chinese society could not be democratized without threatening the CCP's supreme position in the polity. Owing to any of these factors, the views presented at the Eighth Party Congress were likely to be quite transitory.

B. The views of Mao Zedong, 1955–1957

Many argue that Mao Zedong had formulated a consistent strategy of social and economic development by the middle of 1955, or that the line of development equated with Mao Zedong was fully formed by that time.[30] (Central

28. *8PC/D*, pp. 117–39.
29. Ibid., pp. 120–21. Emphasis added.
30. For example, Chesneaux, 1979; Friedman, 1982; Grey, 1973; Howe and Walker, 1977; Reynolds, 1978; and Wheelwright and McFarlane, 1970. Except for Reynolds's, all these accounts equate Mao with a distinct line of development. Reynolds's "internal" model, however, is consistent with the other versions of the "Maoist line," justifying his inclusion here.

elements of this "Maoist line" were mass mobilization for the purposes of developing the economy, emphasis on class struggle, a searing contempt for intellectuals and bureaucracy, and a firm commitment to voluntarism.) This view is belied by the evidence presented here. During the period under discussion, Mao lacked a consistent position and was influenced at various times in 1956 and 1957 by the planners and by the budgeteers, whose positions he presented as his own. Certainly Mao was the moving force behind the upsurge of the collectivization drive in the summer of 1955.[31] His speech on collectivization (and others he and his supporters made in the fall of 1955) certainly revealed a bias in favor of mass movements, or campaigns, for rapid development. Yet as the collectivization drive accelerated, Mao began to develop additional concerns not all in keeping with the "radical" views suggested above. Some of these concerns appear to be contradictory. Because of this uneasy coexistence of competing ideas in his mind, he was capable of abrupt shifts in what policies he supported.

Although Mao spent most of the second half of 1955 and early 1956 railing against conservatism (particularly in the Party's Rural Work Department), he did not neglect the dangers of leftist errors. In January 1956, discussing those dangers he stated:

There are some comrades whose minds are not alert and who are afraid to act on reality. They are afraid of the embarrassing label of rightist opportunism. Once something has undergone investigation and research and has been found to be not feasible, one should dare to say it can't be done. We should dare to stop it and put the plans on a reliable foundation.[32]

Thus, while Mao emphasized the struggle against conservatism, he was not oblivious of the dangers of rashness, although he did not see adventurism as prevalent.

In addition, Mao attacked both the bureaucratism he saw inhibiting progress and cadres who spent most of their time sitting in offices. He called on cadres to become personally involved in leading the masses. He also wanted provinces to compile books of model experiences of cadres who were close to the people, and wanted lower levels to send reports to higher levels. He stated that overall planning was one of the two ways to overcome conservatism (the other being closer contact with the masses).[33] A system that fea-

31. Mao, 1977, pp. 184–207. The idea that Mao actually expected or desired the massive campaign provoked by his speech on agricultural collectivization has been challenged. See Fingar, 1977, ch. 7.
32. Mao, 1978–1979, p. 75. See also Mao, 1977, p. 231.
33. Mao, 1977, p. 222, and Mao Zedong, "Talk Opposing Right Deviation and Conservatism," in *Miscellany of Mao Tse-tung Thought* (hereafter *MMTTT*) (Arlington, Va.: Joint Publications Research Service, no. 61269-1, February 20, 1974), pp. 27–29 (see p. 28).

tured circulating documents and improved planning hardly marked a break with bureaucratic styles of administration.

Mao firmly supported efforts to expand the role of intellectuals in economic construction. He welcomed Zhou Enlai's speech on the problems of intellectuals,[34] and he told the Party that the realization of China's developmental goals required that many intellectuals participate in economic development. "It won't do to rely solely on such untutored people as ourselves," he told the Party meeting on intellectuals. "We can't do without high-level intellectuals. . . . If we are to have large numbers of high-level intellectuals, we must have even more ordinary intellectuals." He conceded that the Party held a number of prejudices against intellectuals, but also stated that with the successful transformation of the economy these prejudices should be excised.[35] He reiterated this theme several days later when he averred:

The people of our country should have a long-range plan that will allow them in several decades of arduous work, to transform the backward economic, scientific, and cultural conditions of our country so that we can speedily reach advanced world levels. In order to achieve this great objective, the decisive factor is whether there are cadres and enough outstanding scientists and technicians. At the same time, we must continue to consolidate and broaden the people's democratic united front and unite with all those forces with whom we can unite.[36]

Thus, during one of the great all-embracing mass movements in the People's Republic of China, Mao saw the intellectuals playing an irreplaceable and decisive role in national construction. And he linked the appeal to the intellectuals with expansion of the united front. At a time when the completion of socialist transformation was imminent, class conflict did not appear to hold a particularly high place in his mind. To him, reliance on, and a greater role for, intellectuals went hand in hand with ideas about the desirability of mass movements.

Nor was Mao opposed to planning and overall balance. He argued that "plans must be feasible and must be built on a foundation with a [solid] base; otherwise we will again end up doing things blindly."[37] In April 1956, he stated:

It is necessary to have national balance. Local independence should not obstruct national balance. Only with national balance can there be partial balance for the localities. Without national balance, the country would be in great chaos. . . . With-

34. Zhou Enlai, "On the Question of Intellectuals," in *Communist China, 1955–1959*, 1971, pp. 128–44.
35. Mao, 1978–1979, pp. 80, 73.
36. "Mao Zedong Zhuxi Zhaoji Zui Gao Guowu Huiyi" (Chairman Mao Zedong Convenes the Supreme State Conference), *Renmin Ribao* (People's Daily), January 26, 1956, p. 1.
37. Mao, 1978–1979, p. 74.

out this balance, it will not be possible to industrialize the nation. When we encourage independence by the localities, we must not lean to one side.[38]

Here Mao counseled that national plans and balance set boundaries for local initiatives. He saw campaigns as consistent with plans and balance, and balance (which he saw as the result of conscious efforts) as essential to the working of the national economy.

From late 1955 through mid April 1956, Mao met with leaders of thirty-four departments of the State Council for a series of discussions that provided the raw material for "On the Ten Major Relationships."[39] The most striking feature of this speech, one of the two or three most important of Mao's post-1949 utterances, was the attempt to strike balances. He argued for slightly more emphasis on agriculture and light industry; slightly more investment in coastal areas; less expenditure on the military; use of material incentives; allocating proper care to all sides in the relations among the state, the production unit, and the individual; correct relations between the upper and lower levels of administration; less chauvinism by Han Chinese cadres toward minority groups; less sectarianism by the Party toward non–Party members; and so forth.[40] Bo Yibo later recalled:

While being briefed, Comrade Mao Zedong said to comrades in charge of light industry: "Your drive in work is not vigorous enough, not as vigorous as that of the heavy industry departments." This criticism reminded us that we who were engaged in heavy industry were so zealous that we brought pressure to bear on others. By saying this, he actually encouraged and supported more vigorous development of light industry.[41]

But while Mao favored greater sectoral balance, he remained fully committed to high targets, fast rates of advance, and high (and rising) levels of investment. At the same time as he called for more balanced development, he

38. *MMTTT*, p. 33.
39. Mao, 1977, pp. 284–307.
40. Barry Naughton has suggested to me that "On the Ten Major Relationships" was not really reflective of Mao's ideas; it was instead a product of the bureaucracy. However, Li Fuchun, as has been noted, objected to many of the economic aspects of the speech (see MacFarquhar, 1974, pp. 61–68). As will be shown, Mao displayed decided preferences before the document was published. He referred favorably to the Ten Major Relationships several times in later years, suggesting that they reflected his ideas and not views imposed on him by the bureaucracy. See, e.g., *MMTTT*, pp. 118, 157, and 310, for the years 1958, 1959, and 1960. Moreover, many of the economic planks of the Ten Major Relationships, such as more investment in agriculture and light industry and more coastal investment, were ignored by the planners, suggesting that they at least were not part of the bureaucratic consensus around the Ten Major Relationships.
41. Bo Yibo, "Respect and Rememberance – Marking the 60th Anniversary of the Founding of the CCP," in Foreign Broadcast Information Service, *Daily Report, China*, July 29, 1981, K 26 – K 36; see K 32.

wanted to add to the already inflated 1956 capital construction budget,[42] and when presented with a draft editorial for *Renmin Ribao* (People's Daily) opposing conservatism and *rash advance,* he scribbled the words "I won't read it" *(Bu kanle)* in the margin.[43] But even though he disapproved of the editorial, he did not attempt to overturn the decision taken by the Politburo to retreat from the small leap.

Thus, Mao's position on economic affairs appeared internally contradictory. On the one hand, he favored a more moderate and balanced pattern of economic investment allocation. Yet on the other hand, he promoted a "high tide" or "wavelike" pattern of advance. The big pushes associated with high tides undermined the moderation inherent in his allocational preferences. At times, he favored bureaucratic methods to cope with the problems of bureaucracy. While principally concerned with the dangers of rightist conservatism, he also warned against the dangers of leftism; and while concerned about class issues in the countryside, he favored a much more extensive role for bourgeois intellectuals in development. He did not rule out any route of advance except laissez-faire capitalism.

Mao's views in 1955–1956 created a climate of ambiguity for China's other decision makers. He had not used his prerogative to define decisively the terms of debate on economic questions. Moreover, after June 1956 he was an even less active participant in economic decision making. To oversimplify, Mao favored balanced but rapid advance. In contrast, the financial coalition championed balanced and stable advance, and the planning coalition favored imbalanced, rapid advance. Mao's position created a situation where the planners and the budgeteers would compete to win him over to their respective points of view.

After the Eighth Party Congress, Mao's views on the economy were even more jumbled than before. He did not devote much attention to specific economic policies, though he was preoccupied with the general question of how to build socialism in China. International relations, ideological questions, encouraging intellectuals to speak out, and improving Party performance were the topics that energized him in late 1956 and early 1957. When he did speak on economic questions, he generally sided with the financial coalition, though aspects of the planners' program also received support.

42. Shi Zhongquan, "Jianxinde Kaitou – Mao Zedong zai 'Wenhua Dageming' Yiqian dui Zhongguo Shehuizhuyi Jianshe Daolude Tansuo" (Arduous Breakthroughs – Mao Zedong's Explorations on the Road of China's Socialist Construction Before the 'Cultural Revolution'), *Dangshi Yanjiu* (Research on Party History), 1987, no. 1, pp. 1–19; see p. 2.

43. Two of the many references to this well-known incident include Deng Liqun, 1981, pp. 11–12, and Wu Leng-hsi, 1969–1970, p. 72.

In his summing-up speech to the Second Plenum of the Eighth Central Committee in November 1956,[44] Mao acceded to the line of development in economic policy making that he had opposed in June, and he favored retrenchment in the 1957 plan. Practically repeating Li Fuchun's statement at the Eighth Party Congress, he averred that economic balance was only relative and that future imbalances would inevitably arise. He stated that the FFYP was basically correct and that perfect plans were impossible. He made no apologies for greatly accelerating the pace of collectivization.

Mao also criticized the budget-making process. He recommended that at least three meetings a year be held where central leaders would review the budget – "Otherwise it will always be the cadres in charge who know them [the contents of the budget] better while we on our part will just raise our hands." In addition, he voiced several nitpicking criticisms of Li Xiannian's report on the budget to the Third Session of the First National People's Congress in June 1956. Li had been one of the first to attack rash advance publicly, and Mao now vented his spleen. He called on Party secretaries (generalists) to play a larger role in finance and planning. He also wanted them to concentrate on grain, pork, vegetables, and agricultural sidelines (the subject of Chen Yun's speech to the plenum). He stated that the peasants' one-sided focus on grain in early 1956 had been wrong. (Actually it was rural cadres who concentrated all efforts on grain.) However, after the price readjustments for agricultural products announced by Li Xiannian at the Eighth Party Congress, the peasants were now ignoring grain. "Low prices for grain hurt the peasants; now that you have set such low prices for grain, the peasants will simply stop growing it. This problem merits close attention." If by this remark Mao meant that the purchase price for grain should be raised, he was fundamentally undercutting the planning coalition. Any increase in the purchase price of grain meant that significant amounts of state monies would be channeled to the rural sector and taken from industry, as Li Xiannian had stated in September 1956. If, on the other hand, he meant that the prices for subsidiary goods would be reduced, then he was supporting the planners against Li's budget redistribution. (In January 1957, Mao supported increasing the grain purchase price.)

Mao also implied that some of his own ideas presented in "On the Ten Major Relationships" might have to be amended. He felt that too much attention was being paid to improving living standards and that insufficient propaganda was being devoted to the idea of "building the country through

44. Mao, 1977, pp. 332–49.

industry and thrift." This contradicted his April view that wages should go up as production increased, and undermined the utility of material incentives.

Mao commented in detail on the international situation (his speech followed shortly after the Polish and Hungarian uprisings) and domestic political affairs. He favored "socialist big democracy," including the right to strike and the right to demonstrate. He felt that the Party should regard strikes and demonstrations as good things because they brought problems to light and facilitated their resolution. He also announced that a rectification campaign was to be launched the following year, targeted at subjectivism, sectarianism, and bureaucratism, the last of which received the most emphasis in his speech.

In early December, Mao, accompanied by Liu Shaoqi, Chen Yun, Bo Yibo, and others, met with leading capitalists.[45] In a conciliatory mood, he began his address by stating, "I am a layman in economics." If the capitalists had troubles now that their enterprises were effectively nationalized, they should report them to the government and Chen Yun would take charge of the matter, he said.

Trying to persuade the capitalists of the need for close Sino-Soviet relations, Mao argued that only the Soviet Union was willing to provide China with designs for large plants, which were beyond the capability of Chinese designers. China was not economically independent. Self-reliance was not part of Mao's agenda at this time.

Mao also proposed an extremely lenient line toward the former bourgeoisie. Not only did he feel that workers should no longer oppose the former capitalists, he also invited the latter to play a full role in the development of China's industry and commerce. All contradictions reflected contradictions among the people. In fact, this theme was ever present in Mao's thoughts during this period. A 1987 source states that at this meeting Mao compared China's economic policies with the Soviet Union's New Economic Policy (NEP associated with market socialism and Nikolai Bukharin)[46] and said that the Soviet NEP period had been too short.[47]

Mao next spoke at a conference of provincial Party secretaries. The first of these talks was on January 18, 1957, the day Chen Yun presented the three

45. *MMTTT*, pp. 36–45.

46. The definitive study is Stephen F. Cohen, 1980, esp. chs. 5 and 6. Bukharin's views were rehabilitated in the Soviet Union only after several years of Gorbachev's rule.

47. Shi Zhongquan (n. 42), p. 15. A March 1957 text of Mao's speech does have a direct reference to China's NEP, stating that it should last another seven years. See MacFarquhar, Cheek, and Wu, 1989, p. 230. I am grateful to Roderick MacFarquhar and Timothy Cheek for providing me with a draft of this volume so that these speeches could be incorporated into my study. All page references are to the published version.

balances to the same conclave; Mao was deeply influenced by Chen's speech. He stated that this conference was designed to discuss three matters: ideological trends, rural questions, and economic issues. Speaking now to a Party audience and not to national capitalists, Mao's view of class questions was a good deal tougher than it had been in December. Many cadres felt discouraged by the problems caused by the upsurge in 1956. Mao singled out Liao Luyan, minister of agriculture, as someone who had lost his courage. He also noted that the preceding year there had been a struggle against conservatism, and in 1956 there had been a struggle against "rash advance." The latter struggle had caused another right-wing deviation. The implication was that it was time for another campaign against conservatism, or at least another production upsurge. Yet when Mao focused on specifics, he was more interested in launching great democracy and convincing provincial secretaries that problems could be solved only if the masses were allowed to voice their complaints.

When Mao turned to agricultural questions on January 27, he sided with the leaders of the financial coalition, who wished to devote more attention and resources to agriculture. He said, "In a sense, agriculture is industry. We should persuade the industrial departments to face the countryside and aid agriculture." His proposals for aiding agriculture included using the law of value and strict economic accounting to increase both accumulation in the collectives and the income of the peasants. He gave a comprehensive exegesis of the linkages between agriculture and the rest of the economy. In unofficial versions of this speech that circulated during the Cultural Revolution, he also called for reviving the Draft Agricultural Program, building chemical fertilizer plants in every province, and raising the procurement price for grain.[48]

This last proposal is particularly important, given the distributive consequences for the entire economy. Mao presented an amalgam of proposals to promote agricultural production. There can be no doubt that he favored paying much more attention to agricultural questions. Although he adopted proposals associated with different coalitions, he seems to have come down on the side of the budgeteers.

In another famous speech, "On the Correct Handling of Contradictions Among the People,"[49] Mao continued his emphasis on agriculture and implicitly criticized the planners. More important than his passing references

48. Mao, 1977, pp. 350–83; *MMTTT*, pp. 46–53, 54–62.
49. The official text, published in June 1957, is in Mao, 1977, pp. 384–421. A text of the original version is in MacFarquhar et al., 1989, pp. 130–89. An analysis of the original version is found in Schoenhals, 1986b. For a reaction to the speech (which also suggests that there are still more versions), see Loh, 1962, pp. 218–22, 261.

to economic concerns, however, was his exposition of the notion of nonantagonistic contradictions, or contradictions among the people. Anyone willing to work for China's development could be a member of the people, even without being in favor of the CCP or socialism. If contradictions developed among the people, they were to be handled through criticism and self-criticism, persuasion, and other relatively gentle methods. Mao agreed with Liu Shaoqi that the period of large-scale mass movements was basically over, and he described how the idea of nonantagonistic contradictions would be applied to various issues in Chinese society.

The official version of the speech contained two parts discussing economic questions. Mao started with a basic point: "In drawing up plans, handling affairs, or thinking over problems, we must proceed from the fact that China has a population of 600 million, and we must never forget this fact. Why do we make such a point of this? Is it possible that there are people who are still unaware of this?"[50] In fact, Mao implied that the planners did not consider the interests of all 600 million Chinese or, since most of the population were peasants, that planners neglected agriculture. He was already on record as wanting industry to face the countryside. He now strengthened his demands.

Mao reiterated the priorities set out in his speech on the Ten Major Relationships and called, at least in the official version of "On the Correct Handling of Contradictions Among the People," for the construction of more medium-size and small enterprises. Interestingly, this reference to medium-size and small enterprises was not present in the original version, and was added only in June 1957 after Li Fuchun and Bo Yibo had campaigned actively for such a policy. Indeed, the original version of the speech suggested that Mao had sympathy for the financial coalition's views, whereas the official version was somewhat more in tune with planning perspectives.

In the original speech, Mao conceded the many problems of collectives and stated that it would take five years of consolidation before they became fully effective. After consolidation, "the state monopoly for purchasing and marketing [of grain] will become a monopoly only for purchasing and not marketing, [and] we will no longer sell grain to the peasants."[51] In other words, the scope of the market would expand. He also advocated freezing state grain procurement at current levels for the foreseeable future, which in combination with other policies would allow "the peasants [to] become richer than workers."[52] This left open the question of how the state could

50. Mao, 1977, p. 407.
51. MacFarquhar et al., 1989, p. 151.
52. Ibid., p. 153; see also pp. 149–52.

extract the resources necessary to fund industrial development and provide raw materials for light industry. The point about peasants becoming richer than workers also revealed Mao's continuing revolutionary optimism (if not outright delusions) about the rural areas. He went on to criticize excessive lowering of standards, especially in engineering projects. (Lowering of standards would be central to the program of Li Fuchun and Bo Yibo, articulated in April and May.) But more radical elements were present too – he wanted to freeze salaries for ten years. This would destroy material incentives, central to both the planners and the budgeteers. Finally, he argued that the "ratio of investments in heavy industry, light industry, and agriculture should be substantially adjusted in comparison with the past."[53] Until 1956, the ratio of investment in heavy industry to that in light industry was 8:1. In his speech on the Ten Major Relationships in April 1956, Mao proposed a 7:1 ratio. Now he suggested a ratio of 6:1. He concluded his discussion of economic issues with strong support for Chen Yun's approach to development.

Give it [economic policy] a bit of flexibility, do more work on markets, let the peasants eat their fill, let the peasants have purchasing power, develop light industry, [and] the peasants [will] produce even more a raw materials for industrial use and produce even more food. [If] peasants increase [their] purchasing power, light industry will have both materials and a market, [and] heavy industry will have a market, too.[54]

After his speech on contradictions, Mao was preoccupied by the question of contradictions among the people, and the Party and the leadership were thrown into turmoil as a result of his advocacy. Indeed, in one of his provincial stops in March 1957, he referred to himself as a "wandering lobbyist" for proper handling of contradictions and for blooming and contending.[55] He did not see class struggle as a major issue, and he did not propose traditional mass movements led by the Party. He sanctioned the unmediated mobilization of the people to express their views, even critical views, to the Party. His ideas on economic affairs were occasional and unsystematic, but he generally favored a more balanced allocation of resources, use of the market, and a moderate pace of development.

Repeatedly in the spring of 1957 Mao argued that the Party must make the transition from emphasis on class struggle to emphasis on the struggle with nature.[56] In a conversation with the Bulgarian ambassador in April, he stated, "Building socialism is really not easy. Building socialism ignoring the

53. Ibid., pp. 185–86.
54. Ibid., p. 187.
55. Ibid., p. 321.
56. Shi Zhongquan (n. 42), p. 1.

people, establishing heavy industry, ignoring the people won't do."[57] Yet he articulated utopian views as well. In the future, he said, the collectives would come under state ownership and would be like factories.[58] Despite increased production, he perceived a strained supply of grain, which required continuing the policy of unified purchasing and marketing. But "neither will it do to have too much [of unified purchase and supply]. [We] plan to have the majority of the [collectives], except in the cash crop regions, handle their own grain, edible oil, and meat by themselves next year."[59] This implied expanding market relations in the countryside. Finally, in April 1957 Mao suggested that he recognized the need to slow the pace of advance. "In the beginning in my mind, I too craved for greatness and success. Only as recently as March and April last year did [I] begin to change."[60]

Thus, until the launching of the Anti-Rightist Campaign in early June, Mao's sporadic interjections on economic affairs increasingly resembled those of Chen Yun and his allies. He voiced no objection to limited expansion of the market and to the use of price policy to increase agricultural production. He favored the redistribution of investment funds to aid agriculture and light industry. He even backed away from a commitment to very high rates of growth. Narrow economic issues were not central to his political activities before June 1957; the overall question of how to build a socialist state was his core concern. He left economic officials alone to manage the economy while he sought to encourage every member of Chinese society to the utmost effort by relaxing the political atmosphere. When relaxation led to strident criticism of the Party, Mao had to rethink his strategy of socialist construction as it had developed from 1956 to June 1957.

Mao Zedong spent much of June and July working on a counterattack against the newly designated rightists. His writings during this period have a knee-jerk quality. Yet at a meeting of Party secretaries in Qingdao in July, he tried to pull the fragmented pieces of the Chinese polity back together and, indirectly, to examine why he had been so wrong about the Hundred Flowers.[61] But he was not entirely convinced that blooming and contending should stop. He warned that "rightists" must be given jobs and not deprived of their civil rights, because, "judging from many events in the past, extreme policies produce bad results." He insisted that most people, even most in-

---

57. Ibid., p. 9.
58. MacFarquhar et al., 1989, p. 314.
59. Ibid., pp. 325–26; quotation, p. 370.
60. Ibid., p. 372. The irony and tragedy inherent in this sentence, in light of future events, are obvious.
61. Mao, 1977, pp. 473–82.

dustrialists and intellectuals, supported the Party, and that certain members of the Party should not overemphasize the strength of the rightists. He called for a rural socialist education movement. He noted that there was danger in both inadequate punishment and excessive punishment but identified the main current danger as excessive leniency. In the rural areas, as well as in the cities, the struggle in the summer of 1957 was a struggle between two roads, capitalism and socialism. In other words, Mao created incentives for cadres to be harsh in their attacks on rightists. As a result, more than 550,000 persons were branded as rightists, several million peasants were labeled "antisocialist elements."[62]

At the conclusion of his speech at Qingdao, Mao directed Party secretaries to devote a great deal of attention to the rural areas. Collectives, grain purchasing, and other questions related to agriculture and the countryside were to be investigated in preparation for the Third Plenum, which he announced would be held in September. He also asked the secretaries to consider whether the National Agricultural Program (the Forty Points on Agriculture) required any revisions, a call Bo Yibo had already issued in June.

Thus, even in July Mao's ideas remained contradictory. He favored mass movements designed to deal with what the Party now defined as the class struggle between the people, led by the Party, and the "capitalist roaders," led by the rightists. But he was still wrapped up in the idea (and convinced of the importance) of contradictions among the people. He was not prepared to renounce the methods and goals he had espoused in early 1957. On economic questions, his views were enigmatic. Mao remained uncommitted to any distinct path of development.

After the Qingdao meeting, Mao went into semiseclusion, perhaps reevaluating the events of 1956 and 1957, and apparently made no major speech until the Third Plenum (September 20 – October 9, 1957). His withdrawal went beyond the ordinary. He all but ignored the thirtieth anniversary of the founding of the People's Liberation Army on August 1, 1957, sending only a one-sentence congratulatory telegram.[63] Thirtieth birthdays are significant in Chinese culture, and it is surprising that Mao had so little to say about an event and an institution in which he had played no small role.

In early September, Mao went to Wuhan to walk across the first bridge to span the Changjiang (Yangtze River) before it officially opened. A Hong Kong communist publication quoted him as asking the director of the bridge-building project if it was possible to build such a bridge without Soviet technical aid.

62. Liao Kai-lung, 1981, pt. 1, p. 81.
63. See *Current Background*, no. 897 (December 10, 1969), p. 57.

The director said yes. Doubting him, Mao asked the question again and received the same answer.[64] Did Mao foresee a breakdown in Sino-Soviet relations? Was he trying to determine China's level of self-reliance? It can only be conjectured that he had painfully reevaluated the policies he and the Party had adopted up to the summer of 1957 and was pondering how to carry out China's socialist political and economic development in light of the failure of the strategy he had endorsed in February. At the Third Plenum, he would begin to articulate his new vision of how to promote China's development.

C. The views of other leaders

C.1. Liu Shaoqi

Compared with Mao Zedong's, the views expressed by other top leaders are much less well documented. Since their deaths, more information about the activities of Liu Shaoqi, Zhou Enlai, and Zhu De has become available, but it is still limited. Deng Xiaoping's activities are particularly obscure, although in the aftermath of the Tiananmen massacre of 1989 a collection of Deng's works from 1938 to 1965 was circulated.

What materials are available are similar to the Mao archive in that economic issues do not play a major role. The leadership focused on issues of contradictions among the people, generally making few or no comments on the economy. Again this suggests that economic officials were not subject to extensive supervision and interference. To be more speculative, it may reflect ignorance of economic matters on the part of some of these leaders, a state of affairs that allowed each economic coalition to press its strategy at every chance.

From December 1956 to May 1957, Liu Shaoqi concentrated on contradictions among the people, and he spent February–April investigating conditions in the five central and southern provinces. Education was also a major concern of his at this time.[65] He argued that more educated young people should be sent to the countryside, because the urban and educational sectors could not absorb their growing numbers. The demand for educated people was well satisfied in urban settings, but rural areas still needed large numbers of educated youths. And sending youth to the rural areas was a mani-

---

64. Gong Jiang, "Chairman Mao Takes a Leisurely Walk Across the Yangtse River," *Wenhui Bao* (Literary Daily; published in Hong Kong), September 30, 1957, in *Survey of China Mainland Press*, no. 1624 (October 4, 1957), pp. 1–3.
65. Liu Shaoqi, 1985, pp. 277–322.

festation of the state's growing concern with agriculture. Indeed, Liu suggested that in the future agriculture would be given greatly increased attention. He was one of the few leaders to mention the Draft National Agricultural Program in the spring of 1957, and he saw the emergence of successive programs for agricultural development that would bring about the mechanization, electrification, and scientific development of the countryside.[66]

Liu gave a 40,000-character speech in Shanghai on April 27, 1957, discussing contradictions among the people. Mao's speech on contradictions comprised about 28,000 characters in the original form and 24,000 in the authorized version.[67] Liu's speech contained a general analysis of contradictions and a long, discursive section on specific social contradictions. In this same passage, he examined a number of economic issues. For example, in addressing the housing question, he argued that it would take more than thirty years to build enough housing to reunite families. People who wanted to deal with this problem immediately should realize, he stated, that China could build housing or it could undertake five-year plans, but not both. He made clear his commitment to high rates of accumulation and planning, but he also suggested that urban workers form collectives to build their own houses, which they would own. He stated that private construction and ownership of houses should also be allowed. He proposed that public housing rents be increased.

In a section on prices, Liu defended recent price increases. He argued that prices of agricultural products had to be increased to spur production. Prices of high-grade materials, particularly cigarettes and woolens, were increased to accumulate more revenue for the state. He refuted the notion that the 1956 wage increase for most workers was consumed by the price increases, suggesting that only 1 percent of the increased wages had been taken away by higher prices.

Liu also examined issues related to free markets. He was one of the few top leaders actually to use the term "free market," but his views were ambivalent. He advocated a policy of "utilizing, limiting, and transforming" the free market. This policy had been used by the CCP toward capitalists prior to socialist transformation in 1956, but at the Eighth Party Congress Chen Yun suggested that such measures should be abolished now that joint state-

---

66. Ibid., pp. 280, 286.
67. On the length of Liu's speech, see *Jiefang Ribao* editorial committee, "Zhengque Chuli Renmin Neibu Maodunde Jiaocai" (Good Teaching Materials on the Correct Handling of Contradictions Among the People), *Jiefang Ribao* (Liberation Daily; published in Shanghai), May 12, 1980, pp. 1, 3. The version of the speech published in Liu Shaoqi, 1985, pp. 295–309, is about 10,000 characters. However, Liu Shaoqi, n.d., contains a complete version (pp. 151–81). On the length of Mao's speech, see MacFarquhar et al., 1989, p. 132.

private ownership existed. Liu's use of these terms, not repeated in other sources, suggests his discomfort with markets. Moreover, he mentioned the existence of "underground factories" and other negative factors as stemming from free markets. On the other hand, he argued that China's planned economy was excessively rigid and inflexible. Plans could only include a limited number of items, and only the market could provide flexibility and stimulate the production of a wide range of products. To increase both flexibility and variety while limiting the market, Liu called for greater autonomy for localities and enterprises in economic decision making. In this way, the state could both compete with private entrepreneurs and use them to improve economic circulation, and ultimately, he felt, force them out of business – the state would prove superior in the marketplace.

Liu addressed many other quite concrete issues in his speech; for instance, he denied that rural living standards were much lower than urban living standards, and spoke of how authorities should deal with people unwilling to work in enterprises and of cadres alienating themselves from the people. His speech demonstrates a much more empirical understanding of contradictions in Chinese society than is found in Mao's comparable address. Liu's views suggest profoundly difficult problems in Chinese society, mostly the result of the revolution of rising expectations and the trade-offs that are a part of economic development.

Liu reiterated many of his views on the market in a conversation with the head of the Higher Party School on May 7, 1957.[68] He commented on the inflexibility of the Soviet planned economy and called on the Chinese to learn from this bad experience. He argued that China's planned economy must be more flexible and diverse than a capitalist economy; if it was not, he asked, how could one say that socialism is superior to capitalism? He called on the Party school to study how to use the market in conjunction with the plan to increase China's economic flexibility and the range of commodities produced while minimizing the market's negative aspects. He upheld the need to use the law of value in allocating and distributing production, and supported private agricultural subsidiary production and private

68. Yang Xianzhen, "Shehuizhuyi Jingji Yaoyou Duoyangxing, Linghuoxing" (The Socialist Economy Should Be Diversified and Lively), *Guangming Ribao* (Illumination Daily), May 23, 1980, p. 3. The information provided in this story is confirmed by several other sources. See, for example, "Wo Guo Nongye Zhanxianshang Liang Tiao Luxiande Douzheng" (The Struggle Between the Two Roads on Our Country's Agricultural Front), *Hongse Nongye Zhanbao* (Red Agricultural Combat News), 1967, no. 1, pp. 1–23 (see p. 13), repr. in *Hongweibing Ziliao*, vol. 15, 1975, pp. 4799–4811, and Zhou Cheng'en, "Bada Qianhou Dang dui Woguo Shehuizhuyi Jianshe Daolude Chubu Tansuo" (Preliminary Examination of the Party's Road for Our Country's Socialist Construction Before and After the Eighth Party Congress), *Dangshi Yanjiu* (Research on Party History), 1986, no. 2, pp. 1–7 (see p. 4). A text of Liu's instructions is found in *Liu Shaoqi*, n.d., pp. 181–86; see esp. pp. 184–85.

plots. The Party school started a study of these points, similar but not identical to many of Chen Yun's ideas, but suppression of the Hundred Flowers halted the work.

C.2. Zhou Enlai

The record of Zhou Enlai's activities between October 1956 and October 1957 is more complete than that of Liu Shaoqi (and Deng Xiaoping). Zhou did address economic issues on occasion, but generally he was occupied with the Hundred Flowers Campaign and united-front policies. He appears to have sided with Chen Yun and the financial coalition on general developments, particularly in his speech to the Second Plenum of the Eighth Central Committee on November 10, 1956.[69] Specifically, he supported sectoral readjustment in favor of agriculture and a slower, more tempered pace of advance.

Zhou argued that plans required revision and that the plan for 1957 would be very lean. He saw imbalance as bad for the economy, particularly the imbalance between heavy industry and agriculture. Citing Mao, he stated that agriculture must be developed to provide the incentives to increase productivity. He suggested that long-term plans might require more time for completion and that this was not a bad thing, since the socialist cause would not be harmed by revising plans downward or prolonging the time to complete them. He pointed out that the Forty Points on Agriculture, Mao's plan for agricultural development in early 1956, required significant modification. Finally, he demonstrated the defects of trying to hasten the pace of development, with a telling example of incorrect sequencing. He noted that the Changchun No. 1 Automobile Plant had been completed early. Early completion had demanded the import of large amounts of machinery from the Soviet Union, which if the plant had been built according to schedule, could have been supplied by machine-building enterprises under construction in China. Moreover, oil and gas production was the one major industrial sector that would not reach its target under the First Five-Year Plan. As a result, the new plant's increased auto production required additional oil and gas imports. "Haste makes waste" was the underlying theme of Zhou's argument.

Zhou, concurrently China's foreign minister and premier, left for two months at the end of 1956 on diplomatic missions to Asia and Eastern Europe. On his return, he met with and escorted a number of prominent foreign visitors,

69. Zhou Enlai, 1984b, pp. 229–38.

and regularly met with non-CCP figures.[70] Economic affairs were at best peripheral to his concerns, with one exception. He did reaffirm the need to train many intellectuals to further China's development, and made interesting comments about Hong Kong's playing an important trade and investment role in China's development. He also saw agricultural development as the precondition for the construction of heavy industry, but he said nothing else about the economy.[71] Zhou, however, was an absolutely tireless worker, the perfect chief of staff; and he undoubtedly kept abreast of economic affairs.[72]

The one break in Zhou's silence on economic affairs was his keynote address to the Fourth Session of the First National People's Congress in mid June 1957. This speech was aimed entirely at rebutting the Hundred Flowers critics. Point by point, Zhou denied their assertion that the Party had mishandled affairs since it came to power. The speech was delivered before the leadership had decided how extensive the Anti-Rightist Campaign should be, and Zhou attempted to strike a balance between the need to suppress the Party's critics and the pressure to continue the Hundred Flowers policy, particularly in regard to science and to allowing intellectuals a larger role in China's modernization. But many in the Party were thirsty for revenge, and Zhou's efforts at balance were quickly rejected.[73]

Conceding the existence of mistakes in China's economic construction, Zhou argued that these certainly did not outweigh the achievements, and he addressed one by one criticisms leveled at the Party in regard to the economy. Some thought that the pace of advance in 1956 had been too rapid and the retreat of 1957 too severe. Zhou argued that this was incorrect – only some targets in 1956 were too high, and the plan for 1957 was accurate. In denying that economic construction in 1956 was overadventurous, he undermined much of the justification for Chen Yun's attempt to restructure the planning system. He then rebutted the charges that the Party had bungled the First Five-Year Plan and the planned purchase and supply of grain, and that China should not have followed the Soviet model. Most of his counterattacks strengthened the hands of the orthodox at the expense of the exper-

70. Huai En, 1986, pp. 390–99. Texts of Zhou's major speeches at this time are found in Zhou Enlai, 1984b, pp. 229–71, and 1984a, pp. 329–88.
71. Zhou Enlai, 1984a, pp. 356–57, 353–55, and 380. Between March 20 and March 23, Zhou conveyed the spirit of Mao's Ten Major Relationships to cadres in Hangzhou, but no text is available.
72. Zhou's workaholic personality is remarked on constantly. See such commemorative volumes as *Jing'aide Zhou Zongli, Women Yongyuàn Huainian Nin*, 1977; *Renminde Hao Zongli*, 1979; and *Huainian Zhou Enlai*, 1986.
73. Zhou Enlai, "Report on the Work of the Government," in *Communist China, 1955–1959*, 1971, pp. 300–329.

imenters in the leadership.[74] Zhou's speech illustrates how the failure of the Hundred Flowers was a vital factor in the weakening of the financial coalition.

C.3. Zhu De and Deng Xiaoping[75]

Recently released materials shed new light on Zhu De's views, which up to now have received little attention.[76] Zhu's role in the policy process remains obscure, however, as does the import of his ideas. He addressed economic questions repeatedly in the period from October 1956 to October 1957. His opinions reflect elements from both the budgeteer and planning coalitions, rather than fall neatly into either camp.

Zhu addressed several issues forcefully and repeatedly during an extensive tour of the provinces between January 7 and March 24, 1957. He was particularly interested in increasing exports, promoting handicraft industries, decentralizing industry, developing mountainous areas, and having defense industries serve civilian needs. He favored the use of price policy, administrative simplification, and the development of tourism to increase foreign exchange earnings. He suggested that even coal be allowed to enter the free market to spur exports, but he argued against foreign borrowing. Price policy and other forms of subsidy were his preferred methods for developing mountainous regions and promoting handicrafts. He wanted more medium-size and small enterprises built, with provinces controlling more of them. He argued that too much emphasis had been put on the processing industries (steel and machine building) and not enough on raw materials. He favored consolidation of the defense industry and encouraging military factories to serve civilian needs.

Zhu's advocacy of price policy, the market (even for coal), administrative simplification, and encouragement of handicrafts and of exports all overlapped with the position of the financial coalition. Yet when touring Yunnan he said, "One aspect of the superiority of our socialist system is that we are able to use planning to organize and develop production, and resolve financial problems. We absolutely cannot allow the resolution of financial problems to hinder production."[77] This certainly was not in accord with Chen Yun's three balances. Zhu's support of medium-size and small industry, of

74. Ibid., esp. pp. 305–9.
75. Chen Yun is discussed in detail in Chapter 4 rather than here, since despite his high rank, he was much less a generalist than were his compatriots on the Politburo Standing Committee.
76. Zhu De, 1986, pp. 349–62, and esp. *Zhu De Nianpu*, 1986, pp. 406–20.
77. *Zhu De Nianpu*, 1986, p. 412.

defense industries serving civilian needs, and of decentralization were congruous with the planners' program. But again his emphasis on raw materials rather than on finished products and use of the market to stimulate coal production put him at odds with the planners. The impact of Zhu's views on policy making is indeterminable; judging from his list of appointments, he spent more time talking to leaders of the planning coalition than to the financial grouping.

Deng Xiaoping's role in Chinese politics during this period, despite recently published materials, remains obscure.[78] He served as a troubleshooter on political questions, especially contradictions among the people. One speech from the period focused on economic questions, though at a high level of generality, and there were other scattered remarks on economic issues. In a speech in Xian in April 1957, he argued for close Sino-Soviet relations and the promotion of heavy industry, but he also criticized the industrial departments for craving only the big and the new. He advocated doing more with less money, and he particularly criticized urban construction plans. Differing with Chen Yun's ideas of January, when Chen suggested that not just the "flesh" (nonproductive investment in things like housing) but also the "bones" (industrial investment) must be cut, Deng favored reducing only nonproductive investment. Nonetheless, he agreed on the need to hold down overall investment figures in 1957 and possibly into 1958 as the "great achievements" of 1956 were consolidated and the problems left over from that year were worked out. He concluded with a vague discussion of how to build socialism according to the reality of conditions in China, and of how to balance the state's need for industrial construction and the people's need for consumption.[79] The lack of specifics in this speech suggests that Deng had little to do with economic affairs in 1956–1957.

One other comment on economic affairs by Deng bears discussion. Speaking to what must have been a hostile audience at Qinghua University in January 1957, Deng noted that the Ministry of Finance had concluded that in the realm of Sino-Soviet economic assistance the Soviets had sought small advantages (*pianyi*) in relations with China. He noted that in isolated cases this was true but that overall the Soviets had made great contributions to China's construction.[80] Indeed, the theme of this speech was a defense of the Soviet Union and of the Sino-Soviet relationship. Unfortunately, no other information is available about this Ministry of Finance analysis, but it reso-

78. See Deng Xiaoping, 1989, pp. 245–67, and 1967, pp. 49–64.
79. See Deng Xiaoping, 1989, pp. 249–57.
80. Deng Xiaoping, 1967, p. 62.

nates with that ministry's opposition to aspects of the Soviet model as applied in China.

D. Conclusion

The ideas of China's top leaders during the period from the Eighth Party Congress to the Third Plenum of the Eighth Central Committee were not clearly articulated. Overall, the leaders expressed vague support for Chen Yun and the financial coalition, particularly on the question of balance. Mao sided with Chen's positions regularly in early 1957. Liu Shaoqi wanted the Party school to study how to develop the economy using diversified forms of ownership, in line with Chen's ideas at the Eighth Party Congress. Zhou Enlai and Chen worked together to stem the rash advance of early 1956, and Zhou was perhaps the leader most sympathetic to the budgeteers' views. Zhu De's feelings were mixed, but he too agreed with part of the financial coalition's position. Deng Xiaoping's views remain opaque, though he seemed sympathetic to the Soviet model.

Two things are more important than this general support for the financial coalition: First, the degree of support expressed by each leader was weak, and the frequency of comments made about the economy was low. No irrevocable commitments were made. Nothing precluded leadership's changing its mind (individually and collectively) about general support for Chen Yun. Second, during this period, all Politburo Standing Committee members except Chen Yun left Beijing to go on provincial tours of inspection. This may have left Chen as the ranking leader in Beijing during the spring of 1957. It also meant that economic officials had the economic agenda to themselves. The best available evidence shows Party leaders concentrating almost exclusively on the issues of contradictions among the people and blooming and contending.

Mao Zedong did not articulate a clear line of development during the second half of 1956 and the first nine months of 1957. Class struggle and mass mobilization were not central to his ideas until after the reversal of the Hundred Flowers. He favored balance, particularly increased attention to agriculture, and he was on record as supporting the expansion of the market. In short, during this period no distinct Maoist model of development existed.

The suppression of the Hundred Flowers Campaign and the resulting Anti-Rightist Campaign undermined the emerging reformist elements in China's political economy. The economic agenda was once again up for grabs, and the planners took quick advantage of the changed political and economic environment. The failure of the Hundred Flowers eliminated or grossly undermined some options for economic development. Policies that weakened Party control over any aspect of life were rejected. Subsumed under this rubric were market-oriented reforms; greater autonomy for technical specialists, scientists, and intellectuals; and an expanded role for bourgeois political parties in state affairs. Whereas this set of choices was denounced formally, the Party adopted policies that revived the social-transformative aspects of the CCP and defined the political situation in the starkest terms of class struggle since at least 1955. In effect, the Party had already biased the decision-making agenda in favor of mass-mobilization campaigns and the economic program of the planners. (Whether Party leaders were aware of this is an open question.) As the summer of 1957 passed, the strength of that bias increased. The Third Plenary Session of the Eighth Central Committee was the occasion for the codification of the planner-Party alliance.

8

The Third Plenum of the Eighth Central Committee and the Great Leap Forward

The two agendas of the CCP in 1956–1957 – economic management and political development – were reintegrated at the Third Plenum of the Eighth Central Committee in September–October 1957. The plenum represented the last stand of the financial coalition in its attempt to change the system of economic control. Its spokesmen made telling points, but the reinjection of political concerns into economic issues doomed their efforts. The planning coalition pushed its program, and Mao decisively sided with the planners, inserting into their scheme his own concern for even faster rates of advance. A temporary alliance among planners, leaders, and the Party was formed, with the planners supplying most of the economic plans and the Party and leadership providing mass mobilization and demands for extremely rapid growth. The alliance proved unstable, and within a short time the leadership and the Party supplanted the planners. Nonetheless, the planning coalition's priorities were still central to the emerging Great Leap Forward; heavy industrial interests, especially the metallurgical industry, were well satisfied by the Leap; and planners did much better politically in the Leap than did budgeteers. Yet when the leadership gradually became aware of the errors in its policies, the leadership and Mao in particular turned to the financial coalition, and above all to Chen Yun, to restore balance.

This chapter concentrates on the deliberations of the Third Plenum and briefly surveys the Great Leap Forward from the perspective of the two main economic coalitions. The Third Plenum marks the end of a stage of Chinese discussions of economic development, and the rejection of one set of options (with one partial exception) for twenty years. At no point in Mao Zedong's remaining years would the policies of the financial coalition be as forcefully expressed as in the twelve months from September 1956 to September 1957.

A. The Third Plenum

The Third Plenum was convened on September 20, 1957. Of the 97 full members of the Central Committee, 91 were in attendance, as were 62 of the 73 alternate members and 416 other CCP leaders from central departments, provincial-level administrations, and prefectural-level units. In CCP parlance, the plenum was a "three-level [cadres'] meeting." The original agenda of the plenum was to focus on how to develop agriculture and how to carry out the rectification campaign, but Mao changed this to how to combine the rectification campaign with all other work. Mao gave an opening address and Deng Xiaoping reported on rectification on September 20; Chen Yun discussed improving the administrative structure of the state and addressed agricultural questions on September 24; and Zhou Enlai examined questions related to labor, wages, and employment on September 26. Mao and Deng delivered closing speeches on October 9. Zhu De, Peng Zhen, Li Fuchun, Li Xiannian, Bo Yibo, Deng Zihui, and other leading figures spoke at various times during the meeting, and Mao Zedong often intervened in the proceedings. During the course of the meeting, the participants broke up into small groups and "enthusiastically" discussed and gave unanimous support to the major reports, by Deng, Chen, and Zhou.[1]

The plenum adopted the National Agricultural Program (in a slightly revised form) in principle. It also endorsed three measures on administrative reform and decentralization, concerning industry, commerce, and finance. Reform of wages and social welfare was also discussed. The drafts of these documents, except for the National Agricultural Program, were to be refined by the State Council and passed on to the Standing Committee of the National People's Congress for final approval.[2] In addition, the Central Committee issued a directive on building irrigation works in the countryside, although discussions of the plenum do not cite this as part of its agenda.[3]

Deng Xiaoping's report on rectification, somewhat misnamed, was the only important pronouncement publicly released at the time of the plenum. Actually, this report summarized most areas of Party work since the Eighth Party Congress. Deng's long speech reviewed the rectification campaign,

1. "The Third Plenum of the Eighth Central Committee," in *Documents of the Chinese Communist Party Central Committee*, vol. 1, 1971, pp. 109–10, and Chen Xuewei, " Bajie Sanzhong Quanhui Shuping" (A Review of the Third Plenum of the Eighth Central Committee), *Dangshi Yanjiu* (Research on Party History), 1986, no. 2, pp. 8–13.
2. "The Third Plenum," pp. 109–10.
3. "Decision of the CCP Central Committee and the State Council to Launch a Campaign for Building Irrigation Projects and Accumulating Manure in [the] Coming Winter and Next Spring" (September 24, 1957), in *Documents of the Chinese Communist Party Central Committee*, vol. 1, 1971, pp. 517–22.

drawing heavily on Mao's speech at the Qingdao Conference in July and admonishing that "the significance of the current criticism of the bourgeois rightists must not be underestimated. This is a socialist revolution on the political and ideological fronts. The socialist revolution on the economic front alone in 1956 (in the ownership of the means of production) was not enough, and it was not consolidated."[4] Deng warned that bourgeois rightists planned to restore capitalism and must be totally defeated. He stated that people should nonetheless not be afraid of full and frank discussion of opinion – this fear was itself defined as a right deviation – that weakened the bond between the CCP and the people. His words marked the beginning of formal rejection of the key contradiction identified at the Eighth Party Congress, between a backward economy and an advanced superstructure. The superstructure was now viewed as imperfect and in need of consolidation through political movements.

Despite occasional signs of moderation, the policies announced by Deng (who was charged with the day-to-day running of the Anti-Rightist Campaign) reflect a consistent set of harsh measures the CCP has taken toward its critics, especially students and intellectuals, over the years, often under Deng's personal leadership.[5] Indeed, many of the policies undertaken in 1957 also appeared after the Beijing massacre of June 4, 1989. Deng stated that the elimination of the bourgeoisie was a fundamental issue in the socialist revolution. The bourgeoisie, and especially its intellectuals, now constituted the main force challenging the proletariat, he argued, and places where intellectuals were concentrated were centers of opposition to the CCP. He concluded his section on the bourgeoisie and intellectuals with the claim that "the rightist offensive showed that most of the bourgeoisie and bourgeois intellectuals were unwilling to accept the leadership of the proletariat and the Communist Party." Yet he cautioned that while the struggle against the rightists must be continued, "we must also prevent the spreading of the scope of attack over too wide an area and the danger of employing simple and crude methods." Nonetheless, expansion of the scope of attack was precisely what happened. Deng also stated that the great majority of intellectuals were willing to advance and must be included among the working class, but this had little effect on the campaign he supervised.[6]

Turning to the rural situation, Deng stated that after the opening of free markets, the trend toward the reappearance of capitalism, especially among

4. Deng Xiaoping, "Report on the Rectification Campaign," in *Communist China, 1955–1959*, 1971, pp. 343–63; quotation, p. 343.
5. On Deng's involvement in suppressing the Chinese people, see Bachman, 1990, pp. 13–17.
6. Deng, "Report," pp. 345–49.

the more well-to-do peasants, had become fairly pronounced and had to be stopped. It was not just the better-off peasants who seemed to deviate from the socialist road, however.

In the recent period, there has existed within the Party a serious rightist deviationist ideology, namely the view that the class struggle in the countryside between the two roads has come to an end, that there is no longer any need to stress the class line and that efforts can be exclusively devoted to production and relaxing socialist education among the peasants.[7]

This undercut basic tenets of financial coalition policies toward the rural sector – implying, in fact, that members of the financial coalition were rightists.

To restrict the development toward capitalism on the part of members of cooperatives, appropriate limitations must be imposed on land retained for self-cultivation [private plots], reclamation of wasteland by individual effort, operation of side-line production individually, and the activities of the free market in the countryside.[8]

"I want to emphasize," Deng said as he delegitimized the financial coalition's policies in the rural areas, "that the class line in the countryside is still of decisive significance."

Yet the struggle between the two roads in the countryside was less pointed than in the urban areas, and the phrase "anti-rightist struggle" had to be avoided in the rural areas, Deng argued. As Mao had done in July, Deng warned against both excessively light and excessively severe punishment for errors, but identified excessive leniency as the more dangerous current problem both in the countryside and toward intellectuals.

He also argued that only when agricultural production expanded considerably could the collectives be consolidated. To spur agricultural production, the National Agricultural Program and the campaign to build water conservation projects were crucial.[9] Only substantial increases in agricultural output would guarantee successful industrialization. Agriculture required greater attention, and more resources for large-scale irrigation and flood-control projects and more chemical fertilizers were necessary. The tendency of Party members to look down their noses at agricultural work was wrong, Deng charged. Efforts by the collectives themselves to build local projects and increase common property (self-investment) were the centerpieces of Deng's views on agriculture.[10]

7. Ibid., p. 350.
8. Ibid., p. 351.
9. See the text of the irrigation directive (n. 3). Deng's speech mentioned the campaign in advance of formal promulgation of the directive. This document had a decisive effect on peasant mobilization in the countryside. The document and the ensuing water conservancy campaign are definitively analyzed in Oksenberg, 1969.
10. Deng, "Report," 349–53.

In discussing the working class, Deng argued that the rectification campaign in factories was a question of raising the ideological level of the workers and improving the work style of workers and managers. This was different in principle from the remolding of the bourgeoisie. He called for the elimination of negative behavior on the part of cadres and for their mandatory participation in production. Regulations and systems that affected production and the unity of the working class, and restricted the initiative of the workers, were to be revised or abolished, with appropriate new management systems replacing them. One such mechanism was for managers, technicians, and workers to form groups, or combinations, to solve the problems of the enterprise.[11] This assault on procedures had ominous implications. A Party cadre could claim that almost any rule or regulation restricted the masses and should therefore be abolished. The power of Party cadres in enterprises was thus greatly enhanced, and during the Great Leap many proper regulations were mistakenly or deliberately displaced, causing severe losses.

Deng stated that a large volume of material relating to defects in the Party had been brought to light during the Hundred Flowers period and that the faults must be corrected. The files on all Party members were to be reviewed in light of their activities during the Hundred Flowers period. Such a review posed the threat of a Party purge and created incentives for cadres to act harshly in the Anti-Rightist Campaign in an effort to compensate for any mistakes they might have made during the Hundred Flowers. Contradicting his statement in September 1956 that Party members with intellectual ability and specialized skills were the backbone of China's (and the Party's) development, Deng now argued that in the past too many of these kinds of people had occupied leadership positions. Inexperienced intellectuals were to be sent down to the basic level to acquire experience. All university and technical school graduates were to work in units of production suited to their specialties for a year or more before becoming officials.[12]

In his concluding section, Deng stated that improving the work style of the Party and carrying out the anti-rightist struggle were of equal importance. A major Party defect revealed in the Hundred Flowers time was the irrationality, impracticality, or mutual incompatibility of many systems and regulations. Lower levels had to play a larger role in Party affairs, since the center could not take charge of everything. In previewing the measures on reform and decentralization to be discussed by Chen Yun and Zhou Enlai at the plenum, Deng saw the basic spirit of their documents as shifting part of

11. Ibid., pp. 353–56.
12. Ibid., pp. 358–60.

the center's power to the local levels to stimulate initiative, strengthening enterprise leadership and overcoming bureaucratism and subjectivism. Deng cautioned that these changes were not to hinder centralized unity or major construction projects. Improved planning and coordination at the local levels, administrative retrenchment, the elimination of special privileges within the CCP, and maintenance of "democratic ties" with the people remained essential. Deng stated that the CCP could not allow the anti-rightist struggle to obstruct the expression of opinion by the people. (But of course it did.) Distinctions between antagonistic and nonantagonistic contradictions must not be blurred. (They were.) Simplistic methods in the Anti-Rightist Campaign were wrong. (But they were widely used.)[13]

Deng's wide-ranging speech presented a picture of developments similar to the one presented by Mao in July. Like Mao, Deng was reluctant to negate the Hundred Flowers experience fully or blooming and contending wholly. Neither Mao nor Deng was willing to see the Anti-Rightist Campaign overshadow nonantagonistic contradictions. Deng was ambivalent about the prime contradiction at the present time in China: Was it the contradiction between the backward economy and the advanced superstructure, or was it the contradiction between the proletariat and the bourgeoisie? In fact, Deng's speech suggested he was groping for some key contradiction from which all policy would flow. It was obvious that Deng and all other Party leaders no longer felt that the superstructure was as advanced and perfect as the Eighth Party Congress resolution had so baldly stated. It was also true, though, that the economy was hindering the consolidation of the socialist system, as Deng's remarks on agriculture demonstrated. At least rhetorically, Deng (and Mao) did not want the struggle against the rightists to be all-embracing. Hope remained for a large number of intellectuals and members of the bourgeoisie. Many had skills that remained in short supply, but they were no longer courted in the way they had been in 1956 and early 1957. The Party agreed that serious class struggle continued to exist in China, but Deng did not answer the question of just how serious and how pervasive that class struggle was. His speech formally ruled out much of the financial coalition's program of development, especially in the rural areas, but the basic definition of the new program of development had not been worked out and so was not presented as the consensus of opinion in his speech.

On September 24, Chen Yun delivered two speeches, one on decentralization and the other on agricultural and consumer goods production.[14] In the first, he discussed the three documents on decentralization (of industrial

13. Ibid., pp. 360–63.
14. Chen Yun, 1986, pp. 66–68, 69–77.

management, commerce, and finance) he had been charged with drafting.[15] Only a small portion of the speech is available, but his views are clearly expressed.

Chen conceded the necessity for decentralization, but he stressed maintaining control and balance after its implementation. "We must strengthen national balance work. Since economic units are scattered, there can be no planned economy without an overall, integrated balance." In the past, he noted, the center had overlooked the localities. But after the reforms were in place, there was danger of the localities' ignoring the whole situation. It was necessary to decentralize, but it was just as important to strengthen overall balance. He stated that local self-sufficiency was a wrong-headed policy because it wasted resources. Consequently, he argued, capital construction projects in the localities had to be approved by the center to ensure that the localities did not squander resources by building redundant plants. Moreover, after decentralization, lower levels should concentrate on agricultural development, not industry.

After financial decentralization, management of funds was to be strengthened. Thorough accounting and supervisory systems would be instituted by the Ministry of Finance, the Ministry of Supervision, and the local areas. Chen's support for an active role by the Ministry of Supervision was significant. At the time of his speech, high-ranking members of the ministry were under criticism because of their activities in the Hundred Flowers period, and he may have been trying to protect the ministry.[16] The plan for financial decentralization was hardly earth-shaking. By 1960, through revenue sharing the localities were to control 3.0 billion to 3.6 billion yuan, or about 10–12 percent of the total state budget for 1957 and about 50 percent of local budgetary expenditures. The revenue-sharing proportions were to remain about the same for 1958–1960, but Chen stated that after a year's experience the figures might be slightly modified. He implied that the greatest danger was of too much money's going to local areas.[17]

15. Ibid., pp. 78–85, 86–89, and 90–95. A 1981 edition of Chen's works includes drafts of only the first two documents (pp. 60–66, 67–69). There are minor differences between the drafts found in this volume and the regulations approved on November 14, 1957. No contemporary text of the financial decentralization regulations was released, but a 1979 collection includes the text. See *Zhonghua Renmin Gongheguo Fagui Huibian*, 1981 (reprint of 1958 original), pp. 391–97 (industry) and 355–57 (commerce). Translations of these are found in *Union Research Service*. vol. 9, no. 18 (November 29, 1957), pp. 269–87. The financial regulations are found in *Zhonghua Renmin Gongheguo Jingji Fagui Xuanbian*, xia, 1980, pp. 252–55.

16. See Schurmann, 1968, pp. 353–64 (esp. p. 354, where Schurmann sees attacks on the ministry as part of the Chen Yun–Mao Zedong power struggle), and pt. v more generally.

17. Chen Yun, 1986, pp. 66–68. The budget figures for 1957 are found in Li Xiannian, "Final Accounts for 1956 and the 1957 State Budget," *Current Background*, no. 464 (July 5, 1957), pp. 28–30. The decentralization regulations adopted in November were not major modifications

Chen saw the reforms and decentralization as being closely controlled by the center. The powers handed down to the local levels were not extensive, and he emphasized at every opportunity how severely circumscribed the action of lower levels would be. He wanted the center to maintain supervisory control and a firm grip on key economic indicators. His reforms sounded more like a limited delegation of authority to the lower levels than like a fundamental change in the administrative system. Overall balance was still central to his economic ideas, and he fought to keep this concept alive in a hostile environment.

Chen's second speech was more inflammatory. It was his last vigorous defense of the financial coalition before it was defeated at the plenum and swept away by the emerging Leap. Even so, his position on certain issues was moving in the direction of the planners. The portion of this speech that is available deals with resolving problems of food and clothing.[18] He began by noting that it would be hard for per capita consumption of food and cloth to increase in the Second Five-Year Plan (SFYP), and that it was possible consumption would even decline. Agriculture was already the weak link in China's economy. While collectivization laid the groundwork for agricultural advance, it did not solve the problem. He noted that there was a time lag of seven to eight years between the initiation of measures to promote agriculture and their yielding full effect. Further delay in dealing with agriculture would only prolong China's backwardness. A delay of five years (i.e., dealing with agriculture seriously only with the onset of the Third Five-Year Plan in 1963) would delay China's progress by fifteen years. He called on local Party committees to devote 80 percent of their energies to agriculture, and noted that even industrial officials were aware of agricultural difficulties. Chen said Mao had recently raised the issue of agricultural mechanization, and he revealed that a five-man central economic work group led by himself was preparing to study the issue. He then outlined four ways to respond to the agricultural situation: develop chemical fertilizers, develop chemical fibers,

---

of the existing system. Many industrial enterprises, especially in light industry, were to be handed over to the localities. Yet at the Eighth Party Congress, Jia Tuofu had stated that 75 percent of light industrial enterprises were already under local control. Enterprises were to be allowed to retain 20 percent of their profits and were not to be required to fulfill as many targets. But 20 percent of enterprise profits came to about 2.5–3.0 billion yuan in 1957, and if the profit-retention figure was applied to industrial enterprises only, the total was only about a billion yuan. See Jia Tuofu, "Guanyu Fazhan Qinggongyede Jige Wenti" (Several Problems in the Development of Light Industry), *Xinhua Banyuekan* (New China Semimonthly), 1956, no. 21, pp. 100–102, and Li Xiannian's budget report. An excellent study of the financial decentralization (Lardy, 1978b) argues that this reform was not a basic change in the structure of the Chinese financial system; this decentralization was largely incremental. In 1958, however, the nature of decentralization changed radically.

18. Chen Yun, 1986, pp. 69–77.

enhance flood-control measures, and expand irrigated cropland. Deng's report and the consensus opposed to the market and price incentives made advocacy of such policies by Chen politically impossible.

Chen now believed that developing the chemical fertilizer industry was the fastest and most important way to develop agriculture. The Chinese had not attached much importance to this – during the First Five-Year plan, the Soviets had supplied China with one 72,000-ton (output) plant, which took five years to construct and for which Chinese industry could supply none of the key equipment. But now China had trial-produced most of the equipment for such a factory, and since February 1957 the Ministry of Chemical Industries had been promoting expanded fertilizer production. After many discussions with that ministry and the First Ministry of Machine Building, the leadership had decided to develop design standards for fertilizer factories in the last half of 1957, to trial-produce equipment in 1958, to begin large-scale fabrication in 1959, and to begin to equip factories with this machinery in 1960. Chen noted that although the technology would be backward, it could be improved gradually. Each 100,000-ton plant would cost a billion yuan but would increase yields by three million tons. In other words, even with much more attention to chemical fertilizer production, the effects of investment in this sector would not be felt for several years, and the state's capacity to build many such factories was limited. (Total investment in the SFYP was slated at 90 billion to 100 billion yuan.)

The situation in cotton textiles was grim, Chen reported. Because of food shortages, cotton acreage was turned over to food production in 1957, so that even further reductions now loomed. It was clear from Chen's comments that the SFYP target of a 50 percent increase in cotton production was impossible. Only development of the chemical-fiber industry offered a way out. This would have important spillover effects in the plastics, pharmaceuticals, dyestuffs, and explosives industries, he opined.

Chen favored flood control as easier to carry out than opening up barren lands. He supported the Central Committee and State Council directive on increasing irrigation, but he went into detail about problems with a campaign to expand irrigation in 1955–1956: It had ignored local conditions; commandism by cadres had been rampant; targets had been excessive; technical guidance had been insufficient; and building of irrigation works had interfered with peasant subsidiary production, reducing peasant incomes (and so undermining their support for water conservancy). He implied that unless the 1957–1958 campaign was carefully managed, such mistakes would reappear. In other words, Chen was doing the most he could possibly do to oppose the emerging campaign without taking the politically impossible step of saying that it should not be launched. He noted that the state had already allocated an additional 100 million yuan to water projects in 1957, and commented that any more appropriations would increase financial, material, and credit imbalances.

In the most significant part of his speech, however, Chen suggested that these measures were only provisional. He stated that they should be thoroughly discussed within the Party and in the newspapers, and that non-Party personnel should be permitted to give their views so that the proposals could be refined. He warned, "We should note: in our history, some things were decided too hastily." The first example of such an improper decision-making style was one for which he himself took responsibility. Stalin had wanted China to expand rubber production quickly to 200,000 tons. (In 1957, China produced only 200 tons of rubber.)[19] Chen unrealistically ordered a drastic expansion of rubber planting without studying the subject, ignoring the fact that it took fifteen to twenty years for rubber plants to become productive. The next example of hasty decision making Chen gave was political dynamite. "Also we suddenly demanded 'more, faster, better, more economical.' That was too impatient. That is a lesson [for us]." This slogan had been formulated by Zhou Enlai and Li Fuchun in late 1955 or early 1956, and it was a favorite of Mao's.[20] Chen thus reaffirmed his commitment to careful, balanced growth, criticizing a slogan that was at the heart of the planners' program. He continued his critique: The SFYP must take feeding and clothing the people as its starting point, but under the plan food and clothing supplies would be "tense"; that is, there would be shortages of these commodities. "If we don't solve the problems of feeding and clothing the people, the cause of our socialist construction will be on shaky ground, and we will certainly have to go back and make amends." He criticized industrial officials for concerning themselves only with industry even when stomachs were empty. It would be very bad for China and the CCP if agricultural problems were addressed after the completion of basic industrialization. "If [China's] economy is not based on having food to eat and clothes to wear, I think construction cannot be stable." But Chen also mildly criticized agricultural officials:

19. State Statistical Bureau, 1986, p. 150. No figure for rubber output is given for the year 1952 (when Stalin was alive), suggesting that Chinese production was negligible when Stalin made his request.

20. Bo Yibo, "Comrade Fuchun Will Always Be with Us," *Renmin Ribao* (People's Daily), January 9, 1980, trans. in Foreign Broadcast Information Service, *Daily Report, China* (hereafter *FBIS*), January 11, 1980, L 11 – L 17 (see L 14), and Gu Zhuoxin et al., "Comrade Li Fuchun's Important Contributions to Planning Work," *Renmin Ribao*, May 22, 1980, trans. in Joint Publications Research Service (hereafter JPRS), *China Report*, no. 75888 (June 17, 1980), "Economic Affairs," no. 64, pp. 73–82 (see p. 75).

Comrades managing agriculture point out, agricultural investment this year is only nine percent of the capital construction fund, it's too little. Can't it be increased [they say] to 12 or 20 percent? Agricultural investment is for providing food and clothing, but solving the problems of food and clothing is not solely dependent on agriculture. Investment should include industry which aids agriculture. For example, chemical fertilizer and chemical fibers should be seen as part of the solution for food and clothing problems. These obviously aren't agriculture, but they are part of the solution to agricultural problems. It is wrong not to see this point, to emphasize only investment proportions.[21]

Chen closed his speech with a call for birth control, a position coming under attack in the Anti-Rightist Campaign.

This was Chen Yun's last public statement on the Chinese economy for more than a year, and it reflected themes he had been articulating since 1956. He reaffirmed the need for balanced, stable growth. Agriculture required much greater attention, and industry (especially heavy industry) was particularly guilty of ignoring agriculture. Rashness was the source of many economic problems, and campaigns to develop the economy required strict supervision. But his proposed solutions revealed political problems in his position. He promised no rapid breakthrough, only years of hard work and tense supplies of basic consumer goods. There was nothing here to excite the imagination, to mobilize the Party and the people. Chen's plans did little to prove the rightists wrong. Indeed, he explicitly supported the rightists on the issue of birth control, and he all but conceded that the CCP had mismanaged the economy. This was Chen Yun at his most outspoken, and it is remarkable that he survived politically.

The financial coalition's position was supported by Deng Zihui's speech on agricultural problems, a portion of which was published at the time.[22] In this text, Deng mentioned a recent meeting of the Party's Rural Work Department and relayed the sense of that meeting to the plenum. The Rural Work Department and Deng Zihui continued to support financial coalition policies despite the changed political environment. For example, three September 14, 1957, directives, products of this work conference but issued in the name of the Central Committee, advocated contract responsibility systems,[23] reducing the size of collectives, and paying attention to the material interests of individual peasants.[24] At the plenum, Deng argued that pigs, the

21. Chen Yun, 1986, p. 77.

22. Deng Zihui, "Guanyu Kuoda Zaishengchan ji Qita Jige Wenti" (On Expanded Reproduction in Agricultural Cooperatives and Several Other Questions), *Renmin Shouce 1958*, 1958, pp. 520–24.

23. Literally *san bao yi jiang*, or "three contracts and one reward," meaning fixed, or contracted, targets for output, number of days worked, and costs, with a reward of some percentage of the output for overfulfillment of the target.

24. "Directive of the CCP Central Committee to Overhaul Agricultural Producer Coopera-

main source of meat in the Chinese diet and a major source of organic fertilizer, should be raised by individuals, and that this was the primary method by which hog production could be increased. (This contradicted Deng Xiaoping's call to restrict individual undertakings in the collectives.) While favoring increases in collective funds for rural capital construction, he stated that such funds should increase only in step with growing individual incomes. He reaffirmed the responsibility system and the flexible assignment of tasks and targets to individual households. Deng Zihui could not advocate free markets and increased procurement prices, but he continued to support an incentivist approach to rural development. Perhaps because his views were increasingly out of step with the mood of the Third Plenum, his report is not mentioned in the plenum communiqué.

Except for Mao's views, reconstruction of other Third Plenum deliberations becomes problematical. Zhou Enlai's report on wages, welfare, and employment has never been released, although an overview implied that Zhou continued to support gradual wage increases (and therefore material incentives).[25] The regulations he introduced to the plenum were mooted in the Great Leap Forward.

No text of the views of anyone from the planning coalition is available. But an article written in 1980, commemorating the twenty-second anniversary of the death of Huang Jing, who in 1957 was minister of the First Ministry of Machine Building, stated that "at a Party Central Committee meeting in 1957, [Huang] made a report on the mechanization of agriculture in China. His report was recommended by Chairman Mao and Premier Zhou."[26] In late October and November 1957, Huang published an article on agricultural mechanization in *Renmin Ribao* and in *Jixie Gongye* (Machine-Building Industry).[27] This article presumably drew on his remarks to the plenum.

Huang sought to include the machine-building industry among the recipients of increased funds allocated to industry to aid agriculture. He argued

tives," "Directive of the CCP Central Committee to Improve Agricultural Producer Cooperative Administration of Production," and "Directive of the CCP Central Committee on Methods of Applying the Policy of Mutual Benefit Among the Cooperative Members," in *Documents of the Chinese Communist Party Central Committee*, vol. 1, 1971, pp. 499–503, 505–10, and 511–15, respectively.

25. Chen Xuewei (n. 1), p. 9.

26. Duan Junyi et al., "Deeply Cherish the Memory of Our Comrade Huang Jing," *Renmin Ribao*, February 23, 1980, trans. in FBIS, March 21, 1980, L 10 – L 15; see L 13. The Third Plenum was the only Central Committee meeting in 1957.

27. Huang Jing, "The Problem of Farm Mechanization in China," *Renmin Ribao*, October 24–25, 1957, trans. in *Survey of China Mainland Press*, no. 1662 (December 4, 1957), pp. 14–24, and "On Agricultural Mechanization in China," *Jixie Gongye*, 1957, no. 21 (November 6, 1957), trans. in *Extracts from China Mainland Magazines* (hereafter *ECMM*), no. 120 (February 24, 1958), pp. 34–43.

that in 1956 many believed that agricultural mechanization would be slow and that the potential for farm mechanization was limited. This view was wrong, he declared, because it ignored the fact that there was often a shortage of labor in the countryside during busy seasons. To increase the multiple-cropping index – one of the main ways to increase the yield per unit area of land – mechanization was required, particularly in South and Southwest China. Mechanization would also speed the construction of irrigation and flood-control projects.

Huang's program, while no doubt aiding agriculture, had the not coincidental effect of defending the investment position of the machine-building sector. An article in April 1957 had argued that prospects for farm mechanization were dim and that implementation would have to wait for the completion of basic industrialization. And Bo Yibo had announced a cut in capital construction for the machine-building industry at the June session of the National People's Congress.[28] Huang apparently managed to reverse this trend at the Third Plenum by jumping on the industry-aiding-agriculture bandwagon. His initiative, endorsed by Mao and Zhou, reversed the view that agricultural mechanization must await China's industrial development. Once again, an element of the planning and heavy industry coalition presented a program responsive to current problems and to the coalition's interests.

Mao Zedong used his prerogatives as Party chairman and his accumulated power and prestige to end the planner-budgeteer debate and to move the Party in the direction of the Great Leap Forward. His views were not fully formed until the last day of the Third Plenum, but he would hold them unswervingly for more than a year afterward.

A strange speech by the Chairman on October 7 illustrates the fluidity of his views up to this point. He stated that class struggle was now the principal contradiction. The Eighth Party Congress Resolution, which said that the contradiction between the bourgeoisie and the proletariat was fundamentally resolved, was not incorrect, but fundamental resolution should not be equated with complete resolution. He resisted, however, publishing the statement that class struggle between the bourgeoisie and the proletariat was the primary contradiction, because it might harm rectification and the airing of views. He did state that questions of the ideological and political power of the proletariat and the bourgeoisie were not yet resolved. Full and

28. Zhao Xue, "The Problem of Agricultural Mechanization in China," *Jihua Jingji* (Planned Economy), 1957, no. 4, trans. in *ECMM*, no. 87 (June 17, 1957), pp. 10–14; Bo Yibo, "Working of the National Economic Plan for 1956 and the Draft Plan for 1957," *Current Background*, no. 465 (July 9, 1957), p. 11.

frank airing of views was a good way to carry out the struggle with the bourgeoisie and perfect the superstructure.[29]

Mao's speech two days later, October 9, provided a summing up of the plenum and represented the most extensive explication of the Chairman's ideas in many months.[30] He wanted rectification and the full airing of opinions to continue, and if these were carried out well, future anti-rightist campaigns would be unnecessary. He told the Party not to be afraid of criticism. Turning to agricultural and industrial questions, he returned the National Agricultural Program to the formal agenda, and stated that he wanted each level of administration to draw up its own plans to carry it out. He also wanted a comprehensive plan drawn up combining industry, agriculture, commerce, culture, and education and coordinating their interrelationships. Mao thus implicitly criticized the five-year plans, for coordinating economic policies in all fields was precisely what they were supposed to do. Apparently the planners were concentrating only on industry. He agreed that heavy industry must have priority in economic construction, but he wanted agriculture and industry to advance simultaneously. More small steel plants were a priority.

Mao then discussed what he called the "two methods": slower and poorer or faster and better. He charged that in 1956, particularly in the second half of the year, the slogan "more, faster, better, more economical" results had been swept away. He claimed that no one in the Party opposed "better" and "more economical." "More" and "faster" were the watchwords that people did not like and labeled rash. But the complete slogan contained built-in self-controlling mechanisms: "better" and "more economical" ensured that waste was not created by "more" and "faster." Accordingly, he called for the entire slogan to be revived. In general, said Mao, it should be the policy of the Party to promote progress, and achieving more, faster, better, more economical results was a major means of accomplishing this. In this way, he defined the financial coalition's program as illegitimate and directly refuted Chen Yun's speech of two weeks before. Through his control of the terms of political debate, Mao took the ground out from under the budgeteers, who knew that "more" and "faster" were, in fact, not restricted by "better" and "more economical."

29. Mao Zedong, "Talk at the Third Plenum of the Eighth Central Committee," in *Miscellany of Mao Tse-tung Thought* (hereafter *MMTTT*), JPRS, no. 61269-1 (February 1974), pp. 72–76. Mao's talk reads like a hodgepodge of diverse comments put together by his editors to make one piece. It is repetitive, and one doubts that Mao really said newspapers and other media ought not to identify the principal contradiction in China or reveal the true nature of class struggle. The speech does show his continued commitment to blooming and contending.

30. Mao, 1977, pp. 483–96. This speech directly contradicts many of the points in Mao's oration of October 7.

In contrast to his October 7 talk, two days later Mao labeled as erroneous the Resolution of the Eighth Party Congress, which had identified the contradiction between the superstructure and the base as the principal one in China. In the second half of 1956, he said, there had been a deliberate slackening in class struggle. This was precisely the time Zhou Enlai and Chen Yun were opposing rash advance, instituting economic retrenchment, and reviving free markets.

Although he did it indirectly, Mao decisively favored the planning coalition. Bo Yibo and Li Fuchun's program promised to implement the slogan of more, faster, better, more economical results. They had all the policies ready to make this slogan into a viable guide to action. The planners were the ones who formulated the ideas about how industry and agriculture could advance simultaneously. Some agricultural development would come from the peasants themselves; the rest would come from greatly expanded industrial inputs that would aid agriculture. No decisive contradiction existed between a more assertive form of Party leadership in the countryside and the planners' program. But Party leadership and mass movements were definitely in conflict with the more market- and incentivist-oriented approach of the financial coalition. In short, Mao had effectively coopted the program of the planners as the Great Leap Forward emerged. His personal contributions to the initial upsurge that led to the Leap were more in the area of style than in that of substance. He injected the idea of proceeding more rapidly, but he did not formulate the plans and programs that could be used to achieve more, faster, better, and more economical results. Mao's cooptation of the planners' program, coupled with the Anti-Rightist Campaign, launched the Great Leap.

The program of the planners was combined with a revitalized social transformation impulse emanating from the Chinese Communist Party. The Anti-Rightist Campaign and the revival of class struggle, the policy of *xiafang* (sending cadres down to lower-level units or to the production front), and Party rectification interacted to put the Party in what might be called a mobilizational mode. In the countryside, that mode was activated by the directive on irrigation released on September 24, 1957. Cadres had been straining at the leash before that order. The directive, plus Mao's calls for faster development, set in motion a train of events that would lead to euphoria and later catastrophe.

The financial coalition was certainly much less responsible for the debacle caused by the Great Leap than were the other two main coalitions. Almost every aspect of the financial coalition's platform was rejected. (Only increased attention to agriculture survived, and that more rhetorically than substantively.) The rejection was not permanent, however, and it was precisely the policies cast aside in 1957 that pulled China out of the depression of the early 1960s.

B. The Great Leap Forward[31]

After the Third Plenum in October, Mao traveled to Moscow to celebrate the fortieth anniversary of the Bolshevik Revolution in November 1957. During his stay in Moscow, he proclaimed that "the east wind prevails over the west wind," meaning that with the first two sputniks and the first operational intercontinental ballistic missile the Soviet Union and its allies had become stronger than the United States and its allies. He was speaking with the knowledge that the Soviets had promised not only to help the Chinese to develop their own nuclear weapons but also to supply them with a sample bomb. His purpose was to encourage the Russians and the rest of the bloc to take more aggressive steps, both at home and abroad, to further consolidate the strength of the East over the West.[32]

China's Soviet and Eastern European allies did not follow Mao's call, but he ensured that China would proceed to build socialism more actively and to oppose the United States more vigorously. In November–December 1957, the Chinese leadership raised the slogan of catching up to Great Britain in output of major industrial products in fifteen years. Targets began to increase. The decentralization regulations stimulated the expectations of the provinces, which hoped to industrialize rapidly.[33] The water conservancy campaign quickly surpassed the early targets set for it, convincing the leadership that more mass mobilization would make for even better results.

The leaders of the coalitions continued to act true to form. Immediately after Liu Shaoqi publicly announced the target of overtaking Britain in fifteen years, Li Fuchun promised that China could produce 40 million tons of steel by the end of that period. Nonetheless, the targets Li announced for the Second Five-Year Plan were generally only marginally higher than those in the proposals for it, and the targets for agriculture were actually lower than those in the proposals.[34]

31. This section draws heavily on MacFarquhar, 1983; Schoenhals, 1987; and He Wenzhen, "Dui 'Sanmian Hongqidè Zai Renshi" (Reflections on the 'Three Red Banners'), *Dangshi Yanjiu* (Research on Party History), 1986, no. 2, pp. 14–20.
32. See MacFarquhar, 1983, pp. 7–19; Lewis and Xue, 1988, esp. ch. 3; Mao, 1977, pp. 514–18; and Schoenhals, 1986a.
33. Provincial excitement over the decentralization regulations is described in Vogel, 1971, pp. 219–31.
34. Li Fuchun, "The Achievements of China's First Five Year Plan and the Tasks and Policy for Future Socialist Construction," trans. in *Current Background*, no. 483 (December 16, 1957),

If there were vestiges of conservatism within the planning and heavy industry coalition, they were roundly criticized by Bo Yibo in an important speech to representatives of the units under the Central Committee and Beijing military leaders on December 19, 1957. Bo frankly called both for a great leap forward in production and for the continued rectification of work styles, particularly among those who felt that mass movements were inappropriate and those who opposed more, faster, better, and more economic results. Cadres, he said, should not be afraid of imbalance. Finally, he implied that targets in the existing state plans were not attuned to the enthusiasm of the workers. Enterprises should set targets higher than the ones given them by the planning agencies.[35] This foreshadowed what was perhaps the most dangerous planning procedure adopted during the Great Leap: the setting of multiple and escalating targets as the plan was handed down from the center to the localities.

The financial coalition did not demonstrate any great enthusiasm for the turn of events after the Third Plenum. In a rather strange development, a third national financial conference was called at the end of December. (Two conferences a year was the norm.) The featured speaker was neither Li Xiannian nor Chen Yun, but Zhu De, the venerable founding father of the Chinese Army. With no background in financial affairs, Zhu, it can only be assumed, was deliberately sent to this meeting to ensure that Li and Chen did not try to restrict the burgeoning movement. Zhu was the classic outsider sent in to enforce conformity with a new political line. He criticized the finance and banking departments for wanting only "reliability" *(wentuo)* and not "enthusiasm" *(jiji)*. He urged the financial departments to be promoters of progress, not opponents of active advance.[36]

In the winter of 1957–1958, Mao journeyed around China, holding major meetings in Zhejiang, Guangxi, Sichuan, and Hubei. During this period, assisted by Liu Shaoqi and others, he worked on "Sixty Points on Work Methods." This document put forward the idea of "uninterrupted revolution." Wave after wave of mass movements was to be launched, transforming China quickly into a fully developed socialist state. The "Sixty Points" also formally introduced the practice of multiple plans, with each level having

---

pp. 1–13. MacFarquhar (1983, pp. 17–19) argues that Li's steel target of 12 million tons by 1962 is an example of planners' resistance to increasing targets. But Mao's Moscow speeches (available after the publication of MacFarquhar's work) reveal that Li's figures for 1962 were in keeping with Mao's, and Li's figure of 40 million tons of steel by 1972 matched the top of Mao's range of targets for that year. See Schoenhals, 1986a, p. 118.

35. Bo Yibo, 1958, esp. pp. 26–27.

36. "Zhu De Fuzhuxi zai Quanguo Caizheng Ting-zhuzhang Huiyishangde Jianghua" (Speech by Vice-Chairman Zhu De to the Conference of Financial Bureau and Department Heads) (December 25, 1957), *Xinhua Banyuekan*, 1958, no. 12, pp. 112–14.

two sets of targets. The first was the minimum plan, the target sent down from above, announced publicly. But all levels were to have a second, un-publicized plan that significantly exceeded the published target. The unpub-lished target was to be the minimum goal for the next lower level. In this way, the targets increased greatly as they were passed from level to level.[37]

In Hangzhou in early January, Mao discussed investment levels.[38] "Ex-actly how large should accumulation [*sic*] be? Some suggest 45%, some 50%, some 55%. The best is half and half."[39] Huge increases in investment, along with mass movements, would propel the emerging Leap.

At the Nanning Conference in January, Mao criticized Zhou Enlai and Chen Yun, chastised the Ministry of Commerce (Chen was still the minister at this time), and attacked economic and financial departments generally.[40] He averred, "Only fifty meters separates those who oppose 'adventurism' from the bourgeois rightists." This made the atmosphere at the conference "very tense"[41] and undermined the positions of Zhou Enlai and Chen Yun. Under Mao's barrage, Li Xiannian offered an implied self-criticism at the Fifth Session of the First National People's Congress, conceding that he had viewed the economic difficulties in late 1956 as much more serious than Mao had; and Zhou Enlai prepared a self-criticism circulated to the Politburo Standing Committee and the Party Secretariat in May 1958.[42] Chen Yun kept silent while the Leap unfolded, and there is no record of his offering a self-criticism.[43] Mao – perhaps to ensure that he would be fully able to mo-bilize provincial leaders in support of his views – dispatched Zhou Enlai, Li Fuchun, and Li Xiannian to investigate flood projects on the Changjiang (Yangtze River). This kept them busy for a critical month so that Zhou and

37. "Sixty Points on Work Methods," in Jerome Chen, 1970, pp. 57–75.
38. Mao used the phrase "accumulation level," which in Marxist accounting means something different from investment. Either Mao was confused or his remarks were incorrectly tran-scribed.
39. MacFarquhar, Cheek, and Wu, 1989, p. 380. Investment ratios were about 40 percent in the First Five-Year Plan, and Bo Yibo at the Eighth Party Congress discussed the appropriate proportion of investment in the state budget, which he argued should be 40 percent or a little higher. In contrast, accumulation (as a percentage of national income) levels during the First Five-Year Plan were about 25 percent. The context and the immense size of the jump from 25 percent to 50 percent lead to my conclusion that Mao confused the terms "accumulation" (which he used in this speech) and "investment," which is what he meant.
40. Bo Yibo, "Respect and Remembrance – Marking the 60th Anniversary of the Founding of the CCP," trans. in FBIS, July 29, 1981, K 26 – K 36 (see K 33); *MMTTT*, pp. 77–84.
41. Quoted in Schoenhals, 1987, p. 6.
42. Li Xiannian, "The Implementation of the State Budget for 1957 and the Draft Plan for 1958," *Current Background*, no. 493 (February 17, 1958), p. 5; "Zhou Zongli Xie Jiantao" (Premier Zhou Writes a Self-Criticism), *Renwu* (Public Figures), 1986, no. 1, pp. 175–77. Chen Yun called Zhou while he was working on this document, but Chen's views have not been revealed. No text of Zhou's self-criticism has been released.
43. Deng Xiaoping, 1984, p. 281.

the others could not mobilize support to restrict the emerging Great Leap Forward.[44]

Unlike the financial coalition's leaders, who either kept silent or bowed to Mao's pressures, the planners responded favorably to the Leap. Li Fuchun "did not *fully* consent to *many* impracticable economic viewpoints and measures put forward during the Great Leap Forward, [but] he implemented them in planning work."[45] In 1981, Bo Yibo conceded that he, like many other leaders, "became careless and arrogant, and overeager for quick results."[46]

The CCP leadership based its ideas about the Great Leap Forward on a false analogy – to the small leap forward of 1955–1956. In the earlier leap, objective conditions had made a short-term production surge possible. The harvest of 1955 was bountiful, providing more resources for light industry. But the harvests of 1953 and 1954 had been fair to poor; as a result, the level of construction in 1955 was relatively low, and significant surpluses of steel and other material were in reserve. Moreover, beginning in 1956, the CCP explicitly encouraged intellectuals to give their all to China's economic development. But 1958 followed a mediocre to poor harvest in 1957; there were considerable shortages of key industrial materials. Intellectuals were under attack. There was no readily available surplus to be exploited. The Party's vehemence in its advocacy of the Great Leap Forward seemed to reflect a need to disprove the objective situation.

By the spring of 1958 the financial coalition had forfeited all of its influence in policy debates. During a restructuring of the State Council in February, Chen Yun lost his portfolio as minister of commerce. Li Xiannian bowed to pressure from Mao and other leaders and did not hinder the development of the Great Leap. As a result, Li Xiannian and Li Fuchun became members of the Chinese Communist Party (CCP) Secretariat. The first economic officials to assume posts in that important body, they symbolized the great role the Party saw itself playing in economic affairs.

When the Second Session of the Eighth Party Congress met in May, Liu Shaoqi codified the elements and the central thinking behind the Great Leap and the idea of uninterrupted revolution to that point:

The fact is that the growth of the social productive forces calls for a socialist revolution and the emancipation of the people; the victory of this revolution and emancipation in turn spurs a forward leap in the social productive forces; and this in turn impels a progressive change in the socialist relations of production and an advance in man's

44. Wang Renzhong, "A Shining Example – Learn from Comrade Zhou Enlai," in FBIS, March 22, 1979, L 14 – L 20; see L 16.
45. Gu Zhuoxin et al., "Comrade Li Fuchun's Important Contributions" (n. 20), p. 75.
46. Bo Yibo, "Respect and Remembrance," K 33.

ideology. In their ceaseless struggle to transform nature, the people are continuously transforming society and themselves.[47]

Liu's speech insisted on high targets and rates of growth. These were combined with mass movements, which not only transformed nature but helped the people of China to transform themselves. Liu revealed the content of Mao's Ten Major Relationships to the public for the first time. Yet the emphasis in Liu's talk and in the Leap itself was on heavy industry.

Liu's speech sealed the alliance between the planning coalition and the Party as agent of social transformation. By May 1958 the basic interests of the planning coalition had not been harmed; in a number of ways, it had benefited from the Leap. For example, the Ministry of Metallurgical Industries had increased its targets before Mao did, thereby justifying greatly increased investment.[48] As Mao told representatives from six Eastern European communist parties in October 1958, "There are so many stupid people in the world, we and I are like them. For so many years we did not know that steel was the key link. Only this year did we realize this. If you grasp steel production, everything else will go along with it."[49] Another example of how the Great Leap served planning coalition interests is the Sino-Soviet defense-technology agreement of October 15, 1957, whereby the Soviets promised the Chinese a sample atomic bomb and other advanced equipment, implicitly guaranteeing that despite the rhetoric about self-reliant development China's heavy and defense industries would have access to Soviet advanced technology and equipment.[50]

The combination of heavy industry and mass mobilization so dominated the unified political agenda that overt opposition was impossible. The financial coalition continued to carry out its tasks as best it could, but it was not in a position to press for its interests until some of the euphoria of the Leap died down. For example, the Ministry of Commerce was forced to adopt the policy "anything produced will be purchased [by the commercial departments]; all that is produced will be purchased."[51] This meant that the Ministry of Commerce was obliged to purchase everything produced regardless of quality. Unfortunately, the retreat from utopia did not occur until late 1958.

47. Liu Shaoqi, "The Present Situation, the Party's General Line for Socialist Construction and Its Future Tasks," in *Communist China, 1955–1959*, 1971, pp. 416–38; see p. 424.
48. He Wenzhen, "Dui 'Sanmian Hongqi de' Zai Renshi" (n. 31), pp. 16–17; Chen Yun, 1986, p. 121; Zhang Wentian, 1985, p. 492.
49. Quoted in Shi Zhongquan, "Jianxinde Kaitou – Mao Zedong zai 'Wenhua Dageming' qian dui Zhongguo Shehuizhuyi Jianshe Daolude Tansuo" (Arduous Breakthroughs – Mao Zedong's Explorations on the Road of China's Socialist Construction Before the 'Cultural Revolution'), *Dangshi Yanjiu*, 1987, no. 1, pp. 1–19; see p. 3.
50. On the agreement and on Sino-Soviet scientific and technical military exchanges, see Nie Rongzhen, 1984, pp. 800–806.
51. Shangye Bu Jingji Yanjiusuo, 1984, p. 169.

Nor was the position of the planners invulnerable. Mao and the Party had largely coopted their program, but once the leadership and the Party took over, the Party was not sure that it needed planners and heavy industrial officials to tell the masses and Party generalists how to carry out construction. The Party put forward the slogan "Politics in command." While this may have been aimed at those who favored balance and greater autonomy for intellectuals in their work – in short, at anyone who denied the primacy of the Party in all affairs – it could also have been aimed at the planning coalition, which sought to maintain control over its own system of allocation and distribution. The planners, like the budgeteers, did not have an effective counter when the Party took off on its extreme flight from reality in the late summer and fall of 1958. But while planning as a means of economic control grew meaningless, investment in heavy industry skyrocketed, and Sino-Soviet trade reached record levels in 1958–1959. Self-reliance was the order of the day, but advanced Soviet technology was clearly appreciated by many.

After the Second Session, in a process still cloaked in mystery, people's communes began to emerge in China's countryside. The huge new structures, generally of 5,000–10,000 households, or fifty to a hundred times the size of the average collective (it is impossible to call them institutions during this period, because their organization was so rudimentary), met the need of the mass movement to build water conservancy projects and the increased demand on the peasants themselves to build mines and industry. In addition to fulfilling a functional need for larger rural units, communes were also associated with an ideological goal. It was no accident that the word "commune" was used for these new organizations. Mao and others saw them as an important step on the road to communism, the means by which agriculture would make the transition from collective to state ownership.

In August, Mao convened an enlarged meeting of the CCP Politburo in Beidaihe. From this meeting came the most extreme utopian claims of the Great Leap.[52] The Beidaihe Meeting called for the formation of communes throughout the Chinese countryside and raised the steel production target once again until it stood at double the 5 million tons produced in 1957. The meeting also supported the launching of more mass movements in the urban and rural areas. Chinese leaders believed they were establishing roots of communism.

In a little over six weeks, most Chinese peasants went from living in collectives to living in communes. Cadres lacked experience in building communes and had no detailed rules for their administration. Incentives were

---

52. MacFarquhar et al., 1989, pp. 397–441.

lacking. Under an expanded supply system, peasants were allowed to eat as much as they wanted without pay. Many able-bodied men were sent off to engage in steel making or the construction of irrigation systems during the harvest season, leaving crops to rot in the field. Cadres did not know how to carry out their vastly increased responsibilities; commandism was the result. In short, the structure and work methods of communes were extremely chaotic. Gradually, despite tremendously inflated claims of production success in all spheres of endeavor, the leadership began to realize the need for some consolidation not only of the communes but also of the other sectors of the economy.

It is particularly interesting to note that Chen Yun was designated to head the newly reconstituted (and slightly renamed) State Construction Commission sometime in the fall of 1958. This might be seen as the first step in the retreat from the Leap. While Chen's political influence had declined during the year, he was still the fifth-ranking member of the Politburo Standing Committee. His task was to bring some order to the fantastically enlarged capital construction front.[53]

An even greater retreat from utopianism occurred in a series of Party meetings in November and December 1958. Orders for commune rectification were issued; talk of sprouts of communism stopped. Conservatism in the economy was still attacked, but calls were now made to improve work style in industry and to overcome difficulties. Nonetheless, the Party Central Committee concluded that even greater victories could be won in 1959.

During the first half of 1959, however, the Party center discovered that things were much less rosy than they seemed. Led by Mao and aided by Chen Yun and others, the Party increasingly tried to consolidate and improve the running of the economy and in particular of the communes. Production brigades in the communes became the key management level. Targets in industry and agriculture were scaled down. The outrageously bloated production "statistics" of 1958 were somewhat reduced. But no fundamental renunciation of the aims and methods of the Great Leap Forward was announced. The theory behind the Leap was still in place; it was defects in implementation that became the target of criticism and modification. On the eve of the Lushan Conference in July 1959, however, Mao Zedong may have begun to question the strategy of the Leap:

One of the major lessons of the Great Leap Forward is the lack of balance. When we walk, both legs should move, but we did not do so. In the national economy, comprehensiveness and balance are a basic problem. Only with comprehensiveness and balance can we have the mass line. There are three balances. . . . Only when we have accomplished these three balances can we fix the ratios in the national economy.

53. Chen Yun, 1986, pp. 100–115.

The order we set in our economic planning in the past has been heavy industry, light industry, and agriculture. Henceforth we may have to reverse the order. Should it be agriculture, light industry, and heavy industry? In other words, we have to do well in agriculture and to change the order of heavy industry, light industry, agriculture, commerce, and communications to agriculture, light industry, heavy industry, communications, and commerce. In this order we have to first develop means of production. This in no way contradicts Marxism. Comrade Chen Yun said, "We should arrange the markets before we go into capital construction." Many comrades disagreed. But now we realize that Comrade Chen Yun was right. We have to solve the problems of clothing, food, housing, utilities, and travel first for they concern the stable life of 650 million people. After we have solved these five problems, the people will live comfortably.[54]

Thus Mao in mid 1959 seems to have reconsidered the ideas of Chen Yun and found them relevant.

Unfortunately, at the Party Work Conference at the resort of Lushan, convened immediately after Mao made the statement just quoted, the minister of national defense, Peng Dehuai, questioned the rationale of the GLF and indirectly attacked Mao. This so provoked Mao that he had Peng replaced, and the GLF was reintensified. Once again, rightist conservatism was roundly criticized.[55]

The Great Leap Forward was never formally terminated, but by mid 1960 it had petered out. Owing to problems with the communes and bad weather, the rural situation had deteriorated so much that no amount of political pressure or unwillingness to accept reality could disguise the need to end the Great Leap and to begin rehabilitative measures. These measures came too late to prevent many millions from dying of starvation or diseases associated with malnutrition. The Great Leap ended not with a triumphant transition to communism but with national famine and economic disaster. Faced with agricultural and industrial collapse, the leadership adopted many of the policies of the financial coalition to save what remained of the Chinese economy.[56]

54. *MMTTT*, p. 183. The preceding paragraphs draw heavily on MacFarquhar, 1983.
55. See Peng Dehuai, 1981, pp. 265–87; Zhang Wentian, 1985, pp. 480–506. The most extensive treatment of the Lushan Meeting is MacFarquhar, 1983, ch. 10. A discussion in Chinese almost as detailed is Su Xiaokang, Luo Shixu, and Chen Zheng, " 'Wutuobang' Ji: 1959 Nian Lushan zhi Xia" (Sacrifice to 'Utopian': The 1959 Summer of Lushan), *Xinhua Wenzhai* (New China Digest), 1989, no. 4, pp. 124–44.
56. The human consequences of the Leap are now extensively documented. See, among the many discussions in English, Kane, 1988, and MacFarquhar, 1983, pp. 326–32. Some views can be found in Chinese in Wang Ping, " 'Da Yuejin' he Tiaozheng Shiqide Renmin Shenghuo" (People's Living Standards During the "Great Leap Forward" and the Readjustment Period), in Liu Suinian, 1982, pp. 162–78, and Liu Suinian and Wu Qungan, 1984.

9

Conclusions

This book has examined the origins of China's Great Leap Forward from the vantage point of the interplay of three different coalitions of political actors. Each coalition presented a program of economic and social change to cope with the problems facing China's political economy in 1956–1957 and the specific difficulties confronting important bureaucracies in carrying out their organizational missions. The top leaders had some autonomy in deciding on policies, but their freedom of choice was circumscribed by the proposals put forward by the coalitions within the state. Thus, Mao Zedong did not think up the Great Leap Forward on his own. Rather, he and the Chinese Communist Party coopted the program associated with the planning and heavy industry coalition and coupled it with demands for mass mobilization in the countryside and a greatly accelerated growth rate.

This chapter expands on the broader historical and analytical findings and issues of this study and covers the larger implications of the patterns of China's political economy as revealed in the origins of the Great Leap Forward. The main sections deal with the choices available to China's leadership in 1956–1957, the nature of China's coalitional politics, larger patterns of China's politics, and the sources of policy evolution and change in China. A brief afterword compares political and economic developments in 1957 with those in 1989.

A. The choices available to the leadership in 1956–1957

The year from September 1956 to September 1957 represents a lost reform in the history of the People's Republic of China. With the completion of the "transition to socialism," the first response of the CCP to defining an independent path of development was a nebulous, inclusivist strategy of incorporating popular views in policy making, coupled with a style of economic growth that included a role for markets. In other words, when Chinese lead-

214

ers and institutions first attempted to put their own stamp on China's future after copying the Soviet model for seven years, they opted for tolerance, balance, and stability, not class struggle, ever-increasing etatization, and heavy industrial mobilization. The achievements and results of this brief period should not be overstated; neither should its long-term influence be minimized.

Many critical aspects of the reformist experience of 1956–1957 were undefined, and significant questions about the stability of the reformist policies can be raised. How could the ideas of intellectuals be incorporated in CCP policy making when intellectuals were dissatisfied with the regime? Does a strategy of change inevitably lead to popular criticism of the Party-state and ultimately to repression? How can the market be linked with a plan in a stable manner? Just how much scope for market activities was sanctioned? How would the state respond to inequalities generated by the market? How would CCP cadres who made a revolution against capitalism respond to a reinvigoration of market transactions and the de facto reappearance of small-scale capitalists? In light of the Anti-Rightist Campaign, it is easy to conclude that the Party-state was incapable of answering any of these questions non-coercively. But what if the harvest of 1957 had been bountiful, Mao had made it clear that only constructive criticisms would be acceptable to the CCP during this period, and institutions had been carefully constructed to handle and mediate the participation of intellectuals and students? Obviously, this question cannot be answered definitively. But the failure of reform in 1956–1957 should not be dismissed as inevitable, or at least failure of reforms in general ought not be subscribed to too hastily.

Moreover, even if the first CCP attempt at reform was inevitably a failure, the significance of the attempt remains. It is not accidental that reformers in the late 1970s and early 1980s drew on the ideas of Chen Yun and Deng Zihui to legitimate, if not actually inspire, agricultural, commercial, and light industrial reforms in the early post-Mao era. Similarly, later ideas about political reform and intellectual freedom drew on the policy of "letting a hundred flowers bloom, letting a hundred schools contend," on Deng's ideas on the nature of classes as expressed at the Eighth Party Congress, and on the need to create "certain systems" so that figures like Stalin or Mao did not reappear. Later political reformers were not explicit about looking to the 1950s for inspiration, but they continued to grapple with issues first placed on the political agenda in the mid 1950s. Indeed, CCP historical journals in the 1980s were flooded with articles about the significance of the Eighth Party Congress line and the reasons it was discarded. Even if reform could not succeed in the 1950s, the significance of the effort was not overlooked by reformers twenty years later; the lost reform legitimated later efforts and provided both policy inspiration and a road map indicating some of the political pitfalls en route to reform. In addition, the failure of reform and the catastrophe caused by the Anti-Rightist Campaign and the Great Leap Forward have provided all Chinese leaders with painful memories of huge errors, and these in turn have served as a partial check on repeating the same errors – although, as we shall see, the leadership's suppression of the people in June 1989 suggests that other lessons were drawn from these memories.

The abortive reform of 1956–1957 also reveals something important about the nature of Mao's leadership and Maoism. Mao was not the "Great Helmsman" successfully navigating the Chinese ship of state through stormy waters, nor was his "thought" the supreme guide to action during this period. Mao's ideas were significantly more flexible and more open than is often thought. To be sure, his preferences for rapid growth and mass mobilization were consistent throughout the 1950s. (The concern for rapid growth disappeared from the late Maoism of the Cultural Revolution decade, and his belief in the efficacy of mass movements as means of economic development also declined.) Except for the issues of speed and mobilization, Mao adopted a consistently "liberal" line on politics and economics in late 1956 and early 1957. In the economic realm, he supported material incentives for peasants, favored use of the market, and advocated balanced growth and material incentives; his political innovations in encouraging intellectuals and others to play a more active role in the affairs of the state are well known. He was willing to accept the idea that widespread class struggle had disappeared, and to substitute education and persuasion. Moreover, he did not view such persuasion and education as a one-way street; the Party was to be remolded by the people, and intellectuals were to hold a privileged position in the process. Again, a tantalizing "what if" question arises. If the Hundred Flowers had succeeded, would Mao have increasingly resembled Tito?

At the very least, the lost reform of 1956–1957 illustrates that Mao's views (and therefore Maoism) were much more flexible and contingent than many argue. Mao's understanding of the sources of tension in the Chinese polity in 1956–1957 was prescient. As in many aspects of his post-1949 career, however, he was far less able when it came to formulating effective policies to address the tensions and to seeing that his ideas were well implemented; and he was less than fully conscious of what effect he had on the policy-making process. In particular, on countless occasions he seemed oblivious of the fact that his personal advocacy induced an excessive response by society, the bureaucracy, or both.

In addition to revealing aspects of the lost reform and Mao's ideas, this study argues that Mao's role in the policy process was circumscribed by the choices presented to him by his advisers and the bureaucracy. Economic officials played the major role in defining the list of available economic alternatives for central decision makers in 1956–1957. The Great Leap Forward program for the economy was thought up not by Mao but by the planners, notably Bo Yibo and Li Fuchun. The Great Leap cannot, then, be seen as the product of the "Maoist model of development," because Mao did not formulate the economic policies of the Leap, except – and it is an important exception – for the communes. Even here, the formation of communes reflects organizational changes caused by *xiafang*, the socialist education campaign in the countryside, the water conservancy campaign, and the interventions of Mao's supporters Chen Boda and Tan Zhenlin. Mao denied in 1959 that he had invented communes.[1]

It might be argued that Mao's role was circumscribed because he and other CCP leaders were devoting inordinate time to the Hundred Flowers during early 1957 and economic officials were given much less supervision than usual. Perhaps. Until studies are made of other periods, no definitive response is possible. The growing complexity and interdependence of the Chinese economy after 1956, however, make it unlikely that central leaders could have formulated the detailed economic policies they eventually adopted. Choices made earlier in Chinese economic development debates precluded certain options and narrowed the scope of what Party leaders could propose.[2] Party leaders could supervise and guide the process under which economic alternatives were formulated, but if they actually tried to frame policies, they risked disaster because they did not fully understand the implications of many of their choices. This is a classic case of insiders' use of expertise effectively precluding generalists from controlling the insiders' area of specialization. Mao's complaints in 1956 and 1958 about the budgetary process, and his unwillingness to read reports to the National People's Congress on the plan and the budget, show that he was not intimately involved in economic policy making after his summing up of the bureaucracy's ideas in the April 1956 speech on the Ten Major Relationships. (Moreover, several of these relationships were immediately ignored by the planners, as we have seen.)[3]

1. See Schurmann, 1968, pp. 464–79; Jane Lieberthal, 1971; MacFarquhar, 1983, pp. 76–88; and Schram, 1974, p. 145.

2. This is one of the main findings of Thomas Fingar's 1977 examination of policy making in 1954–1955.

3. For Mao's complaints in 1956, see Mao, 1977, pp. 334–35. See *Miscellany of Mao Tsetung Thought* (Arlington, VA.: Joint Publications Research Service, no. 61269-1, February 1974), pp. 77–84, for his more biting 1958 views. The Ten Major Relationships are included in Mao, 1977, pp. 284–307.

Why does Mao's lack of understanding of the economy, his flexibility, and his inattention to major economic documents show that he was constrained by the bureaucracy rather than being independent of it? His ignorance of the economy made him dependent on others for ideas about how to run it. His few direct interventions in macroeconomic decision making are hard to identify. He never directed major economic bureaucracies to develop concrete new ideas on overall economic management, and they continued to adhere to their basic views even after his death. Like all leaders, he was dependent on institutions to execute his instructions (when he gave them), and he spent much of the early and mid 1960s excoriating the bureaucracy for blunting or ignoring his instructions, especially in the areas of health, education, literature, and the arts.

Mao Zedong played a decisive role in the development of the Great Leap, but his activities were different from those often portrayed. Mao summed up the situation, brought together various currents in the political system, and combined the disparate elements of the planning coalition's economic program and the Party's mobilization program. He did not initiate either program. He took over the ideas of others and selectively adapted them to his own purposes. He packaged separate policies into a whole, but he did not draw up any of the economic policies associated with the Leap, nor was the "whole" of the Leap very coherent. Even in the case of the communes, as noted, his activities were more complex – more a response to ongoing developments and functional pressures for larger rural units than the outcome of his ideology of permanent revolution.[4]

Through control of the terms of political discussion, Mao succeeded in defining the financial coalition's program as illegitimate. He also decisively influenced the style of policy implementation and injected a tremendous concern for increasing the pace of economic development. But he did not think up the economic policies constituting the Great Leap Forward.

Mao learned the lessons of his own limitations in economic affairs after the Great Leap. His interventions in macroeconomic affairs after 1960 were few and far between, and they reflect ideas associated with the coalitions. Perhaps the most important of Mao's post-1960 interventions in the economy occurred in 1964 when he issued a directive on Third Front industrialization that called for rapid construction of basic industries in the interior. But such a policy was in fact a rediscovery of Stalin-style defense industrialization.[5] Mao also joined with Zhou Enlai and others in arguing in the early 1960s that construction should proceed first in agriculture, then in light industry,

4. See the references in n. 1.
5. See Naughton, 1988.

and finally in heavy industry. But Chen Yun had suggested this first, in 1957. What such a list of priorities meant in practice is not at all clear, and it appears that the planners largely ignored it anyway. Mao's limited activities in regard to the macroeconomy in the 1960s testify either to bureaucratic constraints on him or to his lack of interest in the subject. In either case, economic bureaucracies largely controlled macroeconomic discussions.

B. The nature of coalitional politics

Bureaucratic interests and coalitional politics have been the centerpiece of my analysis of the origins of the Great Leap Forward. Such an approach should not be terribly surprising. Bureaucracies and coalitions are important actors in almost every political system. Yet until recently bureaucratic politics was not a frequently employed point of entry in the analysis of Chinese politics.[6] Among the reasons for relative lack of attention to Chinese bureaucratic and coalitional politics are arguments that the political system under Mao was insufficiently institutionalized to allow bureaucratic politics to exist;[7] that Mao so dominated the political system that it makes little sense to look elsewhere for the origins of policy initiatives;[8] and a related bias in favor of examining the ideological (or in some cases the power-political, or factional) origins of political change but not the organizational sources of political behavior.[9]

The pursuit of bureaucratic interests and coalitional strategies of political activity have been clearly documented here. The Ministry of Finance opposed excessive rates of investment and unbalanced budgets, and its leaders formulated an alternative strategy of development that did not employ them. The Ministry of Machine Building initially opposed diverting some of its productive capacity to serve the rural sector, but once it became apparent that funding for machine tools would decline in 1957 and 1958, its leader argued for increased production of farm implements, linking this with the need for industry to serve agriculture; thereby he would save his own budget. More broadly, planners attempted to convince industry that it should serve agriculture in order to protect the investment share allocated to heavy industry. The policies of self-reliance and emphasis on medium-size and small industrial enterprises that were revived and promoted by the planners in

6. The strongest example of an approach centering on bureaucratic politics is Kenneth Lieberthal and Oksenberg, 1988. Two of the relatively few prereform studies of bureaucratic politics in China are Lampton, 1977, and Whitson, 1972.

7. Domes, 1974, p. 22.

8. For example, Teiwes, 1984, ch. 1.

9. Schram, 1989; Starr, 1979; Pye, 1981.

effect meant increased priority for the steel and machine-tool industries. These examples and the more extensive discussions in Chapters 4 and 5 illustrate the centrality of bureaucratic and coalitional interests in molding preferences for alternative policies.

The case for the primacy of bureaucratic coalitions as key actors in policy making in China is also apparent in these chapters. It was not coincidental that the Ministries of Commerce, Finance, Agriculture, and Light Industry and other units all favored increased agricultural investment, use of the market, and a check on the power of the planning and heavy industry coalition. The Soviet model of economic development created complementary interests and thus natural alliances among planning agencies, the metallurgical sector, and the machine-building industries. Individually, a bureaucracy or commission might face a united front in opposition to its desired policies, but in coalitions there was strength. This is not to say that these bureaucratically based coalitions focusing on economic issues were the only ones in the Chinese polity, but they were certainly the most important in the period under consideration here, and they remained important in later periods.

Instead of the more conventional split between politicians and economic officials,[10] or between "reds" and "experts," this study has identified at least three coalitions, each with its own perspective on the economy. The financial coalition emphasized financial control, balance, and the market; the planning and heavy industry coalition affirmed the Soviet model of development; and Mao, and less clearly the Party, supported rapid but more balanced advance, with mass mobilization as a major source of growth.

It might be argued that the economic officials had long and close personal relations from working on the same general issues for extended periods, and that it was therefore inconceivable for Chen Yun and Li Xiannian to disagree seriously with Bo Yibo and Li Fuchun. This argument can be met in two ways. First, one should not necessarily equate bureaucratic and coalitional politics with life-or-death political struggles. The allocation of resources in any society has many elements of conflict. Certain routines and expectations develop around allocational policies to channel and limit such conflict. Moreover, with a few exceptions, levels of political conflict were not particularly high in China in the 1950s. Within a general framework of elite unity, leaders could object to policies they felt uncomfortable about without paying a high political price.[11]

10. See, for example, MacFarquhar, 1958 and 1974, esp. pt. 1; and Schurmann, 1968, passim. But Schurmann (1974, pt. 2) does depict three different groups or coalitions working to pursue their ideas on policy development.

11. This is argued most persuasively in Teiwes, 1987.

The second rejoinder is more convincing. The empirical evidence shows that, at the very least, budgeteers found aspects of the planning and heavy industry coalition's policies and practices objectionable. The obscure financial official Wang Ziying criticized Bo Yibo's speech at the Eighth Party Congress (without naming Bo) for advocating too high a level of investment. Wang also objected to financial decentralization. Chen Yun objected to the proposed budget figures for 1958 that were drawn up early in 1957 by the State Economic Commission, and he argued for a retrenchment in capital construction that cut the bone (meaning heavy industrial factories) and not just the muscle and skin (investment in housing and other "nonproductive" projects). Chen's emphasis on the three balances directly contradicted Li Fuchun's view at the Eighth Party Congress that all balance was relative and that imbalance should therefore not be of great concern. Evidence of the planners' hostility to the financial coalition is somewhat harder to find; it consists largely of what was not said. The top planners never articulated support for the market or for using prices as incentives; they never favored increased investment in agriculture and light industry; they never supported financial indicators as a means of macroeconomic control. The planners' journal did object to the ending of the production upsurge of late 1955 and early 1956. The planning coalition certainly ignored Mao. It cut investment in agriculture and light industry in 1957 despite Mao's repeated calls for increased investment in the countryside. Its leaders argued for a lowering of construction standards after Mao had warned against that. Mao and the budgeteers criticized the planners for ignoring agriculture. These, and other examples previously discussed, all illustrate differences among the coalitions on economic issues.

C. Larger patterns of Chinese politics

Four larger aspects of Chinese politics are partially revealed in this study of the origins of the Great Leap Forward. First, while the Great Leap forward was the archetypical case, it was one of a number of leaps and retreats that have characterized the Chinese political economy. Second, and related, the Great Leap and the other leaps and retreats were the product of a recurring pattern of coalitional alignment. Leaps (and retreats) occur under particular sets of circumstances and reflect a specific pattern of coalitional alliances. Third, the pattern of leaps and retreats exposes a surprisingly stable series of preferences among the main coalitions concerned with the Chinese political economy. In short, the economic bureaucracy has been highly institutionalized for an extended period. Finally, and most controversially, this

study suggests that organizations and institutions have been a more important source for policy preferences than individual leaders.

C.1. Leaps and readjustments in the political economy of China

The Great Leap Forward was not the first, nor was it the last, of China's
leaps. As a generic event, a leap forward was characterized by a high rate of
investment, particularly in heavy industry. Major changes in rural social organization and mass mobilization were important features of many, if not all,
leaps. Decentralization of power to lower-level Party committees frequently
accompanied leaps. Whether or not there was extensive recourse to mass
campaigns, leaps required the marshaling of societal energies to achieve a
set goal, usually a high rate of economic growth.

Leaps created disproportion and imbalance in the economy. The "storming" aspect of these movements caused the quality of products to fall. The
emphasis on heavy industry meant that light industry was ignored. This, in
turn, undermined incentives: Industrial employment (and hence total social
purchasing power) increased, but consumer goods failed to keep up with the
amount of money in circulation – a classic prescription for inflation. The
idea of going all out, integral to leaps, often spawned commandism by leading cadres, who became so eager to try to achieve perhaps impossible targets
that they felt they must not waste a second, and so constantly ordered people
about. Finally, because of the emphasis on speed, too many investment projects were started without sufficient attention to how to finance them, where
the materials to build the factories would come from, where the raw materials for production would come from, and whether there might be too many
factories in the same product line already in operation. In short, leaps may
have created in the short term unsustainably high rates of growth while pro-
digious amounts of resources were expended for little long-term gain, often
with a net negative effect on the economy.

The center often lost control of events. Local cadres were so responsive
to incentives (which appeared to reward quota overfulfillment highly) that
they greatly exceeded investment plans and created the problems noted.
The national budget often ran a deficit, because most cadres were busy
spending money on investment projects and neglecting revenues. Those who
advocated more caution or financial balance were accused of conservatism.

Leaps were almost invariably followed by readjustments, or retreats, which
were almost the opposite of leaps. During readjustments, emphasis was placed
on restoring economic equilibrium and incentives and on cutting capital construction. More attention was paid to light industry and agriculture, and less

to heavy industry. Efficiency became a major watchword; finances were again balanced. Often the size of agricultural production units was reduced in order to improve incentives. Market allocation was applied to a number of commodities. Somewhat paradoxically, periods of readjustment were often characterized by very strict centralized control of the economy. This seeming paradox can be explained by noting that it was the budget, particularly budgetary expenditures, and investments that were rigorously restrained. The market was reserved for the allocation of goods too varied and therefore too burdensome for state-run commerce to control. The market was also used to stimulate the production of agriculture sidelines, frequently in short supply after leaps.

China's leaps and retreats are similar to, but not identical with, economic cycles in planned economies.[12] In Eastern Europe, such cycles are the regular result of ministries' and enterprises' scrambling to add their pet projects to the long-term plan in the first year or so of its operation. Planners cannot resist the demands of political leaders to include this or that project in the plan. The state quickly exhausts its capacity to fund and supply the now-overburdened plan, and a cutback is announced until the start of the new long-term plan, and so forth. In the Chinese case, the swings in investment were greater, and the leaps and retreats had greater implications for the political positions of various leaders and often involved mass mobilization and changes in rural social organization, which was not the case in Eastern Europe. Moreover, whereas there is a more or less regular periodicity to the economic cycles in Eastern Europe, the PRC's leaps and retreats have occurred more randomly.

At least four leaps and three periods of readjustment have occurred since 1949. Two of the leaps have been discussed here, at least partially: the small leap forward of 1956 and the Great Leap Forward. Other leaps occurred in 1969–1970 and 1977–1978.[13] The 1969–1970 leap might be called the military leap forward. The historical materials on this one are the least satisfactory, but it appears that Lin Biao, Mao's designated successor and commander of the Chinese Army, used the threat of war with the Soviet Union to mobilize resources for defense-industry construction, and not coincidentally to try to consolidate his own position. Pressures arose in the country-

12. There is a very large literature on economic cycles in planned economies, especially those of Eastern Europe. The best short introduction to cycles and their causes in Bauer, 1978. Kornai, 1980, contains a thorough discussion of this and related issues.

13. On the first two leaps, see MacFarquhar, 1974, pp. 15–32, and 1983, passim. On 1969–1970, see Domes, 1977, ch. 4, and Naughton, 1988, pp. 358–67. On 1977–1978, see Dernberger, 1982, esp. pp. 20–35. This section and this abbreviated list of references by no means exhaust either the literature on these leaps or their complexities.

side to abolish all private plots and move the level of commune accounting from the team to the brigade.[14] The 1977–1978 leap has been dubbed the Great Leap Outward because Chinese leaders attempted to carry out economic modernization very rapidly, relying in large part on purchases of factories from foreign countries. Indeed, the leadership planned to invest as much in the 1978–1985 period as had been invested in all the years from 1949 to 1977, with heavy industry receiving the bulk of the resources. Several Chinese leaders compared the early post-Mao period favorably with the Great Leap Forward.[15] In three of these leaps (1958, 1970, 1978) investment in capital construction increased by more than 10 billion yuan over the preceding year. This meant an increase of from 20 to almost 100 percent.[16]

This study has discussed aspects of the first readjustment in detail, especially in Chapter 4. The second readjustment lasted from 1961 until 1964 or 1965.[17] Evidence for a brief readjustment in the early 1970s is weak, though Chinese scholars claim one existed.[18] The most recent period of readjustment lasted from 1979 to 1982.[19]

Rapid, and sometimes excessive, increases in investment expenditures appeared throughout the 1980s, but the prolonged secular decentralization of authority and resources since the Cultural Revolution, the Open Door policy, and the decollectivization of the countryside all changed the institutional and policy-making environment in the decade.[20] Provincial coalitions arose and became, along with the planners and budgeteers, powerful participants in the making of economic policy. And the (relative) development of high-technology industries (fitting neither the light nor the heavy industry cate-

14. The best source on this period is Fang Weizhong, 1984, pp. 449–73. See also Yan Fangming and Wang Yaping, "Qishi Niandai Chuqi Wo Guo Jingji Jianshede Maojin jiqi Tiaozheng" (The Rash Advance of Our Economy in the Early 1970s and Its Readjustment), *Dangshi Yanjiu* (Research on Party History), 1985, no. 5, pp. 55–59. On rural developments, see Zweig, 1989.

15. See Fang Weizhong, 1984, pp. 574–614; *National Conference on Learning from Taching in Industry*, 1977; and Chen Huiqin, "Jishu Yinjinde Fangxiang Bixu Zhuanbian" (The Orientation of Technology Imports Must Shift), *Jingji Guanli* (Economic Management), 1981, no. 4 (April), pp. 22–25.

16. Calculated from State Statistical Bureau, 1986, p. 517. Chinese officials in the early 1980s were well aware of the 10-billion-yuan danger signal. For example, Xu Ming, "10 Billion *Yuan*: A Warning Mark for Capital Construction," in Foreign Broadcast Information Service, *Daily Report, China*, July 20, 1983, K 16 – K 17, and He Jianzhang, "Strictly Control the Scale of Capital Construction," ibid., August 16, 1983, K 3 – K 8.

17. For example, Liu Suinian, 1982, and Fang Weizhong, 1984, pp. 292–404.

18. Yan Fangming and Wang Yaping, "Qishi Niandai Chuqi Wo Guo Jingji Jianshede Maojin jiqi Tiaozheng" (n. 14).

19. See Chen Yun, 1986, pp. 211–14, 220–34, 236–40, and 248–54. For secondary analysis, see Dernberger, 1982.

20. On the decentralization of resources and regional self-reliance, see Naughton, 1987; Lyons, 1987; and Wong, 1985. One case study of the effects of the reforms, illustrating the effects of the Open Door and agricultural reforms, is Vogel, 1989. For an attempt to explain the rapid growth of investment in the 1980s, see Wong, 1986.

gory) and the increasing ability of light industry to grow without agricultural inputs weakened the hold of agriculture in economic policy making.

Chinese leaders knew the Great Leap Forward was a disaster, and many were troubled by the small leap of 1955–1956. Why did the pattern of leaps and retreats persist?

C.2. Coalitional alignments and leaps and retreats

Why did the Chinese leadership follow such a jerky course in its attempts to modernize the economy into the early 1980s? Why did leaps continue to occur after many top-ranking leaders realized how inefficient and costly they were? The answers to these questions lie in the coalitions embedded in the Chinese state, and more broadly in the "materialist" (or environmental) and structural nature of economic politics in China. (See Section D of this chapter.) To overstate the case, leaps strengthened the short-run position of the planning and heavy industry coalition, and readjustments brought the financial coalition to the fore. And leaps were in keeping with the CCP's mobilizational nature. In other words, it was in the political interest of the planning and heavy industry coalition and most members of the CCP to support leaps forward.[21] Through leaps, the primacy of investment in heavy industry was ensured, and the rapid, if short, associated economic expansion provided a chance for cadres to prove themselves. Moreover, there was something deeply compelling to the Chinese Communist Party, and to most Chinese citizens, about the vision of a strong, industrialized China. Leaps were thought to bring that vision closer to reality.

The financial coalition's trouble was precisely that it lacked an appealing vision of the future. Balance is nice, but critics asked how it could create a modern industrialized state. An expanded role for the market, greater use of efficiency criteria, and strict central control all served to limit the role of the Party in economic affairs. Under such a regimen, Party mobility was likely to be much less and recruitment slower than during leaps. The program of the financial coalition might bring order out of economic chaos and balance out of imbalance, but there was little that was positive or compelling in its ideas. It did not tap the primordial forces unleashed by the Chinese revolution. It did little to respond to the Chinese people's strong desire for

21. It might be argued that the "storming" associated with leaps is anathema to the planners' desire to control the economic environment. However, planners have often associated themselves with leaps (clearly in 1958 and 1977), and even if planning organizations are disturbed by leaps, heavy industry, which sees its share of investment increase substantially, is not. Leaps resemble a step-level function. Although there may be some retrenchment after each leap, the base for expansion is enlarged.

rapid advancement. Nor was it likely to appeal to the CCP, which argued in 1956 (and after 1978) that the biggest problem China faced was its backward economy. In short, there was nothing in the financial coalition's views to seize minds or mobilize enthusiasm.

The case study presented here and this brief discussion of the pattern of recurring leaps and readjustments indicate that there was a much greater likelihood that the planning and heavy industry coalition and the Party would enter into an alliance than that the financial coalition and the Party, or the budgeteers and the planners, would. This is not to say that these other combinations were impossible, just less likely. More work needs to be done on when and why various coalitions cooperate and form alliances or united fronts, but some of the reasons why the planning coalition and the Party often worked together can be put forward here.

Rapid economic growth served the interests of both the planners and the Party. Economic upsurges often provided cadres with the opportunity to prove their commitment to the building of socialism. Before Mao's death, most Party members were recruited during periods of mass mobilization. Indeed, ability to contribute to and lead mass movements was almost a prerequisite for Party membership.[22] Pre-1956 campaigns shaped later leaps and the traditions of militarizing activists. The activists often became a constituency for later campaigns and leaps.[23] Leaps also increased the resources allocated to the planning and heavy industry coalition, which could easily support mass mobilization and changes in the size of rural production units because these required no diversion of resources from the heavy industrial sector. One of the fundamental goals of the Party was to transform China from a backward agricultural nation into a modern industrial state. Central to this process was the development of heavy industry. Thus, a significant number of points of contact existed between the planners and the Party.

Many fewer points of agreement existed between the budgeteers and the Party as agent of social transformation. The financial coalition's program for development was slower and much less ambitious than that of the planners. Budgeteer policies provided little opportunity for Party activism and heroism. The idea of politics in command was incompatible with the idea of balance and use of the market mechanism. But when economic conditions deteriorated, central leaders adopted budgeteer policies, or conceded their necessity. Leaders realized that at times high rates of investment could not be sustained, that agriculture must receive more attention, and that balance needed to be restored to the economy. Once balance had been restored, the

22. On this point, see Martin, 1981.
23. I wish to thank Lynn White for this point.

leadership was quick to return to a more ambitious program of economic development.

The planning coalition and the financial coalition had limited areas of agreement. Both may have desired limited Party and leadership intervention in economic administration, but their priorities were at odds. Planners accepted the Soviet model wholeheartedly, while budgeteers expressed a strong preference for balance, stability, and sustained growth, with more emphasis on agriculture and light industry. In principle, the financial coalition did not object to (relative) priority for heavy industry, but in practice the budgeteers strongly objected to the degree of heavy industrial priority and to the speed of advance advocated by the planners.

These basic propensities for alliance provide the conditioning factors essential to an explanation of the pattern of leaps and retreats, but they do not explain the immediate cause of leaps. The record of the four leaps suggests that a crisis in, or a major external challenge to, the political or economic system (in reality, a challenge to the Party's position as ruler of China or a crisis in the economic system, where the primacy of the Soviet model is called into question) was essential to bring about an active alliance between the Party and the planners. In the case of the small leap, the combination of a crisis in the grain supply (threatening all industrial construction) and Hu Feng's criticism of Party leadership in literature and art, which developed into the campaign to eradicate hidden counterrevolutionaries, brought together the Party and the planning and heavy industry coalition. In the case of the Great Leap, the challenge to the legitimacy of CCP rule by the Hundred Flowers critics, the budgeteers' challenge to the planners, and agricultural problems precipitated the Party-planner alliance. The case of the military leap is less clear, but the real danger of war with the Soviet Union posed the greatest threat to PRC security since 1949, and the CCP, as a result of the mass violence of the Cultural Revolution, was in disarray. Finally, the Great Leap Outward of 1977–1978 was a response to the crisis of legitimacy caused by Mao's death and the failure of living standards to improve over two decades.[24]

Of course, many periods of Chinese political history have been characterized by neither leaps nor readjustments. How are "normal" periods accounted for? To some extent, this depends on what is meant by "normal." These periods might be the result of lack of dominance by any single coalition or alliance of coalitions. Normality may be the product of different coa-

---

24. I offer this brief analysis extremely tentatively; it requires in-depth studies of the various leaps and retreats. Nonetheless, the conjunction of crises with leaps and retreats is, to my mind, suggestive of a deep pattern in China's political economy.

litions' focusing on different issues, ineffective leadership by the chief spokesmen of the most powerful coalition (or conversely, effective leadership by the heads of the weaker coalitions), deliberate playing off of one coalition against the other by the leadership, all of these, or some other factors.

A conjunction of propensities to cooperate between the Party and the planning coalition and a challenge or crisis that threatens either grouping's hegemony (for the planners, in the economic realm; for the Party, its right to rule) leads to leaps. The inevitable inability of leaps to sustain themselves, and the severe economic dislocations they cause, create an imperative for the institution of policies associated with the financial coalition. Then, once the immediate economic shortcomings have been ameliorated, the budgeteers find it impossible to institutionalize their position politically, and the planners and the Party reassert their authority over the agenda.

C.3. The institutionalization of Chinese politics

This study and the brief discussion of other leaps and retreats suggest not only that there is a recurring pattern of alliances among the major coalitions involved in economic policy making, but also that there is significant continuity in the positions associated with each coalition over time. Throughout every readjustment, and continuing after the onset of reform, the Ministry of Finance has emphasized stability, balance, and control. Throughout every leap, and continuing into the 1980s, heavy industry has favored high rates of investment, a privileged position in allocational priority, and rapid advance. Other examples of the stability of organizational preferences over time might be adduced.

This may be saying nothing more than that bureaucracies in China differ little from bureaucracies in other countries. They are created to manage certain tasks, they formulate certain procedures and methods to carry out their designated responsibilities, and for good economic and sociological reasons discussed in Chapter 3, these methods and procedures persist. This is not to say that they are immutable or that entrepreneurial bureaucracies do not exist, but that organizations in China, as elsewhere, tend to have stable preferences.

The implications of such a view are perhaps underappreciated in studies of Chinese politics and economics. Choices available to leaders are limited by organizations. Information is selectively compiled and filtered by organizations. Bureaucracies carry out policies and struggle to twist official policy to resemble organizational interests more closely. Bureaucracies often engage in "subterranean" activities of which the leadership may be only vaguely aware. Yet such endeavors may multiply and commit the leadership to policies it may not have authorized formally. For example, in perhaps the finest discussion of the persistence of organizational preferences over time, Lieberthal and Oksenberg show how the Ministry of Petroleum was for more than twenty years interested in outside involvement in China's oil development even though the ministry itself was championing self-reliance.[25]

Thus, Chinese politics must be viewed from below the level of the top leadership, particularly for recurring issues associated with resource allocation. The role of organizations is vital in both the pre- and postdecision phases of policy making. Leaders have discretionary authority, but for particularly complex and interdependent choices, such as plan formulation and budget making, leadership choice is severely circumscribed. Some may argue that it is not really persisting organizational preferences but, rather, the roles and central ideas of key individuals that matter in the end. Key individuals built many of the organizations under discussion throughout this study, and some of these individuals are still alive today and continue to set the course of Chinese politics.

C.4. Organizations versus leaders

Whether the Chinese political system is "system-dominant" or dominated by powerful individual leaders standing above Party and state organizations is a difficult question. Yet in the area of economic policy making, mounting, but so far inconclusive, evidence favors the system-dominant position, and long-term trends favor the growing power of organizations vis-à-vis individual leaders.

It is clear that in the case of the planning and heavy industry coalition there has been significant turnover in leadership but little change in basic interests and program. Yu Qiuli, effectively the chief planning official from 1964 to 1980, was no less eager than Li Fuchun to build heavy industry rapidly. Even in the reform period, leaders of the planning coalition pressed for priority for heavy industry and high rates of centrally controlled investment. The leaders of the production ministries within the planning and heavy industry coalition have changed more frequently than the top planners, and here the evidence is even more persuasive. The Ministry of Metallurgical Industries continues to argue for more steel mills; the Ministry of Petroleum

---

25. Kenneth Lieberthal and Oksenberg, 1988, ch. 5. Their study gives other examples of the persistence of organizational preferences.

wants more money for additional exploration and development of petroleum resources; and so forth.

The case of the financial coalition is much less clear-cut. Chen Yun, Li Xiannian, and Yao Yilin are still alive, and Chen in particular wields great power in the political system when he is healthy. His impact on the organizational interests of the Ministry of Finance is profound. His economic ideas have been highly consistent since 1956. While he is alive, it is impossible to prove that the organizational interests of the ministries in the financial coalition transcend the specific views of its preeminent leader. The same is true of Li and Yao to a lesser extent.

In the next ten years, however, the relative dominance of organizations over leaders will become increasingly manifest. Whereas the octogenarians ruling China today, and in particular Deng Xiaoping and Chen Yun, created many of the organizations making up the state, the fifty- and sixty-year-olds who will succeed them are products of those organizations. The new-generation leaders have narrower career paths and fewer horizontal contacts, and have risen to the top of the Party-state system more slowly than the revolutionary generation. They will be significantly less autonomous political leaders than their predecessors, and the imprint of organizations, and in particular the organization in which each spent most of his or her career, will be much more deeply embedded than for older leaders. To be sure, younger leaders will be better educated than Deng Xiaoping's generation, and as human beings they will possess the ability to imagine and create new alternatives. But in their ability to accrue power in order to transcend the structure of interests in the bureaucratic system, they will be much more strictly limited than Deng, who in turn was much more strictly circumscribed in his choices than Mao. And even Mao had only limited economic choices, as this study has demonstrated.

D. Sources of policy preferences and a "materialist," structural approach to Chinese politics

Where preferences come from is one of the classic questions of politics. This study has answered that preferences come from the interplay of bureaucratic mission and the environment in which the organization operates. Chinese bureaucracies prefer policies that make the achievement of their designated tasks easier. Whether this means larger budgets, reduced demands on the organization, use of the market, or administrative means of allocation depends on the specific task and the situation the particular bureaucracy faces when it attempts to implement policies congruous with its mission. For the

Ministry of Finance, charged with making budgets and controlling inflation, this means financial balances and overall economic stability. For the Ministry of Metallurgy, this means as large a budget share as possible to build new steel mills. These and other examples are discussed more fully in Chapters 4 and 5.

As argued in Chapter 3, however, these narrower bureaucratic interests are generally not sufficiently powerful in themselves to pressure the leadership to favor them. A higher level of preference aggregation is necessary to present these bureaucratic interests to the central leadership forcefully and to limit the ability of the leadership to control the expression and pursuit of bureaucratic interests. These larger aggregations of preferences form around the least common denominator of policies that serve the broad programmatic interests of the bureaucracies joining together in coalitions. This does not eliminate bureaucratic rivalries and conflicts within each coalition, but it does provide an overarching trellis on which disparate and narrow bureaucratic interests and ideologies can be welded together. The process by which the coalitions have formed is still murky, but the leadership contributions by Chen Yun for the financial coalition and by Li Fuchun and Bo Yibo for the planning coalition cannot be denied.

If further studies confirm many of the core arguments in this work – such as the ability of economic coalitions to limit leadership choice, the importance of the economic agenda and of regularized processes of plan formulation and budget making, and the creative tension produced by the political battles between the planning and financial coalitions as the impetus for economic policy changes – then this will indicate that at least in the economic realm analysts of Chinese politics should consider looking at their subject in a new way. That is, they should look in a more "materialist"[26] (or environmental), structural way.

The economic policy debate of 1956–1957 was not about implementing a transcendent ideology, nor was it the product of particular leadership factions not tied to organizational bases, nor a struggle for supreme state and Party power. Power and ideological considerations were not irrelevant, but the fundamental issues were how to increase agricultural production, how to manage the economy, and how to protect or promote the interests of different coalitions of bureaucratic actors. The economic situation – the material foundation of society – determined the key issues in the economic debate. No single easy answer to the problems of scarcity and backwardness

---

26. As used here, "materialist" means coming from the objective economic conditions existing in society, not a Marxian, class-oriented approach (historical materialism). "Environmental" could be substituted for "materialist."

in China existed. Yet it was precisely the issue of how to respond to these basic conditions that energized the economic institutions and their leaders. For one group, the answer was balance and the market; for another, it was heavy industrial aid to agriculture and self-reliance; for yet a third, it was balance in allocations, high speed, and mass mobilization. These programs not only addressed the problems of scarcity and backwardness, they profoundly supported the varied interests of the coalitional groupings that championed them.

It is perhaps not very remarkable that economic policy making, especially in a poor country, is amenable to a "materialist," structural approach. The routines of economic policy making, particularly in a planned economy, where both plans and budgets must be formulated regularly, reinforce organizational interests. Regular staff work, negotiations, tracking of ongoing processes, and allocation of resources with only limited recourse to markets all favor bureaucratic modes of operation rather than the sporadic intervention of individual leaders responding to a wide-ranging and ever varying agenda. Leaders are not powerless in the face of organizational activity, but they are much less autonomous in the realm of economic policy making than is commonly thought. Determining the degree of leadership autonomy and theorizing about the circumstances under which leaders are more or less autonomous (or conversely, the circumstances under which organizations are more likely to determine the policy debate) is a necessary next step in an endeavor to create a "materialist," structural approach to Chinese politics.

Ultimately, the economic agenda of the Chinese state is similar to that of many other poor countries: how to reward the populace in order to increase productivity; how to find jobs for the large number of young people coming into the work force each year; how to extract resources to use for state-building purposes; how to use resources obtained by the state efficaciously; and how to use economic policies to build and consolidate support for the regime. In the Chinese case, additional concerns are linked with the economic agenda, such as how to turn China into a powerful industrial and military power rapidly; whether to use the international system to serve the goal of increasing national power, and how to do so; and what to do about the problem of China's huge population. Certainly such problems do not structure the entire political agenda. Nonetheless, most of the issues confronting the Chinese state flow directly from conditions of scarcity and backwardness; and, arguably, the impact of these basic conditioning factors on the agenda is growing.

A "materialist," structural approach to Chinese politics is not capable of revealing much about the possibility of system change – democratization or degeneration. Yet unless the Chinese political system suffers total collapse, the issues of scarcity and backwardness and the institutions designed to manage them will loom large for any Chinese state. This study, it is hoped, has contributed new perspectives on the relationships among economic issues, bureaucratic organizations, and political leaders. Leaders, even Mao Zedong, were significantly constrained by policy problems and organizational policies to deal with them. Mao tried to ignore economic and technical realities in the Great Leap Forward. The resulting disaster marked the last time he or any other leader would attempt to do so. To the present day, organizational leaders have continued to advocate many of the policies articulated in the 1950s. The generally unchanging nature of the economic problems facing China and the persistence of organizations account for this. The power of institutions and the environment to structure the Chinese political agenda was substantial under Mao, and it is growing significantly under Deng.

E. Aftermath: some thoughts on developments in 1957 and 1989

There are a number of startling parallels between the unfolding of the Hundred Flowers Campaign plus the economic debates of 1956–1957 and political and economic developments in 1989. In both cases, the Chinese people, especially intellectuals, called on the Party to improve itself fundamentally, and they made their demands known in unprecedented numbers. Economic conditions were difficult during both episodes, although the specific problems of each period were different. (In 1957, the main problems were an overheated economy and limited agricultural growth constraining industrial development and consumption levels. In 1989, inflation, corruption, and signs of a stagnating economic reform, despite tremendous rates of growth, were the fundamental issues.) There were continuities between planner and budgeteer positions in 1957 and 1989. Most tragically, both episodes ended in suppression. As noted in this book, the Anti-Rightist Campaign ruined the lives of more than 550,000 persons and left millions of others languishing in prison. The Tiananmen massacre of 1989 and related acts of suppression have claimed more than 1,000 lives, and thousands of others have been imprisoned or subjected to investigation. Finally, two of the key actors in 1957 were also central to events in 1989 – Deng Xiaoping and Chen Yun.

We conclude with a brief examination of the positions of the financial and planning coalitions and the positions of Deng Xiaoping and Chen Yun in 1957 and 1989. Although the overall nature of the Chinese political economy has changed as a result of the Open Door policy, decentralization, reform, and decollectivization, the planning and financial coalitions are still present and, arguably, articulating positions similar to the ones they advanced in 1956–1957. In particular, the financial coalition is recommending today policies almost identical with those it favored in 1957: balanced budgets, centralized control of the economy based on financial indicators, channeling of construction funds through the budget, elimination of extrabudgetary funds, slower and sustainable growth, control over inflation, and the market as a supplement to the plan.

Similarly, the planning coalition favors today a number of policies that it advocated in 1957, although the case is weaker here. Recently, the planners and heavy industry have lost a great deal of their control over the economy because of reforms (however partial and contradictory) and decentralization. The planners have therefore been unable to mobilize resources for their priority targets and projects. They are now largely allied with the financial coalition in an effort to recentralize at least some of the key allocational processes. In this regard, their opposition is now provincial coalitions, particularly a coalition of coastal provinces. In addition, the lack of infrastructural development has become a pressing issue, one that the planners have championed. The development and modernization of steel and machine tools – for their own sake, as part of defense modernization, and as the vital determinant of infrastructural modernization – remain high priorities for this coalition.

In the early aftermath of the Tiananmen massacre, the financial coalition launched yet another period of economic readjustment, using most of the same measures it employed in 1956–1957, with the effect of cooling down the overheated economy. As noted, planners were generally supportive. But once again the financial coalition faces the problem of what vision of the future it can provide to the Chinese people and the CCP. The massacre shattered CCP legitimacy, probably irreparably. Yet all the financial coalition can do is talk about stable and balanced, but slow, growth. This is unlikely to win back hearts and minds for the Party, and in 1990 there were already signs that reform and the Open Door will be revived (at least rhetorically).

Deng Xiaoping's position in 1989 was similar to his position in 1957. Indeed, many of the measures he outlined in his 1957 speech on the rectification campaign (discussed at the start of Chapter 8) are precisely the ones being instituted in the CCP now. Party members' experiences in the democracy movement are now being examined. Party cards are being turned in for examination as part of an attempt to weed out those who do not follow Marxist-Leninist-Mao Zedong thought. As he did in 1957, Deng has excessively expanded the realm of the struggle against those who disagree with him. He has contributed to the revival of ideological concerns in ways that cannot help China in the long run.

Superficially, Chen Yun's role seems to have undergone great change. In 1957, he was the leading advocate of economic reform in China. Today, he is portrayed as the conservative champion of centralized planning. Yet the apparent differences in Chen's position in the Chinese political spectrum are explained much better by the changed nature of that spectrum than by a change in his views. Indeed, I believe Chen's views are basically the same today as they were in 1957. He cherishes balance, based on the three balances. He continues to see the market as a supplement to the plan. He favors financial control and balance rather than material-balance planning, and he remains hostile to excessive heavy industrial investment.

In 1957, Chen was the leader arguing for the most extreme version of economic reform; the planning coalition and Party mobilization were his key targets. Yet Chen and the financial coalition were arguing for quite a tame reform by the standards of the mid 1980s. In the late 1970s, however, Chen's 1956 views were recalled, and they helped legitimize some of the crucial early reforms. In early 1989, the unchanging views of Chen Yun and the financial coalition put them at the conservative end of the political spectrum as ever more radical economic reform proposals were considered. The bold reforms of 1956–1957 are now seen as the epitome of central planning. Nonetheless, Chen's central planning (and that of the alliance of financial and planning coalitions) is quite different from the central planning associated with Li Fuchun and Bo Yibo. The Soviet model is now history in China.

The position of Chen Yun and the financial coalition in China's political system has changed, not because the tendencies and tasks associated with the financial coalition have changed but because new coalitions have arisen in China's political economy, reflecting new environmental and structural conditions. The origins of the Great Leap Forward continue to shed light on Chinese politics today.

Appendix: The constraints on Mao

This book argues that the actions of Mao Zedong were constrained by the workings of institutions in China. This contradicts much of the conventional wisdom about Mao's power, and some may find my statement that Mao was constrained by the bureaucracy problematic. Let me try to explain clearly what I mean by constraints and give evidence of Mao's being constrained.

A. The nature of the constraints on Mao

By constraints I mean limitations on personal autonomy. In particular, in this study I mean, first, Mao's range of choice was significantly narrowed and his choices were channeled along a few limited paths. Second, not infrequently, Mao's explicit preferences were not heeded by the bureaucracy. Finally, Mao perceived himself as being denied a leading role in economic affairs owing to the operations of economic institutions. Evidence on all of these points will be presented shortly.

My use of "constraint" thus goes beyond the trite understanding that in the process of information gathering, organizations bias the representation of reality to serve their interests and distort implementation through the effects of standard operating procedures. To be sure, Mao and other Chinese leaders were constrained in this way. But these constraints are so pervasive that it is hard to imagine any leader of a large country in the twentieth century being free of them.

I do not argue that the constraints on Mao were so powerful that he was effectively denied choice or that economic institutions forced him to make choices he did not want to make. Mao remained a hugely powerful figure until the day of his death. A unified Chinese bureaucracy could not (and did not) approach Mao and say, "You must do not this but something else instead," and expect him to follow its views. And Mao retained the right to make the final choice among all policy options. Instead, the effect of constraint was felt most strongly in the restriction of those options to just two or three.

B. Evidence of the constraints on Mao

As has been argued throughout this study, Mao and the Chinese leadership were effectively presented with three sets of options to deal with the problems of the political economy in 1956–1957. The critical agricultural bottleneck could be addressed by means of markets and price incentives, industrial aid to agriculture, or mass mobilization. Two of these three sets of options might be combined, but not all three. In practice, there was something of a zero-sum quality to each option. Use of the market and price incentives meant taking resources away from industry to supply industrial inputs for the countryside (and vice versa). Markets and mobilization were incompatible. Even mobilization and industry proved incompatible, for the technical expertise required to use industrial inputs successfully in the countryside was often denigrated during mass movements (and again, vice versa). These incompatibilities existed not just in macroeconomic policy toward agriculture but in many other dimensions of macroeconomic policy as well, as is shown in Table 2 of Chapter 3 and in Chapters 4, 5, and 6.

Certainly leaders did try to pick and choose from among the elements of each coalition's policy program, but the compromises proved unsustainable, and the leadership was left with the alternatives of trying to strike a new (and again unstable) compromise or choosing one of the policy programs. Under Mao, the leadership was never able to escape from this structuring of the range of choice and to create new options, no matter how the old options might be discredited.

Not only was Mao's range of choices severely circumscribed, but at times during the period under discussion here his explicit preferences were overridden by other leaders, the bureaucracy, or both. One well-known case was in mid 1956, when the Politburo and others brought the small leap forward under control. Mao said he "would not read" the editorial that announced this retreat from the leap, but he went along with it nonetheless.[1]

In 1956 and 1957, Mao spoke repeatedly about increasing investment in light industry relative to heavy industry, and he also spoke about increasing agricultural investment. Yet Bo Yibo ignored his views and announced cuts in agricultural and light industrial investments in the summer of 1957.[2] In the original version of "On the Correct Handling of Contradictions Among the People," Mao said engineering construction standards should not be cut,

1. See Chapter 7, nn. 43. See also Mao's discussion of the event in Joint Publications Research Service, *Miscellany of Mao Tse-tung Thought* (hereafter *MMTTT*) (Arlington, Va., No. 61269-1, February 1974), p. 83.
2. See Chapter 5, n. 71–72. In absolute terms, investment in agriculture was less in 1957 than in 1956. See *Zhongguo Guding Zichan Touzi Tongji Ziliao, 1950–1985*, 1987, p. 97.

but this is precisely what Li Fuchun and Bo Yibo advocated.[3] The planners ignored Mao's view that more investment should go to coastal areas.[4] In the Ten Major Relationships, Mao called for fewer ministerial orders to the localities, but the number of ministerially allocated products increased.[5] The number of examples here is small, but not trivial, given the generality and contradictory nature of Mao's economic statements in 1956–1957. In any case, Mao's preferences were not always followed by the bureaucracy, suggesting that the bureaucracy constrained his preferences on several important occasions.

Finally, there is Mao's perception that the bureaucracy was trying to prevent him from interfering in its operations or was limiting his influence in economic affairs. As he said in November 1956,

There should be three rounds of discussion before the annual state budget is decided. That is to say, comrades on our Central Committee . . . should hold three meetings to discuss it and make the decision. This will enable all of us to get to understand the contents of the budget. Otherwise it will always be the comrades in charge who know them better while we on our part will just raise our hands. . . .

Both we [the Central Committee] and the secretaries of the provincial, municipal, and autonomous region Party committees should attend to finance and planning. In the past some comrades failed to do so seriously.[6]

More caustically, Mao charged in January 1958:

The finance and economics departments do not keep the Politburo informed, Generally, the reports, too, do not lend themselves to discussion as they do not mention textual research, phraseology and essence. . . .

On the question of reducing personnel, the commercial section and the cooperatives are not responding to political guidance. I have talked about this for several years but they will not reform. . . . The Politburo has become like a voting machine. You give it a perfect document and it has to be passed. . . .

The finance and economics departments do not go into textual research, phraseology, and essence. They must operate in a gentle fashion, giving out information beforehand. With them it has always been a heavy downpour causing washouts. They have always been ungracious, inadequately prepared, and incomplete. This is a blockade. This is a Stalinist method. Ten minutes before the conference opens the document is produced for resolution without any consideration being given to the state of mind of the people. . . . My attack is aimed chiefly at cadres at the ministerial level and above in the central government and it is not levelled at everyone. It is an attack on those who caused heavy downpours and set up blockades.[7]

3. MacFarquhar, Cheek, and Wu, 1989, p. 157. Cf. the views of Bo and Li Fuchun in *Xinhua Banyuekan* (New China Semimonthly), 1957, nos. 11 and 12, pp. 90–91 and 104–5, respectively.

4. See MacFarquhar, 1974, pp. 63–66.

5. Mao, 1977, pp. 292–95, and Zhou Taihe, 1984, pp. 218–22, 502, and 519.

6. Mao, 1977, pp. 334–35.

7. *MMTTT*, pp. 77–81.

Although Mao's rhetoric served political ends, it also seems safe to assume that he felt that the economic bureaucracy did not allow him much input into vital programmatic documents governing decisions about economic allocation. Here, too, Mao was constrained.

Given Mao's leadership style of eschewing close involvement with implementation and paying only sporadic attention to day-to-day economic policy making, he could not help being constrained by the bureaucracy. He could either try to tear it down, as he did in the Cultural Revolution and to a much smaller extent in part of the Great Leap, or be forced generally to work within the system of bureaucratic control of the economy, which constrained his power on economic questions. After the Great Leap, Mao appears to have grown bored with economic issues, and his involvement in macroeconomic questions became increasingly rare. The economic bureaucracy had constrained Mao's power.

Bibliography

Chinese periodicals and newspapers cited

Caizheng (Finance). Beijing. Monthly.
Da Gong Bao (The Impartial Daily). Beijing and Tianjin. Daily.
Dangshi Tongxun (Communications on Party History). Beijing. Monthly.
Dangshi Yanjiu (Research on Party History). Beijing. Bimonthly.
Gongren Ribao (Workers' Daily). Beijing. Daily.
Guangming Ribao (Illumination Daily). Beijing. Daily.
Hongqi (Red Flag). Beijing. Semimonthly or monthly.
Jianshe Yuekan (Construction Monthly). Beijing. Monthly.
Jiefang Ribao (Liberation Daily). Shanghai. Daily.
Jihua Jingji (Planned Economy). Beijing. Monthly.
Jihua yu Tongji (Planning and Statistics). Beijing. Semimonthly.
Jingji Guanli (Economic Management). Beijing. Monthly.
Jingji Yanjiu (Economic Research). Beijing. Bimonthly.
Jixie Gongye (Machine Building Industry). Beijing. Monthly.
Lilun Yuekan (Theory Monthly). Beijing. Monthly.
Nongye Gongzuo Tongxun (Agricultural Work Bulletin). Beijing. Monthly.
Renmin Ribao (People's Daily). Beijing. Daily.
Renwu (Public Figures). Beijing. Bimonthly,
Shangye Gongye (Commercial Industry). Beijing. Monthly (?).
Tongji Gongzuo (Statistical Work). Beijing. Monthly.
Wenhui Bao (Literary Daily). Hong Kong. Daily.
Xinhua Banyuekan (New China Semimonthly). Beijing. Semimonthly.
Xinhua Wenzhai (New China Digest). Beijing. Monthly.
Xinhua Yuebao (New China Monthly). Beijing. Monthly.
Xuexi (Study). Beijing. Semimonthly.

Translation series

Current Background. American Consulate General, Hong Kong. Irregular.
Extracts from China Mainland Magazines. American Consulate General, Hong Kong. Irregular.
Foreign Broadcast Information Service, *Daily Report, China*. United States Department of Commerce, National Technical Information Service. Springfield, Va. Weekdays.
Joint Publications Research Service. United States Department of Commerce, National Technical Information Service. Springfield, Va. Irregular.

Survey of China Mainland Press. American Consulate General, Hong Kong. Irregular.

Union Research Service. Union Research Institute, Hong Kong. Irregular.

Books and English-language articles

Ahn, Byung-joon. 1976. *Chinese Politics and the Cultural Revolution.* Seattle: University of Washington Press.

Allison, Graham T. 1971. *Essence of Decision.* Boston: Little, Brown.

Almond, Gabriel. 1960. "Introduction: A Functional Approach to Comparative Politics." In Gabriel Almond and James Coleman, eds., *The Politics of the Developing Areas.* Princeton, N.J.: Princeton University Press, pp. 3–64.

Almond, Gabriel. 1973. "Approaches to Developmental Causation." In Gabriel A. Almond, Scott C. Flanigan, and Robert J. Mundt, eds., *Crisis, Choice, and Change.* Boston: Little, Brown, pp. 1–42.

Almond, Gabriel, and G. Bingham Powell. 1978. *Comparative Politics.* 2d ed. Boston: Little, Brown.

Andors, Stephen. 1977. *China's Industrial Revolution.* New York: Pantheon.

Bachman, David. 1985a. "The Bureaucratic Origins of the Great Leap Forward." Paper presented to the 37th Annual Meeting of the Association for Asian Studies, Franklin Plaza Hotel, Philadelphia, Pa., March 22.

Bachman, David. 1985b. *Chen Yun and the Chinese Political System.* Center for Chinese Studies Research Monograph no. 29. Berkeley, Calif.: Institute of East Asian Studies.

Bachman, David. 1990. "The Chinese Communist Party: Forty Years in Power." *Fletcher Forum of World Affairs* 14:1 (Winter), pp. 10–17.

Badie, Bertrand, and Pierre Birnbaum. 1983. *The Sociology of the State.* Chicago: University of Chicago Press.

Barnett, A. Doak, with a contribution by Ezra Vogel. 1967. *Cadres, Bureaucracies, and Political Power in China.* New York: Columbia University Press.

Bauer, T. 1978. "Investment Cycles in Planned Economies." *Acta Oeconomica* 21:3, pp. 243–60.

Bedeski, Robert E. 1975. "The Evolution of the Modern State in China." *World Politics* 27:4 (July), pp. 541–68.

Bedeski, Robert E. 1981. *State Building in Modern China.* Center for Chinese Studies Research Monograph no. 18. Berkeley, Calif.: Institute of East Asian Studies.

Bendix, Reinhard. 1978. *Kings or People.* Berkeley and Los Angeles: University of California Press.

Bennett, Gordon, ed. 1978. *China's Finance and Trade.* White Plains, N.Y.: M. E. Sharpe.

Bernstein, Thomas P. 1969. "Cadre Behavior Under Conditions of Insecurity and Deprivation." In A. Doak Barnett, ed., *Chinese Communist Politics in Action.* Seattle: University of Washington Press, pp. 365–99.

Bernstein, Thomas P. 1984. "Stalinism, Famine, and Chinese Peasants: Grain Procurements During the Great Leap Forward." *Theory and Society* 13:3 (May), pp. 339–77.

Binder, Leonard. 1964. "National Integration and Political Development." *American Political Science Review* 58:3 (September), pp. 622–31.

Bo Yibo. 1958. *Guanyu Jingji Bumen Zhengfengde Jige Wenti* (On Several Questions of Rectification in Economic Departments). Beijing: Zhongguo Qingnian Chubanshe.

Borisov, O. B., and B. T. Kolosov. 1975. *Soviet-Chinese Relations, 1945–1973.* Moscow: Progress.

Breslauer, George W. 1982. *Khrushchev and Brezhnev as Leaders.* London: Allen and Unwin.

Brugger, William. 1976. *Democracy and Organization in the Chinese Industrial Enterprise.* Cambridge: Cambridge University Press.

Brzezinski, Zbigniew. 1966. *The Soviet Bloc.* Cambridge, Mass.: Harvard University Press.

Burns, John P. 1987. "China's *Nomenklatura* System." *Problems of Communism* 36:5 (September–October), pp. 36–51.

Cell, Charles P. 1977. *Revolution at Work.* New York: Academic Press.

Chang, Parris H. 1975. *Power and Policy in China.* University Park: Pennsylvania State University Press.

Chao Kuo-chun. 1959. *Economic Planning and Organization in China.* Cambridge, Mass.: Harvard University Press.

Chen, Jerome, ed. 1970. *Mao Papers.* Oxford University Press.

Chen, Theodore H. E. 1960. *Thought Reform of the Chinese Intellectuals.* Hong Kong: Hong Kong University Press.

Chen Xin. 1956. *Shangye Jiben Renwu* (Basic Tasks of Commerce). Beijing: Gongren Chubanshe.

Chen Yun. 1981. *Chen Yun Tongzhi Wengao Xuanbian (1956–1962)* (Selected Manuscripts of Comrade Chen Yun). Sichuan: Renmin Chubanshe.

Chen Yun. 1982. *Chen Yun Wengao Xuanbian (1949–1956)* (Selected Manuscripts of Chen Yun). Hubei: Renmin Chubanshe.

Chen Yun. 1984. *Chen Yun Wenxuan (1949–1956)* (Selected Writings of Chen Yun). Beijing: Renmin Chubanshe.

Chen Yun. 1986. *Chen Yun Wenxuan (1956–1985)* (Selected Writings of Chen Yun). Beijing: Renmin Chubanshe.

Chen Yung-fa. 1986. *Making Revolution.* Berkeley and Los Angeles: University of California Press.

Cheng, Nien. 1986. *Life and Death in Shanghai.* New York: Grove.

Chesneaux, Jean. 1979. *China: The People's Republic.* New York: Pantheon.

Chi Hsi-sheng. 1982. *Nationalist China at War.* Ann Arbor: University of Michigan Press.

Chilcote, Ronald H. 1981. *Theories of Comparative Politics.* Boulder, Colo.: Westview.

Cocks, Paul M. 1975. "Retooling the Directed Society." In Jan F. Triska and Paul M. Cocks, eds., *Political Development in Eastern Europe.* New York: Praeger, pp. 53–92.

Cohen, Paul A., and John E. Schrecker, eds. 1976. *Reform in Nineteenth Century China.* Harvard East Asian Monographs no. 72. Cambridge, Mass: East Asian Research Center, Harvard University.

Cohen, Stephen F. 1980. *Bukharin and the Bolshevik Revolution.* Oxford: Oxford University Press.

Communist China, 1955–1959: Party Documents with Analysis. 1971. Cambridge, Mass.: Harvard University Press.

Compton, Boyd, ed. 1966. *Mao's China.* Seattle: University of Washington Press.

Crozier, Michel. 1964. *The Bureaucratic Phenomenon.* Chicago: University of Chicago Press.

Das, Naranarayan. 1979. *China's Hundred Weeds.* Calcutta: K P Bagchi.

Deal, Terrence E., and Allan A. Kennedy. 1982. *Corporate Cultures.* Reading, Mass.: Addison-Wesley.

Deng Liqun. 1981. *Xiang Chen Yun Tongzhi Xuexi Zuo Jingji Gongzuo* (Learn from Comrade Chen Yun in Doing Economic Work). Sichuan: Zhongyang Dangxiao Chubanshe.

Deng Xiaoping. 1967. *Deng Xiaoping Fandong Yan Xing Huibian* (Collection of Counterrevolutionary Words and Deeds of Deng Xiaoping). Compiled by Xin Beida Gongshe Piping Liu, Deng Liange Zhan (incorrectly dated 1966). N.p. Available at the Fairbank Center, Harvard University.

Deng Xiaoping. 1984. *Selected Works of Deng Xiaoping 1975–1982*. Beijing: Foreign Languages Press.

Deng Xiaoping. 1989. *Deng Xiaoping Wenxuan (1938–1965 Nian)* (Selected Works of Deng Xiaoping, 1938–1965). Beijing: Renmin Chubanshe.

Dernberger, Robert F. 1981. "Communist China's Industrial Policies." *Issues and Studies* 17:7 (July), pp. 34–73.

Dernberger, Robert F. 1982. "The Chinese Search for the Path to Self-Sustained Growth in the 1980s." In U.S. Congress, Joint Economic Committee, *China Under the Four Modernizations*, pt. 1. 97th Cong., 2d sess. Report 91-930. Washington, D.C.: Government Printing Office, pp. 19–76.

Dittmer, Lowell. 1974. *Liu Shao-ch'i and the Chinese Cultural Revolution*. Berkeley and Los Angeles: University of California Press.

Dittmer, Lowell. 1977. " 'Line Struggle' in Theory and Practice." *China Quarterly* 72 (December), pp. 675–713.

Dittmer, Lowell. 1978. "Bases of Power in Chinese Politics." *World Politics* 31:1 (October), pp. 26–60.

Dittmer, Lowell. 1987. *China's Continuous Revolution*. Berkeley and Los Angeles: University of California Press.

Documents of the Chinese Communist Party Central Committee, September 1956– April 1969, vol. 1. 1971. Hong Kong: Union Research Institute.

Domes, Jurgen. 1974. "The Pattern of Politics." *Problems of Communism* 23:5 (September–October), pp. 20–24.

Domes, Jurgen. 1977. *China After the Cultural Revolution*. Berkeley and Los Angeles: University of California Press.

Donnithorne, Audrey. 1967. *China's Economic System*. New York: Praeger.

Donnithorne, Audrey. 1972. "China's Cellular Economy." *China Quarterly* 52 (October–December), pp. 605–19.

Doolin, Dennis, ed. 1964. *Communist China: The Politics of Student Opposition*. Stanford, Calif.: Hoover Institution Press.

Douglas, Mary. 1986. *How Institutions Think*. Syracuse, N.Y.: Syracuse University Press.

Downs, Anthony. 1967. *Inside Bureaucracy*. Boston: Little, Brown.

Eastman, Lloyd E. 1984. *Seeds of Destruction*. Stanford, Calif.: Stanford University Press.

Eckstein, Alexander. 1977. *China's Economic Revolution*. Cambridge: Cambridge University Press.

Eighth National Congress of the Communist Party of China, vol. 2: *Speeches*. 1956. Beijing: Foreign Languages Press.

Eighth National Congress of the Communist Party of China (Documents). 1981. Beijing: Foreign Languages Press.

Evans, Peter B., Dietrich Rueschmeyer, and Theda Skocpol, eds. 1985. *Bringing the State Back In*. Cambridge: Cambridge University Press.

Fang Weizhong, principal ed. 1984. *Zhonghua Renmin Gongheguo Jingji Dashiji, 1949–1980* (Economic Chronology of the People's Republic of China). Beijing: Zhongguo Shehui Kexue Chubanshe.

Faure, Edgar. 1958. *The Serpent and the Tortoise*. New York: St. Martin's.

Fingar, Thomas. 1977. *Politics and Policy-Making in the People's Republic of China.* Unpublished doctoral dissertation, Stanford University.

First Five Year Plan for Development of the National Economy of the People's Republic of China in 1953–1957. 1956. Beijing: Foreign Languages Press.

Friedman, Edward. 1965. "The Revolution in Hungary and the Hundred Flowers Period in China." *Journal of Asian Studies* 25:1 (November), pp. 119–22.

Friedman, Edward. 1982. "Maoism, Titoism, and Stalinism." In Mark Selden and Victor Lippit, eds., *The Transition to Socialism in China.* Armonk, N.Y.: M. E. Sharpe, pp. 159–214.

Ge Zhida. 1957. *Guodu Shiqide Zhongguo Yusuan* (China's Budget in the Transition Period). Beijing: Caizheng Chubanshe.

Geertz, Clifford. 1973. *The Interpretation of Cultures.* New York: Basic.

Giddens, Anthony. 1985. *The Nation-State and Violence.* Berkeley and Los Angeles: University of California Press.

Gilbert, Felix, ed. 1975. *The Historical Essays of Otto Hintze.* Oxford: Oxford University Press.

Gittings, John, ed. 1968. *Survey of the Sino-Soviet Dispute.* Oxford: Oxford University Press.

Goldman, Merle. 1971. *Literary Dissent in Communist China.* New York: Atheneum.

Goldman, Rene. 1962. "The Rectification Campaign at Peking University, May–June 1957." *China Quarterly* 12 (October–December), pp. 138–53.

Goodman, David S. G. 1984. "Provincial First Party Secretaries in National Politics." In David S. G. Goodman, ed., *Groups and Politics in the People's Republic of China.* Armonk, N.Y.: M. E. Sharpe, pp. 68–82.

Goodman, David S. G. 1986. *Center and Province in the People's Republic of China.* Cambridge: Cambridge University Press.

Grey, Jack. 1973. "The Two Roads: Alternative Strategies of Social Change and Economic Growth in China." In Stuart R. Schram, ed., *Authority, Participation, and Cultural Change in China.* Cambridge: Cambridge University Press, pp. 109–58.

Griffin, Patricia E. 1976. *The Chinese Communist Treatment of Counterrevolutionaries, 1924–1949.* Princeton, N.J.: Princeton University Press.

Griffith, Samuel B., III. 1967. *The Chinese People's Liberation Army.* New York: McGraw-Hill.

Griffiths, Franklyn. 1971. "A Tendency Analysis of Soviet Policy-Making." In H. Gordon Skilling and Franklyn Griffiths, eds., *Interest Groups in Soviet Politics.* Princeton, N.J.: Princeton University Press, pp. 335–77.

Halpern, Nina Phyllis. 1985. *Economic Specialists and the Making of Chinese Economic Policy, 1955–1983.* Unpublished doctoral dissertation, University of Michigan.

Hao Mengbi and Duan Haoran, eds. 1984. *Zhongguo Gongchandang Liushi Nian,* xia (Sixty Years of the Chinese Communist Party, vol. 2). 1984. Beijing: Jiefang Jun Chubanshe.

Harding, Harry. 1981. *Organizing China.* Stanford, Calif.: Stanford University Press.

Harding, Harry. 1984. "Competing Models of the Chinese Communist Policy Process." *Issues and Studies* 20:2 (February), pp. 13–36.

Harding, Harry. 1987. "The Role of the Military in Chinese Politics." In Victor C. Falkenheim, ed., *Citizens and Groups in Contemporary China.* Center of Chinese Studies, Michigan Monographs in Chinese Studies no. 57. Ann Arbor: University of Michigan Press, pp. 213–57.

Harding, Harry, and Melvin Gurtov. 1971. *The Purge of Lo Jui-ch'ing.* R 548 PR. Santa Monica, Calif.: RAND Corp.

Harrison, James P. 1972. *The Long March to Power.* New York: Praeger.

He Jianzhang and Wang Jiye. 1984. *Zhongguo Jihua Guanli Wenti* (Problems of Planned Management in China). Beijing: Zhongguo Shehui Kexue Chubanshe.

Hoffman, Charles. 1967. *Work Incentive Practices and Policies in China, 1953–1965.* Albany: State University of New York Press.

Hoffman, Erik P., and Robbin F. Laird. 1982. *The Politics of Economic Modernization in the Soviet Union.* Ithaca, N.Y.: Cornell University Press.

Hongweibing Ziliao (Red Guard Materials), vol. 15. 1975. Washington, D.C.: Center for Chinese Research Materials.

Howe, Christopher, and Kenneth R. Walker. 1977. "The Economist." In Dick Wilson, ed., *Mao Tsetung in the Scales of History.* Cambridge: Cambridge University Press, pp. 174–222.

Hsieh, Alice Langley. 1962. *Communist China's Strategy in the Nuclear Era.* Englewood Cliffs, N.J.: Prentice-Hall.

Hu Hua, ed. 1985. *Zhongguo Shehuizhuyi Geming he Jianshe Shi Jiangyi* (Lectures on the History of China's Socialist Revolution and Construction). Beijing: Beijing Renmin Daxue Chubanshe.

Hu Yaobang. 1980. "Problems Concerning the Purge of Kang Sheng." *Issues and Studies* 16:6 (June), pp. 74–100.

Huai En. 1986. *Zhou Zongli Shengping Dashiji* (A Chronology of Premier Zhou's Life). Chengdu: Renmin Chubanshe.

Huainian Zhou Enlai (Commemorate Zhou Enlai). 1986. Beijing: Renmin Chubanshe.

Huntington, Samuel P. 1968. *Political Order in Changing Societies.* New Haven, Conn.: Yale University Press.

Huntington, Samuel P. 1970. "Social and Institutional Dynamics of One-Party Systems." In Samuel P. Huntington and Clement H. Moore, eds., *Authoritarian Politics in Modern Society.* New York: Basic, pp. 3–47.

Ikenberry, G. John. 1988. "Conclusion: An Institutional Approach to American Foreign Economic Policy." *International Organization* 42:1 (Winter), pp. 219–43.

Jackson, Robert H., and Carl G. Rosberg. 1982. "Why Africa's Weak States Persist." *World Politics* 35:1 (October), pp. 1–24.

Jencks, Harlan W. 1982. *From Muskets to Missiles.* Boulder, Colo.: Westview.

Jiang Boying. 1986. *Deng Zihui Zhuan* (Biography of Deng Zihui). Shanghai: Renmin Chubanshe.

Jianguo Yilai Zhengzhi Jingjixue Zhongyao Wenti Zhenglun (1949–1980) (Disputes on Major Questions of Political Economy since the Founding of the Country). 1981. Beijing: Caizheng Jingji Chubanshe.

Jing'aide Zhou Zongli, Women Yongyuan Huainian Nin (Beloved Premier Zhou, We Will Always Remember You). 1977. 3 vols. Heilongjiang: Heilongjiang Renmin Chubanshe.

Jingji Jianshe Changshi Duben (A Reader in Common Knowledge of Economic Construction). 1956. Beijing: Renmin Chubanshe.

Johnson, Chalmers. 1962. *Peasant Nationalism and Communist Power.* Stanford, Calif.: Stanford University Press.

Joseph, William A. 1986. "A Tragedy of Good Intentions: Post-Mao Views of the Great Leap Forward." *Modern China* 12:4 (October), pp. 419–57.

Jowitt, Kenneth, 1977. "Mobilization and Inclusion in European Leninist Regimes." In Jan F. Triska and Paul Cocks, eds., *Political Development in Eastern Europe.* New York: Praeger, pp. 93–118.

Kane, Penny. 1988. *Famine in China, 1959–1961.* New York: St. Martin's.

Katz, Abraham. 1972. *The Politics of Economic Reform in the Soviet Union.* New York: Praeger.

Kau, Ying-mao. 1969. "The Urban Bureaucratic Elite in Communist China." In A. Doak Barnett, ed., *Chinese Communist Politics in Action*. Seattle: University of Washington Press, pp. 216–69.

Kau, Ying-mao. 1971. "Patterns of Recruitment and Mobility of Urban Cadres." In John Wilson Lewis, ed., *The City in Communist China*. Stanford, Calif.: Stanford University Press, pp. 97–122.

Kaufman, Herbert. 1975. *The Limits to Organizational Change*. University: University of Alabama Press.

Khrushchev, Nikita. 1974. *Khrushchev Remembers: The Last Testament*. New York: Bantam.

Klatt, Werner. 1965. "The Pattern of Communist China's Agricultural Policy." In Werner Klatt, ed., *The Chinese Model*. Hong Kong: Hong Kong University Press, pp. 94–116.

Klein, Donald W., and Anne B. Clark. 1971. *Biographic Dictionary of Chinese Communism*. Cambridge, Mass.: Harvard University Press.

Kornai, Janos. 1980. *The Economics of Shortage*. Amsterdam: North-Holland.

Krasner, Stephen D. 1984. "Approaches to the State: Alternative Conceptions and Historical Dynamics." *Comparative Politics* 16:2 (January), pp. 223–46.

Kraus, Richard Curt. 1981. *Class Conflict in Chinese Socialism*. New York: Columbia University Press.

Ladany, Lazlo. 1988. *The Chinese Communist Party and Marxism*. Stanford, Calif.: Hoover Institution Press.

Lai Ying. 1969. *The Thirty-sixth Way*. New York: Doubleday.

Laitin, David D., and Aaron Wildavsky. 1988. "Political Culture and Political Preferences." *American Political Science Review* 82:2 (June), pp. 589–96.

Lampton, David M. 1977. *The Politics of Medicine in China*. Boulder, Colo.: Westview.

Lardy, Nicholas R., ed. 1978a. *China's Economic Planning*. White Plains, N.Y.: M. E. Sharpe.

Lardy, Nicholas R. 1978b. *Economic Growth and Distribution in China*. Cambridge: Cambridge University Press.

Lardy, Nicholas R. 1983. *Agriculture in China's Modern Economic Development*. Cambridge: Cambridge University Press.

Lee, Rensselear W., III. 1966. "The Hsia Fang System." *China Quarterly* 28 (October–December), pp. 40–62.

Lewin, Moshe. 1974. *Political Undercurrents of Soviet Economic Debates*. Princeton, N.J.: Princeton University Press.

Lewis, John Wilson. 1963. *Leadership in Communist China*. Ithaca, N.Y.: Cornell University Press.

Lewis, John Wilson. 1968. "Leader, Commissar, and Bureaucrat: The Chinese Political System in the Last Days of the Revolution." In Ping-ti Ho and Tang Tsou, eds., *China in Crisis*, vol. 1, bk. 2. Chicago: University of Chicago Press, pp. 449–81.

Lewis, John Wilson, and Xue Litai. 1988. *China Builds the Bomb*. Stanford, Calif.: Stanford University Press.

Li, Choh-ming. 1962. *The Statistical System of Communist China*. Berkeley and Los Angeles: University of California Press.

Li Weihan. 1986. *Huiyi yu Yanjiu* (Reminiscences and Studies). Beijing: Zhonggong Dangshi Ziliao Chubanshe.

Li Xiannian. 1989. *Li Xiannian Wenxuan (1935–1988)* (Selected Writings of Li Xiannian). Beijing: Renmin Chubanshe.

Liao Kai-lung (Liao Gailong). 1981. "Historical Experiences and Our Road to Development." 3 pts. *Issues and Studies* 17:10–12 (October – December), pp. 65–94, 81–110, 79–104.

Lieberthal, Jane. 1971. *From Cooperative to Commune.* Unpublished M.A. thesis, Columbia University.

Lieberthal, Kenneth, and Michel Oksenberg. 1986. *Bureaucratic Politics and Chinese Energy Development.* Prepared for U.S. Department of Commerce, International Trade Administration. Washington, D.C.: Government Printing Office.

Lieberthal, Kenneth, and Michel Oksenberg. 1988. *Policy Making in China.* Princeton, N.J.: Princeton University Press.

Lin, Cyril Chihren. 1981. "The Reinstatement of Economics in China Today." *China Quarterly* 85 (March), pp. 1–48.

Liu Shaoqi. 1985. *Liu Shaoqi Wenxuan,* xiajuan (Selected Writings of Liu Shaoqi, vol. 2). Beijing: Renmin Chubanshe.

Liu Shaoqi. N.d. *Untitled Collection of Texts by Liu Shaoqi.* N.p. Available at the Fairbank Center, Harvard University.

Liu Suinian, ed. 1982. *Liushi Niandai Guomin Jingji Tiaozhengde Huigu* (A Review of the Readjustment of the National Economy in the 1960s). Beijing: Zhongguo Caizheng Jingji Chubanshe.

Liu Suinian and Wu Qungan, eds. 1984. *"Da Yuejin" he Tiaozheng Shiqide Guomin Jingji* (The National Economy During the "Great Leap Forward" and Readjustment Period). Harbin: Heilongjiang Renmin Chubanshe.

Liu Suinian and Wu Qungan. 1986. *China's Socialist Economy.* Beijing: *Beijing Review.*

Loh, Robert, as told to Humphrey Evans. 1962. *Escape from Red China.* New York: Coward-McCann.

Lotveit, Trygve. 1973. *Chinese Communism, 1931–1934.* Monograph Series no. 16. Lund: Scandinavian Institute of Asian Studies.

Lowenthal, Richard. 1970. "Development Versus Utopia in Communist Policy." In Chalmers Johnson, ed., *Change in Communist Systems.* Stanford, Calif.: Stanford University Press, pp. 33–116.

Lyons, Thomas P. 1987. *Economic Integration and Planning in Maoist China.* New York: Columbia University Press.

Ma Yinqu. 1981. *Ma Yinqu Jingji Lunwen Xuanji,* xiace (Selected Economic Writings of Ma Yinqu, vol. 2). Beijing: Beijing Daxue Chubanshe.

MacFarquhar, Roderick. 1958. "Communist China's Intra-Party Dispute." *Pacific Affairs* 31:4 (December), pp. 323–25.

MacFarquhar, Roderick, ed. 1960. *The Hundred Flowers Campaign and the Chinese Intellectuals.* New York: Praeger.

MacFarquhar, Roderick. 1974. *The Origins of the Cultural Revolution,* vol. 1: *Contradictions Among the People, 1956–1957.* New York: Columbia University Press.

MacFarquhar, Roderick. 1983. *The Origins of the Cultural Revolution,* vol. 2: *The Great Leap Forward, 1958–1960.* New York: Columbia University Press.

MacFarquhar, Roderick, Timothy Cheek, and Eugene Wu, eds. 1989. *The Secret Speeches of Chairman Mao.* Harvard Contemporary China Series no. 6. Cambridge, Mass.: Council on East Asian Studies.

MacFarquhar, Roderick, and John K. Fairbank, eds. 1987. *The Cambridge History of China,* Vol. 14: *The People's Republic of China,* pt. I: *The Emergence of Revolutionary China, 1949–1965.* Cambridge: Cambridge University Press.

Magdoff, Harry. 1975. "China: Contrasts with the USSR." *Monthly Review* 27:3 (July–August), pp. 12–57.

Manion, Melanie. 1985. "The Cadre Management System, Post-Mao." *China Quarterly* 102 (June), pp. 203–33.

Mao Zedong. 1965. *Selected Works of Mao Tse-tung*, vol. III. Beijing: Foreign Languages Press.

Mao Zedong. 1969a. *Selected Works of Mao Tse-tung*, vol. IV. Beijing: Foreign Languages Press.

Mao Zedong. 1969b. *Mao Zedong Sixiang Wansui!* (Long Live Mao Zedong Thought!). N.p. Taiwan reprint, 1974.

Mao Zedong. 1971. *Selected Readings from the Works of Mao Tsetung*. Beijing: Foreign Language Press.

Mao Zedong. 1977. *Selected Works of Mao Tsetung*. vol. V. Beijing: Foreign Languages Press.

Mao Zedong. 1978–1979. "Speech at the Conference on the Questions of Intellectuals Convened by the Central Committee of the Communist Party of China." *Chinese Law and Government* 9:4 (Winter), pp. 71–82.

Mao Zedong. 1986. *Mao Zedong Zhuzuo Xuandu*, shang (Selected Readings from the Writings of Mao Zedong, vol. 1). Beijing: Renmin Chubanshe.

March, James G., and Johan P. Olsen. 1984. "The New Institutionalism: Organizational Factors in Political Life." *American Political Science Review* 78:3 (September), pp. 734–49.

March, James G., and Herbert A. Simon. 1958. *Organizations*. New York: Wiley.

Martin, Roberta. 1981. *Party Recruitment in China*. Occasional paper. New York: East Asian Institute, Columbia University.

Marx, Karl. 1972. *The Eighteenth Brumaire of Louis Bonaparte*. In Robert C. Tucker, ed. *The Marx-Engels Reader*. New York: Norton, pp. 436–525.

Meisner, Maurice. 1971. "Leninism and Maoism." *China Quarterly* 45 (January–March), pp. 2–36.

Merton, Robert K. 1952. "Bureaucratic Structure and Personality." In Robert K. Merton, Ailsa P. Gray, Barbara Hockey, and Wanan C. Selvin, eds., *Reader in Bureaucracy*. New York: Free Press, pp. 361–71.

Mommsen, Hans. 1986. "The Realization of the Unthinkable." In Gerhard Hirschfeld, ed., *The Policies of Genocide*. London: Allen and Unwin, pp. 97–144.

Nathan, Andrew J. 1973. "A Factionalism Model for CCP Politics." *China Quarterly* 53 (January–March), pp. 34–66.

National Conference on Learning from Taching in Industry, The. 1977. Beijing: Foreign Languages Press.

Naughton, Barry. 1987. "The Decline of Central Control over Investment in Post-Mao China." In David M. Lampton, ed., *Policy Implementation in Post-Mao China*. Berkeley and Los Angeles: University of California Press, pp. 51–80.

Naughton, Barry. 1988. "The Third Front: Defense Industrialization in the Chinese Interior." *China Quarterly* 115 (September), pp. 351–86.

New China Advances to Socialism. 1956. Beijing: Foreign Languages Press.

Nie Rongzhen. 1984. *Nie Rongzhen Huiyi Lu* (Memoirs of Nie Rongzhen). Beijing: Jiefang Jun Chubanshe.

Nieh, Hualing. 1981. *The Literature of the Hundred Flowers*. 2 vols. New York: Columbia University Press.

Nordlinger, Eric A. 1981. *On the Autonomy of the Democratic State*. Cambridge, Mass.: Harvard University Press.

Nove, Alec. 1969. *The Soviet Economy*. 2d ed. New York: Praeger.

Oksenberg, Michel. 1969. *Policy Formulation in Communist China: The Case of the Mass Irrigation Campaign, 1957–1958*. Unpublished doctoral dissertation, Columbia University.

Oksenberg, Michel. 1970. "Mao's Foreign Policy of Self-Reliance." Paper presented to the First Sino-American Conference on Mainland China, Taipei, Taiwan, December 14–19.

Oksenberg, Michel. 1971. "Policy Making Under Mao, 1949–1968." In John M. H. Lindbeck, ed., *China: Management of a Revolutionary Society.* Seattle: University of Washington Press, pp. 79–115.

Oksenberg, Michel. 1974a. "The Chinese Policy Process and the Public Health Issue." *Studies in Comparative Communism* 7:4 (Winter), pp. 375–408.

Oksenberg, Michel. 1974b. "Methods of Communication Within the Chinese Bureaucracy." *China Quarterly* 57 (January–March), pp. 1–39.

Oksenberg, Michel. 1976. "Mao's Policy Commitments, 1921–1976." *Problems of Communism* 25:6 (November–December), pp. 1–26.

Oksenberg, Michel. 1977. "The Political Leader." In Dick Wilson, ed., *Mao Tsetung in the Scales of History.* Cambridge: Cambridge University Press, pp. 70–116.

Oskenberg, Michel. 1982. "Economic Policy Making in China: Summer 1981." *China Quarterly* 90 (June), pp. 165–94.

Oksenberg, Michel, and James Tong. 1987. "The Evolution of Central-Provincial Fiscal Relations in China, 1950–1983: The Formal System." Unpublished. University of Michigan, Ann Arbor.

Orleans, Leo A. 1982. "China's Urban Population." In U.S. Congress, Joint Economic Committee, *China Under the Four Modernizations,* pt. 1. 97th Cong., 2d sess. Report 91–930. Washington, D.C.: Government Printing Office, pp. 268–301.

Peng Dehuai. 1981. *Peng Dehuai Zishu* (Peng Dehuai's Account). Beijing: Renmin Chubanshe.

Peng Dehuai Yuanshuai Fengbei Yongcun (Marshal Peng Dehuai's Monumental Achievements Will Last Forever). 1985. Shanghai: Renmin Chubanshe.

Pepper, Suzanne. 1980. *Civil War in China.* Berkeley and Los Angeles: University of California Press.

Perkins, Dwight. 1966. *Market Control and Planning in China.* Cambridge, Mass.: Harvard University Press.

Perkins, Dwight. 1968. "Industrial Planning and Management." In Alexander Eckstein, Walter Galenson, and T.C. Liu, ed., *Economic Trends in Communist China.* Chicago: Aldine, pp. 597–638.

Pfeffer, Jeffrey. 1981. *Power in Organizations.* Boston: Pitman.

Prybyla, Jan S. 1970. *The Political Economy of Communist China.* Scranton, Pa.: International Textbook.

Pye, Lucian. 1981. *The Dynamics of Chinese Politics.* Cambridge, Mass.: Oelgeschlager, Gunn and Hain.

Radvanyi, Janos. 1970. "The Hungarian Revolution and the Hundred Flowers Campaign." *China Quarterly* 43 (July–September), pp. 121–29.

Rawski, Thomas. 1975. "China's Industrial System." In U.S. Congress, Joint Economic Committee, *China: A Reassessment of the Economy.* 94th Cong., 1st sess. Report 51–174. Washington, D.C.: Government Printing Office, pp. 175–98.

Rawski, Thomas. 1979. *Economic Growth and Employment in China.* New York: Oxford University Press.

Rawski, Thomas. 1980. *China's Transition to Industrialism.* Ann Arbor: University of Michigan Press.

Reardon-Anderson, James. 1980. *Yenan and the Great Powers.* New York: Columbia University Press.

Renmin Ribao Huiyi Lu (Recollections of *People's Daily*). 1988. Beijing: Renmin Ribao Chubanshe.

Renmin Shouce 1958 (People's Handbook 1958). 1958. Beijing: Da Gong Bao Chubanshe.

Renminde Hao Zongli (The People's Good Primier). 3 vols. 1979. Shanghai: Shanghai Renmin Chubanshe.

Reynolds, Bruce L. 1978. "Two Models of Agricultural Development." *China Quarterly* 76 (October), pp. 842–72.

Riker, William. 1986. *The Art of Political Manipulation.* New Haven, Conn.: Yale University Press.

Riskin, Carl. 1971. "Small Industry and the Chinese Model of Development." *China Quarterly* 46 (April–June), pp. 245–73.

Rothman, Stanley. 1971. "Functionalism and Its Critics." *Political Science Reviewer* 1:4 (February), pp. 236–76.

Schattschneider, E. E. 1960. *The Semi-Sovereign People.* New York: Holt, Rinehart and Winston.

Schoenhals, Michael. ed. and trans. 1986a. "Mao Zedong: Speeches at the 1957 'Moscow Conference.' " *Journal of Communist Affairs* 2:2 (June), pp. 109–26.

Schoenhals, Michael. 1986b. "Original Contradictions – On the Unrevised Text of Mao Zedong's 'On the Correct Handling of Contradictions Among the People.' " *Australian Journal of Chinese Affairs* 16 (July), pp. 99–112.

Schoenhals, Michael. 1987. *Saltationist Socialism: Mao Zedong and the Great Leap Forward, 1958.* Stockholm: Institutionen for Orientaliska Sprak, University of Stockholm.

Schram, Stuart R. 1967. *Mao Tse-tung.* Harmondsworth: Penguin.

Schram, Stuart R. 1971. "Mao Tse-tung and the Theory of Permanent Revolution." *China Quarterly* 46 (April–June), pp. 221–45.

Schram, Stuart R. 1973. "Introduction: The Cultural Revolution in Historical Perspective." In Stuart R. Schram, ed., *Authority, Participation, and Cultural Change in China.* Cambridge: Cambridge University Press, pp. 1–108.

Schram, Stuart R., ed. 1974. *Chairman Mao Talks to the People.* New York: Pantheon.

Schram, Stuart R. 1983. *Mao Zedong: A Preliminary Reassessment.* Hong Kong: Chinese University Press.

Schram, Stuart R. 1989. *The Thought of Mao Tse-tung.* Cambridge: Cambridge University Press.

Schran, Peter. 1975. "On the Yenan Origins of Current Economic Policies." In Dwight H. Perkins, ed., *China's Modern Economy in Historical Perspective.* Stanford, Calif.: Stanford University Press, pp. 279–302.

Schran, Peter. 1976. *Guerrilla Economy.* Albany: State University of New York Press.

Schurmann, Franz. 1968. *Ideology and Organization in Communist China.* Berkeley and Los Angeles: University of California Press.

Schurmann, Franz. 1974. *The Logic of World Power.* New York: Pantheon.

Schwartz, Benjamin I. 1970. *Communism in China: Ideology in Flux.* New York: Atheneum.

Selden, Mark. 1971. *The Yenan Way in Revolutionary China.* Cambridge, Mass.: Harvard University Press.

Selznick, Philip. 1980. *TVA and the Grassroots.* Berkeley and Los Angeles: University of California Press.

Selznick, Philip. 1984. *Leadership in Administration.* Berkeley and Los Angeles: University of California Press.

Seymour, James D. 1987. *China's Satellite Parties.* Armonk, N.Y.: M. E. Sharpe.

Shangye Bu Jingji Yanjiusuo (Economic Research Institute, Ministry of Commerce), ed. 1984. *Xin Zhongguo Shangye Shigao* (Draft History of New China's Commerce). Beijing: Zhongguo Caizheng Jingji Chubanshe.

Sharkansky, Ira. 1970. *The Routines of Politics.* New York: Van Nostrand Reinhold.

Shirk, Susan L. 1986?. "The Central Economic Bureaucracy." In Janet A. Cady, ed., *Economic Reform in China.* New York: National Committee on U.S.-China Relations, pp. 26–32.

Shue, Vivienne. 1980. *Peasant China in Transition*. Berkeley and Los Angeles: University of California Press.

Skocpol, Theda. 1979. *States and Social Revolution*. Cambridge: Cambridge University Press.

Skowronek, Stephen. 1982. *Building a New American State*. Cambridge: Cambridge University Press.

Solinger, Dorothy J. 1981. "Economic Reform via Reformulation: Where Do Rightist Ideas Come From?" *Asian Survey* 21:9 (September), pp. 947–60.

Solinger, Dorothy J. 1983. "Marxism and the Market in Socialist China." In Victor Nee and David Mozingo, eds., *State and Society in Contemporary China*. Ithaca, N.Y.: Cornell University Press, pp. 194–219.

Solinger, Dorothy J. 1984. *Chinese Business Under Socialism*. Berkeley and Los Angeles: University of California Press.

Spence, Jonathan D. 1981. *The Gate of Heavenly Peace*. New York: Viking.

Starr, John Bryan. 1979. *Continuing the Revolution*. Princeton, N.J.: Princeton University Press.

State Statistical Bureau, comp. 1982. *Statistical Yearbook of China, 1981*. Hong Kong: Economic Information and Agency.

State Statistical Bureau, comp. 1986. *Statistical Yearbook of China 1986*. Oxford: Oxford University Press.

Stavis, Benedict. 1978. *The Politics of Agricultural Mechanization in China*. Ithaca, N.Y.: Cornell University Press.

Steinbruner, John D. 1974. *The Cybernetic Theory of Decision*. Princeton, N.J.: Princeton University Press.

Stinchcombe, Arthur. 1965. "Social Structure and Organizations." In James G. March, ed., *Handbook of Organizations*. Chicago: Rand-McNally, pp. 142–93.

Sun Yefang. 1979. *Shehuizhuyi Jingjide Ruogan Lilun Wenti* (Certain Theoretical Questions of Socialist Economics). Beijing: Renmin Chubanshe.

Sun Yefang. 1980. "What Is the Origin of the Law of Value?" *Social Sciences in China* 2:3 (September), pp. 155–71.

Teiwes, Frederick C. 1971. "Provincial Politics in China." In John M. H. Lindback, ed., *China: Management of a Revolutionary Society*. Seattle: University of Washington Press, pp. 116–89.

Teiwes, Frederick C. 1973. "A Case Study of Rectification." *Papers in Far Eastern History* (Australian National University) 7 (March), pp. 71–99.

Teiwes, Frederick C. 1979a. *Politics and Purges in China*. Armonk, N.Y.: M. E. Sharpe.

Teiwes, Frederick C. 1979b. " 'Rules of the Game' in Chinese Politics." *Problems of Communism* 28:5–6 (September–December), pp. 67–76.

Teiwes, Frederick C. 1984. *Leadership, Legitimacy, and Conflict in China*. Armonk, N.Y.: M. E. Sharpe.

Teiwes, Frederick C. 1987. "Establishment and Consolidation of the New Regime, 1949–1957." In Roderick MacFarquhar and John K. Fairbank, eds., *The Cambridge History of China*, vol. 14: *The People's Republic of China*, pt. I: *The Emergence of Revolutionary China, 1949–1965*. Cambridge: Cambridge University Press, pp. 51–143.

Teiwes, Frederick C. 1988. "Mao and His Lieutenants." *Australian Journal of Chinese Affairs* 19–20 (January–July), pp. 1–80.

Terrill, Ross. 1980. *Mao*. New York: Harper and Row.

Tilly, Charles, ed. 1975. *The Formation of National States in Western Europe*. Princeton, N.J.: Princeton University Press.

Tilly, Charles. 1985. "War Making and State Making as Organized Crime." In Peter

B. Evans, Dietrich Rueschmeyer, and Theda Skucpol, eds., *Bringing the State Back In*. Cambridge: Cambridge University Press, pp. 169–91.

Tsou, Tang. 1975. "Prolegomenon to the Study of Informal Groups in CCP Politics." *China Quarterly* 65 (March), pp. 98–115.

Van Slyke, Lyman P. 1967. *Enemies and Friends*. Stanford, Calif.: Stanford University Press.

Vogel, Ezra. 1967. "From Revolutionary to Semi-Bureaucrat." *China Quarterly* 29 (January–March), pp. 36–59.

Vogel, Ezra. 1970. "Politicized Bureaucracy." In Fred W. Riggs, ed., *Frontiers of Development Administration*. Durham, N.C.: Duke University Press, pp. 556–66.

Vogel, Ezra. 1971. *Canton Under Communism*. New York: Harper Torchbooks.

Vogel, Ezra. 1989. *One Step Ahead in China*. Cambridge, Mass.: Harvard University Press.

Walder, Andrew G. 1986. *Communist Neo-Traditionalism*. Berkeley and Los Angeles: University of California Press.

Walker, Kenneth R. 1965. *Planning in Chinese Agriculture*. London: Cass.

Walker, Kenneth R. 1966. "Collectivization in Retrospect." *China Quarterly* 29 (April–June), pp. 1–43.

Walker, Kenneth R. 1984. *Food Grain Procurement and Consumption in China*. Cambridge: Cambridge University Press.

Walter, Carl E. 1981. *Party-State Relations in the People's Republic of China: The Role of the People's Bank and the Local Party in Economic Management*. Unpublished doctoral dissertation, Stanford University.

Waltz, Kenneth. 1954. *Man, the State, and War*. New York: Columbia University Press.

Waltz, Kenneth. 1979. *Theory of International Relations*. Reading, Mass.: Addison-Wesley.

Wang Haibo, ed. 1986. *Xin Zhongguo Gongye Jingji Shi* (A History of New China's Industrial Economy). Beijing: Jingji Guanli Chubanshe.

Wang Heying, Wu Xinjuan, Shu Yumin, and Xu Mingyue, eds. 1987. *Zhonghua Renmin Gongheguo Duiwai Jingji Maoyi Guanxi Dashiji* (Chronology of the People's Republic of China's Foreign Economic Relations and Trade). Nanguan: Duiwai Maoyi Jiaoyu Chubanshe.

Wang Jingzhi. 1956. *Wo Guo Guojia Yusuan* (Our Country's National Budget). Beijing: Tonggu Duwu Chubanshe.

Wang Meng. 1981. "A Young Man Arrives at the Organization Department." In Hualing Nieh, ed., *The Literature of the Hundred Flowers*, vol. II: *Poetry and Fiction*. New York: Columbia University Press, pp. 474–511.

Ward, Benjamin. 1980. "The Chinese Approach to Economic Development." In Robert F. Dernberger, ed., *China's Development Experience in Comparative Perspective*. Cambridge, Mass.: Harvard University Press, pp. 91–119.

Watson, Andrew, ed. 1980. *Mao Zedong and the Political Economy of the Border Region*. Cambridge: Cambridge University Press.

Weber, Max. 1978. *Economy and Society*, ed. Guenther Roth and Claus Wittich. Berkeley and Los Angeles: University of California Press.

Wheelwright, E. L., and Bruce McFarlane. 1970. *The Chinese Road to Socialism*. New York: Monthly Review Press.

White, Lynn T., III. 1978. *Careers in Shanghai*. Berkeley and Los Angeles: University of California Press.

White, Lynn T., III. 1989. *Policies of Chaos*. Princeton, N.J.: Princeton University Press.

Whiting, Allen S. 1975. *The Chinese Calculus of Deterrence*. Ann Arbor: University of Michigan Press.

Whitson, William W. 1972. "Organizational Perspectives on Decision-Making in the Chinese High Command." In Robert A. Scalapino, ed., *Elites in the People's Republic of China*. Seattle: University of Washington Press, pp. 381–415.

Whitson, William W., with a contribution by Chen-hsia Huang. 1973. *The Chinese High Command*. New York: Praeger.

Whyte, Martin King. 1973. "Bureaucracy and Modernization in China: The Maoist Critique." *American Sociological Review* 38:2 (April), pp. 149–63.

Whyte, Martin King. 1974. "Iron Law Versus Mass Democracy: Weber, Michels, and the Maoist Vision." In James Chieh Hsiung, ed., *The Logic of Maoism*. New York: Praeger, pp. 37–61.

Wildavsky, Aaron. 1987. "Choosing Preferences by Constructing Institutions: A Cultural Theory of Preference Formation." *American Political Science Review* 81:1 (March), pp. 2–22.

Wilson, James Q. 1973. *Political Organizations*. New York: Basic.

Womack, Brantly. 1987. "The Party and the People: Revolutionary and Post-Revolutionary Politics in China and Vietnam." *World Politics* 39:4 (July), pp. 479–507.

Wong, Christine. 1985. "Material Allocation and Decentralization." In Elizabeth J. Perry and Christine Wong, eds., *The Political Economy of Reform in Post-Mao China*. Harvard Contemporary China Series no. 2. Cambridge, Mass.: Council on East Asian Studies, pp. 253–78.

Wong, Christine. 1986. "The Economics of Shortage and Problems of Reform in China." *Journal of Comparative Economics* 10:4 (December), pp. 363–87.

Wu Leng-hsi. 1969–1970. "The Confession of Wu Leng-hsi." *Chinese Law and Government* 2:4 (Winter), pp. 63–86.

Wylie, Raymond F. 1980. *The Emergence of Maoism*. Stanford, Calif.: Stanford University Press.

Xue Muqiao. 1979. "Guanyu Yijiuwuba Nian – Yijiuliuliu Nian Guomin Jingji Jianshede Qingkuang he Jingyan" (On the Conditions and Experiences of National Economic Construction from 1958 to 1966). *Jingji Cankao Ziliao-1* (Economic Reference Material). Unpublished. Beijing: Beijing Daxue Jingjixi Ziliaoshi, pp. 1–20.

Yang Bo. 1956. *Guojia Guodu Shiqide Shangye* (The Nation's Commerce in the Transition Period). Beijing: Gongren Chubanshe.

Yeh, K. C. 1967. "Soviet and Chinese Industrialization Strategies." In Donald W. Treadgold, ed., *Soviet and Chinese Communism*. Seattle: University of Washington Press, pp. 327–63.

Zhang Wentian. 1985. *Zhang Wentian Xuanji* (Selected Works of Zhang Wentian). Beijing: Renmin Chubanshe.

Zhao Yiwen. 1957. *Xin Zhongguode Gongye* (New China's Industry). Beijing: Tongji Chubanshe.

Zhong Kan. 1982. *Kang Sheng Ping Zhuan* (A Critical Biography of Kang Sheng). Beijing: Hongqi Chubanshe.

Zhonggong Dangshi Dashi Nianbiao (Yearly Chronology of Major Events in the History of the Chinese Communist Party). 1987. Beijing: Renmin Chubanshe.

Zhongguo Gongye Jingji Tongji Ziliao 1949–1984 (Statistical Material on China's Industrial Economy). 1985. Beijing: Zhongguo Tongji Chubanshe.

Zhongguo Guding Zichan Touzi Tongji Ziliao, 1950–1985 (Statistical Materials on China's Fixed Capital Investment). 1987. Beijing: Zhongguo Tongji Chubanshe.

Zhongguo Renmin Jiefang Jun Dashiji, 1927–1982 (A Chronology of the Chinese People's Liberation Army). 1983. N.p.: Junshi Kexue Chubanshe.

Zhongguo Shehuizhuyi Jingji Jianshe Wenxian Ziliao Xuanbian (Selected Documentary Material on China's Socialist Economic Construction). 1984. Chongqing: Xin-hua Chubanshe.

Zhonghua Renmin Gongheguo Diyijie Quanguo Renmin Daibiao Dahui Disanci Huiyi Huikan (Collected Materials of the Third Session of the First National People's Congress of the People's Republic of China). 1956. Beijing: Renmin Chubanshe.

Zhonghua Renmin Gongheguo Fagui Huibian (Compendia of Laws and Regulations of the People's Republic of China). 1981. Vols. 4–6: July–December 1956; January–June 1957; July–December 1957. Shaanxi: Falu Chubanshe.

Zhonghua Renmin Gongheguo Jingji Fagui Xuanbian, xia (Selected Economic Laws and Regulations of the People's Republic of China, vol. 2). 1980. Zhangjiakou: Zhongguo Caizheng Jingji Chubanshe.

Zhonghua Renmin Gongheguo Jingji Guanli Dashiji (Economic Management Chronology of the People's Republic of China). 1986. Beijing: Zhongguo Jingji Chubanshe.

Zhou Enlai. 1984a. *Zhou Enlai Tongyi Zhanxian Wenxuan* (Selected Works of Zhou Enlai on the United Front). Beijing: Renmin Chubanshe.

Zhou Enlai. 1984b. *Zhou Enlai Xuanji*, Xiajuan (Selected Writings of Zhou Enlai, vol. 2). Beijing: Renmin Chubanshe.

Zhou Taihe, ed. 1984. *Dangdai Zhongguode Jingji Tizhi Gaige* (The Reform of the Economic System of Contemporary China). Beijing: Zhongguo Shehui Kexue Chubanshe.

Zhu De. 1986. *Selected Works of Zhu De*. Beijing: Foreign Languages Press.

Zhu De Nianpu (A Chronicle of Zhu De). 1986. Beijing: Renmin Chubanshe.

Zuo Chuntai and Song Xinzhong. 1988. *Zhongguo Shehuizhuyi Caizheng Jian Shi* (A Basic History of China's Socialist Finance). Beijing: Zhongguo Caizheng Jingji Chubanshe.

Zweig, David. 1989. *Agrarian Radicalism in China*. Cambridge, Mass.: Harvard University Press.

Index

agricultural officials, Chen Yun's criticism of, 200–1

agricultural production: and CCP, 138–9; and consumer goods, 87–92, 198–201, 213; Deng Xiaoping's views on, 194; Deng Zihui's views on, 201–2; and financial coalition, 60–5, 70, 87–92; Liu Shaoqi's views on, 183; Mao Zedong's views on, 177; mechanization of, 120, 202–3; projected targets for, 113, 167–8; structural approach to, 231–2; Zhou Enlai's views on, 185; *see also* National Agricultural Program

agriculture, *see* industry and agriculture

annual plan for 1957, formulation of, 114–15

Anti-Rightist Campaign: and decline of financial coalition, 93–5, 194; development of, 26, 193, 196, 205; effects of, on bureaucracy, 5–6, 195; legacy of, 216; and Tiananmen massacre compared, 233

Bai Rubing, 72

balance: and decentralization, 197, 198, 200; and planning, 172–3, 179; *see also* three balances

banking departments, criticism of, 207

Bo Yibo: background and experience of, 104; and capital construction, 92; and criticism of conservatism, 207; and decentralization, 85; and Economic Transformation System, 49; February 1957 speech by, to National Model Agricultural Workers Conference, 116–17; and Great Leap, 8, 217; and industry and agriculture, 205; and investment cuts, 238; and National Planning Conference of 1957, 126; and planning leadership, 231; and reformulation of planning-coalition position, 26, 121–5; and report to Fourth Session of First National People's Congress, 123–5; speech by, at Eighth Party Congress, 106–8; and support for three balances, 117

bottom-up policy making, 45

budget: balanced, 69; and criticisms of budget-making process, 175; and deficit, 21

budgeteers: ethos and economic positions of, 50–1; Mao's criticism of, 204, 208; objections of, 221, 226; *see also* financial coalition

bureaucracy: and coalitions, 30, 31, 38–41; and commercial system, 88; and cooptation of leaders, 37–8, 44; and development of routines, 38–9; and four sets of interests, 30, 35–6; and Great Leap, 219; and inefficiency, 152, 162, 163, 164, 171; mission of, 230–1; and politics, 228; *see also* leadership; organizations

Caizheng (Finance), 73, 74, 76, 81

Campaign to Eradicate Hidden Counter-Revolutionaries, 15, 227

capital construction: and centralization, 197, 212; formula for, 77, 78, 79; during leaps, 174, 224; phases of, 218–19; and role of intellectuals, 172

career paths of new-generation leaders, 230

central planning, 85–6, 101–3, 197, 212, 223

chemical fertilizer industry, 198–9

Chen Boda, 217

Chen Yu, 111

Chen Yun: and agricultural and consumer-goods production, 198–201; and comparison of 1957 and 1989, 233–5; and construction, 219; and decentralization, 85, 196–8; and Eighth Party Congress, 66–9; as leader of financial coalition, 8, 22–6, 28–44, 48, 63; and leaders and organizations, 230, 231; Mao's criticisms and re-evaluation of, 179, 208, 209, 213; and reformist policies, 87–8, 92, 215, 230; and State Construction Commission, 212; and three balances, 77, 177, 221

Chinese Communist Party (CCP): and agricultural production, 138–9; and collective leadership, 158, 162–3; and control mechanisms, 45–7; and economic issues, 51, 147, 170; and effects of financial coalition, 225–6; Eighth National Congress of, 1, 13, 23–4, 139–46; goals of, 33, 50, 137–9, 146, 153, 226; and Hundred Flowers, 151;

and intellectuals, 161–2, 215; membership of, 134, 137, 139, 165, 226; from October 1956 to October 1957, 146–53; and planning coalition, 210, 211, 226, 227; retooling of, 163–5; social-transformation functions of, 133–4, 139, 154; as system, 134–9; and work style, 20, 145, 192–3, 195–6, 201, 207–8; during Yanan period, 134–5
Chinese model of development, 117–18
Chinese political system, 42–54
circularity problem, 56
class struggle: and Deng Xiaoping, 164–5; and Mao Zedong, 171, 177, 179, 216; principal contradiction of, 190, 203–4; rural vs. urban, 194, 196
coal production, 111
coalitions: and bureaucracies, 39–41; economic differences among, 221; effect of leadership on, 30–1, 54–6; and leaps and retreats, 225–8; political nature of, 48–54, 219–22; recurring patterns of, 221–2, 232
collectives: criticism of, 178; and Mao's intervention, 158, 171; and Party leadership, 161; and private and State ownership, 21–2, 101–2; problems of, 20, 90–1; role of, 180; success and acceleration of, 15–16
commandism, 20, 222
commerce and agricultural problems, 87–92
commodity sales, 168
communes, 211, 212, 217
conservatism, 115–16, 171, 177
constitution, Deng Xiaoping and, 163–5
constraints: explanation of, 237; on Mao Zedong, 217, 233, 237–40
consumer goods, 21, 124–5, 161, 198–201
contract responsibility system, 201, 202
contradiction: handling of, 25, 149, 151, 177–9, 182–4, 196, 238–9; nonantagonistic, 148–9; and socialist system and backward production, 23, 170
cooperatives, 15; *see also* collectives; communes
cooptation, 37–8, 44, 104
cotton production, 113–14
cotton textiles, 199
credit, 80

decentralization: and changes in allocation, 127; Chen Yun's views on, 196–8; and financial coalition, 84–6; and leaps, 206, 222, 224, 234; and light industry, 71; Liu Shaoqi's views on, 160–1; Mao Zedong's views on, 84; and provincial secretaries, 144; Zhou Enlai's views on, 166–7, 169
decision making: bureaucratic constraints on, 229; improper styles of, 200
deficits, 21; and leaps, 222

Deng Xiaoping: agricultural views of, 194; and comparison of 1957 and 1989, 233–5; economic views of, 188–9; and Eighth Party Congress, 43, 158, 164–5; and rectification plan, 28, 192–6; and Social Transformation System (STS), 50
Deng Zihui: and collectives, 90–1; and Eighth Party Congress, 28, 70; and Extraction and Allocation System (EAS), 48; and reformist policies, 215; views of, on agricultural problems, 201–2
distribution: of agricultural and consumer goods, 61–2; of heavy industrial products, 101
Dong Biwu, 49
dual rule, 46–7, 166

economic policy: agricultural, 17–19, 27–8; CCP's role in, 167, 170; and cycles and planned economies, 223; of financial coalition during 1957, 74–83; heavy and light industrial, 18–19; and Mao Zedong, 18–19, 158–60, 216; and Politburo Standing Committee, 158; political and structural nature of, 225, 230–3; and politics, September 1956 – October 1957, 23–8; before September 1956, 17–23; and Soviet model of development, 19
Economic Transformation System (ETS), 34, 49
egalitarianism and development of CCP, 135–6
Eighth Central Committee, Third Plenum of: and agricultural and consumer-goods production, 198–203; and budgeteers and planners, 203–6; and decentralization, 196–8; and rectification program, 192–6; *see also names of specific leaders*
Eighth Party Congress: and Bai Rubing, 72; and CCP, 139–46; and Chen Yu, 111; and Chen Yun, 66–9; and Deng Xiaoping and Party constitution, 163–5; and Deng Zihui, 70; and energy sectors, 110–11; and financial coalition, 65–73; and First Ministry of Machine Building, 108–9; and Jia Tuofu, 71; and Li Xiannian, 69–70; and Liu Shaoqi and Central Committee, 159–63; and machine tools, 108–9; major reports at, 159–70; and Ministry of Metallurgical Industries, 108, 109; and planning and heavy industry coalition, 104–12; and reformist policies, 215; and Resolution on Political Report, 170; and steel industry, 109–10; and transportation sector, 111; and Ye Jizhuang, 72; and Zeng Shan, 72; and Zhou Enlai's Second Five-Year Plan proposals, 165–9
energy sectors, difficulties in, 110–11